SCHOOL FINANCE
A Policy Perspective

SCHOOL FINANCE
A Policy Perspective

THIRD EDITION

ALLAN R. ODDEN
University of Wisconsin—Madison

LAWRENCE O. PICUS
University of Southern California

Boston   Burr Ridge, IL   Dubuque, IA   Madison, WI   New York
San Francisco   St. Louis   Bangkok   Bogotá   Caracas   Kuala Lumpur
Lisbon   London   Madrid   Mexico City   Milan   Montreal   New Delhi
Santiago   Seoul   Singapore   Sydney   Taipei   Toronto

Higher Education

SCHOOL FINANCE: A POLICY PERSPECTIVE, THIRD EDITION

Published by McGraw-Hill, a business unit of The McGraw-Hill
Companies, Inc., 1221 Avenue of the Americas, New York, NY 10020.
Copyright © 2004 by The McGraw-Hill Companies, Inc. All rights
reserved. Previous edition(s) 2000, 1992. All rights reserved. No part of
this publication may be reproduced or distributed in any form or by
any means, or stored in a database or retrieval system, without the
prior written consent of The McGraw-Hill Companies, Inc., including,
but not limited to, in any network or other electronic storage or
transmission, or broadcast for distance learning.

Some ancillaries, including electronic and print components, may not
be available to customers outside the United States.

This book is printed on acid-free paper.

1 2 3 4 5 6 7 8 9 0 DOC/DOC 0 9 8 7 6 5 4 3

ISBN 0-07-282318-6

Vice president and editor-in-chief: *Thalia Dorwick*
Editorial coordinator: *Christina Lembo*
Senior marketing manager: *Pamela S. Cooper*
Project manager: *Christine Walker*
Production supervisor: *Enboge Chong*
Media technology producer: *Lance Gerhart*
Designer: *Sharon Spurlock*
Cover designer: *Laurie Anderson*
Senior supplement producer: *David A. Welsh*
Compositor: *ElectraGraphics, Inc.*
Typeface: 10/12 New Caledonia
Printer: *R. R. Donnelley/Crawfordsville, IN*

Library of Congress Cataloging-in-Publication Data

Odden, Allan.
   School finance : a policy perspective / Allan R. Odden, Lawrence O.
Picus.—3rd ed.
       p. cm.
   Includes bibliographical references (p.) and indexes.
   ISBN 0-07-282318-6 (hc : alk. paper)
       1. Education—United States—Finance. 2. Education—United
   States—Finance—Computer simulation. I. Picus, Larry, 1954–   II. Title.

LB2825.O315 2004
379.1'21'0973—dc21   2003044244

www.mhhe.com

About the Authors

Allan Odden is Professor of Educational Administration at the University of Wisconsin—Madison. He also is Co-Director of the Consortium for Policy Research in Education (CPRE), which is funded by the U.S. Department of Education, the director of the CPRE Education Finance Research Program, and principal investigator for the CPRE Teacher Compensation project, funded by Atlantic Philanthropic Services and the Carnegie Corporation. CPRE is a consortium of the University of Wisconsin—Madison, Pennsylvania, Harvard, Michigan, and Stanford Universities. He was formerly professor of Education Policy and Administration at the University of Southern California (USC) and Director of Policy Analysis for California Education (PACE), an educational policy studies consortium of USC, Stanford University, and the University of California—Berkeley.

Odden is an international expert on education finance, school-based financing, resource allocation and use, educational policy, school-based management, teacher compensation, district and school decentralization, education incentives, and educational policy implementation. He worked with the Education Commission of the States for a decade, serving as assistant executive director, director of policy analysis and research, and director of its educational finance center. He was president of the American Educational Finance Association in 1979–80, and served as research director for special state educational finance projects in Connecticut (1974–75), Missouri (1975–77), South Dakota (1975–77), New York (1979–81), Texas (1988), New Jersey (1991), and Missouri (1992–93). He currently is conducting, with Lawrence Picus, adequacy studies for Arkansas and Kentucky. He also is directing research projects on school finance redesign, resource reallocation, the costs of professional development, and teacher compensation. He was appointed Special Court Master to the Remand Judge in the New Jersey *Abbott* v. *Burke* school finance court case for 1997 and 1998. Odden has written widely, publishing over 200 journal articles, book chapters, and research reports, and 20 books and monographs. He has consulted for governors, state legislators, chief state school officers, national and local unions, The National Alliance for Business, the Business Roundtable, New American Schools, the U.S. Congress, the U.S. Secretary of Education, many local school districts, the state departments of education in Victoria and Queensland, Australia, and the Department for Education and Employment in England.

His books include *Reallocating Resources: How to Boost Student Achievement Without Asking for More* (Corwin, 2001) with Sarah Archibald; *School-Based Financing* (Corwin, 1999), with Margaret Goertz; *Financing Schools for High Performance: Strategies for Improving the Use of Educational Resources* (Jossey-Bass, 1998), with Carolyn Busch; *Paying Teachers for What They Know and Do: New and Smarter Compensation*

Strategies to Improve Schools, second edition (Corwin Press, 2002) with Carolyn Kelley; *Educational Leadership for America's Schools* (McGraw-Hill, 1995); *Rethinking School Finance: An Agenda for the 1990s* (Jossey-Bass, 1992); *School Finance: A Policy Perspective,* second edition (McGraw-Hill, 2000), coauthored with Lawrence Picus; *Education Policy Implementation* (State University of New York Press, 1991); and *School Finance and School Improvement: Linkages for the 1980s* (Ballinger, 1983).

Odden was a mathematics teacher and curriculum developer in New York City's East Harlem for five years. He received his Ph.D. and M.A. degrees from Columbia University, a Masters of Divinity from the Union Theological Seminary, and his B.S. from Brown University.

Lawrence O. Picus is a Professor in the Department of Administration and Policy in the Rossier School of Education at the University of Southern California. He also serves as the director of the Center for Research in Education Finance (CREF), a school finance research center housed at the Rossier School of Education. CREF research focuses on issues of school finance and productivity. His current research interests focus on adequacy and equity in school finance as well as efficiency and productivity in the provision of educational programs for K-12 school children. Picus is past-president of the American Education Finance Association.

Picus' most recent books include: *In Search of More Productive Schools: A Guide to Resource Allocation in Education,* published by the ERIC Clearinghouse on Educational Management in January, 2001; *Leveraging Resources for Student Success: How School Leaders Build Equity,* coauthored with Mary Ann Burke, Reynaldo Baca, and Catherine Jones (Corwin Press, 2003); and *Developing Community Empowered Schools* (Corwin, 2001), coauthored with Mary Ann Burke. Picus is the coauthor of *School Finance: A Policy Perspective,* second edition (McGraw-Hill, 2000) with Allan Odden, and *Principles of School Business Administration* (ASBO, 1995) with R. Craig Wood, David Thompson, and Don I. Tharpe. In addition, he is the senior editor of the 1995 yearbook of the American Education Finance Association, *Where Does the Money Go? Resource Allocation in Elementary and Secondary Schools* (Corwin, 1995). He has also published numerous articles in professional journals.

Picus has worked on the assessment and design of school funding systems in numerous states including Vermont, Washington, Oregon, California, Kansas, Texas, Massachusetts, and Wyoming. He is currently working with Allan Odden on adequacy studies in Kentucky and Arkansas.

To my wife, Eleanor, still best friend, sharpest critic, and loving supporter.

Allan Odden

To Matthew, who is a constant reminder about why this is important.

Larry Picus

Contents

9 ALLOCATION AND USE OF FUNDS AT THE DISTRICT, SCHOOL, AND CLASSROOM LEVELS *280*

10 USING EDUCATION DOLLARS MORE WISELY TO IMPROVE RESULTS *304*

Preface

Public school financing in the United States is a big business; it involved over $379 billion, 59 million children, 3.5 million teachers, and nearly an additional 1.5 million administrators and staff in 2001. School finance has and continues to be a top-priority policy issue at the state and local levels, and one of the top issues the public identifies as needing attention at the national level as well. Further, both adequacy of funding in general and productivity of the use of education dollars in particular are issues leading school finance policy deliberations today.

In this third edition of *School Finance: A Policy Perspective*, we continue the emphasis of the first two editions on the use of education dollars and the need to use current and all new dollars on more effective programs and services—in short to improve the productivity of the education system. Our prime goal in the third edition, however, is to reorient the book to the issues of school principals and other site-based education leaders, as well as to those at the policy level in districts or states. Thus, we have added chapters on budgeting at the district and school levels and on financing facilities, and included more information on the use of resources at the school level. We have streamlined several of the other chapters (sometimes dividing them into two separate chapters) to concentrate on key issues in school finance litigation, definitions of equity and adequacy, revenue raising, and revenue distribution (both state to district and district to school). We also have updated all the material that is included from the second edition.

The book includes a new simulation capacity that allows readers to input staffing and resource data from a *school* and to immediately receive a report indicating whether the school can, via resource reallocation, fiscally afford several comprehensive school designs. In addition, the book continues to include a revised and enhanced school finance simulation that enables students, professors, and researchers to use the World Wide Web (www.mhhe.com/odden3e) to analyze the nature of school finance problems and to simulate the effects of different school finance structures on both a 20-district sample of districts and universe data sets for several states.

The third edition has five major sections:

- three introductory chapters, one providing an overview of key school finance issues, one on the legal issues in school finance litigation, and a chapter that develops an equity and adequacy framework for analyzing state school finance structures;
- one chapter on the raising of revenues for educational purposes;
- three chapters on the distribution of education revenues from states to schools, covering both basic school formulas as well as various adjustments for different

needs, and a chapter with case studies of state school finance problems and their resolution;

- three chapters on issues related to improving the productivity and effectiveness of the education system; and
- four chapters, one on budgeting dollars at the district and school levels, one on allocation and use of educational resources, one on resource reallocation for higher performance, and the last on financing facilities.

1. INTRODUCTION AND OVERVIEW

Chapter 1 serves as an introduction to the topic of school finance. It begins with information on the current status of funding for public K–12 education in the United States, showing how much is spent, the source of those funds, and how levels and sources of funding have changed over time. It shows that as a nation, we spend a great deal of money on K–12 education and that the amount we spend has grown considerably over time. Chapter 1 also discusses the manner in which school finance inequities have changed over the last 30 years. The chapter discusses the "traditional" school finance inequities in several states. In these states, districts with lower property wealth per pupil tend to have lower expenditures per pupil—even with higher school tax rates—than do districts with higher per-pupil property wealth. These high-wealth districts tend to have higher per pupil expenditures even with lower school tax rates.

The chapter then shows that several states today have what the book terms the "new" school finance problem: higher wealth districts with higher expenditures per pupil but also higher tax rates, and lower property wealth per-pupil districts with lower expenditures per pupil but also lower school tax rates. The chapter suggests that remedying these different types of fiscal inequities might require very different school finance reform strategies. Finally the chapter discusses how the issue of "adequacy" has entered the school finance policy agenda.

Chapter 2 reviews the evolution of school finance court cases, from the initial *Serrano* v. *Priest* decision, through the adequacy cases in the late 1990s and early 2000s. The chapter shows how strongly litigation has shifted from equity to adequacy. The chapter is accompanied by a large table on the McGraw-Hill website (www.mhhe.com/odden3e) that includes the education clause in each state and the various school finance cases brought in the state, their status, and the constitutional basis for court decisions.

Chapter 3 begins with a short section on the topic of whether money "matters." This section concludes that this question was more of an issue in the twentieth century when most school finance attention was primarily focused on equity. We argue that today, the adequacy issue directly addresses the "does money matter" question so the issue is not an "add-on" but a core issue in school finance. The second part of this chapter develops an equity and adequacy framework for analyzing state school finance systems. It draws from the Berne and Stiefel (1984) equity framework that was used in the first edition of the text, and adds a discussion of such issues as ex ante versus ex post equity perspectives, the unit of analysis, and various elements of equity including the group, the object, and different measures of horizontal and vertical equity. The chapter includes a new horizontal equity statistic, the Verstegen Index, which measures the variation in the top half of the distribution, compared with the McLoone, which assesses the equity of the bottom half. The chapter also adds the concept of adequacy to the overall framework and presents an adequacy statistic, the Odden-Picus Adequacy Index. The chapter concludes by saying that most analyses of the equity and adequacy of state school finance systems use state and local revenues per pupil, and focus on the degree of revenue per-pupil equality (using the coefficient of variation and the McLoone Index statistics) and the degree of "fiscal neutrality" or the linkage between revenues per pupil and property wealth per pupil.

2. RAISING REVENUES FOR EDUCATION

Chapter 4 reviews the public finance context for school finance, analyzing the base, yield, elasticity, equity, economic effects and administrative costs of income, sales, and property taxes as revenue sources for public schools. It discusses mechanisms to improve the regressive incidence at lower income levels of both the sales and the property tax, and reviews various property tax limitations states have enacted on this primary public school revenue source. It also includes a short analysis of lotteries as a source of school revenues.

3. DISTRIBUTING EDUCATIONAL RESOURCES TO DISTRICT

Chapter 5 begins with a summary of the fact that all levels of government (local, state, and federal) in the United States play a role in funding schools; this system is called fiscal federalism. It then describes the core elements of state school finance formulas: base allocations provided through flat grant, foundation, guaranteed tax base (district power equalizing and percentage equalizing), and combination formulas. The chapter describes these various elements and discusses generally how they work, using a 20-district sample in an updated simulation program. The focus of this chapter is on how different school finance formulas work (i.e., their costs and their effects on horizontal and vertical equity, as well as adequacy). The chapter includes a discussion of four different methods for determining an "adequate" base spending level: the professional judgment approach, the successful district approach, the cost function approach, and the evidence-based approach.

Chapter 6 discusses the rationales for, and types of adjustments for, three categories of special-needs children: those from a low-income background, those with physical and mental disabilities, and those with limited English proficiency. In addition, the chapter discusses various rationales for different adjustments for students at different education levels (elementary, middle, and high school) and adjustments for price differences across states and geographical regions within states, for the latter largely drawing on work conducted by Chambers (1995) and McMahon (1994). The chapter further discusses the issue of scale economies and describes different ways states adjust funding formulas for small/large size or rural isolation.

Chapter 7 uses the analytic tools identified in Chapters 3, 5, and 6 to identify the nature of school finance problems in three states and then, using universe district data from three states representing different kinds of school finance situations, suggests school finance reforms that would remedy the identified problems. This chapter uses the simulation program, available on the McGraw-Hill website (www.mhhe.com/odden3e), adapted for the individual states. Over time, this website should have data sets for more states; it has data for more recent years for the states discussed in the chapter, so professors could have students analyze the nature of the school finance problems with more recent data, and to simulate and propose school finance reforms.

The Vermont state data set discussed in Chapter 7 presents the traditional school finance problem of unequal distribution of funds due to the unequal distribution of wealth. The chapter shows how traditional school finance models can be used to increase horizontal equity, fiscal neutrality, adequacy, and adjustments for different student needs.

The Wisconsin state data set presents the "new" finance problem. In this instance, the wealthiest districts are relatively high spending but also have relatively high tax rate districts, while the poorest districts tend to be low spending as well as exert low tax efforts. The chapter shows how guaranteed tax base (GTB) programs exacerbate fiscal equity for such a state and identifies alternative school finance mechanisms to improve inequity and adequacy.

The Illinois state data present a finance situation that is not only tricky to resolve but also requires substantial additional resources both on adequacy and property tax reduction grounds.

The goal in Chapter 7 is to show how various elements of school finance structures can be used to resolve *different* types of school finance problems. For each state, the chapter includes both an analysis of the kind of school finance problem that the state presents and the effectiveness or ineffectiveness of different school finance formulas in resolving the problem.

One of the problems often encountered in school finance is that funding formulas are either established in a vacuum, or their parameters are the result of available dollars. In the context of these state cases, this chapter uses policy "targets" to help remedy the school finance problems identified. For example, a state might decide it wants to provide a certain minimum level of support for all schools equal to 90 percent of the average spending of a certain type of district. Or alternatively, policymakers may feel that all districts should have access to funds equal to the district at some fixed percentage of wealth. The simulation is used to help students understand and determine logical policy targets and to assess their impact on the school finance problems in the different states.

We encourage any reader or professor to send us data sets from their states that we could convert into a simulation that could be added to the website. Such a universe data set should include the following variables for each school district: number of pupils, equalized property value that is used in the school finance equalization formula, general aid, state categorical aids for disabled students, students from low-income backgrounds, and limited-English-proficient students, and the number of students eligible for free and reduced lunch (or some similar count of students from low-income backgrounds), the number of disabled students, and the number of limited-English-proficient students.

4. BUDGETING AND ALLOCATING DOLLARS FOR EDUCATIONAL PURPOSES

This section includes four chapters: Chapter 8 on budgeting, Chapter 9 on current allocation and use of educational dollars, Chapter 10 on resource reallocation at the site level, and Chapter 11 on financing facilities.

Chapter 8 is a new chapter focused on budgeting educational resources. It focuses more on the nuts and bolts of budgeting and less on research about budgeting processes. The chapter starts with the traditional triangle that structures budgeting—revenues, expenditures, and educational programs—and then discusses how these play out as central issues in school district budgeting. It includes examples of what district budget documents look like, and explanations of the general fund and restricted funds. It also includes descriptions of various ways that districts use to provide resources to school sites, from the more traditional staffing formulas, to emerging needs-based, per-pupil funding formulas. For the latter, it includes short summaries of the operating programs in Seattle and San Francisco. The goal is to help individuals understand the key ways districts resource schools.

Chapter 9 provides a detailed analysis of the way states, districts, and schools allocate and use educational resources. It summarizes research on this topic, using information from national-, state-, and school-level databases. It uses 1994–95 Schools and Staffing Survey data to show how a 500-student elementary school, a 1,000-student middle school, and a 1,500-student high school is typically staffed in different regions of the country. The chapter shows that there are surprisingly common patterns of the uses of the education dollar. It also shows that during the past 30 years the large bulk of new dollars has been used to expand services outside the regular, core instructional program (i.e., to provide extra services for numerous categories of special pupil needs). The chapter concludes that while these uses reflect good values—more money for many categories of special-needs students— the specific uses of those new dollars have not produced much impact on student learning. The implication of this conclusion is that we need to retain the values behind these extra resources but find more effective uses for them.

Chapter 10 addresses this challenge. It discusses the issue of resource reallocation to *school-level* strategies that produce higher student performance. Drawing from the school staffing in Chapter 9, it then describes how a series of new school models are staffed and structured differently, focusing on the two most expensive designs that were developed under the auspices of the New American Schools. It shows how the new school designs use their funds differently to provide educational services and describes the things that schools should consider in implementing these or other school restructuring ideas, including class size reduction. This chapter does not make definitive conclusions about the impact of these new school designs, but does show how these various emerging school designs have a cost structure different from traditional schools, and thus use dollar resources differently.

This chapter also shows that there may be sufficient resources in some regions to fund these emerging higher-performing school models, but insufficient resources in others, thus suggesting that cross-state differences in educational spending need to be considered at some point.

To use the school redesign computer simulation program, readers will need to input staffing and discretionary dollar resources in a school (note that it is just staffing resources and not the school's actual budget), together with the average cost of teachers, administrators, and instructional aides. The simulation will then provide the student with a report analyzing whether fiscally and via resource reallocation, the school could afford an evidence-based model school (Odden, 2000), as well as several other comprehensive school reform models. The chapter will suggest an activity a professor could use as a course paper using these simulation results.

Chapter 11 addresses state approaches to financing educational facilities. It first discusses the differences between financing current and capital expenditures. It also describes how school districts raise funds to build new schools, renovate existing schools, and finance long-term capital improvements to their facilities and grounds. The chapter discusses the complexities of bond financing, the equity issues surrounding the use of property taxes to pay off the principal and interest on bonds levied by school systems, current court rulings on capital funding for schools, and alternative finance options available to states and school districts as they strive to build and maintain adequate school facilities. The chapter concludes with a summary of research on the impact of school facilities on student learning.

5. APPENDIX: THE SIMULATION

An integral part of this book is the school finance simulation designed to accompany the text. We have made a number of improvements to the simulation that accompanied the first two editions of this book. The original 10-district simulation was expanded to include 20 districts. Additionally, two new school finance statistics are provided, the Verstegen Index and the Odden-Picus Adequacy Index. The 20-district simulation is designed to accompany Chapter 5. We found that the previous simulation dramatically improved student understanding of the statistics used by the school finance profession, and helped them better understand the myriad complexities involved in making changes to a state's school-funding system. The 20-district simulation that accompanies this edition should continue that tradition.

The simulation is available on the World Wide Web, from McGraw-Hill's website at www.mhhe.com/odden3e. The appendix describes the general use of the simulation, and provides information on how to access it from the World Wide Web. Additional documentation is available on the website.

In addition to the 20-district simulation, we include data sets for several years for Kentucky, Illinois, Vermont, and Wisconsin for analysis and simulation of alternative school finance reforms.

At the end of the preface of the first edition we said, "We hope this will help the country accomplish its goals of having all students learn to think, solve problems and communicate, graduate from high school, and be first in the world in mathematics and science." We continue this hope with this edition.

ACKNOWLEDGMENTS

Writing a book almost always is the result of activities far beyond those of the authors. To be sure, the authors are primarily responsible for the text, and responsible for errors and omissions, but without insight, assistance, support, and work of others, a book might never see the light of day. We would like to thank the people who played major roles in helping us produce the third edition of this book.

First, Sarah Archibald, a researcher in the University of Wisconsin–Madison offices of the Consortium for Policy Research in Education (CPRE), and Sarah Helvey, a Ph.D. student and a CPRE research assistant, worked tirelessly on most portions of the book, and particularly Chapter 6. They searched out research reports needed for the text revision, they found missing data files crucial to empirical findings, and they filled in details too numerous to mention. Both their careful assistance and continuous encouragement to complete this endeavor are greatly appreciated. We would also like to thank Michael Goetz for his careful proofreading.

Lisa Armstrong, administrative assistant in the UW CPRE offices, and Josie Pedone, a secretary in those offices, were enormously helpful in the word processing needed to produce the final manuscript; they entered the editorial changes, kept track of the most recent files, and produced a faultless final copy. As usual, Lisa was the preeminent citation sleuth, tracking down innumerable citations that either simply needed to be found or needed completion. Without their help, we would still be at the computer or in the library.

At USC, we would like to thank William Glenn, whose efforts in preparing data for the chapters on taxation and budgeting are very much appreciated. His tenacity in finding the often obscure data needed to complete one of the many tables or to help make a point in the text is appreciated.

A special thank you to our reviewers:

David Barnett, *Morehead State University*
Barbara M. De Luca, *University of Dayton*
Len Etlinger, *Chicago State University*
Francis X. Gallant, *University of Idaho–Boise*
Earl B. Kaurala, *Northern Michigan University*
Mary K. McCullough, *Loyola Marymount University*
Kenneth T. Murray, *University of Central Florida*
Jennifer King Rice, *University of Maryland*
Ross Rubenstein, *Georgia State University*
Donald Tetreault, *University of South Carolina*
Sharon P. Wayland, *Wilmington College*

We also would like to acknowledge the many unnamed individuals at the national, state, district, and school level who have allowed us as well as others to conduct research on their use of education resources over the past decade. Without this research, our chapters on resource allocation and reallocation could not have been written. But as we hope will be obvious, the landscape of school finance has changed over the past years. What we know about the nature of these changes has depended on the cooperation of those involved in letting outside individuals intrude into their domain, research what they do, and write up the results.

Finally, we would like to thank our families, who once again have endured our working on the computer rather than engaging in family activities. Their support and sustenance knows no bounds, and we are grateful for their understanding, love, and steadfast support.

Allan R. Odden   Lawrence O. Picus

Madison, Wisconsin   Los Angeles, California

— *Chapter 1* ————————————————————

Introduction and Overview to School Finance

School finance concerns the distribution and use of money for the purpose of providing educational services and producing student achievement. For most of the twentieth century, school finance policy has focused on equity—issues related to widely varying education expenditures per pupil across districts within a state and the uneven distribution of the property tax base used to raise local education dollars. In the 1990s, new attention began to focus on education adequacy and productivity—the linkages among amount of funds, use of funds, and levels of student achievement. As the 1990s ended and the twenty-first century began, policymakers increasingly wanted to know how much money was needed to educate students to high standards; how those dollars should be distributed effectively and fairly among districts, schools, programs and students; and how both level and use of dollars affected student performance. These policy demands are pushing school finance beyond its traditional emphasis on fiscal equity.

This book moves school finance in these new directions. It emphasizes traditional equity issues and also discusses adequacy and productivity issues, including what is known about the linkages among dollars, educational strategies, and student performance. The 1980s and the 1990s were remarkable not only for the intensity of the school reform movement, but also for the duration of interest in educational reform. Today, standards-based education reform, from content standards to charter schools to new accountability structures, seeks to teach students to high levels. In most instances, the implications of these reforms for school finance have not been fully considered, though Odden and Clune (1998) argued that traditional school finance systems were "aging structures in need of renovation." During the 2000s, states and their respective school districts will need to rethink school finance systems to ensure they can adequately meet the productivity expectations and accountability requirements inspired by these reforms.

This book takes a policy approach to school finance analysis. To that end, it emphasizes the actions schools, districts, and states can take—or policies they can enact—

1

to address the equity, adequacy, and productivity issues raised herein. It is important for graduate students in education, as well as educators and education policymakers, to understand both the finance implications of school reform policies, and equally important, to understand how decisions about the distribution of funds to local schools and school districts affect the implementation of those reforms. The book begins with a discussion of traditional school finance issues, including the nature of school finance disparities linked to local financing of schools, legal issues surrounding school finance, analysis of general taxation systems, intergovernmental grants, and traditional school finance formulas. The analysis of school finance formulas is supplemented with a computer simulation designed to allow students the opportunity to simulate the effects of different school finance formulas on a sample of school districts. By designing their own school finance formulas and simulating the impact on a sample of school districts, students will have a more realistic sense of how changes in funding formulas influence school districts across a state. The simulation will help students understand the technical and political complexities that result when one attempts to redesign school-funding programs. In addition to a straightforward 20-district simulation example, there are several state databases available on the McGraw-Hill website (www.mhhe.com/odden3e) that can be analyzed and assessed using the school finance simulation.

20-district simulation and state databases.

The book then moves beyond this traditional approach to school finance. The next three chapters discuss important issues for the 2000s and how they relate to school finance. Included are chapters dealing with budgeting, particularly budgeting dollars to the school level, typical allocation and use of funds at the district and school levels, reallocation of dollars to better uses, and financing facilities, a major issue that emerged during the end of the 1990s. Each of these is a basic school finance issue that principals, superintendents, and other education leaders should understand to be more effective in their jobs.

This introductory chapter has three sections. The first outlines the scope of school finance within the United States. Funding public schools is big business, and the first section outlines its fiscal magnitude. Section two provides a quick history of school finance developments, beginning in the seventeenth century. This section shows how schools evolved from privately funded, parent- and church-run entities to the large publicly and governmentally controlled education systems of today. Section three discusses several examples of the "school finance problem" and how it has evolved from the traditional fiscal disparities across districts to the new issue of education adequacy. The chapter concludes with a summary.

1. THE SCOPE OF EDUCATION FINANCE IN THE UNITED STATES

Education is an enormous enterprise in the United States. It constitutes the largest portion of most state and local governmental budgets; engages more than 100,000 local school board members in important policymaking activities; employs millions of individuals as teachers, administrators, and support staff; and educates tens of millions of children.

Enrollment

Table 1.1 provides detail on public school enrollment, including numbers of school districts and schools during most of the twentieth century. Enrollment was relatively constant during the 1930s and 1940s, but rose quickly after World War II as the postwar baby boom reached school age. After 25 years of rapid growth, public school enrollment declined during the 1970s and then began to grow again in the mid-1980s when the children of the baby boom generation began to enter schools. In 1999–2000, public school enrollment was estimated to be 46.8 million students, a figure slightly higher than the previous peak of 45.6 million in 1970.

Schools and School Districts

One of the major stories of this century has been the consolidation of school districts into larger entities. In 2000, there were just under 15,000 school districts, about the lowest number during the twentieth century. In 1940, by contrast, there were 117,108 school districts. The number of school districts dropped by almost 40,000 between 1940 and 1950 (i.e., after World War II), and then dropped by another 40,000 districts between 1950 and 1960. During the 1970 school year, there were only 17,995 local school districts, and today only about 15,000. The number of districts varies across the states, however, with Texas having 1,041 districts and California having 989 districts in 2002, and Hawaii being one, statewide school district.

Interestingly, as will be discussed here, although school district consolidation also entails consolidation of the local property tax base, remaining inequities in local school financing after the bulk of consolidation had occurred still led courts during the late 1960s and early 1970s to declare finance structures unconstitutional (see Chapter 2).

Table 1.1 also shows that the number of public schools has dropped over time while enrollments have risen, indicating that schools too have grown in size during the twentieth century. There were over 262,000 public schools in 1930, but that number had dropped by a factor of three to around 95,000 schools in 2000. On the other hand, the number of private schools has risen since 1930, from a low of about 12,500 then to around 35,000 today; almost triple the number in 1930.

Impact on the Economy

Funding public schools requires large amounts of dollars. In 2000, public school revenues totaled $378.5 billion, an increase of $170 billion from the 1990 total of $208.5 billion (Table 1.2). Indeed, the data show that public school revenues more than doubled during each decade from 1940 to 1990, a remarkable fiscal record. By way of comparison, in 2000–01, Wal-Mart, the number-one company on the 2002 Fortune 500 list, had total sales of $219.8 billion (Fortune, 2002).

Table 1.2 also shows that during this century, public education consumed an increasing portion of the country's total economic activity (as measured by the gross domestic product), increasing steadily until 1970, dropping slightly during the enrollment decline of the 1970s, and returning to the high reached in 1970 in recent years. The

TABLE 1.1 Historical Data on the Size of the Nation's School Systems, 1919–20 to 1999–2000

Year	Public Student Enrollment (in 1,000s)	Public School Districts	Public Elementary Schools	Public Secondary Schools	Private Elementary Schools	Private Secondary Schools	Private Schools as Percent of Total
1919–20	21,578	—	—	—	—	—	—
1929–30	25,678	—	238,306	23,930	9,275	3,258	5
1939–40	25,434	117,108	—	—	11,306	3,568	—
1949–50	25,111	83,718	128,225	24,542	10,375	3,331	8
1959–60	35,182	40,520	91,853	25,784	13,574	4,061	13
1969–70	45,550	17,995[a]	65,800[a]	25,352[a]	14,372[a]	3,770[a]	17[a]
1979–80	41,651	15,912[b]	61,069[b]	24,362[b]	16,792[b]	5,678[b]	21[b]
1989–90	40,543	15,358[c,d]	61,340[d]	23,460[d]	22,223[d]	8,989[d]	21[b]
1994–95	44,111	14,881[c,e]	62,726[e]	23,379[e]	23,543[e]	10,555[e]	31[e]
1999–2000	46,857	14,928[c]	68,173	26,407	24,685	10,693	—

Source: National Center for Education Statistics, *Digest of Education Statistics, 2001.*

[a]Data for 1970–71.

[b]Data for 1980–81.

[c]Because of expanded survey coverage, data are not directly comparable with figures for earlier years.

[d]Data for 1990–91; for private schools, these data are from sample surveys and should not be compared directly with the data for earlier years.

[e]Data for 1993–94; for private schools, these data are from sample surveys and should not be compared directly with the data for earlier years.

TABLE 1.2 Educational Revenues, GDP, and Personal Income (Billions), 1929–2000

Year	Total Educational Revenues	Gross Domestic Product (GDP)	Revenues as Percent of GDP	Personal Income (PI)	Revenues as Percent of PI
1929	$ 2.1	$ 104.7	2.0	$ 85.3	2.5
1940	2.3	101.3	2.3	78.6	2.9
1950	5.4	294.3	1.8	229.9	2.3
1960	14.7	527.4	2.9	412.7	3.6
1970	40.3	1,039.7	3.9	841.1	4.8
1980	96.9	2,795.6	3.5	2,323.9	4.2
1990	208.5	5,803.2	3.6	4,903.2	4.3
1995	273.1	7,400.5	3.7	6,200.9	4.4
1999	347.3	9,268.6	3.7	7,777.3	4.5
2000	378.5[a]	9,872.9	3.9	8,319.2	4.5

Source: National Center for Education Statistics, *Digest of Education Statistics, 2001.*

[a]National Education Association, *Rankings and Estimates: Ranking of the States 2000 and Estimates of School Statistics 2001.*

same pattern emerges when total public school revenues are measured as a percent of the country's personal income, which peaked at 4.8 percent in 1970 and today represents approximately 4.5 percent of personal income. The 4.5 percent of personal income devoted to education represents a considerable effort on behalf of our schools considering all the other items that individuals could purchase with annual income either for themselves or through government tax revenues.

School Revenues and Expenditures

This important point is supported by the data in Table 1.3. Column 2 shows that *real* expenditures per pupil (i.e., expenditures adjusted by the Consumer Price Index) have increased each decade at extraordinarily large rates: 100 percent between 1920 and 1930, 67 percent during the 1960s, and 35 percent during the 1970s. Even during the 1980s, a decade of government tax and expenditure limitations, expenditures per pupil increased by 36 percent to a total of $6,402 (in 2000–01 dollars) for current operating purposes in 1989–90. At the turn of the century, an average of $6,855 was spent on each public school student. It seems that real resources for public school students are substantial, and rise substantially each decade, although the rise during the 1990s was the smallest of the twentieth century.

These facts certainly are at odds with popular perceptions that schools do not get much more money each year. Though real resources might increase only 1 to 3 percent each year, over a 10-year period, that amounts to nearly a one-third increase in real resources, a substantial increase.

The last columns in Table 1.3 show that the sources of school revenues have changed over the years. Earlier in the century, local districts provided the bulk of school

TABLE 1.3   Educational Expenditures per Pupil and Revenues by Source, 1920–2000

| Year | Expenditures per Pupil | | | Percent Revenues by Source | | |
	Real (2000–01 dollars)	*Nominal*	*Total Revenues (in Millions)*	*Federal*	*State*	*Local*
1919–20	$ 367	$ 40	$ 970	0.3	16.5	83.2
1929–30	734	72	2,089	0.4	16.9	82.7
1939–40	957	76	2,261	1.8	30.3	68.0
1949–50	1,380	187	5,437	2.9	39.8	57.3
1959–60	2,088	350	14,747	4.4	39.1	56.5
1969–70	3,482	750	40,267	8.0	39.9	52.1
1979–80	4,710	2,089	96,881	9.8	46.8	43.4
1989–90	6,402	4,643	208,548	6.1	47.1	46.8
1994–95	6,436	5,529	273,149	6.8	46.8	46.4
1995–96	6,447	5,689	287,703	6.6	47.5	45.9
1996–97	6,527	5,923	305,065	6.6	48.0	45.4
1997–98	6,700	6,189	325,926	6.8	48.4	44.8
1998–99	6,925	6,508	347,330	7.1	48.7	44.2
1999–00[b]	6,855[a]	6,627[a]	378,574	6.9[a]	50.7[a]	42.4[a]

Source: National Center for Education Statistics, *Digest of Education Statistics, 2001.*

[a]Data estimated.

[b]National Education Association, *Rankings and Estimates: Ranking of the States 2000 and Estimates of School Statistics 2001.*

revenues, and the federal role was almost nonexistent. Beginning in the 1960s, the federal government began to increase its financial role, which reached its maximum at 9.8 percent in 1980. Since then, the federal contribution has dropped by almost one-third to approximately 7 percent of the total. Today, the states are the primary providers of public school revenues, outdistancing local school districts sometime during the 1970s' era of school finance reforms. During the 1999–2000 school year, on average the states provided 50.7 percent of public school revenues, local districts (primarily through the local property tax) 42.4 percent, and the federal government 6.9 percent.

These national patterns, however, are very different in each of the 50 states, as shown in Table 1.4. The national average expenditure per pupil was $7,013 in 1998–99, but expenditures ranged from a low of $4,478 in Utah to a high of $10,748 in New Jersey, a difference of almost two-and-one-half-to-one. Note that some data in this figure are different from those in the previous figure because of slightly different data sources.

States also differ in the sources of public school revenues. In Hawaii, for example, 89 percent of revenues derive from the state, while in New Hampshire only 9.3 percent of school revenues come from state sources. States provide over 60 percent of school revenues in 14 states, while local districts provide over 60 percent of school revenues in five states. This variation reflects differences in local perceptions of appropriate state

TABLE 1.4   Educational Expenditures per Pupil and Revenues by Source, by State: 1998–99

		Percent of Revenues by Source		
State	*Expenditures per Pupil*	*Federal*	*State*	*Local*
Alabama	$ 5,512	9.4	62.5	23.2
Alaska	9,209	12.3	62.2	22.9
Arizona	5,235	10.2	44.3	43.2
Arkansas	5,193	10.8	57.7	26.0
California	6,045	8.2	60.2	30.6
Colorado	6,386	5.1	43.4	47.6
Connecticut	9,620	3.9	37.3	56.1
Delaware	8,336	7.6	64.4	26.7
District of Columbia	10,611	16.5	N/A	83.1
Florida	6,443	7.6	48.8	39.7
Georgia	6,534	6.8	51.2	40.1
Hawaii	6,648	8.6	89.0	0.5
Idaho	5,379	7.0	62.7	28.6
Illinois	7,676	6.8	28.5	62.5
Indiana	7,249	4.8	51.4	40.9
Iowa	6,548	5.3	51.3	38.2
Kansas	6,708	5.9	57.9	33.5
Kentucky	6,412	9.6	61.7	26.5
Louisiana	6,019	11.3	50.4	35.9
Maine	7,688	7.0	45.5	46.4
Maryland	7,865	5.2	39.0	52.7
Massachusetts	8,750	5.0	40.7	52.9
Michigan	8,142	6.6	66.0	25.4
Minnesota	7,159	4.9	52.3	39.8
Mississippi	4,871	14.1	55.4	27.1
Missouri	6,393	6.2	39.7	50.1
Montana	6,768	10.2	46.9	38.7
Nebraska	6,856	6.7	33.1	54.7
Nevada	5,934	4.6	31.8	60.1
New Hampshire	6,780	3.8	9.3	84.5
New Jersey	10,748	3.6	39.8	54.3
New Mexico	5,363	13.2	72.2	12.3
New York	10,514	5.4	39.7	53.9
North Carolina	6,088	7.2	67.3	22.7
North Dakota	5,820	12.4	41.1	41.1
Ohio	7,295	5.8	41.2	48.9
Oklahoma	5,684	8.6	61.6	24.5
Oregon	7,787	6.4	56.8	33.6

continued

TABLE 1.4   Educational Expenditures per Pupil and Revenues by Source, by State: 1998–99 (*continued*)

State	Expenditures per Pupil	Percent of Revenues by Source		
		Federal	State	Local
Pennsylvania	8,026	5.9	38.7	53.6
Rhode Island	9,049	5.4	40.1	53.1
South Carolina	6,003	8.5	51.5	35.7
South Dakota	5,613	10.0	35.6	51.4
Tennessee	5,521	8.8	47.7	36.4
Texas	6,161	7.6	44.2	45.8
Utah	4,478	6.9	61.0	29.5
Vermont	7,984	5.2	29.4	63.6
Virginia	6,129	5.2	31.4	60.2
Washington	6,595	6.4	66.0	24.4
West Virginia	7,176	9.2	62.7	26.8
Wisconsin	8,062	4.5	53.7	39.7
Wyoming	7,393	6.7	47.0	44.5
United States	*7,013*	*6.8*	*48.4*	*42.3*

Source: National Center for Education Statistics, *Digest of Education Statistics, 2001.*

and local roles, as well as differences in school finance formula structures (Sielke, Dayton, Holmes, and Jefferson, 2001). These data document one enduring characteristic of state school finance structures: though there are some similarities, the differences are also dramatic. Students of school finance need to understand both the generic similarities and the factors causing the specific differences.

2. EARLY DEVELOPMENTS IN SCHOOL FINANCE

This country has not always had a system of free, tax-supported schools. Free, public education was an idea created in the United States during the nineteenth century, and the large network of public school systems was formed in a relatively short period, primarily during the latter part of the nineteenth and early part of the twentieth century.

Early Actions

American schools began as local entities, largely private and religious, during the seventeenth, eighteenth, and even early nineteenth centuries. As in England, educating children was considered a private rather than a public matter. Providing for education was a mandate for parents and masters, not governments. Eighteenth-century leaders of the new American republic viewed education as a means to enable citizens to participate as equals in affairs of government and thus essential to ensure the liberties guaranteed by the Constitution. Even though Thomas Jefferson proposed creation of free public elementary schools, his proposal was not adopted until the mid-1800s, largely through the efforts of Horace Mann and Henry Barnard, state superintendents of public instruction. Mann spearheaded the development of public-supported "common schools" in Massachusetts, and Barnard did the same in Connecticut.

In the nineteenth century, as education began to assume significance in economic terms, many compulsory attendance laws were passed. Despite these laws, when school attendance became compulsory beginning in the mid-1800s, government financing of schools was not uniformly required.

In 1647, the General Court of Massachusetts passed the famous Old Deluder Satan Act. The act required every town to set up a school, or pay a sum of money to a larger town to support education. It required towns with at least 50 families to appoint a teacher of reading and writing, and required towns with more than 100 families to also establish a secondary school. The act required that these schools should be supported by masters, parents, or the inhabitants in general, thereby establishing one of the first systems of financing schools through local taxation. Pulliam (1987) states that the first tax on property for local schools was levied in Dedham, Massachusetts, in 1648. By 1693, New Hampshire also required towns to support elementary schools.

The Growing Importance of State Governments

Initially, one-room elementary common schools were established in local communities, often fully supported through a small local tax. Each town functioned, moreover, as an independent school district, indeed as an independent school system, since there were no state laws or regulations providing for a statewide public education system. At the same time, several large school systems evolved in the big cities of most states. Even at this early time, these different education systems reflected differences in local ability to support them. Big cities usually were quite wealthy, while the smaller, rural one-room school districts usually were quite poor, many having great difficulty financing a one-room school.

As the number of these small rural and big-city school systems grew, however, and the importance of education as a unifying force for a developing country became increasingly realized by civic and political leaders, new initiatives were undertaken to create statewide education systems. By 1820, 13 of the then 23 states had constitutional provisions, and 17 had statutory provisions pertaining to public education.

In the mid-eighteenth century, several states began to completely rewrite state constitutions, not only calling for creation of statewide systems of public education, but also formally establishing government responsibility for financing schools. Today, all states have constitutional provisions related to free public education.

Creation of free common schools reflected the importance of education in America. It also shifted control over education from individuals and the church to the state. Control over schools was a problematic aspect in crafting statewide education systems. The resolution to the control issue was creation of local lay boards of education that, it was argued, would function in the place of parents and the church.

While local boards basically controlled public schools for the first century they existed, the strength of local control has changed substantially in recent years. In the early twentieth century, much school control was given to the new breed of educational professionals, as the Progressive Era of education sought to take politics out of education (Tyack and Hansot, 1982). Beginning in the 1960s, both the state and federal government began to exert new initiative and control affecting public schools. States continued this trend by taking the lead for education policy throughout the 1980s' education reform period (Doyle and Hartle, 1985; Odden, 1995a). Local boards were for the most part uninvolved in those reforms (Odden, 1995a). In the early 1990s, the president and the nation's governors established nationwide education goals; these were codified into law in 1994 by the U.S. Congress and continue in spirit if not in detail today.

The development of the state-controlled and governmentally financed "common school" also raised many fundamental issues about school finance. The key issues concerned the level of government (local or state) that would support public education and whether new constitutional phrases such as "general and uniform," "thorough and efficient," "basic," or "adequate" meant an equal amount of dollars would be spent for every student in the state, or meant just providing a basic education program for every student, with different amounts of total dollars determined at the local level. As discussed in Chapter 2, this controversy persists today and is resolved in different ways by state legislatures and courts in the 50 states.

Evolution of the State Role in Education Finance

While major differences exist in the specific approaches taken, most states finance public schools primarily through local property taxes. Indeed, in the mid-to-late 1800s, most states required local districts to fully finance mandated public schools through local property taxation. In designing locally administered school systems, states generally gave local governments the authority to raise money for schools by levying property taxes. But when states determined school district boundaries, districts ended up with widely varying levels of property wealth per pupil, and thus large differences in the ability to raise local dollars to support public education. Districts with above-average property tax bases per pupil traditionally were able to spend at above-average levels with below-average tax rates, while districts with below-average tax bases spent at below-average levels even with above-average tax rates.

School finance policy debates throughout the twentieth century, including most school finance texts (see, for example, Alexander and Salmon, 1995; Guthrie, Garms, and Pierce, 1988; Odden and Picus, 1992, 2000, Chapter 1; Swanson and King, 1997) and most court cases, focused on these types of fiscal inequities. To be sure, some individuals pointed to spending differences per se, regardless of whether they were related to varying tax bases, and argued that they should be impermissible in a *state* education system (Wise, 1968). But the bulk of discussion centered on the links between spending differences and local property wealth per pupil (see also Coons, Clune, and Sugarman, 1970).

As discussed at length in Chapter 5, states began to intervene in school financing first through small per-pupil "flat grant" programs in which the state distributed an equal amount of money per pupil to each local school district. The idea was for the state to provide at least some assistance in support of a local basic education program. Over the years, these flat grants became recognized as too small.

In the early 1920s, states began to implement "minimum foundation programs," which provided a much higher level of base financial support and were financed with a combination of state and local revenues (minimum foundation programs and other technical school finance terms used in this chapter are defined and explained more in Chapter 5). These programs were the first in which states explicitly recognized the wide variation in the local property tax base, and designed a state aid structure to distribute larger amounts to districts with a small property tax base per pupil and smaller amounts to districts with a large property tax base per pupil.

These "equalization formulas" were designed to "equalize" differences in local fiscal capacity (i.e., the unequal ability to finance education because of the variation in the size of the local property tax base). But over time, the level of the minimum foundation programs also proved to be inadequate, and additional revenues above the foundation program were raised solely through local taxation. As a result, local educational expenditures per pupil varied widely across local districts in most states, with the differences related primarily to the size of the local property tax base.

Beginning in the late 1960s, these fiscal disparities caused by unequal distribution of the local tax base and inadequate state general equalization programs led to legal challenges to state school finance systems in which plaintiffs, usually from low-wealth and low-spending districts, argued that the disparities not only were unfair but also were unconstitutional (Berke, 1974; Coons, Clune, and Sugarman, 1970). Chapter 2 traces the course of these lawsuits, which spawned a new political channel to improve the ways states financed public education, and which evolved in the 1990s into an "adequacy" strategy to link the funding structure with an education system that could teach nearly all students to high performance.

3. EVOLUTION OF THE SCHOOL FINANCE PROBLEM

This section discusses how the nature of the school finance problem became much more complicated in the 1990s and early twenty-first century. Though many still define the major school finance problem as differences in spending across school districts caused by varying levels of property wealth per pupil, others (e.g., Odden and Clune, 1998) argue that linking finance to an adequate education is the core school finance issue today. Still others argue that educational productivity—determining how to produce higher levels of educational performance with current education resources—is the key school finance goal today (Hanushek and Associates, 1994).

Traditional Fiscal Disparities

This section discusses the nature of school finance inequities in several states, and shows how the nature of these school finance fiscal inequities has changed over time.

California.　　There are many ways to depict the types of fiscal disparities among school districts created by the unequal distribution of the property tax. Table 1.5 shows 1968–69 data that were presented in the original *Serrano* v. *Priest* (Cal. 3d 584, 487 P.2d 1241, 96 Cal. Rptr. 601 [1971]) court case in California (see Chapter 2 for more on this case); at that time, California had a typical minimum foundation program, and most districts raised additional funds to spend at a higher level. These data represent property value per child, the local school tax rate, and resulting expenditures per pupil for pairs of property-rich and property-poor districts in several counties. In each county example, the assessed valuation per pupil—the local tax base—varied substantially: by a factor of almost fourteen-to-one in Los Angeles County and over sixteen-to-one in Alameda County. In each example, moreover, the district with the higher assessed value per child had both the higher expenditures per pupil and the lower tax rate.

　　These examples were selected to show that the California school finance structure produced a situation—similar to most other states at that time—in which districts with a low property tax base usually spent less than the state average even with above-average tax rates, while districts with a high property tax base usually spent above the state average with below-average tax rates. The wealthy enjoyed both the advantages of high expenditures and low tax rates, while the poor were disadvantaged by both low expenditures and high tax rates. The shortcoming of the data in Table 1.5 is that school finance information for only a few districts is shown. While these districts statistically reflected the trends in the system, trends should be analyzed using all of the districts in a state, not selected pairs of districts from different counties.

TABLE 1.5　Comparison of Selected Tax Rates and Expenditure Levels in Selected California Counties, 1968–69

County	Pupils	Assessed Value per Pupil	Tax Rate	Expenditure per Pupil
Alameda				
Emery Unified	586	$100,187	$2.57	$2,223
Newark Unified	8,638	6,048	5.65	616
Fresno				
Colinga Unified	2,640	$33,244	$2.17	$963
Clovis Unified	8,144	6,480	4.28	565
Kern				
Rio Bravo Elementary	121	$136,271	$1.05	$1,545
Lamont Elementary	1,847	5,971	3.06	533
Los Angeles				
Beverly Hills Unified	5,542	$50,885	$2.38	$1,232
Baldwin Park Unified	13,108	3,706	5.48	577

Source: California Supreme Court Opinion in *Serrano* v. *Priest,* August 1971.

TABLE 1.6   Assessed Valuation per Pupil in Colorado School Districts, 1977

Highest: Rio Blanco-Rangely	$326,269
90th percentile: Eagle-Eagle	57,516
Median: Mesa-Plauteau Valley	20,670
10th percentile: Montezuma-Dolores	10,764
Lowest: El Paso-Fountain	4,197
Ratio: Highest/Lowest	77.7:1
Ratio: 90th/10th Percentiles:	5.3:1

Source: Education Finance Center, Education Commission of the States from official data of the Colorado Department of Education.

Colorado.   Another potentially misleading approach in presenting school finance data is to show the extreme cases, as was often done in school finance equity analyses in the 1960s and 1970s. An example is shown in Table 1.6, which displays for Colorado the value of assessed valuation per pupil for the richest and poorest districts, districts at the 90th and 10th percentiles, and the district in the middle. These 1977 data show that the difference between the wealthiest and poorest was 77.7 to 1. This means that at a tax rate of one mill, the wealthiest district can raise $325.27 per pupil, while the poorest district could raise only $4.20! To raise the amount that the wealthiest district produced at one mill, the poorest district would have had to levy a tax rate of 77.7 mills, which is prohibitively high. To blunt the criticism that the extreme cases might represent anomalies, the values for districts at the 90th and 10th percentiles are also presented in Table 1.6. The figures show that property wealth per child still varied substantially, from a high of $57,516 to a low of $10,764, a difference of 5.3 to 1. While these differences are smaller than the range between the very top and bottom, the data clearly indicate substantial differences in school district ability to raise school funds through local property taxes.

This figure also shows the emphasis on variation in the local tax base, per se, in many early school finance analyses. What really matters, of course, is the interaction of the local tax base, local tax rates, and state equalization aid on the final per-pupil spending figure for each district. But even in the first school finance case taken to the U.S. Supreme Court (see Chapter 2), great emphasis was given just to the variation in the local tax base. The data in Table 1.6 *implied* that the Colorado school finance system would have substantial fiscal disparities.

Table 1.7 shows the magnitude of the actual disparities by displaying statistics calculated from a sample of all Colorado school districts in 1977. At that time, Colorado had a guaranteed tax base program (see Chapter 5), but had "frozen" all local expenditures and allowed only modest increases from year to year, letting lower-spending districts increase at a somewhat faster rate than higher-spending districts. This figure organizes all data into groups (in this case five groups, or quintiles), and presents averages for each quintile.[1] Note that each quintile includes approximately an equal percentage of students—not

---

[1]Other studies categorize districts into seven groups (septiles) or 10 groups (deciles). The most common practice today is to use deciles.

TABLE 1.7   Authorized Revenue Base and Current Operating Expenditures per Pupil by Quintiles of Assessed Valuation per Pupil, Colorado, 1977

Assessed Valuation per Pupil	Percent of Pupils	Number of Districts	Authorized Revenue Base	Current Operating Expenditures per Pupil
$ 4,197–12,800	19	33	1,196	$1,532
12,800–15,500	20	25	1,312	1,594
15,500–17,600	14	14	1,299	1,667
17,600–24,500	27	32	1,476	1,742
24,500–326,269	20	77	1,692	2,342

Source: Education Finance Center, Education Commission of the States from official data of the Colorado Department of Education.

districts.[2] Interestingly, though property wealth per pupil varied substantially, both the authorized revenue base (ARB)[3] and current operating expenditures per pupil varied by a much smaller magnitude. Indeed, the ratio between the ARB of the top or wealthiest quintile and that for the bottom or poorest quintile is 1.4 to 1, much less than the 5.3 to 1 ratio of wealth at the 90th to the wealth at the 10th percentile. Further, the ratio of current operating expenditures per pupil at the top quintile to that of the bottom quintile is slightly higher, at 1.5 to 1. Unfortunately, the local tax rate and state aid figures were not provided, so it is not possible to determine whether the more equal revenue and expenditure figures are produced by fiscal-capacity-equalizing state aid, or high tax rates in the low-wealth districts.

New Jersey.   New Jersey data for two time periods—1975–76 and 1978–79—are presented by septiles (seven groups) in Table 1.8. The purpose of these two charts is to show differences in the New Jersey school finance structure three years after the courts, responding to a 1973 court decision overturning the school finance structure, shut down that state's education finance system in 1976, forcing the legislature finally to enact a major school finance reform (see Chapter 2). These figures are somewhat difficult to read because they do not include any typical univariate or relationship statistics (see Chapter 3). Nevertheless, several characteristics are clear from the data. First, in general, expenditures per pupil increased as property value per pupil increased; it seems that both before and after reform, expenditures were a function of local property wealth in New Jersey. But, expenditures per pupil in 1978–79 were nearly the same for the first

[2]Several earlier studies grouped data into categories with equal numbers of districts, and that practice still is followed. However, the emerging practice is to have an equal number of students in each category, to assess the impact of the system on students. See Berne and Stiefel (1984) and Chapter 3 for discussion of the unit of analysis.

[3]The ARB is a Colorado-specific, general fund revenue per-pupil limit that varied for each local school district. It included revenues for the regular education program.

TABLE 1.8   New Jersey School Finance

Relationship between Property Wealth,
Current Expenditures, and Tax Rates, **1975–76**

Equalized Valuation per Pupil	Current Expenditures per Pupil	Current Expenditures per Weighted Pupil	Current School Tax Rate
Group 1: Less than $33,599	$1,504	$1,372	$1.79
Group 2: $33,600–$45,499	1,414	1,324	2.12
Group 3: $45,500–$58,699	1,411	1,347	2.00
Group 4: $58,700–$67,199	1,460	1,401	1.99
Group 5: $67,200–$78,499	1,604	1,543	1.89
Group 6: $78,500–$95,499	1,689	1,628	1.74
Group 7: $95,500 and over	1,752	1,681	1.17
State average	1,550	1,473	1.69

Relationship between Property Wealth,
Current Expenditures, and Tax Rates, **1978–79**

Equalized Valuation per Pupil	Current Expenditures per Pupil	Current Expenditures per Weighted Pupil	Current School Tax Rate
Group 1: Less than $37,000	$1,994	$1,760	$1.67
Group 2: $37,000–$54,999	1,933	1,763	1.57
Group 3: $55,000–$73,999	1,978	1,816	1.55
Group 4: $74,000–$87,999	1,994	1,882	1.58
Group 5: $88,000–$102,999	2,200	2,061	1.69
Group 6: $103,000–$125,199	2,268	2,154	1.67
Group 7: $125,200 and over	2,390	2,262	1.11
State average	2,113	1,959	1.47

Source: Goertz, 1979.

four groups, suggesting that some expenditure-per-pupil equality had been produced for the bottom half by the 1976 reform in New Jersey.

Second, the range[4] increased for both expenditures per pupil and expenditures per weighted pupil between 1976 and 1979; even the range divided by the statewide average increased, suggesting that overall spending disparities increased over those three years.

[4]The difference between the highest and lowest value.

Third, there seems to be wider expenditure-per-pupil disparities on a weighted pupil basis, where the weights indicate special pupil needs (see Chapter 6). Indeed, the weighted pupil count substantially reduces the expenditure-per-pupil figure for the lowest-wealth districts, indicating—correctly, it turns out for New Jersey—that these districts have large numbers of special-needs students.[5]

Finally, and quite interestingly, school property tax rates dropped in New Jersey over these three years, and school property tax rates were almost equal across all but the wealthiest group of districts in 1979.

It seems, therefore, that the major impact of the 1976 New Jersey reform was to equalize school tax rates for most districts, and to increase unweighted expenditures per pupil in the bottom half to about the same level. On a weighted pupil basis, however, spending was not equal in the bottom half, and overall spending disparities seemed to increase. This New Jersey system was overturned by a 1990 state supreme court decision (*Abbott* v. *Burke*), in a case filed in the mid-1980s, but not fully resolved until 1998 (again, see Chapter 2).

Texas.   Texas enacted a major school finance reform as part of a comprehensive education reform during 1984 (Odden and Dougherty, 1984), but that system was challenged in state court a few years later. The 1984 law provided for a minimum foundation program with a higher expenditure-per-pupil level than before 1984, a small guaranteed yield program on top of the foundation program, weights for several different categories of pupil need, and a price adjustment to account for the varying prices Texas districts faced in purchasing education commodities. In the fall of 1987, the court ruled the school finance system unconstitutional, and the state created an Education Finance Reform Commission in early 1988.

The data in Table 1.9 were presented to that commission. The data are organized into groups with approximately equal numbers of children; this time, 20 different groupings are provided, thus showing the impact of the finance structure on each 5 percent of students. The numbers show that, indeed, property wealth per pupil varied substantially in Texas, from under $56,150 to over $440,987, a difference of 7.9 to 1. In fact, the difference was greater, since several districts had assessed valuation per pupil from $800,000 to over $1 million. These very high wealth districts were not anomalies but actual districts that included several of Texas' largest cities and some very wealthy suburban districts. The bottom line in Texas was that the local property tax per pupil clearly was distributed unequally among local school districts.

The column displaying total state and local revenues per pupil shows, however, that while per-pupil revenues tend to increase with wealth, this trend is strongest primarily for the wealthiest districts with 15 percent of the students. For the districts with revenues below that, revenues per pupil vary by about 10 percent above or below a figure of $3,300 per pupil—not a dramatic variation. In fact, it could be argued these data indicate that for the majority of students in the middle, revenues per pupil were basically

---

[5]Many of these districts are large urban districts with large numbers and percentages of poor students, physically and mentally handicapped students, and low-achieving students.

TABLE 1.9 Selected Texas School Finance Variables, 1986–87

Number of Districts	Range of Property Wealth per Pupil	Average Property Wealth per Pupil	Local Revenue per Pupil	State Revenue per Pupil	State and Local Revenues per Pupil	Federal Revenue per Pupil
26	Under $56,150	$ 46,217	$ 508	$2,528	$3,036	$564
57	56,150–79,652	68,793	647	2,309	2,956	426
73	79,653–96,562	87,980	801	2,204	3,005	277
123	96,563–117,462	107,516	1,006	2,092	3,096	269
68	117,463–128,425	120,325	1,050	2,109	3,159	309
73	128,426–144,213	136,285	1,192	2,074	3,266	283
52	144,214–156,931	152,061	1,355	1,864	3,215	227
34	156,932–167,090	161,971	1,610	1,711	3,321	145
46	167,091–177,108	169,925	1,658	1,711	3,369	203
84	177,109–202,136	190,514	1,727	1,643	3,370	171
37	202,137–218,238	208,862	1,904	1,499	3,403	126
44	218,239–239,117	224,173	1,963	1,473	3,436	139
26	239,118–253,338	244,493	2,055	1,403	3,458	130
42	253,339–276,674	260,613	2,281	1,342	3,623	181
36	276,675–308,780	294,373	2,942	1,123	4,065	113
1	308,781–308,862	308,862	2,006	1,125	3,131	312
45	308,863–356,189	330,130	2,494	1,039	3,533	128
45	356,190–436,960	399,954	3,459	830	4,285	89
3	436,961–440,987	440,607	2,862	960	3,822	294
146	Over $440,987	799,896	4,764	418	5,182	143

Source: Texas State Board of Education.

equal. The problem with the system was the low spending of districts at the very bottom, and the high spending of districts at the top. This problem definition requires a different policy response than if disparities are spread across the entire system. Nevertheless, the Texas lower court overturned the system, and that decision was upheld on appeal by a unanimous Texas State Supreme Court in the fall of 1989. This pattern, where even modest variations in spending per pupil that are linked to local property wealth are likely to be overturned by a state court, continues to exist in some states today.

Solutions to School Finance Inequities

We should note that at these times, the underlying school finance problem was seen as the inequality of property wealth per pupil, and many believed that the way to remedy the problem was to make the ability to raise funds for schools more equal across districts. In school finance parlance, the solution was to enact a guaranteed tax base (GTB) or "district power equalizing" program (i.e., a program that guaranteed to all or nearly all districts—rich or poor—some high-level tax base; see Chapter 5). This kind of program allows local districts to tap the same size tax base, and have equal access to revenues at a given tax rate regardless of their actual property wealth per pupil—up to the tax base guaranteed by the state. This allows districts to determine for themselves the level of spending on local education programs, rather than constraining them because they are a low-wealth district.

Under a GTB, higher spending per pupil requires a higher tax rate, but all districts with the same tax rate should have the same revenues per pupil unless their property wealth per pupil exceeds the state guarantee—in which case they could generate more revenue per pupil. While differences in education spending per pupil might remain, these differences would be the result of different choices by local school districts and their voters, not the unequal distribution of the local tax base.

Early school finance reformers anticipated that GTB programs would both reduce spending differences across districts, and would also reduce the linkage between local property wealth per pupil and spending per pupil.

A Different Type of School Finance Problem

These expectations also "assumed" existence of the typical school finance problem or fiscal inequities reflected in all of the previous examples—high property wealth per pupil associated with both high expenditures and low tax rates, together with low property wealth per pupil associated with both low expenditures and high tax rates. But even in the 1970s, this "typical" situation did not hold for all states. The New York school finance situation in 1978 is such an example, as the data in Table 1.10 show. At that time, New York had a school finance system that functioned like a minimum foundation program, but was actually a low-spending level percentage equalizing formula (see Chapter 5). The data in Table 1.10 are presented for all districts, except for New York City, divided into 10 equal groups, or deciles. Each decile has approximately an equal number of students. New York City, with an enrollment of nearly 1 million in a state with a then total

TABLE 1.10   Selected New York School Finance Variables, 1977–78

Deciles of Approved Federal Operating Expenditures per Pupil	Assessed Value per Pupil	Gross Income per Return (1977)	Property Tax Rate (mills)	Property Tax Revenue per Pupil	Other Local Revenue per Pupil	Total State Aid per Pupil	Total Local and State Revenue per Pupil	Total Aid per Pupil
First Decile ($988–$1,389)	$37,957	$12,225	13.01	$485	$54	$1,220	$1,759	$35
Second Decile ($1,390–$1,471)	41,924	12,446	15.34	634	56	1,176	1,866	37
Third Decile ($1,473–$1,542)	46,902	12,422	17.11	770	62	1,107	1,939	58
Fourth Decile ($1,544–$1,640)	50,968	13,527	17.61	862	67	1,081	2,010	40
Fifth Decile ($1,642–$1,789)	57,916	14,190	19.63	1,086	68	1,006	2,160	63
Sixth Decile ($1,790–$1,899)	58,986	13,311	21.68	1,178	72	998	2,248	117
Seventh Decile ($1,903–$2,017)	64,323	15,274	23.48	1,430	81	953	2,464	44
Eighth Decile ($2,021–$2,255)	66,469	16,157	23.69	1,526	178	896	2,600	74
Ninth Decile ($2,260–$2,474)	78,069	16,778	25.26	1,896	102	866	2,864	57
Tenth Decile ($2,475–$5,752)	115,535	21,639	23.84	2,583	154	706	3,443	36
New York City	81,506	13,607	22.52	1,760	41	864	2,665	217
Rest of State	61,732	14,762	20.05	1,240	89	1,002	2,331	57
Statewide Average	67,715	14,412	20.79	1,397	75	960	2,432	105

Source: Odden, Palaich, and Augenblick, 1979.

of 3 million, is shown separately, since if it were included in the deciles, it alone would include over three of the deciles.

Several elements of the data should be noted. To begin, the data are grouped by deciles of spending per pupil; the idea in New York was that expenditure-per-pupil disparities were the final, important variable, and analysis of correlates of that variable should be the focus of the study. Columns 1 and 8 show that revenues per pupil from local and state sources varied widely in New York during the 1977–78 school year, from a low of $1,759 in the bottom spending decile to a high of $3,443 in the highest spending decile, a difference of about 2 to 1. Note that this is a much smaller disparity than the 5.8 to 1 difference in spending between the very top ($5,752) and the very bottom ($988) spending districts.

Second, both spending per pupil and revenues per pupil from local and state sources increase with property wealth, the traditional pattern in school finance. But note also that the school property tax rate also increases; in fact, the school tax rate for the top few deciles is between 50 and almost 100 percent higher than the tax rates in the lowest spending districts. This reality set New York school finance apart from the situation in most other states at that time. Indeed, one of the reasons the wealthier districts spent more per pupil was that they taxed local property at a higher rate. Yes, those districts had a larger property tax base, but they also taxed it more heavily.

It also was true that household income as measured by gross income per return on New York State income tax returns increased with property wealth, and thus with spending and school tax rates. It turns out that higher-income families, not only in New York but also generally, choose to levy higher tax rates for schools. Thus, while higher spending in New York was caused in part by higher local tax effort, that higher tax effort in part was aided by higher household income. Further, household income and property wealth per pupil were highly and positively correlated in New York at that time.

In short, the New York data showed that higher spending occurred in districts with higher property wealth, higher household income, and higher school tax rates, while lower spending occurred in property-poor and income-poor districts with low tax rates. In fact, the correlation between wealth and per-pupil spending was much stronger in New York than in the Texas data displayed in Table 1.9. In the 1970s, a Texas school finance case reached the U.S. Supreme Court (see Chapter 2 for details). That case was ultimately unsuccessful. New York, with a much more clear correlation between measures of wealth and per-pupil spending might have made a better case at the federal level.

These variations from the traditional pattern (i.e., high tax high spending and low tax low spending rather than low tax high spending and high tax low spending) found in New York complicated the formulation of a school finance reform that could pass muster with both the courts and the legislature. When the New York's highest court ruled in 1980 that the system, while unfair, was not unconstitutional, the push for reform abated, and school finance was changed incrementally over time, and still displays these general characteristics.

But New York is not the only state today that exhibits these school finance patterns. Three quite different states—Illinois, Missouri, and Wisconsin—provide additional examples of this "new" type of school finance problem. All three states enacted different versions of school finance reforms over the 1975–95 period. Illinois implemented a generous "reward for effort" GTB-type program in the late 1970s and early 1980s, but then changed it to a foundation-type program in the 1980s and early 1990s.

Missouri implemented a combination foundation-GTB program, which was continuously enhanced over those 20 years so that in 1995, the GTB was set at the 95th percentile of property wealth per pupil,[6] with a minimum required tax rate that resulted in a minimum expenditure of just over $3,000 per pupil.

In 1993, Wisconsin created and implemented a fully funded GTB-type program. The program's major feature guaranteed each district could raise property taxes as if it had the wealth of the district at the 93rd percentile of wealth, and guaranteed spending of at least the 60th percentile of expenditure per pupil.

To greater or lesser degrees, all three states deferred actual spending decisions to local districts, and their school finance structures represent the three major school finance systems: foundation, GTB, and combined foundation-GTB (see Chapter 5 for discussions of these structures). Tables 1.11, 1.12, and 1.13 show the status of school finance in these three states in 1994–95, with the data organized by decile of spending from state and local sources per pupil, again excluding spending for special-needs students.[7] The results indicate that the school finance reforms implemented in these states did not produce the anticipated equity effects. There are still wide spending disparities and, even with major school finance reforms, spending per pupil is still highly associated with property wealth per pupil—the higher the wealth, the higher the spending.

Further, the linkages between spending and tax rates are more like those in New York. In all three cases, although spending per pupil increases with property wealth per pupil, so does the local tax rate for schools. In all three states, the higher the tax rate, the higher the spending. In all three states, higher-property-wealth-per-pupil districts have higher spending per pupil but also have the highest tax rates; conversely, lower-property-wealth-per-pupil districts still have lower spending per pupil but now also have the lowest tax rates.

What happened? First, overall spending per pupil increased in real terms in all three states (122 percent in Illinois, 144 percent in Missouri, and 144 percent in Wisconsin) from 1980 to 1995, using the consumer price index as the deflator. Indeed, school finance reform generally led to higher overall spending (Murray, Evans, and Schwab, 1998). But it seems that the school finance reforms, which would have allowed lower-property-wealth-per-pupil districts to increase their spending to average or higher levels while also lowering their tax rates, were not used for that purpose. Rather, lower-wealth districts appeared to use the potential of the reform programs primarily to lower their tax rates from an above-average to a below-average level. The data show that while

---

[6]This means that every district could levy property taxes and collect per-pupil revenues as if they had the same property wealth as the district at the 95th percentile of wealth.

[7]The data only show local property tax revenues and state equalization aid for these states, and exclude other sources of revenue which in Missouri can average $800 per student. The data also are only for K–12 districts in the three states. The figures are intended to show the final results of school finance reforms implemented over several years. The school finance structure has not changed substantively in any of the states since 1995, though in Wisconsin substantial state revenue has replaced local revenues, but because of spending controls, spending differences have not been altered much. Readers are also referred to Chapter 3 for definitions of the following terms in the figures: horizontal equity and fiscal neutrality.

TABLE 1.11   School Finance in Missouri, 1994–95, K–12 Districts

Decile	Revenues per Pupil[a]	Assessed Value per Pupil (at Market Value)	Local Property Tax Rate (Percent)
1	$2,987	$118,969	1.11
2	3,221	90,120	1.17
3	3,288	103,279	1.17
4	3,426	140,218	1.18
5	3,562	157,524	1.26
6	3,665	150,897	1.34
7	3,829	200,460	1.31
8	4,049	217,998	1.36
9	4,411	254,362	1.44
10	5,973	523,521	1.24

Source: Odden, 1999.

[a]Each district also receives an additional $648 per-pupil flat grant from a state sales tax.

Horizontal equity
   Coefficient of variation: 19.5
   McLoone Index: 0.92
Fiscal neutrality
   Correlation: 0.90
   Wealth elasticity: 0.23

TABLE 1.12   School Finance in Illinois, 1994–95, K–12 Districts

Decile	Revenues per Pupil	Assessed Value per Pupil (at Market Value)	Local Property Tax Rate (Percent)
1	$2,893	$103,238	0.60
2	3,042	126,874	0.61
3	3,130	140,313	0.63
4	3,258	157,754	0.63
5	3,400	207,211	0.67
6	3,632	220,635	0.70
7	3,922	251,595	0.83
8	4,219	280,519	0.86
9	4,687	312,488	0.89
10	5,343	386,903	1.07

Source: Odden, 1999.

Horizontal equity
   Coefficient of variation: 20.4
   McLoone Index: 0.91
Fiscal neutrality
   Correlation: 0.75
   Wealth elasticity: 0.32

TABLE 1.13   School Finance in Wisconsin, 1994–95, K–12 Districts

Decile	Revenues per Pupil[a]	Assessed Value per Pupil (at Market Value)	Local Property Tax Rate (Percent)
1	$4,860	$ 164,138	1.36
2	5,188	179,004	1.45
3	5,310	147,378	1.48
4	5,350	180,601	1.50
5	5,468	172,183	1.53
6	5,569	195,932	1.55
7	5,713	196,185	1.59
8	5,962	196,601	1.73
9	6,231	222,376	1.84
10	6,828	351,184	1.74

Source: Odden, 1999.

Horizontal equity	
Coefficient of variation:	9.87
McLoone Index:	0.95
Fiscal neutrality	
Correlation:	0.59
Wealth elasticity:	0.14

lower-wealth districts still tend to have below-average spending levels, they do so because they also have below-average tax rates. Although the high-level GTBs in both Missouri and Wisconsin would allow these lower-wealth-per-pupil districts to spend at substantially higher levels with only modestly higher tax rates, the districts generally have chosen not to do so. They have chosen low tax rates, which in turn, have produced low expenditure levels. In short, many of the low-wealth districts did not behave as anticipated when provided a major school finance reform program.

The high-wealth districts also seemed to engage in unpredictable behavior. As these states implemented their school finance reforms over the past 20 years, it seems that the higher-wealth districts, which had enjoyed both a spending and tax rate advantage, decided to maintain their spending lead but could do so only by raising their local tax efforts for schools. Yes, some of the exceedingly wealthy districts still can spend at a high level because of their very high wealth, but with the state guaranteeing to all the tax base of the districts at the 93rd–95th percentiles, a wealth advantage exists only for a small percentage of districts, and most of these have a wealth advantage just above what the state will guarantee. For the bulk of the districts in the top third of property wealth per pupil, therefore, the higher spending is primarily produced by their higher tax rates for school purposes, reflecting the desire of their taxpayers to provide a high-quality and expensive education system.

Overall, spending disparities did drop in states that had court cases, and the states responded with school finance reforms (Murray, Evans, and Schwab, 1998). But the decrease was modest, averaging between 16 and 25 percent, depending on the statistical measure used.

In sum, the school finance changes did not do as much to reduce fiscal inequities as expected. Instead, the programs led to overall increases in education spending, and during that process, lower-wealth districts lowered their tax rates to below the average and settled for below-average-spending-per-pupil levels, while higher-wealth districts maintained their spending advantage by raising their tax rates and thus their spending advantages. The result was continued spending disparities, although this time driven more rationally by local tax rate differences rather than by the accident of the distribution of the local property tax base. The outcome also was little or only modest change in these states' fiscal equity statistics—both those measuring spending disparities and those measuring the connection between spending and property wealth.

The School Finance Problem as Fiscal Adequacy

Of course, improving fiscal equity might not be the most pressing school finance issue in these states, as it was for states in the 1970s and 1980s. In fact, delineating what the school finance "problem" is for New York as well as Illinois, Missouri, and Wisconsin has become a major subject of debate. Some argue that the continued existence of spending disparities and their relationship to local property wealth, whatever the cause, remains a problem. But if the "old" problem was the unequal ability to raise revenues to support public schools, and that problem is resolved by the high-level GTB or other kind of school finance reform program, others say that any remaining spending differences are a matter of local taxpayer choice and reflect neither an inherent inequity nor a school-funding problem. Another group may argue that since education is a state function, spending differences per se (as a proxy for education quality) are a problem regardless of whether they are caused by the unequal distribution of the property tax base or local taxpayer choice. Still others focus on the spending of the bottom half of districts, arguing it should be higher.

The problem with all three of these arguments, however, is that they deal simply with money and largely whether base funding is equal or not, and are not related to any other substantive education goal, such as education quality or student achievement. Making this connection is the school finance challenge of today. The driving education issue today is raising the levels of student achievement [i.e., setting high and rigorous standards and teaching students to those standards (Fuhrman, 1993; Massell, Hoppe, and Kirst, 1997; Smith and O'Day, 1991)]. Research from cognitive science suggests that we know how to produce a much higher level of learning, or at least make substantial progress toward this goal (Bransford, Brown, and Cocking, 1999; Bruer, 1993; Siegler, 1998). Given this knowledge, Linda Darling-Hammond (1997) argues that learning to high standards should be considered a right for all children. Moreover, school finance litigation in many states has begun to stress adequacy issues over equity issues (Enrich, 1995; Heise, 1995; Minorini and Sugarman, 1999a, 1999b; and Chapter 2).

Reflecting this student achievement goal, and the education policy and program issues, what curriculum, instruction, incentive, capacity development, organization, and management strategies are required to produce this higher level of student performance? The related finance issue is what level of funding is required for these programmatic strategies?

As both Odden and Clune (1998) and Reschovsky and Imazeki (1998, 2001) argue, the prime school finance problem today is to link school finance to the strategies needed to accomplish the goal of teaching students to higher standards. In new school finance parlance, the challenge is to determine an "adequate" level of spending. The task is to identify for each district/school the level of base spending needed to teach the average student to state standards, and then to identify how much extra each district/school requires to teach students with special needs—the learning disabled, those from poverty and thus educationally deficient backgrounds, and those without English proficiency—to the same high and rigorous achievement standards. As Clune (1994a, 1994b) and Odden and Clune (1998) argue, this requires a shift in school finance thinking from "equity" to "adequacy."

Interestingly, in each of the three sample states discussed earlier, educators and policymakers have begun to raise the issue of school finance adequacy in many ways. Some questioned whether the spending levels of the bottom half of all districts (i.e., those districts with just average or mostly below-average tax rates) were a "problem" (i.e., were too low), or whether those spending levels, even though below average, were "adequate" to teach their students to acceptable standards. Others attempted to calculate a state-supported spending level that can be linked to a specified level of student performance (e.g., it will cost X dollars for 90 percent of students to meet or exceed state proficiency standards in core subjects). In a sense, this is a "back to the future" school finance objective, as many foundation programs have sought to make this linkage throughout this century. Still others explored the degree to which any "adequate" spending level should be supplemented by additional money to provide extra resources to teach students with special needs to high standards.

Chapter 3 discusses the complexities of determining an "adequate" spending level and the various methodologies that are being tapped to determine those levels (see also Guthrie and Rothstein, 1999). Nevertheless, for many, the focus on adequacy constitutes a shift in defining the basic school finance problem—away from the sole focus on fiscal disparities across districts and toward linking spending to what could be construed as an adequate education program (i.e., a program designed to teach students to high levels of achievement).

The School Finance Problem as Productivity

Despite disparities or any other shortcomings of current state education finance systems, many other analysts argue that the most prominent school finance problem is the low levels of system performance and student achievement produced with the relatively large levels of funding in the system (Hanushek and Associates, 1994). These analysts are convinced that, on balance, there is a sufficient amount of revenue in the American public school system, and that the core problem is to determine how best to use those resources, particularly how to use the resources differently to support strategies that dramatically boost student performance. In one sense, much of this book addresses these productivity and adequacy issues. Nearly all chapters address the adequacy issue. Chapter 3 has a section on what is known about improving productivity in education, and Chapter 10 addresses strategies for reallocating resources to produce higher student performance levels—how to use current dollars more effectively.

But it is clear for the next several years that while equity will remain a topic of school finance, the issues of adequacy and productivity will probably dominate. Today, educators need to show how to transform current and new dollars into student achievement results, or the argument that education needs more—or even the current level of—money will be unlikely to attract public or political support.

4. SUMMARY

This chapter showed that public school funding is big business in the United States. Revenues for public schools are almost $400 billion, and consume 3.9 percent of the country's gross domestic product and 4.5 percent of all personal income. Moreover, revenues for public schools grew consistently during the twentieth century, so that by the end of that century and the beginning of the twenty-first century an average of $6,855 was being spent on each public school student. Unfortunately, those dollars were distributed unequally across states, districts, schools, and students. In too many instances, districts with higher property wealth per pupil and/or higher household income were able to raise and spend more money per pupil even at lower tax rates than were districts with lower per-pupil property tax bases and/or households with lower income. These fiscal disparities translated into differences in class size, teacher salaries, program offerings, and quality of buildings, with the wealthier districts having the advantage in each category, even with lower tax rates. As a result, the equity of the distribution of public school resources was the primary topic of school finance for over 100 years.

Although equity is still an issue, the adequacy of education revenues has assumed an even more prominent place on the school finance agenda. Today the key school finance issue in most states is whether there is a sufficient—adequate—amount of dollars for districts and schools to teach students to new and rigorous performance standards that have been developed during the past 10 to 15 years of standards-based education reform. Assuming student achievement goals are ambitious, many argue that if school finance adequacy is met, remaining inequities are not as problematic, but not everyone agrees with this position. Thus, both the equity and the adequacy of school funding are central school finance issues today.

— Chapter 2 —

Legal Issues in School Finance

Differences in educational expenditures per pupil across school districts in a state, identified as problems as early as 1905, remain a concern in most states (Cubberly, 1905). Since 1905, school finance "equity" and "adequacy" have been the center of analytic attention and policy debate across the country, and became the subject of court litigation in the late 1960s. But the topics and focus of school finance litigation have changed over the past 30 years. Initially, the impetus for school finance litigation was the increasing use of the federal equal protection clause to ensure rights for individuals who had been subject to discrimination. Lawyers and education finance policy analysts believed that equal protection constitutional arguments could also apply to school finance inequities and filed several suits to have traditional spending disparities among school districts—long considered unfair—declared unconstitutional as well. But in the past 10 years, litigation on school finance systems has evolved from a focus on fiscal equity to the much more complex issue of adequacy. (The shift from equity to adequacy is covered in detail in Chapter 3.) These lawsuits raise the central question of adequacy: Are there sufficient resources in each district and each school to provide a set of programs and services sufficiently powerful to teach the vast majority of students to higher performance standards? With this change, litigation has become more sophisticated and has broadened its concern from equity to the issues of adequacy and productivity.

This chapter reviews the past 40 years of school finance litigation. It begins with the unsuccessful "educational needs" *McInnis* and *Burruss* cases in Illinois and Virginia, respectively. It then discusses the issues involved in school finance litigation based on federal and state equal protection clauses. Next, it analyzes litigation based on state education clauses, a second channel for legal action that began in the wake of the 1973 U.S. Supreme Court's ruling in the *Rodriguez* case that school finance inequities did not violate the U.S. Constitution. This portion shows how litigation based on education clauses has evolved into the topic of educational "adequacy," which is quite similar to the original "educational needs" cases. The chapter concludes with a summary of the key trends in school finance litigation.

1. THE BEGINNING OF SCHOOL
FINANCE LITIGATION

In the late 1960s, two court cases were filed—*McInnis* v. *Shapiro*[1] in Illinois and *Burruss* v. *Wilkerson*[2] in Virginia—challenging the constitutionality of differences in educational expenditures across each state's school districts. While brought on equal protection grounds, these early cases argued that the systems were unconstitutional because education was a fundamental right and the wide differences in expenditures or revenues per pupil across school districts were not related to "educational need." The suits argued that there was no educational justification for wide disparities in per-pupil education revenues and that while differences in educational expenditures per pupil could exist, they had to be related to "educational need" and not educationally irrelevant variables such as the local tax base.

At trial, however, the court reasonably asked for a standard by which to assess and measure educational need. Plaintiffs did not have a strong response; in fact, at that time, "educational need" was a diffuse term on which there was not even minimal agreement as to either definition or measurement. The wide variations in expenditures per pupil alone were not sufficient to move the court to find the system unconstitutional because there was no way to link expenditures to need. In both cases, therefore, the court ruled that the suits were nonjusticiable because need could not be defined, measured, nor costed out; in short, the court did not have a standard by which to assess the plaintiffs' claims.

These first attempts to use the courts as a route to resolve school finance inequities, thus, were unsuccessful. In nearly all subsequent school finance cases, moreover, one of the defendants' first motions has been to declare the case nonjusticiable, citing *McInnis* and *Burruss* as precedents. School finance litigants, however, continued to use equal protection as the legal route to challenge state school finance structures, but developed standards for courts to use. Section 2 outlines the main issues involved in equal protection litigation (see also Levin, 1977; Minorini and Sugarman, 1999a, 1999b; Sparkman, 1990; Underwood, 1995a, 1995b; Underwood and Sparkman, 1991).

2. EQUAL PROTECTION LITIGATION

The U.S. Constitution was written by individuals who were strong proponents of individual rights. The founding fathers believed that everyone was entitled to life, liberty, and the pursuit of happiness. To give this broad phrase substantive meaning and to protect individuals from governmental actions that might limit them, the Constitution's authors added the Bill of Rights as the first 10 amendments to the Constitution. These amendments specified several rights of U.S. citizens, including the right to free speech, to religion, to a free press, to bear arms, and the right of assembly. Other amendments

---

[1]*McInnis* v. *Shapiro*, 293 F. Supp. 327 (N.O. Ill. 1968) aff'd.
[2]*Burruss* v. *Wilkerson*, 310 F. Supp. 572 Virg. (1969), aff'd., 397 U.S. 44 (1970).

to the U.S. Constitution also identified particular rights of citizenship, including the Thirteenth (prohibition of slavery), Fourteenth (due process and equal protection), Fifteenth (cannot deny right to vote on basis of race), Nineteenth (women's suffrage) and Twenty-sixth (18-year-old voting right). Article 1, Sections 9 and 10 of the Constitution created the rights of habeas corpus and prohibit ex post facto laws. The president also can designate fundamental rights through executive orders.

The U.S. Supreme Court has the responsibility and authority for defining the meanings of the rights identified in the U.S. Constitution, the Bill of Rights, and other amendments, and also for determining whether the president, Congress, or state governors and legislatures exercise their power properly, especially as their actions might impact a right specified in the Constitution.

The equal protection clause of the Fourteenth Amendment provides that no state shall "deny to any person within its jurisdiction the equal protection of the laws." This amendment was enacted in the mid-nineteenth century during the time of slavery, and was designed to make it unconstitutional for states to treat African Americans differently from whites. But as history unfolded, new legislation was enacted that was interpreted as violating the equal protection clause, and suits were filed. Over time, the U.S. Supreme Court created mechanisms for determining whether, and how, governmental actions might violate the equal protection clause.

The equal protection clause *could* be read to mean that governments—local, state, and federal—could not treat individuals differently for any reason. But that is clearly not the case. Laws specify that some individuals with a particular license can drive a car or practice medicine or teach in public schools, and some cannot. In each of these cases, governments have determined that individuals need certain skills or expertise to engage in these activities, and the state provides a license only to those individuals who demonstrate that they have the requisite expertise. All states have some clause in their state constitution that has been interpreted to be the equivalent of an equal protection clause (Minorini & Sugarman, 1999a, 1999b; Underwood, 1995a). Thus, many equal protection cases today, and nearly all school finance court cases, are brought on the basis of either or both federal and state equal protection clauses.

The Rational Test

How, then, does a court determine whether or not a governmental action that treats individuals differently is constitutional? When equal protection suits are brought, the court uses one of three tests to determine whether the equal protection clause has been violated. The first is the rational test. This test simply asks whether the government has a reason for the differential treatment. In the previous examples, the reason for not allowing everyone who wishes to drive a car, practice medicine, or teach in the public schools is that governments feel individuals need to demonstrate that they have some expertise in these areas before engaging in these activities. Courts have accepted these explanations for treating individuals differently. Indeed, states usually can cite some reason for any action they take. Thus, if the court invokes the rational equal protection test, the state action usually is upheld because the state can nearly always identify some basis for its law.

The second is an "intermediate test," which has generally been applied to sex discrimination cases. This test asks whether the practice or policy advances some substantial government interest. Many policies that treated women differently from men have been overturned under this test; governments have not been able to identify any substantial government interest that was served by any differential treatment. It is harder to justify action under this test than under the rationale test, but it is not as hard as the third test, strict scrutiny, discussed next.

The Strict Judicial Scrutiny Test

The third test is "strict judicial scrutiny." When the court invokes strict judicial scrutiny, the government bears a tougher burden. It has to show that there is a "compelling state interest" for its particular action and that there is "no less discriminatory" policy for the state to carry out that compelling interest. This is an onerous test. Unless both parts of the test are met, the statute would be held to violate equal protection. When the court invokes this test, states usually have difficulty both in identifying the compelling state interest and in claiming that no other state policies can be identified that have less discriminatory impacts. Indeed, when strict judicial scrutiny is invoked, the state usually loses the case. The strict judicial scrutiny test usually overturns the governmental action that is the basis of the suit.

The key, then, is to identify the circumstances under which the court can invoke strict judicial scrutiny. Courts invoke strict judicial scrutiny in only two circumstances: (1) when governmental action affects a "fundamental right" or (2) when governmental action creates a "suspect classification" of individuals.

Fundamental Rights.   Fundamental rights, as just discussed, are those identified in the Constitution or, over time, in equal protection litigation as the subject of a U.S. Supreme Court ruling. Fundamental rights today include the right to practice any religion, the right of free speech, the right of a free press, the right of assembly, and the right to due process.

Through equal protection litigation during the 1950s and 1960s, the Court created two new fundamental rights: the right to vote and the right to appeal a court case. Many states had required individuals to pay a poll tax in order to register to vote. Poor individuals were unable to pay the tax and thus lost the opportunity to vote. Cases challenging this governmental requirement to pay a poll tax were brought on two grounds: (1) that voting was a fundamental right of U.S. citizens and (2) that the poll tax created a suspect classification (defined in the next section) of poor and nonpoor individuals. The court ruled that voting was indeed a fundamental right, and that there were less discriminatory ways for the state to collect the small amount of revenues acquired through the poll tax, and the poll tax was ruled to be unconstitutional.

During that time, some states required individuals who lost a lower court case to pay for a reproduction of the court transcript if they wanted to appeal the court decision. Individuals without the economic means to do so thus lost their opportunity to appeal. Cases challenging this governmental requirement again were brought on two grounds: (1) that the right to appeal was a fundamental right of U.S. citizens and (2) that the requirement to pay for a reproduction of the lower court transcript as a condition of appeal created a suspect classification (defined in the next section) of poor and nonpoor individuals. The court ruled that the right to appeal was indeed a fundamental right, and that there were less discriminatory ways for the state to collect the small cost for reproducing the transcript (e.g., the cost could be borne by the government), and ruled unconstitutional the practice of requiring individuals to pay the cost of the transcript as a condition to appeal. In both of these cases, the U.S. Supreme Court identified new fundamental rights and overturned state actions that differentiated among individuals in their exercise of these fundamental rights.

Suspect Classification.   The second situation for invoking strict judicial scrutiny is when government action creates a "suspect classification" of individuals. The Constitution directly prohibits government actions that affect individuals differently in terms of their religion or national origin, but is silent on race. It was the 1954 U.S. Supreme Court decision in the *Brown* v. *Board of Education*[3] desegregation case that identified race as a suspect class. In this decision, the court ruled that "separate but equal" schools created in many southern states violated the equal protection clause of the U.S. Constitution because it classified individuals according to race. In overturning the practice of segregating schools, the court created a new suspect class—race—that effectively overturned all state laws that treated individuals differently solely on the basis of race.

Income, while raised as a potential suspect class in both the poll tax and right to appeal cases as a suspect class, has not been recognized by the U.S. Supreme Court as a suspect class. While the decisions in both of these instances showed sympathy toward recognizing personal income as a suspect class, the cases turned on the fundamentality of the rights affected, not on the classification of poor and nonpoor. Thus, today individual income is not recognized as a suspect classification.

School Finance Equal Protection Litigation

In the wake of *McInnis* and *Burruss*, school finance litigation had two general challenges: to determine a strategy that would place challenges to interdistrict school finance expenditure per-pupil disparities directly in the mainstream of equal protection litigation, and to identify standards that could be used by courts to decide whether school finance realities met equal protection requirements.

Arthur Wise (1968), then a doctoral student at the University of Chicago, argued that education was a fundamental right, and that the equal protection clause required that education must be provided equally across all school districts. He further argued that variations in educational expenditures across districts in most states did not reflect uniformity of educational offerings, because expenditure variations were not related to educational need. But as just discussed, the educational need argument was not accepted by the court.

---

[3]*Brown* v. *Board of Education of Topeka*, 347 U.S. 483 (1954).

At about the same time, John Coons, then a law professor at Northwestern University, and two law students, William Clune (now an emeritus law professor at the University of Wisconsin–Madison) and Stephen Sugarman (now a law professor at the University of California–Berkeley), began to frame another argument, namely that education funding created a suspect classification defined by district property wealth per pupil (Coons, Clune, and Sugarman, 1970). They argued that local school districts were creations of state governments and that by making school financing heavily dependent on local financing, states gave school districts unequal opportunities to raise educational revenues because the property value per child varied widely across school districts. Coons, Clune, and Sugarman argued that school-financing systems needed to be "fiscally neutral" (i.e., that expenditures per pupil could not be related to local district property wealth per pupil). Put differently, they argued that education could not be dependent on local wealth, but only on the wealth of the state as a whole.

This argument created two major new "hooks" for school finance litigation. First, it suggested district property wealth per pupil as a suspect classification. Second, and as importantly, it created a new standard—the fiscal neutrality standard—that holds that the quality of education could only be a function of the wealth of the state as a whole, not local wealth. More concretely, the fiscal neutrality standard required that there be no relationship between educational spending per pupil and local district property wealth per pupil. Both of these variables were easily measured, both were used in nearly all state school finance systems, and there were standard statistical measures to identify the magnitude of the relationship between these two variables. Thus, Coons, Clune, and Sugarman gave school finance litigation a standard that the court could use and added the suspect class hook to the litigation arsenal. In addition, the Coons, Clune, and Sugarman strategy clearly identified aspects of a school finance system that could not exist and left wide legislative discretion to design a school finance structure that could pass constitutional muster.[4]

Under the Coons, Clune, and Sugarman strategy, school finance litigation based on either federal or state equal protection clauses makes two arguments before the court. The first is that education is a fundamental right and must be provided equally to all individuals. The second is that state school finance structures create a suspect classification based on property wealth per pupil, which makes the quality of education higher for students in districts high in property wealth per pupil, and lower for students in districts low in property wealth per pupil.

While creative from the legal perspective of equal protection litigation, this school finance litigation strategy faced several challenges. First, litigants were asking the court both to recognize a new fundamental right—education—and to recognize a new suspect classification—property wealth per pupil. Second, the suspect class not only was a new one, but a different kind of suspect class. District property wealth per pupil related to governmental entities—school districts—and not individuals, to which all previous suspect classes had pertained, and was an economic measure that had not yet been recog-

---

[4]Chapter 5 details several different school finance systems, and discusses the degree to which they will create constitutional structures.

nized as a suspect class. Again, even though the court had appeared sympathetic to individual income as a suspect class, it had not recognized individual income as one. But even if the court had, district property wealth per pupil would still be different, both because district property wealth related to a government entity and not an individual, and because it related to wealth—property valuation—and not income. Even though this school finance equal protection strategy was devised during a time when the U.S. Supreme Court was expanding its list of fundamental rights and suspect classifications, the Court nevertheless tends to take a conservative stance. School finance litigants knew they would need to develop a litigation strategy on a case-by-case basis that would help lead the Court to make these two new additions to equal protection litigation.

Serrano v. Priest.   The first case filed using the Coons, Clune, and Sugarman strategy was *Serrano* v. *Priest*[5] in California. The case was filed in 1968. There was an immediate motion to dismiss, claiming that school finance cases were nonjusticiable, citing *McInnis* and *Burruss* as precedents. The trial court dismissed the case on that basis. The dismissal was appealed all the way to the California Supreme Court, which rendered an opinion in August 1971. In that opinion, based both on the Fourteenth Amendment to the U.S. Constitution and the equal protection clause in the California constitution, the court ruled that: (1) the case was justiciable, using the fiscal neutrality standard; (2) education was a fundamental right and property wealth per pupil was a suspect class; and (3) the California school finance system was unconstitutional. This was a precedent-setting opinion, gaining nationwide media, policy and legal attention, and immediately spawning a series of similar court cases in other states.[6]

It is important to understand that neither the *Serrano* opinion (nor subsequent school finance court cases) found that use of the property tax per se in financing schools was unconstitutional. Unfortunately, this policy implication was raised in several media reports on the *Serrano* opinion, but it was incorrect. As Chapter 5 indicates, there are several ways states can use the local property tax to help finance schools and still create a fiscally neutral, or constitutionally acceptable, system. It is only when there is heavy reliance on local property taxes, and there is no state aid program to offset the differences in the amounts districts can raise with a given tax rate, that systems can become unconstitutional (i.e., that strong relationships evolve between expenditures or revenues per pupil and local property wealth per pupil).

Rodriguez v. San Antonio.   One case filed after the *Serrano* opinion was *Rodriguez* v. *San Antonio School District*[7] in Texas. This case was taken directly to a three-judge federal district court panel, with the next stage being a direct appeal to the U.S.

[5]*Serrano v. Priest*, 96 Cal. Rptr. 601, 487 P.2d 1241, 5 Cal. 3d 584 (1971).
[6]Arizona (*Shofstall* v. *Hollins*, 1973); Connecticut (*Horton* v. *Meskill*, 1977); Idaho (*Thompson* v. *Engleking*, 1975); (*Blase* v. *Illinois*, 1973); Kansas (*Knowles* v. *Kansas*, 1981); Minnesota (*Van Dusartz* v. *Hatfield*, 1971); New Jersey (*Robinson* v. *Cahill*, 1973); Oregon (*Olsen* v. *State*, 1976); Texas (*Rodriguez* v. *San Antonio*, 1972); Washington (*North Shore School District No. 417* v. *Kinnear*, 1974); Wisconsin (*Buse* v. *Smith*, 1976).
[7]*San Antonio School District* v. *Rodriguez*, 411 U.S. 45 (1972).

Supreme Court.[8] The district court found for the plaintiffs, finding education to be a fundamental right, and property wealth per pupil to be a suspect classification. The decision held that the Texas school finance system violated the equal protection clause of the U.S. Constitution and ordered the legislature to devise a constitutional system.

The state of Texas immediately appealed the case to the U.S. Supreme Court, before any other school finance case had been appealed to a state supreme court. In March 1973, in a split 5–4 decision, the U.S. Supreme Court held that the Texas system did not violate the U.S. Constitution. The majority opinion held that important as education was for U.S. citizens and for discharging the responsibilities of citizenship, it was not mentioned in the Constitution, and the Court was unwilling, on its own, to recognize it as a fundamental right. Further, the decision held that property wealth per pupil was not a suspect class, in large part because it related to governmental entities (school districts) and not individuals, and because property wealth was so different from individual income.[9]

Thus, the Court did not invoke strict judicial scrutiny. Instead, it invoked the rational test. As was the practice then (and now) for states being sued, Texas responded that the existing method of funding education by local property taxes reflected the principle of local control. And this response, as are most responses to a rational test, was accepted as reasonable by the courts.

The *Rodriguez* decision undercut hopes that had been raised by the *Serrano* opinion about the efficacy of reforming school finance inequities through the federal courts. Just 18 months after the precedent-setting opinion in the *Serrano* case, the *Rodriguez* case eliminated the U.S. Constitution as a legal route to school finance reform. The decision threw all school finance cases out of the federal courts and back to state courts, to be argued state-by-state on the basis of state equal protection clauses, as well as state education clauses.[10]

Indeed, the *Rodriguez* decision somewhat encouraged litigation at the state level. One part of the decision suggested that states could find education to be a fundamental right because, unlike the federal government, most state constitutions not only mentioned education, but had constitutional clauses explicitly creating student access to a free, public education.

Robinson v. Cahill.   As if responding to the U.S. Supreme Court's ruling, the New Jersey Supreme Court rendered a decision in *Robinson* v. *Cahill*[11] in April 1973, just one

---

[8]Some have argued that the *Rodriguez* case should not have been filed so as to force an appeal to the U.S. Supreme Court so early in the process of school finance litigation, that it would have been better to win several cases at the district and state level and to show that states could respond to a decision overturning the school finance system and that such decisions would not simply put a state's education system into a state of disarray.

[9]In addition, the state of Texas showed that low-income children did not generally attend schools in low-wealth districts. Indeed, many low-income children attended school in districts—the big-city districts—that had quite high property value per pupil. Thus, if the court had been inclined to recognize income as a suspect class, the data did not allow plaintiffs to argue that low income and low property wealth were correlated.

[10]All states have some sort of education clause requiring states to create a system of public schools.

[11]*Robinson* v. *Cahill*, 303 A.2d 273 (N.J. 1973).

month after the *Rodriguez* decision. This was the first case to reach a state supreme court.[12] A loss in *Robinson,* while not eliminating litigation in other states, would have been a further blow for litigants, following so closely in the wake of *Rodriguez.* The New Jersey court recognized the *Rodriguez* test invoking the strict scrutiny test under state equal protection—laws which either (1) operate to the disadvantage of suspect classes, or (2) interfere with the exercise of fundamental rights and liberties explicitly or implicitly protected by the constitution. As to the issue of fundamental rights, the court in *Robinson* acknowledged that education was mentioned in the New Jersey constitution but found that "the fact that the obligation to furnish the service is the state's could not serve as an index to the 'fundamental' nature of the right to that service . . . Nor can it matter that the service is expressly mandated by our State's Constitution." As to the issue of suspect classification, the court held that although rich and poor school districts had, respectively, above- and below-average spending per pupil, property wealth per pupil was not a suspect class. Thus, the *Robinson* court found that the New Jersey school finance system did not violate the New Jersey equal protection clause.

However, the court did overturn the New Jersey school finance system, citing the state constitution's education clause that required the state to create a "thorough and efficient" public education system. The court held that a school finance structure that allowed for wide disparities in spending per pupil that were strongly linked to local property wealth per pupil was not a "thorough and efficient" system, and sent the case to the state legislature to design a new system. The court also found that the school finance system must allow schools to provide "educational opportunities that will prepare [the student] for his role as citizen and as competitor in the labor market (*Robinson* I, 1973: 293)." But despite this phrase foreshadowing subsequent adequacy cases, the court went on to rule the system unconstitutional largely on the basis of spending differences, as those were the only criteria available to judge whether or not the system was thorough and efficient.

This case was important for three reasons. First, it kept school finance litigation alive just after *Rodriguez* seemed to toll its death knell. Second, it paved the way for challenging school finance systems on the basis of state education clauses, a substantively different strategy than using the equal protection clause. Third, it hinted at a new standard, which subsequently evolved into adequacy litigation.

Interestingly, the New Jersey legislature procrastinated in its response to *Robinson.* The state did not have an income tax, and each year the state budget was short of the level of funds needed for the enhanced state fiscal role needed to finance a constitutionally permissible school finance structure. In July 1976, therefore, the New Jersey Supreme Court, in a dramatic but largely symbolic action, shut down the entire New Jersey school system.[13] In response, the legislature designed a new school finance structure and enacted a new tax system to fund it, as well as provide local property tax relief.

---

[12]Remember that the *Serrano* ruling simply overturned a motion to dismiss the case. The California Supreme Court remanded the case back to the superior court for trial.

[13]Since this occurred during the summer break, only summer schools were affected. The action, however, indicated the serious posture of the supreme court and was highly symbolic.

3. SCHOOL FINANCE LITIGATION BASED
ON STATE EDUCATION CLAUSES

Challenging state school finance structures under the state education clause entails additional legal strategies beyond those used for equal protection litigation. Some cases use the education clause to frame a fiscal neutrality argument (i.e., to find that education is a fundamental interest and/or property wealth per pupil is a suspect class). Others use the education clause to buttress arguments about the fundamentality of education and wealth as a suspect class made under the equal protection clause. The cases in both Arkansas[14] and Wyoming[15] in the early 1980s were largely based on these arguments, as were the Texas[16] decisions from the late 1980s until the mid-1990s, and the Vermont[17] case in 1997.

The Texas *Edgewood* v. *Kirby* decisions entailed some fascinating interactions between the court and the legislature, and led to a legal decision and new finance structure that was unique. The Texas clause, "support and maintenance of an efficient system of public free schools," was initially used to overturn the system on fiscal neutrality grounds, but many analysts claimed that the Texas system was quite equal except for the bottom and top 50 districts. As the legislature submitted plan after plan to create a new structure for the overall system, the court kept rejecting these proposals. When the legislature then enacted a system that "recaptured" funds from the highest-wealth districts, which the court decision seemed to require, the court subsequently found the system in violation of another section of the constitution prohibiting the legislature from reallocating local revenues. Finally, the legislature created a two-tiered pupil-weighted system (Picus and Toenjes, 1994) that was similar to the original system, but required the wealthiest districts to voluntarily, with voter approval, give some of their wealth or revenues to lower-wealth districts as a condition for receiving any state aid. This system, which largely focused on the top and bottom 50 districts and which the court identified as the core of the problem at the beginning of the litigation process, was finally approved. As discussed in the next paragraph, this was the first time that a court overturned a state's school finance system because of its impact on only a small number of districts.

Nevertheless, the use of the state education clause to make the same arguments as the fiscal neutrality cases was not successful in most courts. Courts seemed to want more than fiscal differences arguments, and wanted plaintiffs to show some "injury" rather than just a relative difference in educational offerings. Indeed, in rejecting the fiscal neutrality arguments as reasons to overturn state school finance systems, several of the court decisions in the 1990s (e.g., Maine, Minnesota, Virginia, Wisconsin, and Wyoming) suggested they might be more sympathetic to a different type of argument: namely, an adequacy argument.

[14]*Dupree* v. *Alma School District No. 30*, 651 S.W.2d 90 (Ark. 1983).
[15]*Washakie County School District No. 1* v. *Herschler*, 606 P.2d 310 (Wy. 1980).
[16]*Edgewood Independent School District* v. *Kirby*, 777 S.W.2d 391 (Tex. 1989); *Edgewood* v. *Meno*, 893 S.W.2d 450 (Tex. 1995).
[17]*Brigham* v. *State*, 692 A.2d 384 (Vt. 1997).

Giving Meaning to the Education Clause

The third use of the education clause is to inject substantive meaning into a state education clause, which subsequently led to the "adequacy" cases that emerged in the 1990s. The language of education clauses varies substantially across the states, with some calling for the creation of an education system, and others calling for "thorough and efficient," "thorough and uniform," or "general and uniform" school systems. Yet all states have some requirement for the state to create a system of public schools. Though McUsic (1991) argued that the specific wording of the education clause could lead to stronger or weaker interpretations of the substantive meaning of the clause, both Sparkman (1994) and Underwood (1995a, 1995b) concluded that the meaning of the education clause is state specific and depends on its political history and prior interpretation. There are three aspects to challenging the school finance system on the basis of the state education clause.

Historical Meaning of the Education Clause. The first is to analyze the debates at the constitutional convention as they relate to the phrasing of the education clause to determine how authors of the state constitution viewed education. In some states, the "general and uniform" clause appears to have been merely an attempt to create one statewide system of public schools. Prior to most states' nineteenth-century constitutional conventions, there was no state education system. Education systems were local entities that differed from district to district. Sometimes there were city and noncity school districts, or regional groupings of districts, but there was no statewide system. States then began to consolidate these diverse systems into one statewide system, defined primarily by state laws, rules, and regulations, especially as they pertained to school accreditation and teacher licensure. In these states, the "general and uniform" type clauses simply meant one, statewide education system. The phrase had no particular implications for school finance or differences in per-pupil education spending; indeed, in these states, the financing system usually continued to rely heavily on local property taxes, with small state roles provided via a flat per-pupil grant (see Chapter 5).

In other states, however, such clauses meant much more than simply creating one statewide system. Records from debates surrounding the creation of the constitution indicated that the constitutional framers envisaged a statewide uniform system, with equal spending per pupil, often fully financed with state funds. Especially in western states, there was hope that proceeds from the Northwest section lands and other land grants could provide all the funds needed for the public school system. In these states, "thorough and uniform" and "general and uniform" could reasonably be inferred to mean something close to equal spending or equal access to core educational opportunities across all school districts.

Unfortunately for school finance litigation, there is no single answer to the type of education and education finance system state constitutional framers meant to create when they wrote state constitutions, including the education clauses. Nevertheless, one avenue both plaintiffs and defendants explore in litigation based on state education clauses is to review the constitutional history and determine whether the constitutional framers had specific ideas in mind about the nature of the state education system, the type of school finance structure that would support it, and whether those notions are relevant to current school finance legal issues.

Education Clauses Requiring More Than Just an Education System.   The second route to school finance litigation based on state education clauses seeks to inject substantive meaning into education clauses. Though state constitutional framers might or might not have implied specific school finance structures, today state supreme courts decide what state education clauses require in terms of modern school finance structures. Thus, the task for school finance litigants is to convince the court to accept variations of what the education clause could require.

One strategy is to argue that the education clause places an "affirmative duty" on the legislature to create more than just an education system, which all states have created. This argument was used in the 1973 *Robinson* case, in which the court argued that the "thorough and efficient" clause required an education system that allowed all students equal opportunities to compete in the labor market. It was used again by the New Jersey court in the 1990 *Abbott* v. *Burke*[18] case (subsequently discussed in detail) to ensure higher educational attainment for low-income and minority students in the state's property-poor and low-income central-city school districts. In both instances, the court overturned the state's education finance structure. But a Georgia Supreme Court in a 1981 case[19] concluded that the state education clause that required state provision of an "adequate education" placed no affirmative duty on the state to equalize educational opportunities and upheld the state's school finance system. An Idaho court in 1975[20] ruled that it was the legislature's and not the court's prerogative to interpret the education clause. A 1976 Oregon court[21] ruled that their school finance system could be justified on the basis of local control. Similarly, the Colorado Supreme Court in *Lujan* v. *Colorado*[22] found that the state's "thorough and uniform" clause was met when an education program was provided in each school district, even though the quality of the programs varied substantially.

Substantive Demands of the Education Clause—Adequacy Arguments.   The third strategy has been to focus explicitly on the substantive demands of the education clause, and it is this strategy that led to the actual term "adequacy" and its definition in school finance litigation in the 1990s and early twenty-first century. The first decisions using this strategy were those in the 1978 Washington[23] and 1973 New Jersey cases. Minorini and Sugarman (1999a, 1999b) argue that these two cases actually were the precursors of the 1990's adequacy cases, though the term "adequacy" was never used in these cases. These decisions began to expand the notion of school finance equity beyond finance to the delivery of an education program that would provide students a fair op-

---

[18]*Abbott* I: *Abbott* v. *Burke*. 100 N.J. 269 (1985); *Abbott* II: *Abbott* v. *Burke*, 119 N.J. 287 (1990).
[19]*McDaniels* v. *Thomas*, 285 S.E.2d 156 (Ga. 1981).
[20]*Thompson* v. *Engleking*, 537 P.2d 635 (Idaho 1975).
[21]*Olsen* v. *State*, 554 P.2d 139 (Ore. 1976).
[22]*Lujan* v. *Colorado State Board of Education*, 649 P.2d 1005 (Colo. 1982).
[23]*Seattle School District No. 1 of King City* v. *State*, 585 P.2d 71 (Wash. 1978).

portunity to learn to high standards. It took New Jersey more than two decades to define what that education program would be, but Washington defined their program as the staffing that the average district had been providing its schools together with a statewide teacher salary schedule.

It was not until the 1982 *Pauley* v. *Bailey*[24] West Virginia case that a more specific definition of such a program was developed. This definition was quite similar to later definitions of "adequacy" that emerged in the 1990s through school finance litigation and the standards-based education reform movement. On an initial motion to dismiss (again based on *McInnis* and *Burruss*), the West Virginia Supreme Court ruled that the case was justiciable, but required the trial court first to determine what a "thorough and efficient" (T & E) education system was, and then to assess the degree to which the existing system met the T & E test. The trial court concluded that T & E required equal programs and services across all school districts, and found that the existing finance system did not provide such equality. Even though it was only a lower court that had overturned the West Virginia school finance system, the state did not appeal. In response, the state department of education, with the support of the governor, created numerous committees around core education programs—all the core subject areas, such as mathematics, science, social studies, language arts; all categorical programs such as compensatory education, special education, and bilingual education, as well as vocational education, and all other programs—and asked them to define standards that would represent a quality, or thorough and efficient, program. An overview committee then took the reports from the various subcommittees, and compiled them into what became the state's Master Plan of standards for all operating programs, as well as for facilities. Funding this plan would have required the state to nearly double education resources in West Virginia, so the plan was only partially implemented. But in 1997, 15 years after the Master Plan was proposed, a court ordered the state finally to fully fund the plan.

The adequacy approach to interpreting the requirements of the state education clause matured during the 1990s. Four major cases represent what has become the adequacy approach. In 1989, the Kentucky Supreme Court[25] not only overturned the state's school finance system, but also found the entire state education system to be unconstitutional, including its curriculum, governance, and its management. Although this case began as a fiscal neutrality case, the court decision turned it into an adequacy case. The court held that school finance equity required that all students should have access to an adequate education program, and included this language about what such a program would include:

- sufficient oral and written communication skills to enable students to function in a complex and rapidly changing civilization;
- sufficient knowledge of economic, social, and political systems to enable the student to make informed choices;

---

[24]*Pauley* v. *Bailey*, C.A. No. 75-126 (Cir. Ct. Kanawha Cty., W. Va. 1982), initially decided as *Pauley* v. *Kelly*, 255 S.E.2d 859 (W. Va. 1979).
[25]*Rose* v. *Council for Better Education, Inc.*, 790 S.W.2d 186 (Ky. 1989).

- sufficient understanding of governmental processes to enable the student to understand the issues that affect his or her community, state, and nation;
- sufficient self-knowledge and knowledge of his or her mental and physical wellness;
- sufficient grounding in the arts to enable each student to appreciate his or her cultural and historical heritage;
- sufficient training or preparation for advanced training in either academic or vocational fields so as to enable each child to choose and pursue life work intelligently; and
- sufficient levels of academic or vocational skills to enable public school students to compete favorably with their counterparts in surrounding states, in academics, or in the job market.

In response, the state completely redesigned the education system, including not only the finance structure, but also the governance, management, and curriculum programs. Moreover, the Kentucky reforms also reflected the kind of education reform that first was known as "systemic reform" (Fuhrman, 1993; Odden, 1995a; Smith and O'Day, 1991) and later evolved into standards-based education reform (Massell, Hoppe, and Kirst, 1997). They included, in addition to a new three-tiered finance system that was accompanied by a large infusion of new money, content standards for the curriculum in all major subject areas, performance standards for students including a new testing system, changes in school governance and management including much more school-based decision making, and a new accountability system with rewards and sanctions at the school-site level (Adams, 1994, 1997).

At least five aspects of the overall Kentucky policy response were and continue to be significant. First, the system focused on student performance outcomes. The primary goal was not just dollars and education inputs but high levels of student achievement in a variety of educational areas. Second, school sites gained substantial discretion for allocating and using dollars with many finance decisions decentralized from the district to the school. Third, schools were rewarded financially (on an unequalized wealth basis) for meeting performance improvement goals, and sanctioned—including being taken over by the state—for consistently not meeting goals (Kelley, 1998a; Kelley and Protsik, 1997). Fourth, preschool, which is essentially an additional grade, was provided at substantial new cost. Fifth, the finance system included a substantially increased foundation program for base expenditures across all districts. And the state limited local add-ons to about an extra 50 percent, for which the first 15 percent was "equalized" by the state through a guaranteed tax base. Many of these programmatic elements became the core of standards-based education reform and the basis for a definition of adequacy.

Shortly after the 1989 Kentucky decision, the Alabama[26] and Massachusetts[27] Supreme Courts overturned state education and school finance systems on the basis of adequacy arguments. Interestingly, the decisions in both states used the same language

---

[26]*Alabama Coalition for Equity, Inc. v. Hunt*, 1993 WL 204083 (Ala. Cir.).
[27]*McDuffy v. Secretary of the Executive Office of Education*, 615 N.E.2d 516 (Mass. 1993).

from the Kentucky decision in defining what the court meant by an adequate education program. Massachusetts immediately enacted a comprehensive standards-based education and school finance reform, but Alabama was not able to muster the political support to enact a similarly comprehensive reform program, and by the end of 1997 had not acted in response to the court order.

In Wyoming,[28] acting on a new case, the court again overturned that state's education finance system and this time required an adequacy response by stating that "the legislature must first design the best educational system by identifying the proper education package each Wyoming student is entitled to have. The cost of that educational package must then be determined and the legislature must then take the necessary action to fund the package." So while not specifying what an adequate education package should be, as did the courts in Kentucky, Alabama, and Massachusetts, the Wyoming court did stipulate that the legislature had to define the program and, once defined, it then had to fully fund it. In response, Wyoming used the professional judgment (see Chapter 3) approach to determine the adequacy expenditure level (Guthrie et al., 1997; Management Analysis and Planning, 2002).

Five other state courts overturned school finance systems on the basis of adequacy arguments—Arizona,[29] Ohio,[30] New Hampshire,[31] North Carolina,[32] and Tennessee[33]—using their own rather than Kentucky's language for defining "adequacy." The courts in Florida,[34] Illinois,[35] and Rhode Island[36] rejected cases based on the adequacy argument, and four state courts—Maine, Virginia, Minnesota, and Wisconsin—suggested successful arguments could be made on the basis of educational adequacy when rejecting plaintiffs' arguments in fiscal neutrality cases.

New Jersey represents yet another twist and advance on the adequacy front. As stated earlier, though the 1973 New Jersey case foreshadowed adequacy by interpreting the T & E clause to mean an education system designed to produce students who could compete in the evolving labor market, most of the *Robinson* I decision focused largely on financial disparities. Further, the 1976 legislative response sought to address those disparities and the first subsequent court challenge to the new school finance law actually upheld those financial elements of the new system (Minorini and Sugarman, 1999a, 1999b). But in that subsequent decision and in the multiple decisions beginning in 1989 and continuing through 1998 that systematically overturned the New Jersey system in six different *Abbott* v. *Burke* decisions,[37] the state supreme court focused more and

---

[28]*Campbell County School District, State of Wyoming, et al.,* v. *State of Wyoming,* 907 P.2d 1238 (Wyo. 1995).

[29]*Roosevelt Elementary School District* v. *Bishop,* 1994 WL 378649 (Ariz. 1994).

[30]*DeRolph* et al. v. *State,* 677 N.E.2d 733 (Ohio 1997).

[31]*Claremont School District* v. *Governor,* No. 92-711 (N.H. 1993).

[32]*Leandro* v. *State,* 472 S.E.2d 11 (N.C. 1996).

[33]*Tennessee Small School System* v. *McWherter,* 851 S.W.2d 139 (Tenn. 1993); *Tennessee Small School System* v. *McWherter,* S.W.2d 894 S.W.2d 7374 (Tenn. 1995).

[34]*Coalition for Equity* v. *Chiles,* 680 So.2d 400 (Fla. 1996).

[35]*Committee* v. *Edgar,* 673 N.E.2d 1178 (Ill. 1996).

[36]*Pawtucket* v. *Sundlun,* 662 A.2d 40 (R.I. 1994).

[37]*Abbott* I: *Abbott* v. *Burke,* 100 N.J. 269 (N.J. 1985); *Abbott* II: *Abbott* v. *Burke,* 119 N.J. 287 (N.J. 1990); *Abbott* III: *Abbott* v. *Burke,* 136 N.J. 444 (N.J. 1994); *Abbott* IV: *Abbott* v. *Burke,* 149 N.J. 149, 168 (N.J. 1997); *Abbott* V: *Abbott* v. *Burke,* 153 N.J. 480 (N.J. 1998), *Appendix* I; *Abbott* VI: *Abbott* v. *Burke,* 153 N.J. 480 (N.J. 1998).

more on the substantive meaning of that T & E education clause. In addition, the 1989 decision (*Abbott* I) overturned the system for just the 28 "special-needs" districts (i.e., the districts with the highest concentrations of low-income and minority students) thus joining Texas in finding the school finance system unconstitutional for just some districts in the state.

Abbott I required the state to raise the spending per pupil of the special-needs districts so that it approached the average of the wealthiest, suburban districts. The subsequent legislative response, the Quality Education Act of 1990, moved in that direction, but the state was not able to raise sufficient funds to finance it. Thus, the plaintiffs returned to the courts and were successful in obtaining two additional decisions in the early 1990s (*Abbott* II and *Abbott* III) that required a revised system that could raise sufficient funds, and the court gave the state a late 1996 deadline by which to comply. In essence, the court wanted the state to define and then to fund an education program that would teach students in the 28 special-needs districts to high performance standards.

In response to both the court case and to the evolution of education reform, the state began in 1996 to create curriculum content and student performance standards in six different subject areas, and a new state testing system that would measure performance to those standards. They also designed a new finance system, called the Comprehensive Educational Improvement Finance Act (CEIFA), which was intended to be sufficient for districts and schools to implement the standards. In CEIFA, the state identified the staffing for an elementary, middle, and high school that it felt was sufficient to teach students to the new standards, and used statewide average costs to determine what that amount would provide for each of the 28 special-needs districts. The resultant figures increased funding for the special-needs districts but not to the level specified by the court. Nevertheless, the state argued in court that the proposal was sufficient to accomplish the educational goals of the new state's program, which was the ultimate intention of the school finance court case.

In early 1997, however, the court in *Abbott v. Burke* IV ruled that the CEIFA program was unconstitutional largely because CEIFA did not reflect a program specific to the needs of the special-needs districts. Indeed, the CEIFA school models were patterned after practices in districts with very few similarities to the education challenges faced by the special-needs districts, which enrolled very large percentages of low-income and minority students. The court then ruled that the only effective schooling model they knew of was that of the highest spending districts, which were successful in teaching their students to high standards. So the court used that model as a de facto standard and mandated the state to raise the spending in each of the special-needs districts to the average level of the most advantaged districts, which was $8,664 in 1997–98, concluding that such a level of funding would be sufficient for the special-needs districts to devise a quality, core educational program. This was the "parity" standard. The court then required the state to identify the supplementary programs students in these districts would need, beyond parity, in order to offset their educational disadvantage caused by the poverty environment of their local urban neighborhoods. The court left open the possibility of adopting something different for the parity standard, but wrote that the state would have to prove the sufficiency of any new proposed standard. The court also asked a remand judge to hold hearings to identify the supplemental programs and their costs.

During those hearings, the state retained the general CEIFA structure, but replaced the staffing proposal with the staffing for a whole school model that had been specifically designed for the needs of low-income and minority students in urban locations, including language minority students—the Roots and Wings/Success for All program (Slavin, Madden, Dolan, and Wasik, 1996)—and showed that this model could be funded by the dollars provided by the parity standard. After a lengthy remand hearing concerning this proposal, as well as debates about which additional programs would be required, such as preschool, summer school, and school-based youth services, which were recommended by the remand judge in *Abbott* V, the New Jersey Supreme Court ruled in *Abbott* VI in May 1998 that:

- parity funding would be retained until a different standard was proposed and accepted,
- the state proposal to use an urban specific, whole school program as the way to implement school finance reform and determine whether there was sufficient funding was now appropriate, and that the state had made a substantive case with the Roots and Wings/Success for All program,
- each school would need to offer both full-day kindergarten and a half-day pre-school program to all children aged 3 and 4,
- the state was responsible for improving the physical facilities in all the *Abbott* districts, at a cost of billions of dollars, and
- that if schools could still demonstrate need for additional funds, they could make a request for more through the commissioner of education.

There are several important aspects of the New Jersey experience as it evolved from a fiscal equity to an educational adequacy case. First, it focused only on the most disadvantaged districts. Second, it included a new and unique approach to defining "educational adequacy," namely a comprehensive, whole school design that could be made compatible with state content and performance standards (see Stringfield, Ross, and Smith, 1996 for descriptions of additional school designs, and see Odden and Busch, 1998 and Odden, 2000 for a discussion of their costs). Further, because the school design was quite specific in all of its strategies and elements, its cost could be determined and then used as the basis for calculating the amount of money a district and each school in it needed. In this way, New Jersey began a process of defining "adequacy" not only generally, as the types of standards that would need to be met, but also specifically, as the needs of a proven effective, comprehensive school design with a cost structure that could be used to determine a spending level that could be incorporated into a school finance formula. Third, the court expanded the notion of "educational adequacy" by requiring the state to provide preschool services to children who fell outside the 5–17 age bracket specifically mentioned in the education clause. Finally, New Jersey showed that rather than shy away from the complexities of defining "educational adequacy," the court wanted the state to confront those detailed issues, and their definitions helped the court resolve this 25-year-old case.

Although the language of the court decision was quite specific, New Jersey has experienced difficulties implementing the 1998 court decree. Erlichson, Goertz, and Turnbull

(1999) and Erlichson and Goertz (2001) found that schools, districts, and the state faced several challenges in having schools select comprehensive school reforms and reallocate resources in order to fund them with the level of resources at their disposal.

Finally, the *Leandro* decision in the North Carolina adequacy case has taken adequacy to even more specific levels than perhaps even New Jersey.[38] One implementing decision requires preschool for all low-income 4- and perhaps even 3-year-olds. Another implementing decision requires school sites to first allocate funds to the educational needs of students from low-income backgrounds before making other uses of those dollars. The objective was to ensure that the first draw on education dollars was for the base program and next the extra services low-income students require in order to perform to the state proficiency student performance standards. The point here is that courts in both North Carolina and New Jersey have been comfortable delving into the specifics of how education dollars are used in the attempt to link funding levels to student achievement outcomes.

Does Adequacy Require Equal Outcomes?

Another important issue is whether adequacy cases require equal education outcomes, or having all students actually achieve to some high minimum standards. Legal analysts claim that they do not (Clune, 1994a, 1994b; Minorini and Sugarman, 1999a, 1999b; Underwood, 1995b). They argue that adequacy means a level of resources for a district or school that would allow it to provide the type of program that should be sufficient to teach students to high minimum standards. Compliance would require a new education system with content and performance standards; a testing system to assess performance to those standards; some set of management, governance, and incentive changes; and a finance system to fund the programs. Thus, compliance would demand some type of comprehensive reform program that was designed to teach nearly all students to high-performance standards, such as the comprehensive education reforms enacted in Kentucky, Massachusetts, and Missouri in the early 1990s, or the comprehensive school design approach of New Jersey.

At the same time, we suggest that it is entirely possible that some court in the future might require the "acid test" of some uniform, minimum but high level of student achievement as a result of a new finance structure. This would be a natural evolution of the adequacy issue, and the ultimate test of whether a comprehensive education program actually could deliver student achievement results.

The Education Clause and Absolute Deprivation

Finally, courts are asked to determine whether, under the education clause, a state's school finance system functions to deprive plaintiffs of an education program, despite allowing fiscal and programmatic disparities across districts to exist. Such courts usually find that state education clauses require only provision of a basic education program, and that anything more than that is conditioned on local control of schools. The 1982

---

[38]*Leandro* v. *State*, 468 S.E.2d 543 (N.C. App 1996), aff'd in part, rev'd in part, 488 S.E.2d 249 (N.C. 1997).

Court of Appeals in New York[39] (which is New York's highest state court) held that "if what is made available by this system may properly be said to constitute an education, the constitutional mandate [for a system of free common schools] is met." In 2002, the same court[40] made essentially the same argument in overturning a lower court's decision[41] which struck down the school finance system because it did not provide adequate revenues for New York City. In effect, this decision found that evidence was insufficient to prove that educational inadequacies deprived students of a sound basic education.

At the same time, we should note that the adequacy cases actually move constitutional requirements beyond provision of just some kind of an educational program. An adequacy ruling requires states to define and fund a program or plan that meets an absolute standard (i.e., adequacy, rather than just "something" versus "nothing").

A School Finance Legal Scorecard

Key school finance court cases.

A chart located on this text's website (www.mhhe.com/odden3e) summarizes the key school finance court cases since 1968 and indicates whether the system was overturned or upheld, and the constitutional basis for court action. The chart shows that school finance cases have been decided in 42 states, and existing school finance systems were upheld in about half the cases and overturned in the other half. Thus, school finance litigants are batting about 0.500 in their attempts to overturn state school finance structures that allow wide variations in educational expenditures linked to local property wealth per pupil, or in education programs and services. In several states, moreover, second and third rounds of litigation have been filed, and many of these second-generation cases have been successful in making their claims. Arizona, Connecticut, Minnesota, Missouri, New Jersey, Texas, and Washington are just some of the states where second and third cases were filed that finally convinced a court to overturn the school finance system. In short, the court route to reforming state school finance systems is alive and active, and one motto could well be, "If at first you don't succeed, try, try again."

In terms of the constitutional route to overturning school finance structures, the score was about even in 1990 in terms of which strategy was the most successful in overturning systems. At that time, about half the courts had used the state education clause as the basis for their decision, and half had used equal protection, with those using equal protection holding that education was both a fundamental right and that property wealth per pupil was a suspect classification. Four states (Arkansas, Connecticut, West Virginia, and Wyoming) used both clauses. Yet only Wyoming created an equal expenditure per-pupil standard that the school finance system must meet. Though many assumed that *Serrano* required substantially equal per-pupil expenditures, the actual court decree required only that "wealth-related" per-pupil spending differ by no more than $100,[42]

[39]*Board of Education, Levittown Union Free School District* v. *Nyquist,* 94 Misc.2d 466, 408 N.Y.S.2d 606 (1978), aff'd, 83 A.D.2d 217, 443 N.Y.S.2d 843 (1981), rev'd, 57 N.Y.2d 27, 439 N.E.2d 359, 453 N.Y.S.2d 643 (1982), appeal dismissed, 459 U.S. 1139 (1983).
[40]*Campaign for Fiscal Equity, Inc.* v. *State,* 744 N.Y.S.2d 130 N.Y.A.D. 1Dept., 2002.
[41]*Campaign for Fiscal Equity, Inc.* v. *State,* 719 N.Y.S.2d 475 (N.Y.Sup., 2001).
[42]Later court rulings have allowed this $100 "band" to be adjusted for inflation. For the 1997–98 school year, this inflation adjusted band was $324.

which suggests that spending could differ according to local tax effort, if the yield were "power equalized" by the state (see Chapter 5).[43]

Since that time, however, nearly all cases have been tried on the basis of state education clauses, and most have been successful in overturning state systems. Minorini and Sugarman (1999a) concluded that between 1973, when the state constitution became the basis for school finance litigation, and 1998, the scorecard has been about even with 15–17 courts overturning systems and 15–17 upholding systems, though at least 13 states overturned state systems in the 1990s (Alabama, Arizona, Arkansas, Massachusetts, New Hampshire, New Jersey, New York, North Carolina, Ohio, Tennessee, Texas, Vermont, and Wyoming).

4. SUMMARY

In short, school finance litigation has evolved over time, initially using state and federal equal protection clauses to focus on inequities of resource distribution across school districts, and then using state education clauses to argue substantive issues linking school finance to education programs and services. Today, almost all school finance litigation is based on state education clauses, adequacy oriented, and is delving into intricate issues of education programs and services.

Using the education clause in school finance litigation is different from using the equal protection clause, and generally raises issues about the substance and quality of the education program required for all school districts in the state (see also Wise, 1983; Clune, 1995). Further, litigation based on state education clauses is a state-by-state strategy that is heavily dependent on the state's history, the types of arguments made by plaintiffs on what "adequacy" could mean, and the individuals who happen to sit on the particular state's highest court at the time the case is heard and decided.

It also should be noted that courts are moving away from the traditional fiscal disparities cases and toward the more complicated educational adequacy cases. Indeed, courts seem to prefer the more complex and more demanding issues involved in adequacy litigation, with several courts rejecting fiscal neutrality cases and inviting cases to be brought on adequacy grounds. Courts are aided in these endeavors by the evolving and increasingly sophisticated standards-based education reform movement, which through professional associations endorsed by policymakers, is creating standards that define education quality. Thus, courts can venture into the adequacy arena, draw upon standards developed by professional educators, and have instruments to both assess an education system and to determine the funding for it. In this way, the evolution of the adequacy litigation strategy concurrently with the standards-based education reform movement dovetailed nicely for plaintiffs and courts receptive to the adequacy argument.

Finally, as Minorini and Sugarman (1999a) conclude, the prominence of the adequacy cases does not mean courts have shifted away from the equity argument. It means

---

[43]Such a system would also require a change in California's Proposition 13, which currently prohibits increases in the local tax rate.

only that the courts have turned from equity defined only in dollar terms to equity defined in terms of programs and services or school design, to which a dollar figure can be attached. Though this is clearly an advance, it also harkens back to the "education needs" cases at the beginning of school finance litigation. Indeed, it could be argued that the adequacy approach, together with standards-based education reform and school designs, is simply the updated version of the old education needs argument, except today it has standards and measures and has been quite successful in the courts.

A Framework for Assessing Equity and Adequacy in School Finance

There are many ways to assess the equity and adequacy of a state's school finance system. Behind this concern, of course, is the question: Does money matter? Traditional assessments of school finance, particularly during most of the previous century, assumed that money did matter and focused largely on equity (i.e., whether money was distributed fairly across school districts and students). During the latter quarter of the last century, however, questions were raised about the assumption that money mattered; indeed, many policy analysts, particularly a group of economists, raised questions about that assumption and, after reviewing large bodies of literature, concluded there was little research support for the assumption that money mattered. During about the same time, the policy interest, and as shown in Chapter 2, the course of litigation, began to focus on the adequacy of school finance systems, directly addressing the issue of how money would matter and how much money would be required.

This chapter has three parts. The first quickly reviews the literature on whether money matters. It concludes that money does matter, but that it is the way money is used that determines the power of differential levels of education dollars linked with differential levels of student learning.

Since equity in school finance is still a driving policy issue, the second section draws from the work of Berne and Stiefel (1984, 1999) and develops an equity framework that can be used to determine the degree of school finance equity of a state's school finance structure. Although Berne and Stiefel have not been the only scholars to outline a school finance equity framework (see also, for example, Wise, 1968, 1983; Garms, 1979; and Alexander, 1982), theirs is the most comprehensive and has been used by many analysts to conduct empirical studies of the equity of state school finance structures (see, for example, Adams, 1997; Goertz, 1983; Goldhaber and Callahan, 2001; Hickrod, Ramesh, Chaudhari, and

Hubbard, 1981; Kearney, Chen, and Checkoway, 1988; Odden, 1978, 1995b; Picus and Hertert, 1993a, 1993b; Rubenstein, Doering, and Gess, 2000).

Section three of the chapter addresses the issue of school finance adequacy. This approach to assessing a state's school finance system expressly attempts to link the finance side of district and school operations more directly to the program, curriculum, and instruction side, as well as to the student achievement that is produced. Put a different way, it explicitly tries to show how money does matter and to show how these conclusions lead to the design of "adequate" state school finance structures.

1. DOES MONEY MATTER?

One huge question that always has surrounded school finance is: Does money matter in terms of student performance? Most educators would say yes, but the policy and research communities have been more skeptical. The fact is there has been disagreement among researchers as to whether or not a statistical link can be found between student outcomes and money (or, what money buys, such as class size, teacher experience and degrees, etc.). Production function research constitutes the largest body of research evidence on this issue, and the conclusions from this research are mixed (Monk, 1992).

A production function is an economic tool used to measure the contribution of individual inputs to the output of some product. It is possible to estimate an educational production function with this form:

$$P = f(R,S,D)$$

where

> P = a measure of student performance
> R = a measure of resources available to students in the school or district
> S = a vector of student characteristics
> D = a vector of district and school characteristics

One possible measure of R would be the class size at a school or school district. In fact, actual class size is in many ways a good choice for this particular variable as it provides a proxy for the level of resources available for children (i.e., it is highly correlated with per-pupil spending).

Although several methodological problems are associated with production function research—determining the correct measure of results, controlling for sociodemographic variables, statistically adjusting for variables measured at different levels in the system (student, classroom, school, and district), conducting longitudinal rather than cross-sectional analyses, and correctly specifying input factors (pupil-teacher ratios, for example, are not good proxies for actual class sizes)—there nevertheless are large numbers of production function studies that can be used to help answer the question of whether money or resources matter.

The most often cited research in this field is the synthesis work of Eric Hanushek (1981, 1986, 1989, 1997). Hanushek has consistently argued that there does not appear to be a systematic relationship between the level of funding and student outcomes (see also Hanushek, 2002, on the class size debate).

Hanushek has now analyzed 90 different studies, with 377 separate production function equations over a 20-year period. In his 1997 publication, he continued to argue that "These results have a simple interpretation: There is no strong or consistent relationship between school resources and student performance. In other words, there is little reason to be confident that simply adding more resources to schools as currently constituted will yield performance gains among students" (Hanushek, 1997, p. 148).

Hanushek essentially divided the 377 different findings into two major categories: those indicating a positive and those indicating a negative relationship. He compared the numbers in each category and found more negative than positive findings. He then concluded that the variation in findings was such that a systematic relationship between money and outcomes had not yet been identified. He stated:

> The concern from a policy viewpoint is that nobody can describe when resources will be used effectively and when they will not. In the absence of such a description, providing these general resources to a school implies that sometimes resources might be used effectively, other times they may be applied in ways that are actually damaging, and most of the time no measurable student outcome gains should be expected. (Hanushek, 1997, pp. 148–9)

He suggested that what is needed is a change in the incentive structures facing schools so that schools and teachers in them are motivated to act in ways that use resources efficiently and that lead to improved student performance.

Others have analyzed the same studies as Hanushek and reached opposite conclusions. Hedges, Laine, and Greenwald (1994a, 1994b; see also Greenwald, Hedges, and Laine, 1996a, 1996b; and Laine, Greenwald, and Hedges, 1996) concluded that in fact, money can make a difference. They calculated the effect size of the different studies and, rather than counting the number of positive and negative findings, calculated an average effect size; their results produce a significantly positive effect size. The larger effects of the "positive" studies are greater than the smaller effects of the "negative" studies. Relying on this and other evidence, Hedges, Laine, and Greenwald (1994a) concluded that school spending and achievement are positively related. In his rejoinder, Hanushek (1994b) argued that while there is evidence that the relationship exists, there is not evidence of a strong or systematic relationship. We side more with Hedges, Laine, and Greenwald than with Hanushek, viewing the "effect size" as the way to summarize across studies.

Differences in analytic methods and conclusions also characterize some of the debate over class size (see Hanushek, 2002 and Krueger, 2002). On this issue, we also side with those concluding that class size does make a difference, but note that the research shows only that class sizes of 15 students and only for kindergarten through grade 3 boosts student performance (Achilles, 1999; Finn, 2002; Grissmer, 1999; Kreuger, 2002).

Other economic research bolsters the positive conclusions that money matters. Ferguson (1991) analyzed spending and the use of educational resources in Texas. He concluded that "hiring teachers with stronger literacy skills, hiring more teachers (when students-per-teacher exceed 18), retaining experienced teachers, and attracting more teachers with advanced training are all measures that produce higher test scores in exchange for more money" (Ferguson, 1991, p. 485).

In a more recent study, Wenglinsky (1997) used regression analysis to analyze three large national databases to see if expenditures had an impact on student achievement of fourth- and eighth-graders. He found that the impact of spending was in steps or stages. For fourth-graders, Wenglinsky concluded that increased expenditures on instruction and on school district administration increased teacher-student ratios (more teachers per same number of students). Increased teacher-student ratios (smaller class sizes) in turn led to higher achievement in mathematics.

In the eighth grade the process was more complex. Specifically, Weglinsky found that increased expenditures on instruction and central administration increased teacher-student ratios (reduced class size). This increased teacher-student ratio led to an improved school environment or climate, and the improved climate and its lack of behavior problems resulted in higher achievement in math.

Equally interesting was Wenglinsky's (1997) finding that capital outlay (spending on facility construction and maintenance), school-level administration, and teacher education levels could not be related to improved student achievement.

In summary, we side with those who conclude that the research suggests there is a positive connection between resources and student achievement, so that the distribution of educational resources discussed in the remainder of this chapter is important for both equity and effectiveness reasons. But we also conclude that the money-results connections are not all that strong, and we show in Chapter 10 that there are numerous ways to use money more effectively. In addition to the strategies we discuss in Chapter 10, there also are ways to pay teachers differently that would lead to better instruction and higher levels of student learning (see Odden and Kelley, 2002 and Gallagher, 2002).

2. EQUITY IN SCHOOL FINANCE

Berne and Stiefel's (1984) original framework for assessing a state's school finance structure required answers to four key questions:

1. *Who* is the group for whom school finance should be equitable? There are two major groups: (a) children who attend the public schools, and (b) taxpayers who pay the costs of public education. The equity issues for each group are quite different. Equity for children was discussed largely within an educational opportunity framework. Equity for taxpayers was discussed largely in the public finance context of tax burden, as it is in Chapter 4 of this book.

2. *What* resource objects or educational services should be distributed equitably among the group of concern? The traditional answer to this question for children is dollars or revenues per pupil. But educational

processes such as curriculum and instruction are also key educational resources. Outcomes such as student achievement also are possible objects to analyze. Deciding on the specific object is important to assessing the degree of school finance equity. Some objects could be distributed equitably, and others inequitably.

3. *How* is equity to be defined, or what are the specific equity principles used to determine whether a distribution is equitable? There are three equity principles: (a) *horizontal equity*, in which all members of the group were considered equal; (b) *vertical equity* in which differences (for which unequal resource distributions are legitimate) among members of the group were recognized; and, (c) *equal opportunity*, which identified variables such as property value per pupil that should not be related to resource distribution. Because the term "equal educational opportunity" has been used in several nonschool finance contexts and has multiple meanings, the school finance version of this term has become known as *fiscal neutrality*.

4. *How much* equity is in the system, or what is the specific status of equity? This component includes the specific statistics used to measure the degree of equity in the system.

As Berne and Stiefel (1984) demonstrated, different answers to these four questions could result in different conclusions about the equity of the system. One major objective in developing and using a school finance equity framework is to help clarify how one analyst could declare a system equitable while another, using the same data, could declare it inequitable. The reason could simply be that they had different answers to these four key questions. The framework helps to sort out the issues and to show how these more complex conclusions could be made.

Solid as the framework was, it nevertheless became problematic as it was used over the subsequent 20 years. First, because wealth or fiscal neutrality was such a central issue in both litigation and school finance policy deliberations, it was difficult to establish it as just one of four different equity concepts. Second, though the framework was amenable for use with any unit of analysis—district or school—it came to be too strongly associated with the district and thus seemed out of date or inappropriate as concern moved to school-level finance (Busch and Odden, 1997a; Goertz and Odden, 1999). Third, as adequacy emerged as a preeminent issue in both school finance litigation and education policy, the framework appeared obsolete as it seemed only to address equity and not the outcome aspect of what was popularly perceived as central to adequacy. In short, largely due to how the framework was used and defined in practice, it needed some refurbishing in order to incorporate evolving school finance issues.

Thus, in the late 1990s and as part of assessing the history of equity in school finance, Berne and Stiefel (1999) updated the framework, recasting some of its elements, and also explaining how it actually could incorporate nearly all of the salient new issues in both school finance litigation and policy deliberations. This chapter draws largely from their recent work. Berne and Stiefel suggested that school finance analysis address six key topics:

1. ex ante versus ex post analyses;
2. the unit of analysis in terms of state, district, school, or student;
3. the objects of interest, whether they be input fiscal variables, educational process variables, or student achievement variables;
4. the group of concern in terms of children or taxpayers;
5. equity concepts, but now leading with fiscal neutrality, while also incorporating horizontal and vertical equity; this chapter will include measures of equity under this general heading, and
6. the concept of adequacy, even though nearly all of its elements could be incorporated into the preceding five issues. Adequacy is addressed in section three.

Ex Ante Versus Ex Post

Ex ante versus ex post analysis addresses the issue of whether the assessment of the school finance system is done on the basic structure, concepts, variables, and parameters prior to or before (ex ante) they are actually applied in practice, *or* on data, numbers, and results that emerge after (ex post) a system is implemented. Few analysts make this somewhat arcane but important distinction, though it is critical. Indeed, nearly all empirical analyses of state school finance systems use actual data and thus are ex post analyses.

An example might help clarify the distinction. Take the historic issue in school finance: the unequal distribution of the property tax base and the resultant linkage between spending levels and wealth levels. As Chapter 1 discussed, and as is discussed further in Chapter 5, a high-level guaranteed tax base (GTB) program, such as at the 95th percentile, would be highly equitable from an ex ante perspective. Such a program would eliminate the traditional problem of the unequal access to a school tax base, and make the tax base that could be tapped for education purposes the same, at least for 95 percent of districts and children.

At the same time, as Chapter 1 also showed, such programs tend not to eliminate spending differences across districts nor reduce all statistical links between spending and property wealth per pupil. Thus, from an ex post perspective, such a system could have inequity statistics only slightly better than the system before such a high-level GTB was put in place. In this example, then, the system could be deemed eminently fair from an ex ante, formula parameter analysis, but unfair from an ex post, empirical analysis. This is the dilemma that underlies assessments of the equity of the Missouri school finance system (Odden, 1995b) as well as the Wisconsin system (see Chapter 7).

A similar dilemma could arise under the emerging adequacy issues. For example, suppose this definition of "adequacy" is used: sufficient funds to allow provision of a set of programs, services, and instructional efforts deemed sufficient to have students achieve to state performance standards. Then suppose that school districts did not translate these dollars into appropriate programs and services. Such a system could correctly be characterized as adequate from an ex ante fiscal perspective but not adequate from an ex post, programs, services, and student-results perspective.

The point is that beforehand (ex ante) analyses are quite different from after-the-fact, empirical (ex post) analyses, and finance policy analysts should make the distinction explicit in any report or study. Particularly if an analysis is conducted using actual data after full implementation, it should be made clear that an ex post analysis is being presented (such as those in Chapter 7); indeed, the conclusions could be compared to an ex ante analysis, even if findings about the equity and adequacy of the system were different.

Unit of Analysis

There are two aspects to the discussion of the unit of analysis. The first concerns the primary unit at which measures of the object are taken (i.e., whether the measure is at the state, district, school, or student level). The second is a statistical issue of how to appropriately calculate statistical measures.

As to the first issue, historically and traditionally, measures in school finance, such as revenues and expenditures, have been taken at the district level, making the district the unit of analysis. Moreover, usually the analysis is conducted across school districts within a state. Recently, however, analyses of school finance equity have been conducted at the district level but across the entire country without respect to state boundaries (Hertert, Busch, and Odden, 1994; Murray, Evans, and Schwab, 1998; Odden and Busch, 1998), and these analyses generally show that most fiscal disparities are due to cross-state rather than within-state differences. Since there is a virtually national goal to teach students to high standards, and since the primary issues of both equity and adequacy concern cross-state differences, this national focus might gain more attention in the future.

In addition, as education policy increasingly focuses on the school site, more analysis using the school site as the primary unit will likely emerge, as in for distributing revenues (e.g., Odden, 1999; Odden and Busch, 1998), for analyzing fiscal equity (Hertert, 1996; Odden and Busch, 1997; Rubenstein, 1998), or for assessing the efficiency and effectiveness of resource use (Miles and Darling-Hammond, 1997; Odden, 1997b; Odden and Busch, 1998; Speakman et al., 1997).

Nevertheless, we expect most analyses of school finance issues likely will continue to be conducted with measures taken at the district with increasing numbers of analyses at the school-site level, though gathering good school-level data is difficult (Berne, Stiefel, and Moser, 1997; Cohen, 1997; Farland, 1997; Goertz, 1997; Monk, 1997; Picus, 1997b; Rubenstein, 1998).

But whatever the unit at which measurement occurs, most analyses of school finance systems, and most of the discussion in the remainder of this chapter, are concerned with the impact of the system on students, and thus there is somewhat of a mismatch between the unit at which measurement occurs (districts or schools) and the unit of primary concern (children).

The challenge, then, is how to assess the impact on children. A statistical solution is to "weight" the district or site measure by the number of students in order to give larger districts or schools more influence on the statistical results. If this statistical weighting is not done, each district regardless of size is treated as one observation. Thus, in New York State for example, New York City with a million students and about one-third of all students in the state would affect the statistical findings exactly as much as would a small, rural district with only 100 students. That simply does not make sense, although for years analyses of school finance systems used district data without statistical weighting by the number of students.

Thus, to produce more accurate results, the usual and recommended approach is to statistically weight each district or school measure by the number of students in it, an option provided by nearly all statistical software packages. In the preceding example, this procedure gives New York City more impact on the analytic conclusions than the small district with only a few students; indeed, this procedure actually turns the number of observations into the total number of students, with New York City accounting for 1 million observations and the rural district only 100. This approach also indicates more accurately how the overall resource distribution system impacts students.

To be sure, this strategy makes the assumption that all students within a district or school receive the level of resources indicated by the district or school measure. Though this is a bold assumption, 35-plus years of experience with federal Title I and Chapter 1 regulations requiring districts to distribute base resources equally among all schools and students makes this assumption reasonable. But since districts also legitimately distribute categorical dollars differently to schools based on variations in student need, the measures used for analysis either should exclude these additional resources, or some other adjustment should be made to ensure that these legitimate differences do not cause statistical inaccuracies (see subsequent discussion on vertical equity).

This statistical weight should not be confused with the pupil-need weight discussed below and in Chapter 6 that reflects different student need. Both the unit of analysis-statistical weight and the pupil-need weight must be considered and addressed separately in equity analyses.

Objects

Berne and Stiefel (1984) used three categories of children's equity objects: (1) inputs, such as fiscal or physical objects; (2) outputs, such as student achievement; and (3) outcomes, such as lifetime incomes. This chapter uses these three categories but combines the last two and suggests additional variables such as the curriculum content taught and measures of teacher quality. In this way, children's school finance equity objects would include the key variables needed for determining educational adequacy.

We should note explicitly that equity analyses need not be confined to educational inputs, such as dollars per pupil or even the enacted curriculum. Outcome variables that include measures of student achievement could easily be the object of analysis, to determine, for example, the distribution of average levels of achievement or the percentage of districts or schools that have taught students achieving to new, high student performance standards. Further, because objects can include measures of educational provision (curriculum, instruction, teacher quality) as well as results in terms of student performance, this framework also can be used to assess different definitions of educational adequacy.

Fiscal and Physical Inputs.　　There are a wide variety of fiscal and physical inputs that could be targeted for analysis as school finance equity objects. The traditional object of analysis has been some measure of educational dollars. Dollars, however, can be categorized in several ways, each of which can lead to different conclusions about the equity of the system.

First, dollars can be divided into two categories: dollars for current operating expenses and dollars for capital outlay or debt service. Analysis of current and capital dollars is usually done separately. Current dollars are analyzed on an annual basis since education services need to be provided each year. Capital and debt service dollars are usually (or should be) analyzed on a multiple-year basis because schools are built only periodically, last for decades, and are paid for incrementally over several years. Other capital items, such as buses and computers, are purchased periodically and also can be used for several years.

Second, dollars can be divided into revenues or expenditures, which are similar but technically quite different. Revenues are usually identified by (1) source—local, state, and federal and (2) type—general/unrestricted aid (i.e., for any educational purpose) or categorical/restricted (i.e., for specific purposes such as special education for the handicapped or special services such as transportation). Many studies analyze current unrestricted revenues from local, state, and federal sources, and leave categorical or special-purpose dollars out of the analysis. Other studies use only state and local general revenues. These general revenues, it is argued, are the revenues that support the regular or core education program, which is one key issue of concern across districts. Further, since the focus is on the equity of the *state* school finance system, federal dollars should be excluded from the analysis. Other studies analyze total current revenues from all sources, arguing that dollars are partially fungible, and that total dollars are what districts have to run the entire education program. Using different revenue figures can yield different conclusions about the equity of the system.

Expenditures, which usually include dollars from all three government sources, can be analyzed on a total basis (current operating expenditures per pupil), or by function (expenditures on administration, instruction, operation and maintenance, transportation, etc.) or by program (regular, special education, compensatory education, bilingual education, etc.). It also would be desirable to analyze expenditures by level of education or school-site level (i.e., elementary, middle/junior high school, and high school). Though there has been much discussion of the need to collect data at the site level (Busch and Odden, 1997a; Goertz and Odden, 1999), only a few states (e.g., Florida, Kentucky, Ohio, Oregon, and Texas) provide such fiscal data.

Collecting resource data by school level is important for both state and nationwide education policy. Many argue that if the education system were successful in educating all students at the elementary and middle school levels, high school and college education could be much easier. Many states, however, still spend between 25 and 33 percent more for high school students than elementary school students (see Chapter 6), and insufficient public money supports preschool services for poor children. Perhaps a shift of dollars already available toward the lower grades could improve overall student achievement. Knowing and being able to analyze educational expenditures by school site could help the country, states, districts, and schools decide how to allocate scarce dollar resources to accomplish its ambitious student performance goals.

Most school finance equity studies that use an expenditure figure rely on total current operating expenditures per pupil or instructional expenditures per pupil, largely because these figures are commonly available. But other, more detailed expenditure figures are preferred, especially expenditures by program and school level. The latter are the key policy issues.

At any rate, different choices of dollar input variables can lead to different conclusions about the equity of the system. For example, Park and Carroll (1979) found a much more equitable distribution of instructional expenditures per pupil in their study of school finance equity in six school finance reform states, than they did for either total revenues per pupil or total current operating expenditures per pupil. But Speakman and colleagues (1997) often found more inequality in expenditure when the data were analyzed at the school-site level.

Physical objects traditionally include, for example, teacher-pupil ratios, administrative-teacher ratios, support staff–pupil ratios, numbers of books in the library, and square footage of instructional space or of total space. The most common figures used are teacher-pupil ratios. But care should be given to defining the ratio used. The total professional staff–pupil ratio includes several professionals who do not teach in the classroom; ratios that include these professional resources not only imply a much smaller class size than actually exists, but also that more teachers are provided for core instruction than actually may be the case. Nevertheless, the pupil-professional ratio indicates the level of professional staffing in a school, a very important overall measure of professional educational resources as discussed in Chapter 9. A more accurate indicator of class size and a good measure of core instructional services is the classroom teacher-student ratio (i.e., the average or median number of students actually in a teacher's classroom).

A new variable that will become available in the future will be the number and percentage of different types of teachers. Several districts are adopting Charlotte Danielson's (1996) Framework for Teaching, and can identify teachers as being at the basic, proficient, or advanced levels of performance. Other teachers are becoming board certified by the National Board for Professional Teaching Standards (Buday and Kelly, 1996; Rotberg, Futrell, and Lieberman, 1998). The board assesses individual teachers to high professional standards, and a board-certified teacher is an individual who has demonstrated expertise of classroom practice that reflects accomplished teaching. These and other such measures and identifiers indicate the quality of the faculty in a school or district.

Key fiscal and physical input variables to analyze.   Though any fiscal and physical input variable could be analyzed, these key variables in per-pupil terms are suggested:

- total revenues from local, state, and federal sources,
- total revenues from local and state sources,
- total general revenues from local and state sources (i.e., total state and local revenues minus restricted revenues [categorical aids]),
- total current operating expenditures,
- total instructional expenditures,
- total expenditures for the core instructional program, if available,
- pupil–professional staff ratio,

- average actual class size, and
- number or percentage of basic, proficient, advanced, and board-certified teachers.

Achievement or Outcome Variables.   This category includes the results of the education process—student achievement or performance in the short run, and labor market, family, and civic performance in the long run. Though Berne and Stiefel (1984) discuss longer-term outcomes such as an individual's income, job, occupational status, ability to compete in the labor market, and so on, the connections between these outcomes and K–12 schooling are somewhat tenuous (Burtless, 1996). In the long term, showing connections between K–12 schooling and longer-term outcomes should be a research topic. As the connections are developed, analysis of the outcomes and their link to the distribution of school resources could be included in school finance equity analyses.

Shorter-term education system outcome variables include student achievement. Variables could include student achievement in different content areas (mathematics, science, etc.) or more global achievement, such as the overall measure from a standardized, but not necessarily norm-referenced, achievement test. High school graduation rates are also an important output measure. The number of academic courses taken is another outcome indicator that is closely linked to student learning (Madigan, 1997). Finally, postsecondary attendance rates are outcome measures that indicate behavior in the year immediately following high school graduation.

Several issues arise in deciding how to measure these variables. The most debated are those related to student achievement. Traditionally, norm-referenced measures of student achievement have been used. These measures can be developed at different grade levels and in different content areas, but they indicate how an individual compares to other individuals at the same age or grade. They do not indicate the degree to which a student knows a certain content area, or indicate knowledge and skills to a set standard.

Norm-referenced measures of student achievement are gradually being replaced by criterion-referenced measures, which indicate what a student knows in a certain content area. Nearly all states are creating or using new student testing systems covering numerous subject areas, and providing the data at both the district and school and sometimes even individual student level. Further, as tests expand from just multiple choice to include expanded multiple choice, short answer, writing, and actual student performance tasks, the tests will be able to indicate not only what students know but also what they can do (e.g., whether they can conduct a laboratory experience, solve multiple-step mathematics problems, or write a persuasive paragraph). As these more sophisticated measures of student achievement become available, they should be the measures used in a school finance analyses for both equity and adequacy purposes.

Whether norm- or criterion-referenced, the most useful test scores are those that are "equated" across each grade level. Equated tests use the same scoring metrics, so a higher score on a grade 4 test, for example, as compared to a grade 3 test would indicate that the student had advanced in their achievement—beyond a normal year's expected growth. Indeed, such tests will be more useful to district and school leaders in determining whether students make "adequate yearly learning progress" under the 2002 No Child Left Behind federal law (see Chapter 6 for more on No Child Left Behind).

A new way to present achievement data has been suggested for monitoring nationwide and state progress in achieving the country's educational goals. The new way is to identify the percent of students who are performing at different levels on criterion-referenced tests, such as basic, minimal, proficient, and advanced levels. The argument is that the country needs a workforce with a certain level of skills and that the measures of student performance should indicate the degree that the educational system produces student achievement, on average, with that range of skill levels (Murnane and Levy, 1996). As states adopt this strategy, and several have moved in that direction, outcome measures for schools, districts, or states could be the percent of students performing at basic, minimal, proficient, and advanced levels on criterion-referenced assessments of what students need to know and be able to do, although the more continuous scale scores on these tests also could be used. Wide variations in such achievement could reveal economic or other variations in student performance that could lead either to additional adjustments in resource allocation to compensate for different needs (see Chapter 6) or reallocation to ensure that all schools, districts, and states meet those targets.

Key student achievement measures to analyze.   These measures are suggested:

- high school graduation rate,
- postsecondary attendance rate, and
- percent correct, scale scores, or percent scoring at basic, minimal, proficient, and advanced levels on equated measures of student achievement in mathematics, science, language arts (including reading in elementary grades), writing, history, and geography at the elementary, middle, and high school levels.

The Group

Children are just one, but undoubtedly the most important, group for whom the equity of a state's school finance system is an important policy issue. Children are a group of primary concern because they are the "customers" of the education system; the system is designed to educate children. Further, the ability of children to compete in the labor market and, ultimately, their incomes are determined significantly by what they do—by what they learn—in schools and classrooms (Murnane and Levy, 1996; Odden, 1995). Thus, school finance equity, particularly the emerging concern with adequacy, emphasizes equity for children and generally is the primary group of focus in this book.

But children also differ, so equity analyses focused on children should make appropriate distinctions among categories of students: the "average" student, the disabled, students from low-income backgrounds, students with limited English ability, minorities versus nonminorities, gifted and talented, and so on. This book will address only the first four categories of children.

However, children are not the only group for whom school finance equity can be an issue. Taxpayers—both those who have children in public schools and those who do not—pay for public education services. They clearly are another important group for whom school finance equity is an important policy issue. Chapter 4 discusses taxpayer equity, in terms of the burden various taxes place on different taxpayers, within the public finance context. But as an element of fiscal neutrality, this chapter also discusses taxpayer equity in terms of the equal yield for equal effort concept. "Yield" could include dollars or expenditures, but also programs, services, and student achievement.

Teachers increasingly are another group for whom the equity of a state's school finance system is important. The level and distribution of teacher salaries; the state role in supporting minimum teacher salaries; the distribution of teacher quality, knowledge and skills, including the percentage of teachers certified by the National Board for Professional Teaching Standards; and other policies designed to promote teacher productivity and teacher professionalism are all salient teacher policy issues (Darling-Hammond, 1997; National Commission on Teaching and America's Future, 1996; Odden and Kelley, 2002) and possible issues around which to assess a state's overall school finance structure. As school finance unfolds in the twenty-first century, it is likely that the equity of the school finance system as it relates to evolving teacher policy will become a more salient issue within school finance.

The list could continue. Nevertheless, children are the dominant group and have received the most attention in school finance. This chapter primarily discusses issues related to school finance as they apply to children and the three subcategories of disabled children, children from low-income backgrounds, and English-language learners.

Equity Concepts

Once an object has been selected, an approach to assessing equity needs to be determined. This entails defining and selecting an equity principle. There are three different but related children's equity principles:

- fiscal neutrality,
- horizontal equity, and
- vertical equity.

This section discusses several issues surrounding each of these principles.

Fiscal Neutrality for Children.   This principle targets the traditional school finance problem and states that resources, or educational objects, should not vary with local fiscal capacity, such as property wealth per pupil, property value per pupil, household income, or any other measure of local fiscal capacity. This equity principle derives from the standard fiscal disparities that have plagued state school finance structures throughout the twentieth century, and directly relates to the legal standard of fiscal neutrality typically, as discussed in Chapter 2, used in most school finance court cases.

Assessing the degree of fiscal neutrality entails analyzing the relationship between two variables: (1) the object chosen and (2) the variable identified as something that should not be linked to resource differences. Traditional fiscal neutrality analysis assesses the relationship between current operating expenditures per pupil and property wealth per pupil, or local plus state general revenues per pupil and property wealth per pupil. But analysis of the relationship between any object just discussed and any measure of fiscal capacity, such as household income or even the sales tax base per capita, reflects analysis according to the fiscal neutrality principle. Analyzing fiscal neutrality is different from analyzing either horizontal or vertical equity, because the former requires at least two variables, whereas the latter requires only one variable.

Fiscal neutrality statistics. To measure the degree of fiscal neutrality, statistics that indicate the relationship between two variables are necessary. Two have become increasingly common in school finance:

- the correlation coefficient and
- the elasticity (i.e., the elasticity calculated from a simple one-variable regression).

For both statistics, measures of two variables are needed: (1) the measure of the object of concern, such as current operating expenditures per pupil; and (2) the measure of fiscal capacity, such as property value per pupil. Both fiscal neutrality statistics indicate whether the educational object is a function of some variable to which it should not be related, such as the local tax base.

The simple correlation is a statistic that indicates the degree to which there is a linear relationship between two variables (i.e., whether as one variable increases the other increases, or decreases). It ranges in value between minus 1.0 and plus 1.0. A value of +1.0 or close to +1.0 indicates a positive relationship (e.g., as property wealth increases so does expenditures per pupil). A negative correlation indicates that as one variable increases, the other decreases; it indicates that there is an inverse relationship between the two variables. In school finance, there is usually a negative correlation between state aid per pupil and property wealth per pupil, indicating that state aid is inversely related to wealth, that the poorer the district, the greater the state aid. A correlation coefficient of zero indicates that there is no linear relationship between the two variables.

While a correlation coefficient indicates whether or not there is a linear relationship between two variables, the elasticity indicates the magnitude or policy importance of that relationship. For example, expenditures and wealth could be strongly related, but if a tenfold increase in property wealth resulted only in a small increase in revenues, one could argue that the magnitude of the relationship was not significant or of little policy significance.

Technically, the elasticity indicates the percent change in one variable, say expenditures per pupil, relative to a 1 percent change in another variable, say property value per pupil. It is a statistic that usually ranges in value from zero to any positive number, although it also can be negative. In school finance, an elasticity that equals 1.0 or higher indicates that spending increases in percentage terms at the same or higher rate as property wealth. Elasticities below 1.0 indicate that spending does not increase at the same percentage rate as local property wealth.[1]

---

[1] This might be a somewhat different definition of elasticity than is the case in economics, but it has become the approach used in school finance circles.

The simple elasticity between a dollar object, such as expenditures per pupil and property wealth per pupil, can be calculated using the slope of the simple linear regression of expenditures on wealth; the elasticity equals the slope (the regression coefficient for wealth) times the ratio of the mean value of property wealth per pupil and the mean value of expenditures per pupil.

It often is wise to assess the correlation coefficient and elasticity jointly. If the correlation is high and the elasticity is low, there is a relationship between the two variables—fiscal neutrality does not hold—but the relationship is not of policy importance. On the other hand, if the correlation is low and the elasticity is high, even the tenuous link might have policy significance. If both the correlation coefficient and elasticity are high, then fiscal neutrality clearly does not exist—the two variables are linked and the magnitude of the link is strong.

A correlation less than 0.5 with an elasticity less than 0.1 could function as a standard to determine whether a state system met the fiscal neutrality standard.

Berne and Stiefel (1984) discuss other relationship statistics for fiscal neutrality. Further, more complex econometric methods can be used to quantify the relationship between educational objects such as revenues per pupil and (1) property wealth, (2) the composition of the local property tax base (residential, commercial, and industrial property), and (3) household income (Adams and Odden, 1981; Feldstein, 1975; Ladd, 1975; Yinger, 2002).

Fiscal Neutrality for Taxpayers.   Fiscal neutrality for taxpayers would indicate whether the funding system allowed districts to raise equal dollars (or any object) per pupil for a given tax rate (see also Berne and Stiefel, 1979). The measure would generally be local plus state dollars per unit of tax effort, or the appropriate measure of the object per unit of tax effort. If this measure were the same across districts, it would indicate that fiscal neutrality for taxpayers would have been provided.

Since this is a single variable, the measures of dispersion discussed under "Horizontal Equity" would be the statistics used to determine whether the system met the test of fiscal neutrality for taxpayers, using the same standards for each statistical measure.

Link to litigation and school finance structural remedies.   Recall that fiscal neutrality has been a major focus of many school finance court cases, even though adequacy recently has taken the lead position in court cases. For both fiscal neutrality for children and fiscal neutrality for taxpayers, moreover, the implied school finance structural remedy is a guaranteed tax base (GTB), district power equalizing (DPE) or percentage equalizing program, each of which is discussed more fully in Chapter 5. These programs attempt to make the ability of districts to raise revenues at a given tax rate as close to equal as is practical. School finance equity analyses, at least most of those focusing on within-state equity, nearly always include measures of fiscal neutrality.

Horizontal Equity.   This principle is similar to the horizontal principle in public finance; indeed, Berne and Stiefel (1984, 1999) used traditional public finance principles and concepts to construct their school finance equity framework. Horizontal equity provides that students who are alike should be treated the same: "Equal treatment of equals" reflects the horizontal equity principle. Horizontal equity requires that all students receive equal shares of an object, such as total local and state general revenues per pupil, total current operating expenditures per pupil, instructional expenditures per pupil, or equal minimum scores on student criterion-referenced assessments. Horizontal equity is embedded in the standards-based education reform goal of teaching all students to high standards.

When horizontal equity is used, one assumes that all students are alike. While this is a crude assumption at best, it is implied when it is argued that spending should be equal across school districts or schools. Thus, horizontal equity has been widely used in school finance, despite its assumption that all students are alike.

The principle of horizontal equity is best used for subgroups of students (e.g., all elementary students in the regular program, all high school students in an academic track, or all students performing below the first quartile on a student achievement measure). For carefully selected subgroups of students, it is reasonable to require equal distribution of resources, or the object selected for equity analysis. Of course, care must be taken to create a legitimate subgroup of students, for which homogeneity claims are accurate.

Assessing the degree of horizontal equity entails measuring inequality or dispersion. Such statistics measure aspects of the distribution of one variable, specifically the object chosen for analysis.

Horizontal equity statistics.   There are numerous statistics that assess the degree of equality for one variable, such as expenditures per pupil in school finance. Berne and Stiefel (1984) identified several and analyzed their various properties. Five statistics are discussed here, although many more are discussed by Berne and Stiefel.

1. The first is the *range*, which is the difference between the value of the largest and the smallest observation. The larger the range, the greater the inequality. This statistic indicates the maximum difference in the distribution of this variable among students in a state. That also is a disadvantage. It indicates the difference between only two observations, the top and the bottom. The fact is that there are a few outlying districts in every state: some very poor, low property wealth and low-income rural districts, and some very wealthy districts that might have a nuclear power plant or oil wells and few students. These districts are anomalies, and do not reflect common circumstances.

    The range does not indicate the degree of equality or inequality for any of the other observations, and thus is a poor indicator for assessing the degree of equity of the *system*. Furthermore, the range increases with inflation. As inflation occurs, and all other structural variables remain the same, the range will increase. Indeed, one reason the range statistic might be used in some school finance court cases is that each year the range generally increases. An increasing range is interpreted (incorrectly we believe) to indicate a system with increasing inequality. Nevertheless, although used extensively and routinely by many school finance analysts, and showing the maximum degree of inequality in a distribution, the range has several detracting features and is not a desired horizontal equity statistic.

2.   The second horizontal equity statistic is the *restricted range,* which is the difference between an observation close to the top and an observation close to the bottom, such as the difference between the 5th and 95th percentile, or the 10th and 90th percentile. The restricted range generally avoids the problem of outliers that afflicts the range, but the restricted range still measures the degree of inequality between just two observations, and not the overall system. Further, just as with the range, the restricted range increases (i.e., worsens with inflation), even if all other characteristics of the finance system remain the same. If a range statistic is used, the restricted range is preferred to the unrestricted range, but neither are good indicators of the equality of the distribution of the object for the entire education system.

A variation of the restricted range is the *federal range ratio,* which is the restricted range divided by the observation at the 5th percentile. Though the federal range ratio shares most advantages and disadvantages of the restricted range, because it is a ratio it eliminates the inflation problem (i.e., the federal range ratio does not increase with inflation). In addition, the federal range ratio has been a statistic used to determine whether states can include federal Impact Aid in calculating state equalization aid (Sherman, 1992).

3.   The third horizontal equity statistic is the *coefficient of variation (CV),* which is the standard deviation divided by the mean (i.e., the average); it can be expressed in decimal or percent form. Its value usually varies between zero and one, or in percentage terms, from zero to 100, although the values can be larger. A coefficient of variation of zero indicates that the object is distributed uniformly among all children.

The CV indicates the percent variation about the mean. For example, a coefficient of variation of 10 (or 0.1) percent indicates that two-thirds of the observations have a value within one standard deviation of the mean (i.e., 10 percent above or below the value of the average), and 95 percent of the observations have a value within two standard deviations of the average (i.e., 20 percent above or below the mean).[2] So if the average expenditure per pupil is $6,000 and the CV is 10 percent, it means that two-thirds of all districts have an expenditure per pupil between $5,400 ($6,000 minus 10 percent) and $6,600 ($6,000 plus 10 percent).

The coefficient of variation is a statistic that includes all values of a data set, unlike the range, which includes only selected values. Also, the coefficient of variation does not change with inflation, an attractive

---

[2]These comments assume a normal distribution.

characteristic. Thus, if the structural properties of a school finance system remain constant, but all economic and dollar variables rise with inflation, the coefficient of variation would remain the same, correctly indicating that the equity of the system had not changed. The coefficient of variation is also easy to understand. Because of these attractive features, the coefficient of variation is increasingly being used by analysts.

Another issue, however, is determining the value that indicates an equitable or fair distribution of school funds. Determining a standard for the coefficient of variation is a value judgment. Berne and Stiefel (1984) suggest a variety of ways to determine what the standard should be. The key distinction is whether to use a relative standard, which would compare districts in the top, middle, and bottom quartiles, or an absolute standard, which would establish a cut-off point for determination of equity. The problem with a relative standard is that some observations are always at the bottom, no matter how small the degree of inequality. An absolute standard provides a cut-off point, which separates equitable from inequitable resource distribution patterns. It is difficult to determine an absolute standard. Nevertheless, an absolute standard of about 10 percent for the coefficient of variation is generally used throughout this text. This is a high standard, because few states have a coefficient of variation for revenue-per-pupil figures below 10 percent. It is worth remembering that standard setting is an issue of both values and politics; different states and different analysts might reasonably set different levels as an acceptable coefficient of variation.

4. A fourth horizontal equity measure is the *Gini Coefficient,* a statistic taken from economists' measures of income inequality. To determine the Gini Coefficient, a graph is made by plotting the cumulative value of the measure of the object as a percent of the total value on the vertical axis and the percent increments of the number of observations on the horizontal axis. The resulting graph indicates the degree to which the object is distributed equally to children at various percentiles; put differently, the graph indicates the degree to which children at different percentiles have the same amount of the object. If the object is perfectly distributed, the Gini graph would be a straight, 45-degree line. If the object is not perfectly distributed, the Gini graph would be a concave curve below that line. In school finance, the measure on the vertical axis is typically the cumulative percentage of school district expenditures, and the measure on the horizontal axis is typically percent of students enrolled in the state, as shown in Figure 3.1.

The Gini Coefficient is the area between the Gini curve and the 45-degree line divided by the area under the 45-degree line. Its value ranges from 0 to 1.0 with a completely equitable distribution occurring when the Gini coefficient equals zero. Most values in school finance are in the 0.1 to 0.2 range. The Gini Coefficient includes all observations and is insensitive to inflation (i.e., it remains the same when inflation is the only intervening variable).

The Gini Coefficient is challenging to understand conceptually. What does it mean when the area between the Gini curve and the 45-degree

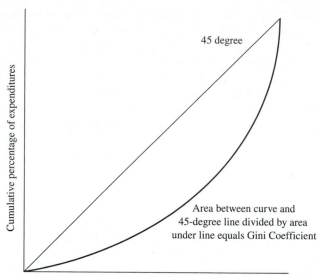

FIGURE 3.1   **Example of a Graph Used to Determine a Gini Coefficient**

line—even in a system with what most would call large differences in expenditures or revenues per pupil—is 0.1 or very close to zero? A value close to zero suggests equality, but the system may, in school finance terms, be quite unequal. Nevertheless, the Gini Coefficient is a popular horizontal equity statistic in school finance. A standard for it has not been set, although a value less than 0.05 is probably desirable. The smaller the Gini Coefficient, the more equal the distribution of the object.

5.   A fifth measure of horizontal equity is the *McLoone Index,* which is a statistic unique to school finance, actually created by and named after Eugene McLoone, an economics professor emeritus at the University of Maryland. The McLoone Index was created to provide a measure of the bottom half of a distribution, to indicate the degree of equality only for observations below the 50th percentile. Since the American political culture often shows more interest in the condition of those at the bottom, the McLoone Index is a statistic that reflects that perspective.

   Technically, the McLoone Index is the ratio of the sum of the values of all observations below the 50th percentile (or median) to the sum of all observations if they all had the value of the median. It ranges in value from zero to one, with a one indicating perfect equality.[3] The value of the

---

[3]A value of 1.0 for the McLoone Index indicates that per-pupil expenditures in the lowest-spending districts containing 50 percent of the state's children is equal. A value of less than one implies that among the low-spending districts with that 50 percent of schoolchildren, expenditures vary. The smaller the McLoone Index, the larger the spending differential among the low-spending districts.

McLoone Index for most school finance data sets is generally in the 0.7 to 0.9 range. Again, a standard has not been set for a "good" McLoone index, but higher than 0.95 is desirable.

Though Berne and Stiefel (1984) analyzed other standard statistics that are sensitive to changes in the bottom half of the distribution, the more complex statistics are difficult for policymakers to understand. Because the McLoone Index is a measure of the equity of the distribution for the bottom half and is more straightforward, it has become popular in school finance and is included in many school finance equity analyses.

6. A new horizontal equity statistic is the *Verstegen Index,* which is the opposite of the McLoone Index, in that it is a measure of disparity in the top half of the distribution. Nearly all analyses of school finance assess either characteristics of the entire distribution, or characteristics of the bottom half of the distribution. But as discussed in Chapter 1, an issue that is gaining more attention is the behavior of the districts in the top half of the distribution. It seems that in some states, the differences in fiscal resources among these districts have increased over time, even while the disparities for those in the bottom half have diminished (Verstegen, 1996). The result is a McLoone Index closer to zero but a larger CV. Since the CV has become such a popular school finance equity statistic, a rising CV could indicate that fiscal disparities are increasing, but such an interpretation would not reflect the differences in the nature of the distribution among the top and bottom half.

    The Verstegen Index helps to show this phenomenon; it is the ratio of the sum of the values of all observations above the median to the sum of all observations if they were all at the median. It has a value of 1.0 or greater, and, like the McLoone and CV, does not increase with inflation. It would increase as disparities in the top half increase. A careful analyst would calculate all three statistics: the CV, the McLoone, and the Verstegen Indices, and determine whether overall disparities have improved (a lower CV), whether differences below the median have improved (a higher McLoone), and whether differences in the top half have improved (a lower Verstegen).

Link to litigation and school finance structural remedies.   Horizontal equity is most closely associated with two legal issues: the equal protection argument that education is a fundamental interest, and the adequacy argument as the intended meaning of a state's education clause. The general legal thrust is that the core or regular education program should be provided equally to all students, or that all students should have access at least to an "adequate" education program.

School finance structures that respond to these arguments are full-state funding, a very high foundation program, and an even broader federal role to ensure adequacy across all states. Full-state funding is the primary implication of the legal finding that education is a fundamental right because if it is, it should be provided equally to all students and there would be no (or only an extraordinary) reason for allowing some students to have a better education than others. A high foundation is the primary implication of the adequacy argument, in that all students should have, at the minimum, a basic education sufficient to teach the average student to high standards. As Odden and Busch (1998) show, if the adequacy issue were considered nationwide, it might raise anew the need for a new federal role in education, as very preliminary analysis shows that many states are not providing, and might not be able fiscally to provide, any of their districts with sufficient resources to fund an adequate school program.

Studies of horizontal equity.   There have been dozens of studies of the degree of horizontal equity within a state. Several studies have analyzed the status of school finance equity within the 50 states (Brown et al., 1977; Evans, Murray, and Schwab, 1997; Murray, Evans, and Schwab, 1998; Odden and Augenblick, 1981; Odden, Berne, and Stiefel, 1979; Schwartz and Moskowitz, 1988). Brown (1977) was one of the first studies that used a 50-state sample. It found that expenditure disparities actually increased nationwide from 1970 to 1975, a time of intensive school finance reform. Further analysis, however, showed that for states that underwent school finance reform in the early 1970s, expenditure disparities might have increased more than they did had the states not changed their school finance systems. The Odden, Berne, and Stiefel study, using data from only 35 states, showed that several school finance reform states improved both horizontal and fiscal neutrality over a multiple-year period during the mid-1970s. The Odden and Augenblick study used 1977 NCES data for all 50 states and found that state school finance equity ratings changed depending both on the equity object selected and statistic used. The Schwartz and Moskowitz study compared data from all 50 states for the years 1976–77 and 1984–85 and concluded that school finance fiscal equity had stayed, on average, about the same, for both horizontal and fiscal neutrality principles and for several different statistics (primarily the ones just discussed). Wyckoff (1992) then found that although fiscal neutrality was stable, horizontal equity improved modestly between 1980 and 1987. The 1997 General Accounting Office study (1997) identified bigger improvements in fiscal equity, but Hertert, Busch, and Odden (1994) showed that substantial disparities remain.

The most comprehensive study of school finance disparities analyzed 20 years of data and concluded that fiscal disparities had been reduced over this period but only by 16–25 percent and largely in those states with court cases (Evans, Murray, and Schwab, 1997; Murray, Evans, and Schwab, 1998). This study together with others (Odden and Busch, 1998) make a further advance in adjusting all dollar variables by a geographic price factor (Chambers, 1995; McMahon, 1994) to better compare differences in "real" resources across districts. Finally, Murray, Evans, and Schwab (1998) show that the majority of fiscal differences, after adjusting for cost differences, are caused by inter- rather than intrastate disparities, so that even if all within-state disparities are eliminated, two-thirds of the disparities will remain, which supports Odden and Busch's (1998) conclusion that disparities across states exceed those within states.

Numerous authors have used the Berne and Stiefel (1984) framework, or variations of the framework, to study the equity of the school finance structure within states (see, for example, Goldhaber and Callahan, 2001; Hirth, 1994; Johnson and Pillianayagam, 1991; Porter, 1991; Prince, 1997; Rubenstein, Doering, and Gess, 2000; Sample and Hartman, 1990; Verstegen and Salmon, 1991; Wood, Honeyman, and Bryers, 1990). Picus, Odden, and Fermanich (2002) conducted a 10-year equity analysis of the Kentucky finance system enacted after the court decision overturned the system in 1989, and found that equity had indeed improved over the 1990s. These studies generally use a fiscal object, such as state plus local revenues per pupil. They also typically use two or three measures for horizontal equity, including the coefficient of variation, the McLoone Index, and the Gini Coefficient, as well as two measures of fiscal neutrality, the correlation coefficient and the wealth elasticity. The Picus, Odden, and Fermanich study also used pupil-need weights and a geographic price adjustment—two adjustments for vertical equity, discussed next.

Vertical Equity.   Vertical equity specifically recognizes differences among children and addresses the education imperative that some students deserve or need more services than others.[4] "Unequal treatment of unequals" has been a traditional public finance way to express the vertical equity principle. What this phrase means is that in some circumstances or for some reasons, it is acceptable to treat students differently, or to provide more services to some students (or districts) than others. A key step in vertical equity is to identify the characteristics that legitimately can be used as a basis for distributing more resources, or more of the specific object selected. Three categories of characteristics have been identified: (1) characteristics of children; (2) characteristics of districts; and (3) characteristics of programs.

Characteristics of children that could lead to the provision of more resources include physical or mental disabilities, low achievement perhaps caused by educational disadvantage from a low-income background, and limited English proficiency. It is generally accepted in this country, and around the world, that students with these characteristics need additional educational services in order to perform better in school. More controversy surrounds the characteristic of gifted and talented. Some argue that these students learn more from regular instruction and do not need additional resources; others argue that the best and brightest should be given some measure of extra services.

District characteristics that could lead to provision of more resources include issues such as price, scale economies, transportation, energy costs, and enrollment growth. As Chapter 6 shows, some districts face higher prices than others, and they need more money simply to purchase the same level of resources as other districts. Some districts also face higher costs either because of factors caused by very small size, such as a one-room school in a sparsely populated rural area, or factors caused by large size, such as most large-city school districts. While size adjustments can be controversial—some argue that small districts should be consolidated and that large districts should be divided into smaller entities—differential size can be a legitimate basis for allocating some districts more resources than others. Finally, transportation costs vary widely across most districts. Sparsely populated districts must transport students long distances and face higher per-pupil transportation costs, and big-city districts often must bus for racial desegregation. States often recognize these different district circumstances by allocating additional funds, usually to be used only for a specified purpose.

---

[4]Chapter 6 discusses how adjustments can be made in school finance formulas to recognize vertical equity issues.

Some programs also cost more than others. For example, vocational education; laboratory sciences; small classes in specialized, advanced topics; and magnet schools tend to cost more than "regular" programs. State and district decisions to provide these programs can be a legitimate reason for allocating more resources for some students than others.

Although there is general agreement that additional funds should be provided in most of the circumstances discussed in preceding paragraphs, controversy surrounds other school and student distinctions. For example, differential treatment on the basis of race or sex is generally viewed as illegitimate. The question however, remains as to whether additional funds should be provided on the basis of race to foster desegregation (such as more money for magnet schools) or on the basis of sex to foster greater female participation in school athletics and in mathematics and science. Also controversial are issues about whether cost differences due to grade level (see Chapter 6) should be continued.

In school finance, it is generally agreed that additional resources should not be available because of fiscal capacity, such as property value per pupil, household income, or other local economic factors. On the other hand, there is more controversy surrounding tax rates as a legitimate reason for resource variation. Those who support local control argue that higher local tax rates are a legitimate reason for having more resources; others argue that from a child perspective, educational resources should not vary because of local taxpayer preference for education.

In short, vertical equity, though simple on the surface, is difficult to implement. There is substantial agreement on some of the reasons for providing more resources to some students or districts than to others, but disagreement remains on several variables. Thus, implementing vertical equity entails making significant value and political judgments, many of which have no widespread consensus as to what is deemed "right."

Measuring and assessing vertical equity.   There are two major ways to assess vertical equity. The first is to provide a pupil-need weight to all students who need extra services (see Chapter 6) and then to conduct a horizontal equity analysis using the number of weighted pupils as the pupil measure. This approach combines vertical and horizontal equity in a joint analysis. Vertical equity is reflected in the weights; having recognized factors that can lead to different resource levels and made appropriate adjustments, equality of resources per weighted child indicates the degree of resource equality.

This approach can be used only when there are good data to quantify the degree to which students with different needs require different levels of resources. This approach is strengthened if some independent analysis is made of the weights themselves, to assess whether they accurately represent the degree of extra services needed. It is more valid when the different weights have been calculated relative to the statewide average expenditure per pupil. The 1997 GAO study and the National Center for Education Statistics (1997) studies used this approach, weighting each handicapped student an extra 1.3, and each low-income student an extra 0.2.

Alternately, categorical revenues for extra services and programs can be eliminated from the object, and analysis conducted for just general revenues, or educational expenditures for the regular instructional program. This approach assesses the degree of equality of the base program for all students, but essentially skirts analysis of vertical equity.

If price differences are part of the state aid formula, the equity analysis should be conducted with price-adjusted dollars, not with nominal dollars, which is the usual approach (Barro, 1989; Chambers, 1995; McMahon, 1994). Furthermore, all dollars should be price-adjusted, not just those that might be adjusted by a state formula price factor. This approach was taken by the General Accounting Office (1997), Odden and Busch (1998), Murray, Evans, and Schwab (1998), and Picus, Odden, and Fermanich (2002).

Link to litigation and school finance structural remedies. Vertical adjustments are integrally embedded in the adequacy approach to school finance litigation; in fact, Underwood (1995b) argued that vertical equity was educational adequacy. Although we would not limit educational adequacy to vertical equity, we certainly would agree that any comprehensive definition of educational adequacy would include some degree of vertical equity adjustments, to ensure that students who could learn to high standards, but needed additional resources to do so, would be provided those resources.

It is not clear that vertical equity is an integral part of fiscal neutrality and the legal arguments about education as a fundamental right have not been the arguments that have led either to the legal right to appropriate education programs for the disabled (that is provided by the federal Individuals with Disabilities in Education Act [IDEA]), and certainly has not created a right to extra educational services for students from low-income backgrounds or students with limited English proficiency (again, provided by federal law and regulatory requirements).

As Chapter 6 shows, there are two primary ways to address vertical equity in school finance structures. The first is to weight by pupil need different categories of students in a way that quantifies, relative to the base level of expenditure, the additional resources that are needed. The second is to provide a separate program, like a categorical program, that provides revenues specifically for such services.

Studies of vertical equity. Chapter 6 discusses the studies that pertain to vertical equity adjustments for students, districts, or programs, including the issues and controversies surrounding them.

3. ADEQUACY

This principle was not included in Berne and Stiefel's (1984) equity framework largely because adequacy had not appeared directly on the school finance agenda at that time. Today, however, as Chapter 2 showed, adequacy is the key focus of school finance litigation, and increasingly of school finance policy as well. Adequacy is thus an additional principle with which to judge a state's school finance system.

As we have suggested, the notion of adequacy is the provision of a set of strategies, programs, curriculum, and instruction, with appropriate adjustments for special-needs students, districts, and schools, and their full financing, that is sufficient to teach students to high standards. As Berne and Stiefel (1999) suggest, the notion of adequacy has its roots in the 1983 *Nation at Risk* report (National Commission on Excellence and Equity in Education), which added excellence to what had been a 20-year focus on equity. Adequacy could be viewed as having both an inputs orientation as well as an outputs orientation: the inputs being the programs, curriculum, and instruction that are sufficient to teach students to high standards, and the outputs being the measurement of the results that are achieved. Indeed, as the education excellence reforms of the 1980s transformed into systemic and standards-based education reform of the 1990s (Elmore, 1990; Fuhrman, 1993; Massell, Hoppe, and Kirst, 1997), the concept of educational adequacy matured. It continued with the Clinton Administration's Goals 2000 programs and the Bush Administration's No Child Left Behind legislation.

Link to Litigation and School Finance Formulas

A definition of "adequacy" as a high level of inputs—programs, services, curriculum, instruction, classroom, and school organization—certainly can be justified as part of a definition of "adequacy." This definition evolves from standards-based education reform. Standards-based education reform enhances the rigor of these inputs through curriculum content, student performance standards, and changes in school management, organization, finance, and accountability. These latter dimensions of educational adequacy appeared explicitly in most of the 1990s' adequacy cases discussed in Chapter 2. Moreover, Minorini and Sugarman (1999a, 1999b) argue that from the legal perspective, adequacy pertains only to inputs. They claim that the courts are neither requiring equal outcomes, nor outcomes for all students who are at or above some high, minimum level.

An input definition of "adequacy" would also include a range of appropriate adjustments for special-needs students, schools, and districts. Indeed, "adequacy" in the legal context certainly requires adjustments for low-wealth and low-spending districts. Further, since the cases include the phrase or notion of "all students" achieving to high standards, adjustments for special-needs students are required.

Once a set of programs and services and other adequate educational elements are identified, it is straightforward to price them and calculate a dollar amount that could be used for each district or school as the foundation, or "adequate" base spending amount per pupil. In this way, the foundation school finance formula and educational adequacy seem to fit well with each other.

At the same time, the notion of adequacy as outputs can also be argued. Nearly all written discussion of adequacy includes the notion of students achieving to some set of performance standards, implying that "adequacy" also could be defined as a set of educational strategies and their funding that are successful in teaching students to some set of achievement standards. Odden and Clune (1998) and Verstegen (2002) argue that this means the school finance system needs some adequate high foundation base, with appropriate supplements for special-needs students, as well as some performance-improvement mechanisms, such as more school authority over the use of resources to allow for site reallocation to higher performance programs, changes in teacher compensation toward providing salary increases for more knowledge and skills, and school-based performance incentives to reward schools for improving student achievement results. Economic analysts (e.g., Duncombe, Ruggiero, and Yinger, 1996; Reschovsky and Imazeki, 1998, 2001) suggest that this means moving to a "performance-based funding system" that formally links spending levels and adjustments for special needs to a specified level of output of the system.

An adequacy approach can be applied to all districts and schools, as has been done in Kansas, Maryland (Augenblick and Meyers, 2001a, 2001b) and Wyoming (Guthrie et al., 1997; Management Analysis and Planning, 2002) but also could be more focused on selected populations or places, such as low-income students (Clune, 1995) or the special-needs districts in New Jersey.

One major difference between equity and adequacy is that equity implies something about a relative difference, while adequacy implies something about an absolute level. For example, a state system could have base resources distributed quite equally, such as in California and Alabama, but still not be an adequate system. Similarly, one could conceive of a state or education system (perhaps New Jersey when its response to its 1998 court case is fully implemented) with substantial differences in resources, but with the lowest-spending districts still spending above some adequacy level.

Finally, given all these issues, adequacy requires some link between inputs and outputs, a set of inputs that should lead to certain outputs, or some level of spending that should be sufficient to produce some level of student achievement. This highlights the need to learn more about the input-output linkages.

Measuring Adequacy

There has been little if any work on developing measures of educational adequacy in a statistical context. Thus, we propose an approach that we will call the Odden-Picus Adequacy Index (OPAI). Arithmetically, it draws from the McLoone Index but uses an "adequate" spending level rather than the median. The idea behind the OPAI is to calculate an index that roughly indicates the percentage of students educated in schools or districts that are spending at an "adequate" level. If the calculation is conducted on the basis of weighted students, or if all expenditures are adjusted by an overall "cost function" index (see Chapter 6), then the OPAI includes vertical equity as well.

The OPAI is calculated as listed here:

1. identification of an "adequate" spending level,
2. identification of the percent of students/district spending above that level,
3. calculation of a McLoone-type ratio for those below that level, but using the "adequate" expenditure level rather than median, therefore calculating the ratio of all those spending below the adequate level to what it would be if they were spending at the adequate level; this ratio would then be multiplied by the percent of students/districts below the adequacy level, and
4. calculation of the sum of these two numbers.

Assume that an adequate expenditure level has been determined. Next, assume that 60 percent of students/districts are spending above that level. So, variable #2 above is 0.60. Assume, that the McLoone-type calculation would produce a ratio of 0.8, which would mean the students/schools/districts below the adequacy level would have 80 percent of the revenues needed for full adequacy. This would then be multiplied by 40 percent, the percentage below adequacy, which would equal 0.32 in this example. Then the OPAI would be 0.92 (i.e., 0.60 plus 0.32). It would indicate how close the system was to providing an adequate level of funding for all students.

Actually, the OPAI would show that if revenues were increased by 8 percent of the adequacy level, and given just to those students, schools, or districts spending below the adequate level, everyone could be raised to the adequate level. So it could be used in a very specific way to show how close the finance system is to providing an adequate base for all students.

If a weighted-pupil count were used, the adequacy index would include an assessment of vertical equity as well. Moreover, if the pupil-need weights themselves were adequate and calculated relative to the adequacy expenditure level, then the adequacy index could be used to indicate the degree to which the school finance system was adequate for all students, both "regular" students and students with special needs who needed more than the regular revenue level to learn to the proficiency standards set by the system for them.

The OPAI is about the same size as the McLoone but covers the entire distribution. It also is not subject to inflation, a positive characteristic of the CV and McLoone Index that was mentioned previously.

Studies of Adequacy

There has been both conceptual and empirical research on educational adequacy. Clune (1994a, 1994b, 1995) produced some of the most thoughtful conceptual analysis of how educational adequacy and school finance can be linked. Although his work has emphasized the importance of adequacy for low-income students, conceptually his work addresses the adequacy issue for all children.

But there also has been a segment within school finance that always has been concerned with adequacy (i.e., how high the foundation expenditure level should be, whether at a minimum, basic level, as was discussed years ago, or at an adequate level, as is discussed today). Four methodologies have been used to determine an adequate foundation expenditure level: (1) the input or professional judgment approach; (2) the successful district approach; (3) the cost function approach; and (4) the evidence-based approach (for longer discussions, see Guthrie and Rothstein, 1999; Odden and Picus, 2000).

The input approach began nearly two decades ago when the Washington school finance system was declared unconstitutional, and that state's top court required the state to identify and fund a "general and uniform" education program. In response, the state essentially identified the average staffing (teachers, professional support staff, administration, etc.) in a typical district and, using statewide average costs, determined a spending level. To a substantial degree, Washington still uses this approach.

A more sophisticated input approach was the Resource Cost Model (RCM), created by Jay Chambers and Thomas Parrish (1994). Using groups of professional educators, the RCM first identified base staffing levels for the regular education program, and then identified effective program practices and their staffing and resource needs for compensatory, special, and bilingual education. All ingredients were priced using average price figures, but in determining the foundation base dollar amount for each district, the totals were adjusted by an education price index. This method was used to propose a foundation spending level for both Illinois and Alaska, but the proposals were never implemented. This method is very similar to what has been termed "activity-led staffing" in England, which is an English version of the RCM approach to school financing (Levacic, 1999).

Most recently, Guthrie et al. (1997) made a further advance on the professional input approach as part of a response to the Wyoming Supreme Court's finding that the state's finance system is unconstitutional. Guthrie and colleagues also used a panel of professional education experts. In identifying the base staffing level for typical elementary, middle, and high schools, however, they relied on the findings of the Tennessee STAR class-size-reduction study results to set a class size of 15 in elementary schools (Finn, 1996; Grissmer, 1999), and then used the panel to determine additional resources for compensatory, special, and bilingual education. They, too, adjusted the dollar figures by a constructed price factor. As previously noted, similar types of adequacy studies have been conducted recently for Kansas, Maryland, and South Carolina.

The advantage of all of these input approaches is that they identify a set of elements that an amount of dollars would be able to purchase in each school district, including additional resources for three categories of special-needs students, all adjusted by a price factor. The disadvantage is that the resource levels are connected to student achievement results only indirectly through professional judgment and not directly to actual measures of student performance.

The second approach to determining an adequate spending level attempts to remedy this key deficiency of the input approach by seeking to identify a spending level directly linked to a specified level of student performance. The successful district approach first determines a desired level of performance using state tests of student performance, identifies districts that produce that level of performance, from that group selects those districts with characteristics comparable or close to the state average, and then calculates their average spending per pupil. Such studies have been conducted in Illinois (Augenblick and Myers, 2001b; Hinrichs and Laine, 1996), Maryland (Augenblick and Meyers, 2001a; Management, Analysis and Planning, 2001), and Ohio (Alexander, Augenblick, Driscoll, Guthrie, and Levin 1995; Augenblick, 1997). Interestingly, in most of these studies, the level of spending identified was approximately the median spending per pupil in the state.

A major advantage of this approach is that it identifies what is required to produce student performance results. A disadvantage is that, other than expert educational judgments, the strategies and ingredients have no clear link to actual performance levels. However, expert judgments can vary both across and within states (see Augenblick and Myers, 2001a, 2001b; Guthrie, 1997; Management, Analysis, and Planning, 2001) depending on how the process is conducted.

Further, atypical districts often are eliminated from such analysis, which usually include the highest and lowest spending and highest and lowest wealth districts, as well as large, urban districts. The result is that the districts identified are usually nonmetropolitan districts of average size and relatively homogeneous demographic characteristics, which generally spend below the state average. The criticism of this approach is that the adequate expenditure level typically identified is difficult to relate to the fiscal adequacy needs of big-city and small rural districts, even with adjustments for pupil needs and geographic price differentials.

The third procedure uses the economic cost-function approach. This approach seeks to identify a per-pupil spending level sufficient to produce a given level of performance, adjusting for characteristics of students and other SES characteristics of districts. This method also can be used to calculate how much more money is required to produce the specified level of performance by factors such as special needs of students, scale economies or diseconomies, input prices, and even efficiency. The results produce an adequate expenditure per pupil for the average district, and then, for all other districts, adjust that figure to account for differences in pupil need and educational prices as well as diseconomies of both large and small size. The expenditure level is higher (lower) as the performance level is higher (lower). This analysis usually produces an adjustment for city districts of two to three times the average expenditure level, which when combined with the complex statistical analysis, makes its use problematic in the real political context.

No state currently uses this approach, though cost function research has been conducted for several states, including New York, Wisconsin, Texas, and Illinois (Reschovsky and Imazeki, 1998, 2001; Duncombe, Ruggiero, and Yinger, 1996). Research showed that there was substantial variation in the average adequacy level due to student and district needs, ranging from a low of 49 percent to a high of 460 percent of the average in Wisconsin, and a low of 75 percent to a high of 158 percent of the average in Texas. In both states, the adequate expenditure figures for the large urban districts were at the highest levels.

Moreover, these studies used different methodologies and had different definitions of "adequate" performance levels—in Wisconsin, it was teaching students to the average on state tests, and in the other two states it was teaching at least 70 percent of students to state proficiency standards. But all studies sought to identify a spending level that was associated with a desired, substantive education result—student achievement to a specified standard, and in general that spending level was close to the respective state's median spending level.

The fourth approach to determining an adequate expenditure level, one that the authors have developed, is to identify *research- or other evidence-based* educational strategies, cost them out and then aggregate them to identify adequate school-site, district, and state expenditure levels. This approach more directly identifies educational strategies that produce desired results, so it also helps guide school sites in how to use dollars in the most effective ways. Initially, this strategy used the ingredients of "high-performance" school models (Odden and Picus, 2000; Stringfield, Ross, and Smith, 1996) to determine an overall cost level, often "whole school" designs created by the New American Schools models (see Odden, 1997a, and the New American Schools website). And the costs of these models generally fell within the revenues available to the average elementary, middle, and high school in the country (Odden and Busch, 1998).

New American
Schools

More recently, the "state-of-the-art" approach merged research findings on effective educational practices with common features across several "comprehensive school designs," which themselves are compilations of research and best practice knowledge. This approach identifies a set of ingredients that are required to deliver a high-quality instructional program, and determines an adequate expenditure level by placing a price on each ingredient and aggregating to a total cost (e.g., Odden, 2000). It identifies these services and ingredients for adequately funding each school, normalizing on a school of 500 students:

- one principal;
- two instructional facilitators, coaches, or mentors;
- preschool for three- and four-year-olds, at least for children from lower-income backgrounds, with a teacher and an educational assistant for every 15 students;
- teachers for a full-day kindergarten program;
- teachers to provide for class sizes of 15 students in grades K–3, and 25 for all other grades;
- an additional 20 percent of teachers to provide for planning and preparation time for the above teachers and to teach art, music, physical education, and other noncore academic classes, with the requirement that a substantial portion of such time be used by regular classroom teachers for collaborative instructional improvement work;
- tutors (professionally licensed teachers) for struggling students, at a rate of one tutor for every 20 percent of students from low-income backgrounds, with a minimum of one tutor for each school, which should provide sufficient resources to serve slow learner, mildly disabled, and/or English-language-learning students;
- sufficient funds for all severely disabled students;
- an additional $2,000 per teacher for the training component of professional development (the above facilitators provide the ongoing coaching within the school);
- about $125,000 for computer technologies (hardware and software) to cover purchase, upgrading, and repair;
- one to five positions for a pupil support/family outreach strategy, with one position for each 20 percent of students from a low-income background, with a minimum of one position; and
- other resources for materials, equipment, and supplies; operation and maintenance; and clerical/secretarial support.

This level of funding would allow schools to deploy just about every strategy research has shown to have statistically significant impacts on student learning, and to deploy just about any comprehensive school reform model that exists (see, for example, Erlichson and Goertz, 2001; Erlichson, Goertz, and Turnbull, 1999; Odden, 2000). It was used as the basis for the 1998 final New Jersey Supreme Court decree in that state's 25-year-old school finance case. And a variation of this approach has just been proposed for Wisconsin (Norman, 2002) and Kentucky (Odden, Fermanich, and Picus, 2003).

To be sure, additional work is needed to identify "adequate" expenditure levels. Each approach just discussed has strengths and weaknesses, and none has been perfected.

Any state would need to select one of the previous approaches, or choose some other approach, and determine what their level of adequacy would be. But at their core, these new approaches to school finance seek to link spending with student achievement results.

4. SUMMARY

This chapter has two emphases: first, to argue that money does matter in education, and second, since money is provided in both unequal ways and insufficient amounts to districts and schools, to identify various ways to assess the degree of equity and adequacy of a state's school finance system. In terms of whether money makes a difference, we side with those analysts who conclude that it does, but we also side with the critics who argue that the way money is used makes the most important differences and, as we show in Chapter 10, there are more effective ways to use money in most schools.

In general, as is shown most clearly in Chapter 7, equity and adequacy are most commonly assessed from an ex post perspective, and focused on the impact of the system on students. The most common fiscal variable analyzed is state and local revenues per pupil. Fiscal neutrality is assessed by calculating the correlation coefficient and simple elasticity between this revenue-per-pupil figure and property value per pupil. Horizontal equity is usually assessed with such measures as the coefficient of variation and the McLoone Index. Vertical equity is assessed by providing need-based pupil weights and then conducting horizontal equity analyses. Four different approaches can be used to determine an adequacy expenditure level, and the Odden-Picus Adequacy Index can be used to measure the degree of adequacy for the school finance system.

Table 3.1 summarizes the equity/adequacy framework in chart form, and Table 3.2 provides a summary of the statistics used to measure the degree of equity/adequacy. Both charts portray the key aspects of the framework and important statistics, but there are several related issues, many of which this chapter has discussed. These issues will be discussed further in Chapters 5 and 7. Chapter 5 goes into more detail on formula options for school finance structures, and Chapter 7 discusses how state finance systems can be improved.

TABLE 3.1   School Finance Equity Framework—Summary and Examples of Variables

Factors	Components	Variables and Statistics
Group (who)	Children Taxpayers Teachers Parents	District value weighted by the number of students
Objects (what)	Inputs–Fiscal (per pupil)	• Total revenues from local, state, and federal sources • Total revenues from local and state sources • Total general revenues from local and state sources • Total current operating expenditures • Total instructional expenditures • Total expenditures for the regular programs
	–Physical Outcome (student achievement)	• Average student/classroom teacher ratio • High school graduation rate • Postsecondary attendance rate • % correct on criterion-referenced measures • % scoring at basic, proficient and advanced levels by content area
Principles (how)	Horizontal equity	• Equal treatment of equals –equal distribution of resources
	Vertical equity	• Unequal treatment of unequals –legitimate needs for children (handicaps, low achievement, limited English), districts (price, size, transportation, enrollment growth), programs (voc ed, lab science, advanced topics)
	Fiscal neutrality	• Linear relationship between object and fiscal capacity variable • Magnitude of the relationship
Statistics (how much)	Horizontal equity	• Range • Restricted range • Federal range ratio • Coefficient of variation • Gini Coefficient • McLoone Index • Verstegen Index
	Vertical equity	• Weighted pupils for needs • Elimination of categorical revenues in the analysis • Price-adjusted dollars
	Fiscal neutrality	• Correlation coefficient • Elasticity
	Adequacy	• Odden-Picus Adequacy Index

TABLE 3.2   Assessing Equity Statistics

Statistic	Calculation	Value	Other Attributes	Overall Evaluation
Range	Subtract value of highest observation from that of lowest observation.	Maximum difference in observations. The larger the range, the greater the inequity.	Based on only two observations—highest and lowest. Can reflect anamolies. Sensitive to inflation.	Poor.
Federal range ratio	Difference between observation of 95th and 5th percentile, divided by value of 5th percentile.	Ratio of the range between 95th and 5th observation. Ranges from 0 to any positive number.	Based on only two observations. Not sensitive to inflation.	A good range statistic.
Coefficient of variation (CV)	Standard deviation divided by the mean.	Ranges from 0 to 1.0, or 0% to100%. Zero indicates equal distribution. Equitable if CV less than 0.1.	Includes all values; does not change with inflation.	Good.
McLoone Index	Ratio of sum of all observations below median (50th percentile) to sum if all observations had value of median.	Ranges from 0 to 1. One indicates perfect equality. Most school finance data sets are between 0.7 and 0.95; 0.9 desirable.	Compares bottom half of the districts to the median (50th percentile).	Good, sensitive to bottom half of distribution.
Verstegen Index	Ratio of sum of all observations above median (50th percentile) to sum if all observations had value of median.	Ranges from 1 and higher. One indicates perfect equality. Most school finance data sets are between 1.2 and 1.5.	Compares top half of the districts to the median (50th percentile).	Good at indicating variation in top half of distribution.

TABLE 3.2 Assessing Equity Statistics *(continued)*

Statistic	Calculation	Value	Other Attributes	Overall Evaluation
Gini Index	Area of the graph between Gini curve and 45-degree line divided by area under 45-degree line.	Ranges from 0 to 1.0; value close to 0 suggests equality, but in school finance values usually less than 0.5.	Indicates degree to which children at different percentiles have same amount of the object. Includes all observations. Insensitive to inflation.	Complicated but a good statistic.
Correlation coefficient	Measure of linear relationship between two variables.	Ranges from -1.0 to $+1.0$. Values close to 0 indicate no relationship; values closer to -1 or $+1$ indicate a strong positive or negative relationship.	Includes all observations. Insensitive to inflation. Not good for indicating a nonlinear relationship.	Good for indicating existence of relationship, but not magnitude of relationship.
Elasticity	Ratio of percent increase in one variable to percent increase in another.	Ranges from 0 to a number above that; can exceed 1.0. Numbers greater than or equal to 1.0 indicate an elastic relationship.	Includes all observations. Insensitive to inflation.	Good for indicating the magnitude of the relationship. If correlation is low and elasticity is high, there is an important link between the two variables.
Odden-Picus Adequacy Index	Percentage of sum of all observations below adequacy level to sum if all observations at adequacy level.	Ranges from 1.0 or 100% to a percentage less than 100. Numbers close to 100 indicate a more adequate system.	Virtually includes all observations, but focuses on those below adequacy. Insensitive to inflation.	Good for indicating how close or far the system is to providing an adequate spending level for all districts.

Chapter 4

The Public Finance Context

Public K–12 education in the United States is a big business. As was shown in Table 1.2 (Chapter 1), revenue raised by all levels of government for K–12 education in 2000–01 amounted to more than $378.5 billion (National Education Association, 2001). This is approximately the same amount spent by the federal government for defense in fiscal year 2000–01 (Moody, 2002). These revenues are raised as part of the larger federal fiscal system in the United States. Under our federal system, governments at the local (city, school districts, etc.), state, and federal levels all raise and spend public tax dollars. In calendar year 2000, total governmental receipts from all levels of government amounted to over $2.89 trillion (see Table 4.1). As this shows, revenues for K–12 education constitute only 13 percent of total governmental revenue.

Although responsibility for the education of our children almost always rests with the nearly 15,000 local school districts across the nation, nearly half the money spent on K–12 education is now provided by the governments of the 50 states. It is only in the last 30 or so years that the state has become an equal partner with local school districts in financing education.

States have taken a more significant role in the finances of schools for a number of reasons. In response to lawsuits across the nation, states have either been forced, or have voluntarily agreed, to use their financial resources to equalize differences in the property tax–raising capacity of their school districts. As local taxpayers have grown more reluctant to increase property taxes to finance local services, including education, states have filled in, either providing additional funds for schools or using their resources to provide property tax relief. Often these two efforts work hand-in-hand, with increases in state revenues being used partially to reduce local property tax burdens and partially to increase educational spending. In addition, movements for educational reform and increased educational accountability have led to a growing state role in the provision of school services. In many instances, this growing state role is supported with additional funds.

Local school districts have traditionally financed almost all of their share of educational revenues through property taxes. This is because property is fixed in location, and values tend to change slowly, giving relatively small units of government—such as

TABLE 4.1   Tax Revenue by Source and Level of Government, 1957–2000

Year	Total— All Governments	Federal Government	State Governments Own Source	Local Governments Own Source	School Districts[c]
Total Tax Revenue (in Billions)					
1957[a]	$ 108.6	$ 79.8	$ 14.5	$ 14.3	$ 4.5
1967[a]	209.8	148.8	31.9	29.1	10.8
1977[a]	531.6	355.6	101.1	74.9	27.1
1987[a]	1,159.5	854.4	246.9	158.2	51.8
1997[b]	2,307.9	1,579.3	444.2	284.4	93.4
2000[e]	2,893.2	2,025.2	539.7	328.3	106.5
Property Taxes (in Billions)					
1957[a]	$ 12.9	—	$ 0.5	$ 12.4	$ 4.4
1967[a]	26.0	—	0.9	25.2	10.6
1977[a]	62.5	—	2.3	60.3	26.4
1987[a]	121.2	—	4.6	116.6	50.5
1997[b]	218.8	—	10.3	208.5	90.4
2000[e]	246.2	—	11.0	235.2	102.0
Sales, Gross Receipts, and Customs (in Billions)					
1957[a]	$ 20.6	$ 11.1	$ 8.4	$ 1.0	$ —
1967[a]	36.3	15.8	18.6	2.0	—
1977[a]	83.8	23.2	52.4	8.3	0.2
1987[a]	192.7	48.4	119.9	24.5	0.5
1997[b]	336.5	74.8	216.4	45.3	d
2000[e]	385.0	88.8	252.1	44.1	d
Individual and Corporate Income Taxes (in Billions)					
1957[a]	$ 59.5	$ 56.8	$ 2.5	$ 0.2	$ —
1967[a]	103.5	95.5	7.1	0.1	—
1977[a]	250.0	211.6	34.7	3.8	0.2
1987[a]	582.8	476.5	96.7	9.7	0.4
1997[b]	1,112.7	919.8	175.7	17.2	d
2000[e]	1,459.5	1,211.8	227.1	20.6	d
Social Insurance (Federal Only)[e]					
1957	$ 10.0	$ 10.0	—	—	—
1967	32.6	32.6	—	—	—
1977	106.5	106.5	—	—	—
1987	303.3	303.3	—	—	—
1997[b]	539.4	539.4	—	—	—
2000[e]	652.9	652.9	—	—	—

(continued)

TABLE 4.1   Tax Revenue by Source and Level of Government, 1957–2000
(continued)

Year	Total— All Governments	Federal Government	State Governments Own Source	Local Governments Own Source	School Districts[c]
		Other Sources of Revenue (in Billions)			
1957[a]	$ 5.6	$ 1.9	$ 3.1	$ 0.7	$0.1
1967[a]	10.3	3.8	5.3	1.8	0.2
1977[a]	23.5	9.0	11.7	2.5	0.3
1987[a]	47.8	14.5	25.7	7.4	0.4
1997[b]	80.4	22.2	41.8	13.4	3.0
2000[e]	149.5	71.7	49.5	28.3	4.5

[a]*Source:* Advisory Commission on Intergovernmental Relations (1988). *Significant Features of Fiscal Federalism,* Volume II. Washington, D.C.: ACIR, p. 64; and U.S. Bureau of the Census, Government Finance in 1986–87. Washington, D.C.: U.S. Bureau of the Census, p. 7

[b]*Sources:* Office of Management and Budget (2003). Budget of the United States Government, Fiscal Year 2003: Historical Tables. *http://w3.access.gpo.gov/usbudget/fy2003/pdf/hist.pdf;* State and Local Data: U.S. Bureau of the Census (2000). *Compendium of Government Finances: 1997 Census of Governments,* Volume 4, Government Finances. *www.census.gov/prod/gc97/gc974-5.pdf;* and School District Data: U.S. Bureau of the Census (2000). *Public Education Finances: 1997 Census of Governments,* Volume 4, Government Finances. *www.census.gov/prod/gc97/gc974-1.pdf.*

[c]Figures for school districts are included in the state and local government totals. Total—All Governments column represents the sum of Federal, State, and Local columns and includes school districts.

[d]Data for all other tax sources are included in Other Sources of Revenue for 1997 and 2000.

[e]*Sources:* Federal Data for 2000 and Social Insurance Data for all years: Office of Management and Budget (2003). Budget of the United States Government, Fiscal Year 2003: Historical Tables. *http://w3.access.gpo.gov/usbudget/fy2003/pdf/hist.pdf;* State Data: U.S. Census Bureau. (2002). State Government Tax Collections: 2000. *www.census.gov/govs/statetax/0000usstax.html;* Local Government Data: Calculated from U.S. Census Bureau (2002). Quarterly Summary of State and Local Government Tax Revenue, Tables 1 and 2. *www.census.gov/govs/www/qtax.html;* and School District Data: U.S. Census Bureau (2000). Public Elementary–Secondary Education Finances: 1999–00. *www.census.gov/govs/school/00fullreport.pdf.*

Please note: Visit the text's website at *www.mhhe.com/odden3e* for updates to these or any other URL references included in the text.

school districts—a stable source of revenue (Monk and Brent, 1997). States, which have a larger base upon which taxes can be levied, have been able to use other taxes, in particular sales and income taxes, to finance their operations. Moreover, these broad-based statewide taxes make it possible for the state (through equalization grants discussed in Chapter 5) to more efficiently ensure that educational spending in individual districts is more a function of the wealth of the entire state and not of the individual school district.

The purpose of this chapter is to set the context within which revenues for education are raised. The major reason for studying how governments raise revenue is that taxes are the primary source of dollars for public schools. While the focus of the chapter is on raising tax revenues, taxes can be used for other purposes as well. Taxes can be a means to redistribute income from the wealthy to the poor. Taxes also can be used as a regulatory tool. For example, rather than regulate manufacturing plant emissions, pollution could be controlled by taxing those emissions, or alternatively, providing tax breaks for companies that take steps to minimize pollution. In other words, taxes can be used for a variety of purposes. However, this chapter focuses on taxes as a source of revenues for public schools.

This chapter has three sections. The first provides an overview of trends in federal, state, and local taxes from 1957 to 2002. The second section presents the public finance criteria commonly used to evaluate specific taxes, while the third section uses those criteria to assess the individual income tax, sales taxes, and property taxes. The third section also contains a discussion of state lotteries, which are increasingly popular mechanisms for raising governmental revenues, and other alternative revenue options being considered.

1. TAXATION OVERVIEW

This section provides a short overview of the magnitude of local, state, and federal taxation, as well as changes in tax structures over time.

Trends in Federal, State, and Local Taxation

During the past 40 years, there have been significant changes in the tax revenues raised by different governmental levels. Table 4.1 exhibits tax revenues by type of tax for all levels of government, including school districts, from 1957 to 2000. Several trends in this figure are worth noting. First, total tax revenues for all levels of government more than doubled in each of the first four decades presented in the figure, and increased by over half a trillion dollars between 1957 and 2000, an increase of $81.6 billion when adjusted for inflation. These figures reflect government growth over that period. Second, nominal (not adjusted for inflation) state government revenues have increased at a faster rate than revenues for either the federal or local governments, rising by over 3,600 percent between 1957 and 2000.

Another trend displayed in this figure is that property taxes are the primary source of tax revenues for local governments. The federal government does not collect any property taxes, and state governments collect a small amount of property taxes. Further, over 41 percent of all property taxes were collected by school districts in 2000.

Table 4.1 also shows that most sales and gross receipt taxes are raised by state governments. Local sales taxes, though, have grown in importance as a revenue source since 1977. Sales taxes comprised the largest single source of tax revenues for state governments in 2000. School districts raise very little revenue directly through sales taxes.

Finally, individual income taxes raise the largest amount of governmental tax revenues, and the bulk of income taxes are raised by the federal government. But income taxes are rising at both state and local levels. Federal individual and corporate income taxes grew from $59.5 billion in 1957 to nearly $1.5 trillion in 2000 ($244.8 billion in 1957 dollars). Federal individual and corporate income taxes accounted for 83 percent of that amount. Income taxes have historically comprised a minuscule amount of local school district revenues.

This discussion suggests that sources of tax revenue have been changing over the past 40-plus years. In 1957 governments at all levels collected a total of nearly $109 billion and by 2000 total tax collections were nearly $2.9 trillion ($473.2 billion in 1957 dollars). Despite the changes, the individual income tax is the primary tax source for the federal government, the sales tax the primary revenue source for state governments, and the property tax the prime revenue producer for local governments, including school districts. It is important to remember these relationships as we discuss sources of revenue for schools later in this chapter.

Changes in Tax Structures

Federal, state, and local tax structures have experienced significant structural changes over time. At the federal level, there have been shifts in the proportion of taxes paid by individuals compared with business. There have also been changes in marginal tax rates as well as the number of rate categories that are part of the tax system. The number and level of deductions, exemptions, and tax-sheltered items, as well as the treatment of capital gains, have also changed a number of times in the last 40 years. There have been a host of other modifications that alter the amount of money collected by the federal tax system and how the taxes collected impact different individuals with different levels and sources of earnings. Most of these changes have affected federal, personal, and corporate income taxes, and the social security tax.

At the state level, tax structures have experienced even more changes. Over time, states have added new taxes, including on occasion a new income or sales tax. They also have changed tax rates, enacted a variety of mechanisms to alleviate tax burdens on low-income families, conformed their income tax structure to the ever-changing federal tax structure, and modified their tax systems to buffer increases and decreases in federal intergovernmental grants. In addition, during the recent period of economic growth, many states have taken steps to reduce taxes and/or curtail the growth of tax revenues. Although public finance economists urge governments to create stability in the tax structure so households and the business community can make decisions in a more stable fiscal environment, political leaders have difficulty heeding this advice. Change seems to be a hallmark of state and federal tax structures and seems to be catalyzed by both economic and political variables.

In recent years, states have become more dependent on income (and to some extent sales) taxes than in the past. At the same time, because measures of individual household income seem to be changing—with more households owning and trading stocks and bonds—state revenues seem to fluctuate with changes in the economy more than in the past. The result during the 1990s was substantial state revenue deficits during the recession at the beginning of the decade, followed by considerable state revenue surpluses in the middle and end of the decade when the economy was strong and growing. During this time, many states cut tax rates, which has resulted in even larger state revenue deficits early in the 2000s as the economy has weakened.

At the same time, as pointed out in Chapter 1, states continue to expand their share of public school revenues, making local school districts more dependent on swings in the economy and hence swings in state revenues than in the past. Although school districts have always had to cope with some variation in revenue over time, the recent swings have been proportionally much larger and complicated the task of long-term planning at the same time that districts face increased calls for greater accountability. One of the challenges faced in public finance today is finding ways to smooth out the gyrations in state revenue that appear to be a new factor in raising and spending government resources.

2. ASSESSING AND UNDERSTANDING TAXATION

Raising taxes is not a simple endeavor. Not only are actions to increase tax revenues—or institute new taxes—unpopular politically, new taxes often have side effects that may create economic inefficiencies (Musgrave and Musgrave, 1989). In looking at the revenue potential of any tax, policymakers consider both the tax rate and the tax base.

The rate is the level of taxation. The tax base is the entity to which the tax rate is applied. The relationship between tax rate and tax base is crucial to understanding the yield of any tax, and can be captured in a simple equation as follows:

$$\text{Tax Yield} = \text{Tax Rate} \times \text{Tax Base}$$

Policymakers seeking to increase revenue can increase either the rate or the base, or both, to garner that revenue. The decision they make will have differential impacts on individuals in different circumstances. It is important to understand what those impacts might be before recommending that changes in tax rates or tax bases be implemented. In general, economists argue that the most efficient taxes, which are those that create the fewest inefficiencies in the economy, are those with low rates and broad bases (see, for example, Musgrave and Musgrave, 1989; Rosen, 2001).

Public Finance Criteria for Evaluating Taxes

Public finance economists use several analytic criteria to evaluate taxes. These criteria are commonly accepted as both the economic and policy assessments needed when analyzing a tax (see Musgrave and Musgrave, 1989, or Rosen, 2001, for an example). These criteria include:

- the tax base,
- yield,
- equity,
- the economic effects of the tax, and
- administration and compliance issues.

This section discusses each of these in some detail.

Tax Base.   The tax base is the entity to which a tax rate is applied. For example, a tax could be based on the number of cars or television sets a person owned. The rate, then, could be a fixed dollar amount per car or television. Usually tax bases are related to some economic category such as income, property, or consumption. Broad-based taxes, such as property, income, and sales taxes, are taxes with broad or comprehensive bases. There are four major tax bases: wealth, income, consumption, and privilege.

Wealth.   There are many forms of wealth, some typically taxed and others not taxed. In economic terms, wealth represents an accumulation of value, or a stock of value, at any one point in time. Net worth—the sum of all economic assets minus all economic liabilities at some fixed point in time—is one measure of wealth. A wealth tax could then be levied on an individual's net worth. Proposals for net worth taxes have been made over the years but have never been enacted into law.

Another common measure of wealth is property. Property can be divided into two general categories: real property and personal property. Real property includes land and buildings. For individuals, personal property includes assets with a shorter life span, such as automobiles and other vehicles, and household items, such as furniture, video equipment, computers, rugs, and appliances. For businesses, personal property includes machinery and equipment, furniture and other office supplies, and inventories. Stocks, bonds, and other financial instruments—certificates of deposit, notes, bank accounts, etc.—are other forms of wealth that could theoretically be taxed. The value of an inheritance is yet another form of wealth that often is taxed.

A pure tax on wealth would tax all of these different categories. The United States does not have and has never had a wealth tax. Financial instruments such as stocks and bonds have rarely been taxed. Large portions of real property owned by the government and religious organizations are not taxed. And there has been an increasing tendency on the part of states to exempt some types of real and many forms of personal property from taxation.

The property tax comes closest to a wealth tax in this country. But the property tax generally covers only real property. The trend during the past three decades has been to eliminate both individual and business personal property from the property tax.

Income.   Income represents another tax base. Compared with wealth, which is a measure of economic worth at one point in time, income is a measure of an economic flow over time. The net value of income minus expenses over a time period represents the change in net worth over that period. Income includes salaries, interest from financial instruments, dividends from stocks, gifts, money from the sale of an item of wealth including both property and a financial instrument, and other forms of money flow. Earned income is typically money earned through work, such as wages and salaries. Unearned income represents money received from the returns on financial assets and investments, such as stocks, bonds, and mutual funds.

While income from salaries is rather easy to identify, income from business activities is more complicated, since net income is determined by subtracting legitimate expenses from gross receipts or sales. While conceptually straightforward, defining "gross receipts," "sales," and "legitimate expenses" is technically complex, and income can vary substantially depending on the specifics of the definition.

Regardless of how "income" is defined, it is generally viewed as the measure of ability to pay. This measure of ability to pay refers to all forms of taxation, not just income taxes. For example, if the value of a person's wealth is fixed, such as the value of a home, some current income is needed to pay a tax on that element of wealth. If current income is insufficient to pay the tax, the element of wealth would need to be sold, or partially sold, to meet the tax liability. Alternatively, the individual would need to borrow funds to pay the tax or alter his/her consumption patterns to be able to pay the taxes. This would likely result in a reduced ability to purchase other goods and services. The same is true for a sales or consumption tax; that tax is paid from an individual's current income, so the greater the tax, the fewer other things an individual can purchase with current income sources.

An important factor in using income as a measure of ability to pay is the period over which income is measured. Typically income is measured in annual amounts, and most tax structures assume yearly income to be both the tax base and the measure of ability to pay. But individuals and businesses purchase capital items such as homes, cars, manufacturing plants, factories, and equipment on a longer-term basis, often with the assumption that average income will increase over time. For example, assuming their income would rise over the next decade, a family might purchase an expensive home with a mortgage that consumes a high proportion of their current income. Their assumption that income will grow over time means that in a few years the cost of the mortgage (monthly payments) will be less burdensome, eventually being a smaller portion of their monthly expenses. This suggests to many economists that some measure of long-term, or lifetime income, might be a better measure of ability to pay, rather than annual income which is generally used in such analyses today (see, for example, Musgrave and Musgrave, 1989; Rosen, 2001).

Consumption.   Theoretically, a tax on consumption would include taxation of all goods and services purchased by individuals and businesses. A consumption tax is usually called a sales tax if it applies to a broad range of items that can be purchased. Most state and local sales taxes fall into this category. A consumption tax is usually called an excise tax if it applies to specific items, such as beer, alcohol, cigarettes, furs, jewelry, luxury cars, etc.

A broad-based consumption tax would tax income less savings—all income spent on purchases for current consumption. The United States does not have a broad-based consumption tax at the present time although there have been a number of calls for such a tax to be implemented. While most state sales taxes come the closest to this definition, they generally exclude services that are an increasing component of current consumption, and they include both small and large products such as food, prescription medicine, and cars. Thus, sales taxes in this country are more aptly described as broad-based selective sales taxes.

Privilege.   A small portion of revenues for federal, state, and local government services are raised by granting individuals or businesses a privilege and charging a fee for that privilege. A driver's license fee is paid for the privilege of driving a car; a car license plate fee is paid for the privilege of owning a car. Privilege fees are paid for a variety of other purposes such as franchise fees for running certain businesses, fees for using park facilities, fees for a permit to operate a taxicab, and fees for using port facilities. A privilege tax is similar to an excise tax, the major difference being that the privilege tax is paid for the privilege of engaging in some activity, while an excise tax is paid for the privilege of purchasing and owning or using some product.

Yield.   The yield is the amount of revenues a tax will produce. Yield is equal to the tax rate times the tax base. Rates are usually—but not always—given in percentage terms. Examples include a 5 percent sales tax, a 10 percent gasoline tax, a 33 percent marginal federal income tax rate, or a 4 percent state income tax rate. Given a defined tax base, it is straightforward to determine the yield for each percent of tax rate on that tax base. Knowing the revenue-raising or yield potential of a tax (given a defined tax base) is important information for policymakers. Economists argue that it is preferable to be able to raise substantial revenues at low or modest rates, arguing for broad-based taxes rather than taxes with narrowly defined bases.

Broad-based taxes by definition can produce high yields even at modest rates, whereas selective taxes, such as a cigarette tax, are limited in the amount of revenue they can produce. A tax that produces a large amount of revenue, such as a property tax, is difficult to eliminate (a proposal often made for the unpopular property tax). This is because doing so would require either large cuts in governmental services or substantial increases in other tax rates. Neither option is politically popular. Indeed, broad-based taxes may make it easier to raise new revenues since it would only require a small tax rate increase.

Other aspects of tax yield include revenue stability and the elasticity of the tax. Stability is the degree to which the yield rises or falls with national or state economic cycles. Stable tax revenues decrease less in economic downturns but also increase less during economic upturns. The property tax historically has been a stable tax since property values consistently increase over time and fall only in deep, major recessions. Sales taxes on products tend to rise and fall more in line with economic cycles, as do taxes on income. Corporate income taxes follow economic cycles even more closely and thus tend to be an even more volatile revenue source. In the current economic environment, both income and sales tax receipts appear to have become less stable.

Elasticity measures the degree to which tax revenues keep pace with change in either their base, or more commonly, the change in personal income. To measure the income elasticity of a tax, one compares the ratio of the percentage change in the tax yield to the percentage change in personal income. An elasticity less than one indicates that tax revenues do not keep pace with income growth; an elasticity equal to one indicates that tax revenues grow at the same rate as incomes; and an elasticity greater than one indicates that tax revenues increase faster than income growth. Since prices and demands for governmental (including school) services tend to at least keep pace with income growth, an income elasticity of at least one is a highly desirable feature of any tax. Individual income taxes, especially if marginal rates are higher for higher incomes, tend to be elastic, while sales tax revenues generally track income growth. Over time, property taxes have exhibited elasticities of approximately one.

To some degree, a trade-off exists between stability and elasticity. Elastic taxes tend to be less stable since their yield falls in economic downturns when personal income also tends to fall or at least grow more slowly. Stable taxes are less elastic. As a result, their yields remain steadier during economic fluctuations.

Tax Equity.   Tax equity addresses the issue of whether the tax is fair, treating individuals or businesses equitably. Although conceptually simple, it is difficult to determine with preciseness the degree to which a tax treats all fairly. There are two primary aspects of tax equity: horizontal equity and vertical equity.

Horizontal equity concerns equal tax treatment of individuals in the same, or equal, circumstance. For example, if an income tax met the horizontal equity test, individuals with the same taxable income ($40,000, for example) would pay the same amount of tax ($4,000, for example). Or, two families with a home with the same market value would pay the same amount of property tax. But as will be discussed later, these two simple examples mask a variety of technical issues. In the income tax case, the issue is determining taxable income. At both the federal and state level, there are a variety of exemptions, deductions, and adjustments made to gross income in determining taxable income. If there is disagreement about any of those modifications, the preceding conclusion about horizontal equity could be challenged. As a result, even horizontal tax equity is difficult to attain.

Most individuals are not equally situated. Vertical equity is the principle used to describe how a tax treats individuals in different economic situations. Determining vertical equity is more complex than estimating horizontal equity. The first issue is to decide on the criterion for differentiating tax treatment. That is, if taxes are to burden some individuals more than others, what variable should determine those differences? The degree to which the tax would vary is a value judgment. But determining on what basis a tax should vary is an important tax policy decision.

One possible criterion would be benefits received—that is, taxes should vary with the benefits received—where the greater the benefits, the higher the tax paid. A gasoline tax burdens drivers but meets the benefits-received criterion since individuals who drive benefit from use of public roads and highways. Moreover, the more they drive, the more they benefit from the roads, and the more they pay in gasoline taxes as they consume more gasoline.

By definition, a fee-for-service tax meets the benefits principle—the fee is simply the tax for the service (or benefit) received. Appealing as the benefits-received criterion is, it is difficult, if not impossible, to measure the individual benefits received for a broader array of services. For example, police and fire services generally benefit the individuals within the locality where police and fire protection are provided. But education, which is another locally provided service, provides benefits not only to individuals in the form of higher incomes but also to society in general in the form of economic growth and lower needs for social services (Cohn and Geske, 1990). Even if education benefits accrued only to individuals, today most individuals move from the city where they are educated, making it difficult to have anything other than a national tax related to those benefits.

At broader levels, the benefits principle becomes more problematic. For example, how do we measure the individual benefits from spending on national defense, public transportation systems, interstate highway systems, a statewide higher education system, or an interstate system of waterways for transit and agriculture? It would seem foolish to increase the taxes for individuals receiving public assistance (welfare) benefits since taxation of their benefits would defeat the purpose of providing the assistance in the first place. For these reasons, a benefits principle, though appealing to economists, has not been implemented as a basis for differential tax treatment, at least for broad-based income, sales, and property taxes.

Instead, ability to pay has been adopted in this country as the criterion for vertical tax equity. Ability to pay generally is measured by income. If taxes differ among individuals, they should differ because of differences in their ability to pay—that is, because they have different income levels.

Vertical tax equity can be measured by comparing taxes expressed as a percent of income. Vertical equity is broadly defined by the terms "progressive," "proportional," or "regressive." Progressive tax burdens increase with income—as income rises, so does the tax liability as a percent of income. Proportional tax burdens would impose the same percentage tax burden regardless of the level of income. Regressive taxes are the opposite of progressive taxes in that individuals with lower incomes pay a higher percentage of their income in taxes than do those with higher incomes. They may not pay more in total taxes, but as a portion of their income, more goes to taxes. For example, if an individual with $10,000 in income paid a 12 percent income tax and an individual with an income of $100,000 paid 10 percent income tax, the tax would be regressive. However, the total dollar tax burden would be $1,200 for the low-income individual and $10,000 for the individual with the higher income.

In this country, it is generally agreed that regressive tax burdens should be avoided. It is widely felt that the poor, or low-income individuals or households, should not pay a larger percentage of income in taxes than average or above-average individuals. It is also generally agreed that the tax system should be at least proportional, and probably progressive, although support for progressive tax burdens has waned in recent years as initiatives at both federal and state levels have reduced the degree of progressivity of many taxes. For example, in the 1990s there was considerable interest in a flat tax rate for federal income taxes. While a progressive tax burden has generally been sanctioned in the past, there is less consensus for that position today.

Measuring vertical tax equity entails an additional series of technical problems. First, one needs to distinguish tax impact from tax incidence or tax burden. Put differently, one needs to differentiate between who actually pays the tax to the tax collector from who actually bears the burden of the tax. The latter is commonly referred to as the tax incidence. For example, merchants actually submit sales tax payments to governments, but individuals who purchase products almost always bear the burden or incidence of the sales tax. Likewise, companies or organizations usually remit income tax payments to state and federal governments, but working individuals almost always bear the burden of that tax since income taxes are withheld from periodic salary payments. The issue of tax incidence or tax burden for other taxes is not as clear cut.

Tax incidence for the property tax is the most complex. Four different types of property are taxed: owner-occupied homes, residential rental property, business and industry property, and commercial property. The property tax on individuals who own homes is not only paid by homeowners, but they also bear the full burden of the tax. But property taxes on the other components can be shifted. For example, property taxes on rental property might be shifted to renters in the form of higher rents. Depending on competitive conditions, property taxes on industries and corporations could be shifted forward to consumers in the form of higher prices or backward to workers in the form of lower wages, or could be borne by stockholders in the form of lower dividends and stock prices.

A similar issue exists for corporate income taxes: are they shifted forward to consumers into higher prices, or backward to stockholders and/or workers? Likewise, depending on competitive conditions, property taxes on local commercial activities could be shifted forward to consumers, or backward to owners. It turns out that shifting assumptions and patterns produce widely varying conclusions about property tax and corporate income tax incidence, from being steeply regressive to steeply progressive.

Another issue to consider in assessing tax equity is income transfers. The federal government and many state governments have programs that transfer income from the broader group of taxpayers to the poor. Welfare programs, income tax credits, food stamps, rent subsidies, and child-care supports are just some examples of income transfer programs. Thus, a comprehensive assessment of tax equity would consider taxes as well as income transfers. This is because although the poor might pay a large percentage of their incomes in sales taxes and in assumed shifted property taxes, that regressivity could be counterbalanced by receipt of income from a variety of transfer programs. Likewise, average and above-average-income individuals pay more taxes to support income transfer programs but receive none or few income transfer benefits.

Economic Effects.   While taxes are imposed by governments and thus by definition distort the free functioning of the competitive market, some taxes and specific tax designs distort economic decision making more than others. The general goal is for taxes to have a neutral impact on the economy. So another criterion for assessing a specific tax structure is the degree to which it has neutral economic impacts.

Most taxes have some elements that are not economically neutral. The federal income tax allows homeowners to deduct interest on home mortgages, thus encouraging housing consumption over other kinds of consumption. Since interest from savings is taxed at both the federal and state levels, consumption is encouraged over saving. Since most sales taxes cover only products, consumption of services is favored over consumption of products. Since business purchases, even of equipment and items that will be put into products for resale, are frequently (but not always, depending on the individual state sales tax structure) subject to the sales tax, vertical integration is somewhat encouraged if those costs are less than the costs of paying the tax. In California, property taxes are based on market value at the time of purchase rather than current market value. As a consequence purchase of a new home entails a high cost and is discouraged, while remaining in one's home is encouraged by that state's property tax system.

Differences in taxes across state borders also can encourage business investment and individual location. In metropolitan areas near state boundaries, individuals are economically encouraged to live in the state with the lowest sales and/or income tax rates in order to minimize their tax liability.

In short, almost all tax structures have elements that encourage or discourage a variety of economic behaviors. The goal is to structure the tax to neutralize its economic incentives or at least to minimize its economic distortions.

Administration and Compliance.   Finally, both the administration of the tax, and individual or business compliance with tax requirements, should be simple and as low cost as possible. Often simplicity is gained at the cost of some tax equity and vice versa. Further, the more complex the tax, the greater the costs of both administration and compliance. Mikesell (1986) identifies seven factors in tax administration and compliance:

1. maintaining and gathering records,
2. computing the tax liability,
3. remittance of the tax liability,
4. collection,
5. audit,
6. appeal, and
7. enforcement.

Depending on the tax in question, responsibility for each of these steps falls on individual taxpayers or governmental agencies. Ideally, both administration and ability to comply with the tax requirements should be simple. Monk and Brent (1997) point out that the more complicated the tax system, the greater the costs of administration and compliance.

An example of a revenue source with high administration costs is a lottery, which is increasingly popular across the country. Lotteries are poor sources of revenue because of the high costs of administration. To sell lottery tickets, a wide variety of prizes must be offered to individuals who purchase tickets. In most states, the prize payouts comprise 50 percent of all lottery sales. Put differently, for every $1 raised through lottery sales, fully 50 cents is allocated to prizes. Further, most merchants who sell lottery tickets earn a commission, which takes more away from other governmental uses. Other administrative costs also add to expenses. For example, in California, prizes are required to be 50 percent of sales, and administrative costs (which include commissions to sales agents) are capped at 16 percent of lottery ticket sales. Assuming the state lottery administration costs are equal to the full 16 percent of ticket sales, only 34 percent of each lottery dollar is available for other uses.

All other broad-based taxes, such as the income, sales, and property taxes, while requiring administrative costs for both the government and individuals, provide a much higher net yield, somewhere in the high 90 percent range. To be sure, there are ways of increasing and decreasing administration costs of these taxes, but in all cases they are dramatically lower than those of a lottery.

States could nearly eliminate income tax administrative costs if they simply made the state income tax a fixed percent of federal tax liability. States could eliminate sales taxes altogether, and thus sales tax administrative costs, by adopting a general consumption tax that could be administered entirely through the income tax. Short of these more dramatic choices, streamlining federal and state tax administration, though, is an important objective for any specific tax structure, as well as change in tax structure.

3. ANALYSIS OF INDIVIDUAL TAXES

This section uses the previous framework to analyze the key features of each of the following taxes: income, sales, property, and lotteries. The basis, yield, equity, economic effects, and administration of each is discussed.

The Income Tax

The individual income tax is the largest revenue producer for the federal government and is also used by 41 states. Another three states apply the income tax only to interest, dividends, and/or capital gains (i.e., on income from capital assets but not on earned income). Eleven states allow local governments to levy income taxes. As displayed in Table 4.1 (see page 83), in 2000, individual and corporate income taxes produced $1.212 trillion for the federal government, $227.1 billion for state governments, and $20.6 billion for local governments. In the following analysis, we focus primarily on the federal income tax. The discussion of income taxes ends with comments on trends in state income taxes and needed changes for the future.

Basis. Income is the base for both federal and state income taxes. But defining "income" and determining taxable income is a complex activity driven by federal and state tax codes that are revised frequently and consume thousands of pages of law. Defining "gross income" and determining taxable income requires a series of modifications, including income adjustments, both standard and itemized deductions, and exemptions. While an income tax generally meets the horizontal equity standard since individuals with the same taxable income pay the same amount of tax, horizontal equity would be violated if any of the income modifications are deemed unjustified. In addition, both the federal and state governments have different tax schedules for individuals and for famililes (individuals generally paying higher tax rates than families under the assumption that it costs less for one individual to maintain a household than it does for a family). Horizontal equity is violated if there is disagreement over the particular mechanism for differential treatment of individuals and families in either the federal or state income tax structures.

Income adjustments, standard and itemized deductions, and various exemptions at first blush seem reasonable modifications to make to determine taxable income. Most would agree that two families with, for example, an income of $50,000 should pay a different amount of tax if one family consists of just husband and wife with few medical expenditures and the other consists of husband and wife, four children, a live-in parent, and high medical costs. But a reasonable deduction or adjustment for one person can seem unreasonable or unfair to another. For example, in the past, several types of investments provided large deductions for taxpayers, often exceeding the dollar amount of investment made. While such tax shelters encouraged investment in those activities, some having good social values like low-income housing, the proliferation of tax shelters and their use primarily by higher-income individuals gave a perception over time that they were simply unfair.

Yield.   Individual and corporate income taxes are the largest source of revenue for the federal government. Table 4.2 shows that both federal and state income taxes have grown considerably over time. However, as a percentage of personal income, total individual and corporate income taxes have remained relatively stable—actually dropping from 16.6 percent of personal income in 1957 to 14.9 percent of personal income in 2001. This suggests that income taxes take approximately the same "bite" out of household income today as they did in the 1950s. However, inspection of the last column in Table 4.2 shows that income taxes as a percentage of personal income have increased by about 3 percent, suggesting a substantial drop in corporate income taxes over time.

The income tax is an elastic tax. As income rises, income tax collections generally rise faster. Table 4.3 shows that the individual income tax elasticity exceeded one (that is, tax collections grew at a faster rate than personal income grew) in each decade between 1957 and 1987. That pattern was reversed between 1987 and 1994 when the elasticity of the income tax amounted to only 0.73. This is due largely to the income tax revisions of 1986, which substantially flattened the tax brackets and left the highest bracket at 31 percent during the recession of the early 1990s, and the indexing of income tax brackets so that increased marginal tax rates impacted only taxpayers whose incomes grew at a rate faster than the rate of inflation. The figure shows that between 1994 and 2001 the elasticity increased dramatically. This is the result of increases in the top marginal tax rate to 39 percent and the dramatic growth in personal income attributable to the large number of individuals who received stock options as part of their compensation package.

Income taxes, even though they are elastic, have historically been quite stable. Even in past economic downturns, personal income does not drop tremendously across the nation. As a result, individual income taxes tended to drop little, if any at all. As just described briefly, this pattern seems to have changed during the 1990s where the combination of income tax cuts during high growth periods and changes in the structure of personal income have changed the realities of both federal and state revenue generation.

TABLE 4.2   Income Taxes as a Percent of Personal Income, 1957–2001

Fiscal Year	Total Individual and Corporate Income Taxes (in Billions)	Total Individual Income Taxes (in Billions)	Personal Income (in Billions)	Total Individual and Corporate Income Taxes as a Percentage of Personal Income (%)	Total Individual Income Taxes as a Percentage of Personal Income (%)
1957	$ 59.5	$ 37.4	$ 359.3	16.6	10.4
1967	103.5	68.3	650.4	15.9	10.5
1977	250.0	189.5	1,637.1	15.3	11.6
1987	582.8	476.5	3,962.5	14.7	12.0
1994	840.6	671.9	6,200.9	13.6	10.8
2001	1,290.8	1,188.9	8,685.3	14.9	13.7

Sources: Advisory Commission on Intergovernmental Relations (1988). *Significant Features of Fiscal Federalism,* 1988 Edition, Volume II, Washington, D.C. ACIR, p. 64; Table 59; U.S. Bureau of the Census (1988). *Government Finance in 1986–87,* Washington, D.C.; U.S. Bureau of the Census, p. 7; *Economic Report of the President,* January 1989, p. 333; Moody, Scott, ed. (1998). *Facts and Figures on Government Finance,* 32nd edition. Washington, D.C.: Tax Foundation, Tables C23 and D22; Bureau of Economic Analysis (1998). *Survey of Current Business.* Washington, D.C.: U.S. Department of Commerce. *www.bea.doc.gov/bea/ ARTICLES/NATIONAL/NIPA/1998/0898nip3.pdf/* Table 1, p. 147; U.S. Bureau of the Census (2002). *United States State Government Tax Collections: 2001.* Washington, D.C. *www.census.gov/govs/statetax/0100usstax.html;* Bureau of Economic Analysis (2002). *Regional Accounts Data: Annual State Personal Income.* Washington, D.C.: U.S. Department of Commerce. *www.bea.gov/bea/regional/spi/;* and Bureau of Economic Analysis (2002). Personal Income and Its Distribution: Table 2.1, and *National Income and Product Accounts Tables: Table 3.2. Federal Government Current Receipts and Expenditures.* Washington, D.C.: U.S. Department of Commerce. *www.bea.gov/bea/dn/nipaweb/selecttable.asp?SelectedTable* (select table, then select annual and "Refresh Table").

Please note: Visit the text's website at *www.mhhe.com/odden3e* for updates to these or any other URL references included in the text.

Since corporate profits fluctuate much more in recessions and economic growth periods, corporate income taxes tend to be less stable than individual income taxes. Thus, the trend toward making individual income taxes a larger portion of the total of individual and corporate income taxes works to make the tax more stable.

Equity.   Horizontal equity was previously discussed. In terms of vertical equity, the federal individual income tax is clearly progressive due to the use of marginal income tax rates that increase with income. Most state individual income tax structures are also progressive, although they tend not to be as progressive as the federal income tax, since

TABLE 4.3   Income Tax Yield Elasticity, 1957–2001

Year	Individual Income Taxes (in Billions)	Personal Income (in Billions)	Percent Change from Previous Period Individual Income Taxes	Personal Income	Elasticity: Ratio of Percent Change in Tax Collections to Percent Change in Income
1957	$ 37.4	$ 359.3	—	—	—
1967	68.3	650.4	82.6	81.0	1.02
1977	189.5	1,637.1	177.5	151.7	1.17
1987	476.2	3,962.5	151.3	142.0	1.07
1994	671.9	6,200.9	41.1	56.5	0.73
2001	1,188.9	8,685.3	76.9	40.1	1.92

Sources: Advisory Commission on Intergovernmental Relations (1988). *Significant Features of Fiscal Federalism,* 1988 Edition, Volume II, Washington, D.C. ACIR. p. 64; Table 59; U.S. Bureau of the Census (1988). *Government Finance in 1986–87,* Washington, D.C.: U.S. Bureau of the Census, p. 7; *Economic Report of the President,* January 1989, p. 333; Moody, Scott. ed. (1998). *Facts and Figures on Government Finance,* 32nd edition. Washington, D.C.: Tax Foundation, Tables C23 and D22; and Bureau of Economic Analysis (1998). *Survey of Current Business.* Washington, D.C.: U.S. Department of Commerce. *www.bea.doc.gov/bea/ ARTICLES/NATIONAL/NIPA/1998/0898nip3.pdf/* Table 1, p. 147; U.S. Bureau of the Census (2002). *United States State Government Tax Collections: 2001.* Washington, D.C. *www.census.gov/govs/statetax/0100usstax.html;* and Bureau of Economic Analysis (2002). Personal Income and its Distribution: Table 2.1, and *National Income and Product Accounts Tables: Table 3.2. Federal Government Current Receipts and Expenditures.* Washington, D.C.: U.S. Department of Commerce. *www.bea.gov/bea/dn/nipaweb/selecttable.asp?SelectedTable* (select table, then select annual and "Refresh Table").

Please note: Visit the text's website at *www.mhhe.com/odden3e* for updates to these or any other URL references included in the text.

many states have targeted income-tax-relief programs for low-income families (Johnson, 2000.) Since individuals cannot shift the income tax, tax impact and tax burden are identical (i.e., those who pay the tax also bear its burden or economic incidence).

In addition to the marginal tax rate brackets, progressivity in the federal income tax system is increased through the use of exemptions and standard deductions. The personal exemption spares a portion of income from taxation under the theory that individuals need some income to pay their living costs and thus should be able to do so without the burden of taxation. Vertical equity among households is achieved to some degree by allowing an exemption for each individual in the household. The standard deduction also reduces taxable income using the same logic; however, it applies to an entire household. Families with high deductible expenses such as mortgage interest costs or medical bills generally choose to itemize their deductions to further reduce their taxable income.

State income tax rates are not nearly as progressive as the federal tax rates. However, Monk and Brent (1997) show that they are generally progressive. Only ten states have indexed income brackets, and the relatively low level of income subject to the highest tax rates in many states further reduce progressivity (Gold, 1994). States that use the federal tax liability as the basis for their own income taxes tend to have more progressive tax structures—in line with the progressivity of the federal system. Another way to look at the progressivity of the federal income tax is to consider who pays the taxes. Data from the Tax Foundation (*www.taxfoundation.org/prtopincometable.html* [January 4, 2003]) shows the percentage of total federal individual income taxes paid by different numbers of taxpayers in both 1989 and 1999. For 1999, the numbers show that the top 5 percent of taxpayers (i.e., the 5 percent of tax returns with the highest incomes) paid 55.5 percent of the total federal individual income taxes. That top 5 percent of taxpayers earned 34.0 percent of total income. This shows that the highest earners in the country pay a substantially higher portion of the taxes than their share of total income. On the other side, the bottom 50 percent of tax returns (those with the lowest incomes) paid 4 percent of the federal individual income tax despite earning 13.3 percent of total income. This pattern suggests a strongly progressive tax structure. The Tax Foundation table shows that the average tax rate declines steadily as income declines.

State tax burden studies have not been as detailed as those at the national level in large part because gathering such data for all 50 states is very costly. Nevertheless, Phares (1980) calculated indices of progressivity for state individual income taxes for 1977 and found state individual income taxes to be the most progressive state tax. Indeed, Phares found that only state tax structures with a major individual income tax were progressive overall.

Economic Effects.   To the degree that deductions and income adjustments are limited, the income tax can be quite neutral in its economic effects. Nevertheless, there are several economic impacts created by both the federal and most state income taxes. First, as stated previously, the deduction of home mortgage interest, though quite popular, encourages home purchases more than would be the case if the deduction were eliminated. Second, including interest earned from savings as well as returns from investments in taxable income produces some deterrent to savings. While there is reasonable debate over these tax provisions, if neither were taxed, savings and investments probably would increase and arguably would help improve the productivity of the country's economic system.

Administration and Compliance.   The federal income tax is complex and costly to administer for businesses and most individuals. Continual changes to the tax code make the system more, not less, complex. Large percentages of individuals use accountants and other services to fill out income tax forms, and businesses have large accounting departments that spend considerable time keeping tax records. Often, tax requirements are different from good accounting requirements. The costs borne by individuals and corporations reduce the economic efficiency of the income tax.

Income Tax Trends and Issues at the State Level.   While state sales tax increases received the most attention during the mid-1980s, the state income tax increased both as a percent of personal income and as a percent of total state taxes, as shown by the data

**TABLE 4.4   State Income Taxes as a Percent of Personal Income and as a
Percent of Total State Taxes, 1957–2001**

Fiscal Year	*State Income Taxes as a Percent of Personal Income (%)*	*State Income Taxes as a Percent of Total State Taxes (%)*
1957	0.7	17.2
1967	1.1	22.2
1977	2.2	34.3
1987	2.6	39.2
1994	2.7	38.2
2001	2.8	42.8

Sources: Advisory Commission on Intergovernmental Relations (1988). *Significant Features of Fiscal Federalism.* 1988 Edition, Volume II, Washington, D.C. ACIR, p. 64; Table 59; U.S. Bureau of the Census (1988). *Government Finance in 1986–87.* Washington, D.C.: U.S. Bureau of the Census, p. 7; *Economic Report of the President,* January 1989, p. 333; Moody, Scott. ed. (1998). *Facts and Figures on Government Finance,* 32nd edition. Washington, D.C.: Tax Foundation, Tables C23 and D22; Bureau of Economic Analysis (1998). *Survey of Current Business.* Washington, D.C.: U.S. Department of Commerce. *www.bea.doc.gov/bea/ARTICLES/ NATIONAL/NIPA/1998/0898nip3.pdf/* Table 1, p. 147; U.S. Bureau of the Census (2002). *United States State Government Tax Collections: 2001.* Washington, D.C. *www.census.gov/govs/ statetax/0100usstax.html;* and Bureau of Economic Analysis (2002a). *Regional Accounts Data: Annual State Personal Income.* Washington, D.C.: U.S. Department of Commerce. *www.bea.gov/bea/regional.spi/.*

Please note: Visit the text's website at *www.mhhe.com/odden3e* for updates to these or any other URL references included in the text.

in Table 4.4. Between 1957 and 2001, state income taxes rose from 0.7 percent to 2.8 percent of personal income, and from 17.2 to 42.8 percent of total state taxes.

These trends emerged in part because few states have reformed their income tax structures. Maximum tax rates were reached in nearly half the states when taxable incomes reached only $10,000 and the value of personal exemptions was low. Thus, inflation in the late 1970s together with general wage increases pushed individuals into the top income tax brackets. These realities interacted with rate increases in the early 1980s to combat revenue losses caused by recession and federal aid cuts, and income tax revenues rose. An unanticipated result, in part also due to unchanged income tax structures, was that increasing numbers of low-income households faced income tax burdens for the first time. While a few states began to reform their income tax in 1987, the strength of the economy in the late 1990s has led to a number of state tax reductions.

Despite the changes that have occurred over time in the structure of the state income tax, the tax should continue to provide a stable source of revenue. Four themes characterize the need for state income tax reform:

1. Broaden the base to improve horizontal equity, increase political and popular perceptions about the fairness of the tax, and negate the trend to narrow the base through exclusions.

2. Rate reduction in both numbers and levels, which will increase public perception of the tax and help improve the business climate.
3. Increase the values of personal exemptions, standard deductions, and earned income credits to eliminate the poor from income tax rolls.
4. Index the entire structure to require political votes to increase revenues rather than have tax revenue increases occur as a by-product of inflation.

Conclusions About the Income Tax.   The income tax historically has been perceived as a fair tax and is the nation's and most states' most progressive tax. During the 1970s and 1980s, it was increasingly viewed as unfair. Many viewed the income tax as proliferating exclusions; special tax shelters, inflation, and privileged treatment drove most individuals into higher tax brackets, put the poor on the income tax rolls for the first time, and allowed many rich individuals and corporations completely to avoid paying any income taxes. Federal tax reform efforts in the 1980s and 1990s began to reverse those trends and to restore the income tax as a fair and continued high revenue–producing tax. States began to reform state income taxes in 1987. In the 1990s, the federal income tax became slightly more progressive than it was in the late 1980s. States are relying on it for more of their revenue as well.

The Sales Tax

The general or retail sales tax is the single largest source of state revenue today. In fiscal year 2000, states collected $252.1 billion in sales, gross receipts, and customs taxes (see Table 4.1). The sales tax is the most common state tax, currently in use by 45 states. Only one of the five states that does not have a state sales tax, Alaska, allows for local sales tax levies (Due and Mikesell, 1994). In fiscal year 2001, general sales taxes represented 32.1 percent of total state revenue, while selective state sales taxes, such as those on motor fuel, tobacco, and alcohol sales, accounted for another 14.1 percent of total state revenue (Federation of Tax Administrators, *www.taxadmin.org/fta/rate/01taxdis.html* [January 4, 2003]).

Historical Context.   Mississippi was the first state to enact a sales tax. In 1932, it introduced a 2 percent sales tax designed to replace a low-rate business tax (Due and Mikesell, 1994). This action introduced a new form of taxation to the United States. Initially a desperation measure designed to help states fund essential services during the Great Depression, the sales tax has become the single largest source of revenue for states. At the same time, states have typically transferred authority for property taxes to local governments (Monk and Brent, 1997).

Despite protests by retailers, sales taxes spread rapidly. Between 1933 and 1938, 26 more states, plus Hawaii (which was not yet a state), imposed a state sales tax (Due and Mikesell, 1994). Five states allowed the taxes to expire after one or two years, although they eventually reimposed them. The sales tax was particularly favored during the Great Depression when income tax yields fell due to declining incomes, and local governments needed the revenues from property taxes.

Following the Depression and World War II, there was a slow trend toward renewed adoption of sales taxes. By 1963, 10 additional states had imposed sales taxes, and three of the five that allowed it to expire had renewed them, bringing the total to 37. The mid-1960s was a period of growth in state use of sales taxes with eight more states either introducing or reimposing a state sales tax. In 1969, Vermont was the 45th and last state to introduce a sales tax. Today, only Oregon, Montana, Delaware, New Hampshire, and Alaska do not have state general sales taxes, and in Alaska, there is substantial use of the sales tax at the local level. In many cases, local sales tax rates in Alaska are comparable to state sales tax rates in other states. Local sales taxes are feasible in Alaska because communities are fairly widely separated. This limits the possibility of avoiding the tax by making purchases in an adjoining no or low sales tax community. This is generally not the case in most of the other 49 states.

Basis and Yield.   State sales tax rates and revenue levels vary considerably (see www.taxadmin.org/fta/ for current information). In 2001, state tax rates ranged from a low of 3 percent in Colorado to a high of 7 percent in Mississippi and Rhode Island.

All general sales taxes are not alike. Many states offer exemptions for food and prescription (and nonprescription) drugs in an effort to reduce the regressive characteristics of the sales tax. The most common exemption is for prescription drugs. With the exception of New Mexico, all of the 44 remaining states that levy a general sales tax exempt prescription drugs. Ten states exempt nonprescription drugs as well. Food is exempt from sales taxation in 27 of the states.

In addition to general sales taxes, all 50 states levy one or more of a variety of additional sales and excise taxes. These are not general sales taxes, but represent additional levies on specific items. The exact nature and level of the taxes vary considerably. For example, gasoline taxes range from a low of 8 cents a gallon in Alaska to a high of 38 cents a gallon in Connecticut, while cigarette taxes vary from 3 cents a pack in Kentucky to 82.5 cents a pack in Washington. Even the five states without general sales taxes—Alaska, Delaware, Montana, New Hampshire, and Oregon—tax gasoline, cigarettes, and alcohol (Moody, 2002). Current information on state tax rates can be found at the Federation of Tax Administrators website.

Federation
of Tax
Administrators

Thirty-four states allow local jurisdictions to levy sales taxes as well. Local taxing authority varies substantially among the states, but cities and counties are typically granted some leeway in levying local sales taxes. In some states, other jurisdictions such as transit agencies or special districts are also allowed to levy sales taxes. There is frequently a limit on the tax rate any jurisdiction may levy, and in a number of states, there is a cap on the total local sales tax that may be levied.

The elasticity of the sales tax is considerably lower than the elasticity of the income tax (Gold, 1994). This means that as the economy of a state grows, the more dependent the state is on income taxes compared to sales taxes, the faster state revenues will grow. The actual elasticity of a sales tax depends on the composition of its tax base. If food is taxed, elasticity tends to be relatively low since food consumption is not responsive to income growth (Gold, 1994). On the other hand, if services are taxed, the sales tax will be more elastic since demand for services is increasing more rapidly (Dye and McGuire, 1991).

TABLE 4.5   General Sales Taxes as a Percent of Personal Income, 1957–2000

Fiscal Year	Total General Sales Taxes (in Billions)	Sales Taxes as a Percent of Personal Income (in Billions)	Personal Income (%)
1957	$ 8.6	$ 356.3	2.4
1967	21.4	644.5	3.3
1977	64.0	1,607.5	4.0
1987	150.3	3,780.0	4.0
1995	243.6	6,072.1	4.0
2001	321.2	8,678.3	3.7

Sources: Advisory Commission on Intergovernmental Relations (1988). *Significant Features of Fiscal Federalism,* 1988 Edition, Volume II, Washington, D.C. ACIR, p. 64; Table 59; U.S. Bureau of the Census (1988). *Government Finance in 1986–87,* Washington, D.C.: U.S. Bureau of the Census, p. 7; *Economic Report of the President,* January 1989, p. 333; Moody, Scott. ed. (1998). *Facts and Figures on Government Finance,* 32nd edition. Washington, D.C.: Tax Foundation, Tables C23 and D22; Bureau of Economic Analysis (1998). *Survey of Current Business.* Washington, D.C.: U.S. Department of Commerce. Federation of Tax Administrators *www.taxadmin.org/fta/rate/00stl_pi.html/.*

Please note: Visit the text's website at *www.mhhe.com/odden3e* for updates to this or any other URL references included in the text.

Table 4.5 shows that in 1957, general sales taxes represented 2.4 percent of personal income. This figure grew to 4.0 percent by 1977 and remained at that level until the late 1990s when it began to decline slightly. In 2001, general sales taxes represented 3.7 percent of personal income.

Stability.   A desirable characteristic of any tax is for it to produce revenue steadily without large fluctuations from year to year. If revenue is unstable, the taxing jurisdiction will have more trouble balancing its budget (Gold, 1994). Sales taxes are clearly affected by changes in the economy. In times of recession, consumers have fewer dollars to spend, and business is less likely to purchase new equipment. On the other hand, when the economy is growing, consumer purchases tend to increase as well. Consequently, it appears that sales tax revenues are probably not as stable as property tax receipts, yet are impacted less by changes in personal income than are income taxes (see Musgrave and Musgrave, 1989; Rosen, 1992).

The tax base for an individual state's sales tax also impacts how revenues respond to changes in the economy. For example, sales taxes in states that exempt food are more sensitive to economic downturns because individuals will continue to purchase food, and in many cases will shift purchases from prepared meals (e.g., restaurant meals, which are taxed) to grocery store purchases (which are not taxed). In times of economic growth, sales tax receipts may grow more slowly than income tax receipts since individuals with higher personal incomes may consume more services, which as is discussed below, are taxed less often under state sales tax systems.

Equity.   Horizontal equity—the equal treatment of individuals in the same situation— is generally not a substantial problem with sales taxes since tax rates tend to be uniform across a state. Where local sales taxes are permitted, there may be differences, but they are relatively small, and they too are uniform across a taxing jurisdiction.

Vertical equity is a problem for the sales tax. There is considerable evidence that sales taxes are regressive. Since states generally obtain more income from taxes on consumption (sales taxes) than taxes on income, most state tax systems are regressive (Gold, 1994). Regardless of the analysis, the sales tax is a major source of that regressivity. While this regressivity may be lessened by the progressive, or less regressive, nature of other parts of the tax system, the sales tax places a greater burden on those in low-income categories.

Reducing Sales Tax Regressivity.   There are three approaches that could be considered, either alone or together, in attempting to mitigate the regressive tendencies of a sales tax. One is to reduce the tax rate, the second is to expand the tax base to include more items consumed by those with high incomes, and the third is to tax services, which also will increase the yield.

Reducing the tax rate.   Since individuals in low-income categories consume a higher portion of their income, and are less likely to consume items not currently subject to sales taxation (e.g., professional services), they tend to pay a higher proportion of their income in taxes. This makes the tax regressive (see Pechman, 1985 and 1986, for example). Lower tax rates would mean that a smaller percentage of household income would be devoted to sales taxes generally, reducing the regressivity of the tax overall. While this would have some impact on the vertical equity of the sales tax, it comes at the expense of lower revenues as well, unless the tax base is increased. As the discussion will show, the tax base can also be used to moderate the potential regressivity of the sales tax.

Changing the tax base.   A number of tax exemptions have been implemented by states to reduce the level of sales tax regressivity over the years. The most frequently discussed, and largest in terms of revenue impact, is the exemption on food. On the other hand, efforts to tax services that are consumed in greater proportion by those with high incomes and would thus improve the vertical equity of the sales tax have generally met with little or no success. This discussion focuses first on ways to broaden the tax base through taxation on services to improve vertical equity, and then shifts to alternatives that tend to narrow the sales tax base to achieve greater vertical equity.

Taxing services.   There are a number of alternative services that can be, and often are, taxed by states. Services that are taxed can include custom-written computer programs, the time of an accountant or lawyer, or the costs of utilities such as phone or electricity service. The Federation of Tax Administrators has conducted a number of studies of the taxation of services. They have identified 164 different services that are taxed by one or more of the states.

As the number of services taxed increases, the tax base is broadened, leading to greater levels of revenue per penny of sales tax rate. In Florida, efforts to broaden the sales tax to include virtually all services ended in failure and repeal of the law. As Gold (1994) points out, one of the services subject to taxation was advertising. Not surprisingly, the advertisers, not wanting to see the costs of their services increase (or alternatively, their profits diminish), devoted considerable advertising resources toward defeating the tax measure. California's experience with a more limited tax on snack foods, which was also repealed in a campaign focused on the complexity of defining snack foods, shows that changes in what is and is not subject to sales taxation can be a very controversial decision. As the role of services in the economy expands, taxation of those services will yield greater revenues for states.

One problem with broadening the tax base is that it can make the sales tax more regressive (Gold, 1994). Taxation of food and utilities increases regressivity. However, if the tax is expanded to include services used more often as income increases, the regressivity is reduced. Regardless of how reliant a state is on sales tax revenues, any attempt to increase sales taxes must address the regressive tendencies of the tax. Broad exemptions for food and other items are one approach, but the downside of these alternatives is a substantial reduction in revenue. States would be better off using some form of tax refund based on income, or in the case of states that do not have income taxes, direct payments to low-income individuals like Wyoming uses, or some form of property tax relief such as that used in Kansas.

Economic Effects.   A routine argument against any tax is that it makes an area less competitive in attracting new business and thus economic growth. To the extent that sales taxes are levied on products that are highly mobile, it can make an area less attractive for new business to locate. If the item taxed is highly mobile (for example, items that can be procured via mail order), an individual can avoid paying sales tax by purchasing the item from the provider not subject to the local jurisdiction's sales tax. In this case, the local business must bear the burden of the tax to remain competitive—if the business tries to pass the sales tax on to consumers, they will purchase the item from another provider.

On the other hand, if a sales tax is levied on products that require close proximity of customers and providers, those products can be taxed with little concern the producers will relocate. Such taxes, however, do add to the cost of doing business in that jurisdiction, making it somewhat less attractive for the business to relocate or expand in the future. Even if the seller of the product is able to shift the entire tax burden to purchasers of the product, there are still costs of collecting the sales tax and remitting the tax receipts to the state (see the next section on administrative costs).

Administration and Compliance.   The administrative cost of a tax is the amount of money expended by the taxing jurisdiction to collect the tax from taxpayers. Administrative costs of a sales tax are generally lower than for income and property taxes (Due and Mikesell, 1994). Income taxes require filings by all individual taxpayers, and property taxes require accurate assessments of real, and, in some states, personal property. On the other hand, many of the collection costs of a sales tax are borne by retailers, and the state has fewer tax returns to audit. Moreover, total sales are generally easier to measure than income and property value.

Many studies suggest that compliance with sales tax laws is quite high due to the relatively low cost of compliance and the relative ease with which sales can be audited. Because sales tax rates are generally quite low (ranging from 3 to 7 percent), many argue there is little incentive to avoid compliance. If tax rates or the costs of compliance were to increase, avoidance activities would also likely increase.

Political Acceptability.   If additional revenue is needed for schools, policymakers need to find a way to generate support for raising those additional funds. In today's political climate, no tax is viewed as a "good" tax. Increasing taxes to generate additional state and/or local revenue continues to be a political challenge.

When faced with using income taxes or sales taxes to replace property taxes for schools in 1994, Michigan's voters elected to increase the state sales tax from 4 percent to 6 percent rather than pay higher income taxes. Although this action does not appear to be in the best interest of those with the lowest incomes, as sales taxes tend to be more regressive than income taxes (see the previous discussion of fairness), support for the sales tax over the income tax seems to have been widespread in Michigan. In Ohio, voters turned down a one-cent increase in sales taxes in 1998. The tax increase was to be split—half a cent for schools and half a cent for property tax relief.

Broadening the sales tax base through the taxation of more goods, and in particular, more services, does not appear to be particularly popular with taxpayers either. California's effort to increase the sales tax base by subjecting snack goods to taxation resulted in failure.

Exportability.   Taxes are exportable to the extent that someone else has to pay them. Taxes can be exported either to the federal government, or to nonresidents of the taxing jurisdiction. Exporting a tax to the federal government is possible if they are deductible on corporate or individual income tax returns. The federal government does not actually pay the taxes; rather, the deduction reduces federal revenues, meaning it must either borrow more money, spend less, or increase other tax sources. Since the elimination of the sales tax deduction for federal income taxes, it is no longer possible to export a portion of sales taxes to the federal government.

Sales taxes are ideal for export to other individuals. Tourists, business travelers, and other visitors to an area will purchase goods and services during their visit. To the extent these goods and services are taxed, someone other than those in the taxing jurisdiction pays the tax. This same principle accounts for the popularity of hotel taxes, parking taxes, and taxes on automobile rentals. If others can be forced to pay taxes to support local services, local taxpayers will have to pay less themselves. The downside to this type of taxation is that it is more sensitive to economic fluctuations than many other sales taxes, as travel is one of the first things that is cut back in a declining economy, whether it is travel for business or leisure.

Conclusions About Sales Taxes.   This discussion shows that there are a number of important issues that must be carefully considered before relying on an increase in the sales tax rate or an expansion of the base to provide additional funds for education. Moreover, as tax rates increase, issues of fairness or equity, exportability, and compliance become more difficult. States often enact politically motivated, broad-based exemptions, reducing the potential yield of the new tax. An alternative is to broaden the base subject to sales taxation. One way to do this is to establish a sales tax on services as well as on products. To the extent that there is a trend away from consumption of goods toward purchase of more services, this will also make the tax more elastic (see Dye and McGuire, 1991).

The Property Tax

The property tax has been and remains today the mainstay of local government financing. In 2000, property tax collections represented 28.6 percent of total state and local tax collections (*www.taxadmin.org/fta/rate/slsource.html* [January 5, 2003]). Alabama and Louisiana rely more on sales and gross receipts tax revenues for local governments than do the other states. In the District of Columbia, property, sales, and income taxes represented almost identical shares of own-source revenue in 2000.

For years, the property tax produced the largest percentage of revenues for schools, but that role was ceded to state governments during the flurry of school finance reforms enacted in the 1970s. Nevertheless, the property tax produces large amounts of steady local revenue and, except for the few local governments that can levy sales and income taxes, it is the only broad-based tax that most local governments, including school districts, can use to raise tax dollars. This section analyzes the property tax in terms of its base, yield, equity, economic effects, and administration and compliance costs. It ends with a summary of state approaches to property tax relief for the poor and a brief discussion of the impact of California's Proposition 13, enacted in 1978.

Basis.   The basis of the property tax generally is wealth. Except for the inheritance tax, which is being lowered and eliminated in many states, the property tax is the closest approximation to a wealth tax in this country. But because so many elements of wealth are not included in the property tax and because the elements of wealth that are included are primarily property, the tax historically has been called a property tax.

There are three categories of wealth or property: (1) real or land, (2) tangible, and (3) intangible. Referring to land as real property derives from the medieval times when all land was owned by royalty; "real" is actually a derivative of "royal." Tangible property includes improvements on land, such as buildings, homes, business establishments, factories, and office buildings, as well as personal property, such as automobiles, furniture, other household items, and business inventories. A value can be placed on all tangible property. Intangible property refers to items that represent a value but which itself has no value, such as bank deposits, certificates of deposit, stock certificates, bonds, etc. The property tax base usually includes the bulk of real property or land, portions of tangible property (primarily land improvements but usually not personal property), and little if any intangible property.

In terms of horizontal equity, the property tax does not treat all wealth holdings equally. An individual with greater amounts of financial investments as compared to real estate would pay less property tax than an individual with a portfolio mostly in real estate. Similarly, individuals with larger portions of their wealth in personal property exempt from the property tax base will likely pay less in property taxes than will those with larger portions of their holdings in land and buildings. In short, the property tax treats holders of wealth differently primarily based on the composition of their wealth across real, tangible, and intangible property.

These generalizations mask other aspects of the property tax. A considerable amount of real property and land improvements escapes property taxation, driving up the property tax rate for the remainder that is taxed. Property and buildings owned by the government—federal, state, or local—are exempt from the property tax, as are land and buildings owned by religious and some charitable organizations. Further, there are substantial numbers of additional exemptions. Many states provide a homestead exemption that eliminates a certain amount of a home's value from the property tax altogether. There are exemptions for certain kinds of business activities. Several localities, especially cities, have enacted property tax abatements under which new business buildings are exempt from the property tax rolls for a fixed number of years, often as long as 20 years. These exemptions or exclusions add to large totals over time. Thus, while all property that is on the tax rolls is taxed equally (except for the issues subsequently described), the large portions of property not on the tax rolls avoid the property tax altogether, further violating horizontal equity.

The Assessment Process.   Additional issues enter the picture because property is taxed on the basis of what is called assessed valuation, and the assessment process is riddled with technical challenges and problems. The assessment process basically has three steps:

1. All parcels of land across the country are identified, plotted, and recorded by local taxing jurisdictions, usually city or county government agencies.
2. Those parcels subject to the property tax are given a value, usually a value approximating the market value; both land and their improvements (buildings) are included in assigning a value.
3. An assessed valuation is assigned, which is some percentage of true or market value.

The sum of the assessed valuation of each parcel in a taxing jurisdiction is the local property tax base. The process seems simple, but actually determining assessed valuation is a complex technical and political process.

Determining market or true value.   Conceptually, determining a true value for a piece of land and its improvements is straightforward. True value is the market value; true value is what an individual would have to pay to buy the piece of property. That process is pretty straightforward for homes. The market value of a home is the value for which it would sell. Since records are kept of home sales, determining the market value of homes that sell is relatively straightforward.

But what about placing market values on homes that are not sold? The use of comparable homes that have sold in recent months provides an excellent way to estimate the value of a house in a given neighborhood and is frequently used to estimate the market value of all houses in an area. While technically this is fairly simple, as most real estate agents would attest, keeping up-to-date market values on the tax rolls requires a process that would continually update the figures. Computer programs exist to provide such updating, but political pressures frequently mitigate against full record updating. Some feel it is unfair to tax a homeowner on unrealized home value gains, as happens when updating of tax files occurs regularly. That leads to the question of how often tax rolls should be updated—every year, every other year, once a decade, or some other time frame? If annual updates do not occur, horizontal equity may be violated as homeowners who do not move pay a decreasing portion of the local property tax. But annual updating costs money and creates some public displeasure.

Valuing homes is simple compared with placing values on other properties. Consider small commercial buildings or small businesses that use land and buildings that are rarely sold. Since a market value does not exist, a process called capitalizing income or capitalizing rents is often used. If net income or profits are 10 percent, the value then becomes total sales divided by 10 percent (which would be total sales multiplied by 10). That is, the value is linked to the profits that are earned by using the land and buildings. Another somewhat different method links the value of commercial buildings to the rents that can be charged for using the building. Rents are divided by an average rate of return to determine true or market value; indeed, this process often determines the building's market price if the owner decides to sell. Capitalized values are determined by two critical variables: sales and net profit, or rents and assumed rate of return. Values can be increased or decreased by changing either of these two figures.

Determining market value for factories or plants provides more complex challenges. While capitalized valuation is one possible approach, it is difficult to allocate profits and sales just to one plant for a business with multiple plants. So an alternative process, replacement costs less depreciation, is often used. Replacement costs would be an estimate of what it would cost completely to rebuild the plant. In many respects, just replacement costs updated each year would indicate the true value of that type of property. But unlike homeowners, businesses are allowed to depreciate plants and factories in order to reinvest and improve properties over time. So true values for a plant or factory would be replacement costs minus accumulated depreciation.

Utilities, such as gas and electrical lines, represent yet an additional technical challenge. While such lines have little worth in themselves, they represent a distribution network allocated by governments to utility companies, and the distribution networks have substantial value, just as plane routes and airport gates in the airline industry have a value that far exceeds the value of the item itself. States have taken a variety of approaches to valuing utilities and often use a combination of capitalized valuation and replacement costs less depreciation.

Farmland presents another set of issues. While a market usually exists for farmland, often times the actual selling price exceeds the farming value of the land, even for farms far from growing urban areas. In addition, even if the market value of farmland equaled the farming capitalized price, a drought or other type of natural disaster could reduce a farmer's income to zero in any one year, making it quite difficult to pay property taxes on farmland that still retained a value. Further, for farmland that does not turn over, if the selling price of nearby farmland is used as the basis for identifying a value, care must be taken to compare similar types of land. Land that can only be used for grazing should not be compared with land used for agriculture; and different types of agriculture, which often depend on the specific characteristics of the soil, produce different net returns for farmers. All of these factors must be considered in valuing farmland. Several states use some type of market value, and several also use the lower of market value or actual use value.

In short, determining property values is conceptually straightforward, but technically, socially, and politically complex. In many cases, there are no "right" processes; technical approaches interact with value judgments. As a result, the question of whether horizontal equity is met requires both a technical and a political/social conclusion.

Determining assessed valuation.   Once a value is given to a piece of property, an assessed value must be ascribed because that is the value that officially becomes part of the tax base. In the best of all worlds, this step would be eliminated, and the determined value would be the measure that becomes part of the property tax base. But for a variety of reasons, fractional assessment practices exist across the country. That is, property is assessed at some fraction or percent of actual value; percentages can range from as low as 10 percent to as high as 100 percent, which is the actual market or true value. Public finance economists argue for 100 percent valuations, and that should be the goal for most state property tax systems.

Fractional assessments have no inherent economic justification; they are simply a complicating factor and often a factor fraught with substantial inequities. Fractional assessments have been used primarily to hide some of the realities of the property tax since most individuals are not aware of the details of the local assessment process. For example, if the practice is to assess property at 25 percent of market value, a homeowner with a $100,000 home receives a tax notice showing the assessed value to be just $25,000. Most homeowners think their house is undervalued since it is assessed so far below market value, when in fact the home is assessed at the correct level. While the tax rate applied to assessed valuation to raise a fixed amount of revenue would need to be four times the rate if it were applied to full or market value, the homeowner usually takes more comfort in a perceived valuation below market levels than the actual level of the tax rate. In addition, tax rates are often limited to some maximum level. So if assessment levels are artificially low, the government reaches the maximum tax rate more quickly, and thus local taxes are kept artificially low. But this gives political decision making to the local assessor and not the local policymaking bodies, where tax rate decisions should be made.

This problem is clear in California, where Proposition 13 limits assessed value to the value of the property in 1975–76, with increases limited to no more than 2 percent a year. Property can only be reassessed at market value when it is sold. As a result, the assessed value of most property is substantially below its market value. Since property taxes are limited to 1 percent of assessed value, there is a substantial difference between the taxes actually collected and the potential tax collections if all property were assessed at its true market value. Since homes and other properties sell at different times, it is possible for individuals living in identical houses next door to each other to pay substantially different amounts of property taxes based on the length of time they have owned the house. Additionally, since residential property is sold more frequently than commercial and industrial property, and thus reassessed more frequently, a growing proportion of the property tax base in California is shifting to residential property. This means that a greater share of the property taxes paid by California's citizens are paid by homeowners.

Fractional valuations can mask a host of related inequities. If the popular assumption is that most homes are assessed far below market value, two individuals with the same $100,000 home, one with an assessed value of $25,000 and another with an assessed value of $20,000, might both feel that they are being given a "deal," when in fact the latter is being unfairly assessed 20 percent less than legal requirements. This situation often happens as homes grow older and families do not move, and these kinds of differences often are popularly accepted as fair.

Differential assessment practices create significant problems for state school finance systems that are designed to provide relatively more state education aid to districts low in assessed value of property per pupil versus districts with average or above-average levels of local property tax wealth per pupil. If two districts are alike in all characteristics, the district that assessed at the lowest fraction of market value would look poorer and thus be eligible for more state aid. That would be unfair, and state school finance systems need to adjust for such inequitable differences.

Consider two districts, A and B, with assessed valuations of $34,500,000 and $50,000,000, respectively. Just looking at these numbers would suggest that district B is wealthier in terms of total valuation. But further assume that district A assesses property at 25 percent of true value, and district B assesses at 50 percent. To determine the real true or market value, or adjusted or equalized assessed value as it is called in school finance, the assessed valuation figures must be divided by the assessment ratios. Thus, the true valuation in district A is $138,000,000 ($34,500,000 ÷ 0.25), and the true valuation in district B is $100,000,000 ($50,000,000 ÷ 0.50), which shows that district A actually has more wealth than district B. In other words, the unadjusted assessed valuations did not give an accurate picture of relative total wealth between these two districts.

For school finance purposes, the property tax base is divided by the number of students to determine relative ability to raise property tax dollars for school purposes. Assume that district A has 2,500 students, and district B has 1,500 students. If the state used just assessed valuation per pupil, district A would have a value of $13,800 ($34,500,000 ÷ 2,500), and district B would have a value of $33,333 ($50,000,000 ÷ 1,500). District B would appear nearly three times as wealthy as district A. But if equalized or adjusted assessed valuations are used, as they should be, district B would appear just slightly more wealthy than district A, at $66,667 (district B) compared with $55,200 (district A).

Thus, it is important for the state to recognize that local assessing practices can vary from required state practice, to collect data to identify the variations, and to make adjustments in school finance formulas to adjust for the differences. Usually this adjustment is accomplished through what is commonly called a State Equalization Board, which monitors local assessing performance. The monitoring usually consists of gathering sales data and comparing them with assessed valuations and calculating assessment/sales ratios to determine the degree to which local assessment practices reflect state requirements. Since assessment/sales ratios are available, the state legislature can and usually does use them to adjust local assessed valuations in determining state aid calculations.

In summary, numerous issues are associated with determining the local property tax base. The property tax base is primarily land and improvements on the land, although government, religious, and charitable organization–owned land is exempt. Further, tax abatements and homestead exemptions further erode the local property tax base. Determining true or market value of many types of property is a technically complex undertaking, and raises social and political issues as well. Fractional assessments are widely practiced but serve only to mask the actual functioning of the property tax. Actual property assessments tend to differ within classes of property, across classes of property, as well as across areas within local taxing jurisdictions, leading to horizontal inequities. And differential fractional assessments across local taxing jurisdictions require state adjustments in order to allocate state education aid in an equitable manner.

Yield.   The property tax is a stalwart revenue producer, providing $246.2 billion in revenues for state and local governments in 2000 (see Table 4.1). Table 4.6 shows total property taxes and property taxes as a percent of personal income between 1957 and 2001. Property tax yields rose from $12.9 billion in 1957 to $261.2 billion in 2001 ($41.5 billion in 1957 dollars).

Interestingly, property taxes represent a lower portion of personal income today than they did 30 years ago. While property taxes as a percent of personal income rose from 3.6 percent in 1957 to 4.0 percent in 1967, during the next decade when property taxes more than doubled, they dropped slightly to 3.8 percent. By 1987, property taxes consumed only 3.1 percent of personal income, and that figure remained the same in 1995. By 2001, property taxes represented only 3.0 percent of personal income. The drop since 1977 probably reflects the tax- and expenditure-limitation fever after 1978.

Property tax rates.   Expressed as a percent, a property tax rate is easy to use to determine the property tax yield. If the tax rate were 1.5 percent, and assessed valuation were $50,000, the yield would be 1.5 percent times $50,000, or expressing a percent as a decimal, 0.015 times $50,000, or $750.

Unfortunately, the property tax rate is not always given as a percent of assessed valuation. Property tax rates are usually stated in "mills" and "dollars per hundred" dollars of assessed valuation. These rate units further add to the complexity surrounding the property tax. A tax rate in mills indicates the rate applied to each $1,000 of assessed valuation. Thus, if the tax rate is 15 mills, and assessed valuation is $50,000, the yield is 15 times $50, or $750. In many respects, the mill rate is useful because the mill rate can be multiplied by the assessed valuation with a decimal point replacing the comma that indicates the thousands. Technically, a mill is "one-thousandth," so a tax rate in mills, say

TABLE 4.6 Property Taxes as a Percent of Personal Income, 1957–2001

Fiscal Year	Total Property Taxes (in Billions)	Personal Income (in Billions)	Property Taxes as a Percent of Personal Income (%)
1957	$ 12.9	$ 359.3	3.6
1967	26	650.4	4.0
1977	62.5	1,637.1	3.8
1987	121.2	3,962.5	3.1
1995	193.9	6,200.9	3.1
2001	261.2	8,685.3	3.0

Sources: Advisory Commission on Intergovernmental Relations (1988). *Significant Features of Fiscal Federalism*, 1988 Edition, Volume II, Washington, D.C. ACIR, p. 64; Table 59; U.S. Bureau of the Census (1988). *Government Finance in 1986–87*, Washington, D.C.: U.S. Bureau of the Census, p. 7; *Economic Report of the President*, January 1989, p. 333; Moody, Scott. ed. (1998). *Facts and Figures on Government Finance,* 32nd edition. Washington, D.C.: Tax Foundation, Tables C23 and D22; Bureau of Economic Analysis (1998). *Survey of Current Business.* Washington, D.C.: U.S. Department of Commerce. *www.bea.doc.gov/bea/ARTICLES/ NATIONAL/NIPA/1998/0898nip3.pdf/* Table 1, p. 147; Bureau of Economic Analysis (2002). Personal Income and its Distribution: Table 2.1, and *National Income and Product Accounts Tables: Table 3.2. Federal Government Current Receipts and Expenditures.* Washington, D.C.: U.S. Department of Commerce. *www.bea.gov/bea/dn/nipaweb/selecttable.asp?SelectedTable* (select table, then select annual and "Refresh Table").

Please note: Visit the text's website at *www.mhhe.com/odden3e* for updates to these or any other URL references included in the text.

15 mills, expressed as a decimal would be $15 \times 1/1,000$ or $15/1,000$ or 0.015 (note this is the same as the decimal expression for 1.5 percent). If that representation of the rate is used, the yield would be just the rate times the base, or $0.015 \times \$50,000$ or still $750.

The same tax rate given in units of dollars per hundred would be $1.50. Thus, the yield would be the rate, $1.50, times the number of hundreds of dollars of assessed valuation ($50,000 ÷ 100 or $500) or again, $750. Notice that this rate is similar to the rate given as a percent; for both, the number 1.5 is used.

This may seem confusing, even though the end result is the same regardless of which method is used. Table 4.7 is designed to help clarify matters by showing how tax rates are expressed in different formats. The first column of Table 4.7 displays the tax rate expressed as a percentage of assessed value. The next three columns display the same tax rate in mills, dollars per hundred dollars of assessed value, and dollars per thousand dollars of assessed value. The fifth column of Table 4.7 shows the decimal value to use when multiplying the tax rate times the assessed value to determine the property tax yield or revenue.

Mills and dollars per hundred were used in part because assessed valuation figures were so large. Such a rate helped reduce the number of figures needed to calculate results. But these two rates are confusing, especially in comparing rates across jurisdictions

TABLE 4.7   Tax Rate Equivalents for Determining Tax Yield

Tax Rate (%)	Mills	$/100 of Assessed Value	$/1,000 of Assessed Value	Value to Use in Calculations
1.0	10	$ 1.00	$ 10.00	0.010
1.5	15	1.50	15.00	0.015
2.0	20	2.00	20.00	0.020
2.5	25	2.50	25.00	0.025
3.0	30	3.00	30.00	0.030
100.0	1,000	100.00	1,000.00	1.000

and across states. If it were possible, shifting to a simple percentage rate, as was done in California, would simplify matters. Then all tax rates—income, sales, and property—would be given in the same units that could be compared.

Property Tax Elasticity.   One of the major criticisms of the property tax has been that it is not responsive to economic growth (Mikesell, 1986). Mikesell estimated that the elasticity of the property tax is substantially less than one, meaning that as income increases, revenue from property taxes rises more slowly. This means that governments that are heavily dependent on property taxes (most school districts) need to raise their rates to meet increases in the demand for their services, such as education (Monk and Brent, 1997).

Property Tax Stability.   In terms of stability, the property tax has some ideal characteristics. In times of economic slowdowns, it produces a steady revenue stream, largely because property values maintain their levels except in very deep recessions. On the other hand, in times of economic growth and/or inflation, property values rise so property tax revenues rise. In other words, property tax revenues relative to the business or economic cycle are stable on the downside and increase on the upside.

Property Tax Equity.   For years, the property tax was considered a regressive, actually a steeply regressive, tax (Netzer, 1966). In the 1970s, a new view of property tax incidence was developed, which concluded that it had a progressive incidence pattern (Aaron, 1975; Mieszkowski, 1972). Since the mid-1970s, analysts have essentially divided into two camps, those claiming an overall progressive incidence pattern and those claiming a regressive incidence pattern. More recently, Zodrow published an article describing three views of the incidence of the property tax that readers can consult for more information on this issue (2001). There is, however, general consensus that at very low household income levels, generally less than $20,000, the property tax is regressive.

Economic and Social Effects.   For homeowners, the property tax is a tax on housing consumption. As such, it raises the price of housing and thus discourages housing investments. On the other hand, the property tax, which consumed 3.0 percent of personal income in 2001, is a smaller burden than the sales tax, which consumed about 5 percent of personal income, and thus a much smaller burden than if housing consumption were simply rolled into the sales tax base, a policy for which good arguments could be made. Further, property tax payments can be deducted from federal income tax payments, thus offsetting the property tax impact. At the present time, sales taxes are not deductible for federal tax purposes. In addition, states have enacted a wide-ranging array of adjustments designed to reduce the property tax impact on homeowners and to encourage housing consumption. While all of these latter mechanisms might not fully offset the regressive effect of the tax, they certainly help.

Further, the costs of property taxes are offset by the benefits in local services that they support. Indeed, both taxes and services are capitalized into the price of property, with taxes decreasing the price, and services increasing them. Research shows that the capitalized impact of services is substantial (Wendling, 1981a).

Property taxes on the business sector raise a series of additional economic issues. A general issue is that businesses that rely more heavily on physical capital (land, buildings, equipment, machinery, including inventories) than human capital (lawyers, accountants, computer-service vendors, etc.) bear the impact of higher costs from property taxation and thus have some economic disadvantages in the marketplace. This reality raises the overall issue of how businesses should be taxed. During the past several years, states have generally exempted business inventories as well as machinery and equipment from the property tax rolls, thus including only land and buildings owned by the business sector.

Administration and Compliance. The administration burdens of the property tax consist of recording all property parcels, maintaining a record of changing ownership, and assessing property, which is fraught with technical and political challenges. Technically, tools exist to keep up-to-date values on just about any kind of property, and thus to maintain assessed values reasonably close to current market values. But, as noted, practice generally is otherwise. Appointed, rather than elected, local assessors with clear requirements for the skills needed to qualify for appointment; some degree of funding for the local assessment process with computer facilities to store, maintain, and update records; and a State Equalization Board to conduct periodic assessment-sales studies and provide equalization ratios for state school-aid purposes are the minimal requirements for good property tax administration.

Individual compliance is probably the most straightforward for any tax. A tax bill is submitted once a year, and property owners pay, sometimes in annual and sometimes in semiannual payments. Some homeowners have the bank collect property tax liabilities monthly with their mortgage payment; in these cases, the bank pays the bill annually. The annual nature of property tax bills contributes to the unpopularity of this tax. Individuals would rather pay taxes in smaller amounts, as they do for the sales tax. That said, Monk and Brent (1997) point out that between 1987 and 1997, missed payments of school property taxes increased dramatically in a number of states, with the number increasing by as much as 40 percent in New York State during that period.

Low-Income Property Tax Relief Programs.   For years, states have enacted a variety of programs that ostensibly provide property tax relief for some if not all homeowners, but often only to low-income homeowners, the elderly, veterans, or the disabled. Public finance economists generally criticize these programs on a variety of grounds, but the programs remain and actually proliferate. Ebel and Ortbal (1989) summarized these programs from a detailed update by the Advisory Commission on Intergovernmental Relations (1989b). Johnson (2000) also discusses a number of income tax relief programs targeted to low-income families.

Generally, property tax relief includes a variety of programs designed to reduce reliance on the property tax to raise local revenues. As such, the programs are designed to benefit all local property taxpayers as well as to target additional relief to low-income households to reduce property tax regressivity. There are two categories of property tax relief programs: direct and indirect. Direct programs include homestead exemptions or credits, circuit breakers, tax-deferral plans, and classification of the property tax base. These programs reduce property tax bills directly. Indirect programs include intergovernmental aid programs (which include school finance equalization programs at the state level), tax and spending limitations (for a review, see Gold, 1994), and local option sales and income taxes.

Homestead exemptions and credits.   Reflecting the value this country places on homeownership, 48 states have some type of homestead exemption or homestead credit that simply reduces the property tax for an individual who owns his/her home. Homestead exemptions or credits are one of the oldest property tax relief programs. For the homestead exemption, the assessed valuation is reduced by a fixed amount, often several thousand dollars. This reduces the property tax bill, and the cost is borne by local governments. Some, but not many, states reimburse local governments for these revenue losses through a homestead credit, whereby the local government reduces the homeowner's property tax bill by the amount of the homestead exemption times the tax rate and then bills the state for the total amount for all local taxpayers. Since several of the programs are financed locally, a total cost of these programs has not been calculated.

Interestingly, a number of the states that provide this type of property tax relief do not link it to income (i.e., do not have a "needs" test—all homeowners, rich or poor, benefit from the homestead exemption or credit). Further, only 17 of the 48 states extend the program to all homesteads; others limit the program to the elderly (again rich and poor), the disabled, the poor, and/or veterans or disabled veterans (Monk and Brent, 1997).

Circuit breaker programs.   As the name suggests, a circuit breaker program of property tax relief is designed to protect homeowners from property tax overload, which could happen if current income falls in a year due to illness or unemployment or drops for several years due to retirement. Circuit breakers typically relate property tax bills to a taxpayer's income; circuit breaker relief is then some portion of the property tax bill that exceeds a given percentage of income. Such programs can help reduce regressive residential property tax burdens.

Most states link the circuit breaker program to the state income tax through a separate schedule, but several states administer the circuit breaker program separately and send cash refunds to those who qualify. Still other states have the local government provide the property tax relief, and then reimburse the local government for the total amount.

By 1994, 36 states had enacted some type of circuit breaker program. That number remained constant in 2001. Wisconsin enacted the first program in 1964; Michigan currently has the most comprehensive program. All 36 states make all homeowners eligible, and 21 states make renters eligible (assuming that landlords shift property tax bills to renters). Some states target relief to the elderly or disabled. Monk and Brent (1997) found that the average level of benefits granted in the states that reported such figures ranged from a high of $593 in Maryland to a low of $80 in California, with a median of $257 in Pennsylvania (Monk and Brent, 1997).

Tax deferrals.   A tax-deferral program extends the period over which property taxes can be paid. The taxpayer is given the option of paying the current tax bill or deferring the payment to some future time, usually when the property is sold. At that time, past property tax payments plus interest are due. Legally, these deferred property tax payments are liens on the property. Another way tax deferrals are used is to continue to assess property based on its current use as long as the qualifying use continues. If there is a change in use, the property owner is responsible for deferred taxes on the property. For example, if a farmer or parking lot owner sells the property for development, the taxing jurisdiction will collect back taxes, based on the highest and best use valuation of the property prior to the sale (Monk and Brent, 1997).

Tax deferrals are the most recently enacted property tax relief programs. In 1979, only nine states had such programs; the number increased to 31 by 1991 (Monk and Brent, 1997). Tax-deferral programs have the "best" economic characteristics of all the property tax relief programs because they entail minimal governmental interference in housing consumption, reflect the social goal of homeownership and staying in one's home even when income drops, and maintain governmental revenues, at least over time.

Unfortunately, as with most tax relief programs that have the best economic features, they are not so popular. Deferral programs have few participants; it seems that the negative features of placing a lien on one's home for deferred tax payments is not outweighed by the positive features of location stability and continued homeownership.

Property tax limitations.   A commonly used indirect form of property tax relief is a limitation on property taxes. Many states impose a variety of limits on property taxes and taxing jurisdictions. According to the Advisory Commission on Intergovernmental Relations (1995), the most common types of limits are:

- Overall property tax rate limits that set a ceiling that cannot be exceeded without a popular vote: these limits apply to the aggregate rate of tax on all local governments.
- Specific property tax rate limits that set a ceiling that cannot be exceeded without a popular vote: these limits apply to specific types of local jurisdictions (e.g., school districts or counties).

- Property tax levy limits that constrain the total revenue that can be raised from the property tax.
- Assessment increase limits that control the ability of local governments to raise revenue by reassessment of property or through natural or administrative escalation of property values.
- Full Disclosure or Truth in Taxation provisions that require public discussion and specific legislative vote before enactment of tax rate or levy increases.

Classification of the property tax base.   The basic goal of a property tax classification program is to tax different elements of the property tax base—residential, commercial, industrial, farm, utilities, etc.—at different effective rates. Typically, the goal is to tax residential property at lower rates or, put differently, to tax nonresidential (i.e., business property), at higher effective tax rates. A classification system is often called a "split roll" system. In many states, this is prohibited constitutionally. However, 19 states and the District of Columbia use some kind of classification scheme.

The number of classifications of property varies substantially, from a low of two to what used to be a high of 34 in Minnesota. Minnesota's system was so complex that some analysts had suggested the state actually had created 70 property classifications (Bell and Bowman, 1986). In 1989, Minnesota changed its classification system, reducing the number of classes to about 10.

Summary of property tax relief programs.   As this discussion suggests, property tax relief programs for all homeowners, as well as programs targeted to the elderly, the poor, veterans, or disabled are popular and are increasing, rather than decreasing, in numbers. Several major policies are associated with these programs. The first is that most provide aid or relief to all homeowners—regardless of income level. Put differently, classification systems in which all residential property is taxed less than nonresidential property and general homestead exemptions and credits provide aid to the rich and poor alike. Other programs target certain groups (the elderly, veterans, and the disabled) for protection usually without needs (i.e., income tests), and exclude other groups with low property tax burdens and low incomes from assistance. On economic grounds, such programs can be challenged; these programs clearly weigh the social goals of homeownership over the economic goals of a good tax system. A public finance economist would argue that all of these programs should be linked to income (i.e., that the overall policy objective should be to reduce regressivity and thus relief should be targeted in increasing amounts to low-income property tax payers). Most public finance economists, however, go beyond this recommendation and argue that housing goals should be excluded completely from property tax adjustments and handled through other public policies (Musgrave and Musgrave, 1989).

Further, many of these programs, especially circuit breaker programs, make it easier for local governments to raise property taxes; the circuit breaker effectively cuts in for all taxpayers if residential property tax payments exceed the fixed percent of income. Thus, the programs become indirect state support for local choices either for more services or for higher-quality services.

Another example of an attempt to bring property tax relief, different from those previously discussed, is California's Proposition 13. Enacted in June 1978, Proposition

13 rolled back assessed valuations to the 1975–76 market value. Growth in assessed value was limited to 2 percent a year, with reappraisal to market value occurring only when property was sold. The tax rate was fixed at 1 percent of assessed evaluation. In passing this proposition, California shifted to an acquisition-based assessment system, under which property is assessed at market value only when it changes ownership.

Drawing on data over 10 years, Phillips (1988) analyzed the effects of this approach. Phillips' research showed that by 1981 the tax base relative to market value dropped by nearly 50 percent. By 1986, the effective tax for a long-term owner was just 0.31 percent of market value, while a recent buyer faced a burden more than three times higher at 1.0 percent. Further, assessment/market values were inversely related to property value, meaning that individuals with the higher-valued homes had lower relative assessed valuations, so that the rich benefited more than the middle- or lower-income household. Therefore, the result of California's Proposition 13 or switch to an acquisition-based system of property tax assessment was to significantly lower the tax base over time and violate horizontal equity in directions that make the property tax even more regressive overall.

In sum, except for state-financed circuit breakers, most of the programs discussed in this section reduce the local property tax base. Thus, they make it more difficult to raise local tax revenues for schools as well as other functions.

Conclusions About the Property Tax.   The property tax has never been a popular tax; for most of this century, it has been the most unpopular tax. Yet it has been and continues to be the pillar of local government and school finance. It likely will continue to play that role. It produces large amounts of revenues, maintains those revenue levels in economic downturns, and then produces revenue increases during economic growth periods. Its burden is proportional in the middle-income ranges, and its regressivity can be reduced by circuit breaker and other income tax-credit programs. While its unpopularity engendered property tax relief and reform during the 1970s, it also contributed to the tax and spending limitation in the late 1970s. But, as the federal government cut real federal aid during the 1980s, and education improvement became a national imperative, states tapped the property tax for substantial new revenues. Property taxes are crucial for funding local government services but are rarely popular taxes. They are needed even though they are not liked.

Lotteries

First introduced in 1964 in New Hampshire, lotteries have grown in popularity and importance in terms of state revenue since that time. Indeed, many lotteries earmark their receipts to education funding. Although they represent a relatively small portion of total educational revenues (generally no more than 4 percent in any given state), many think that their implementation will (or has) solve education's funding problems. This is not so.

Monk and Brent (1997) argue persuasively that lotteries are a tax. They point out that the voluntary nature of the game does not make a difference and is no different than paying the sales tax on a meal consumed in a restaurant. That is, an individual voluntarily chooses to play the game or eat the meal, but in doing so, agrees to pay the tax.

Lotteries have changed dramatically from New Hampshire's first effort, which was designed to slow down increasing property tax–rate growth in that state. In New Hampshire and New York (which was the second state to introduce a lottery in 1968), participants had to register to play, tickets were expensive, and drawings took place only a few times a year. The result was they were relatively unpopular and raised little money.

In 1971, New Jersey introduced a number of changes, which made lotteries more successful. Among the new features were lower-priced tickets, instant winners, and aggressive promotional campaigns. By 1998, 37 states and the District of Columbia had introduced lotteries. According to Monk and Brent (1997), 12 of those states earmark the proceeds of the lottery to education. The form of that earmarking varies. California, for example, provides the funds to school districts and institutions of higher education on a per-pupil basis. Georgia, on the other hand, uses the proceeds of the state lottery to provide Hope scholarships. These scholarships pay the tuition of Georgia students who attend Georgia public institutions of higher education.

Today, lottery proceeds are not derived from a single lottery, but from a variety of games each designed to attract different groups of players. Lotto games, where participants select (or have a computer randomly select for them) six numbers are the largest and most popular games. If there are no winners for several cycles of the game, in which drawings are generally held twice a week, the size of the jackpot grows. In some instances, lotto prizes have topped $100 million. A new version of lotto, called Powerball, has combined 20 states for one drawing. In 1998, one group of 13 individuals won a Powerball payout of over $250 million.

Other lottery games include instant game tickets where players scratch off numbers to see if they win an "instant" prize; numbers games where three to five numbers are drawn daily for prizes; and video lottery terminals (VLTs), which have recently been introduced. These machines allow lottery players to participate "online." These machines may be the fastest-growing sector of the lottery industry, and it appears that the states with the largest growth in lottery proceeds between 1990 and 1994 were those with VLTs.

Most research claims lotteries are regressive. It is generally argued that poorer individuals are more likely to play and to spend a greater portion of their income on lotteries than are wealthier individuals. Borg and colleagues (1991) indicate that as lottery prizes grow, more higher-income individuals play, lessening the regressivity of the lottery. Monk and Brent (1997) suggest this makes sense intuitively since the appeal of a lottery is that if you win, you get rich. Rich people have less incentive to play than do poor people. As the size of the winnings grow, more and more individuals find the prize attractive and begin to play. In a recent analysis of Georgia's lottery, Rubenstein (2002) found that lower-income and nonwhite households tend to have higher purchases of lottery products, yet receive lower benefits from the lottery, in large part because higher-income and white households are better able to take advantage of the Hope scholarships that pay for a student's tuition at a public Georgia university.

The stability of lottery proceeds is also problematic. In general, following the initial introduction when interest is high, revenues from lotteries tend to taper off. Between 1990 and 1994, state lottery revenues (adjusted for inflation) increased 24.2 percent. However the share of revenues retained as proceeds declined 1.7 percent. Total sales were down more than 15 percent in eight states. Total revenue grew by substantial amounts in Minnesota, Oregon, and South Dakota, but only 11 states saw increases in net proceeds between 1990 and 1994 (Demographics.com, 1996). In California, lottery proceeds at one time amounted to 4 percent of school district expenditures. Today, that figure is approximately 2 percent.

Lotteries are expensive to administer from the state point of view, although for individuals, there is virtually no compliance cost—you either buy a ticket or you do not. As just suggested, the lottery is very inefficient given the substantial sums of money that must be returned in the form of prizes and the high costs of administration. These administrative costs include commissions paid to vendors, usually on the order of 5 percent of sales. They also include the printing of tickets, holding drawings, and promoting the games. Combined, between 30 and 35 percent of total sales are available to the government agencies benefiting from the revenue sales.

In summary, many states have enacted lotteries to help fund public services, often earmarking funds for education. As a form of taxation, lotteries are very inefficient since over half of the revenues are used either for prizes or administrative costs. In California, only 34 cents of each dollar collected finds it way to schools. In addition, after an initial burst of excitement, most lottery sales decline somewhat. Combined with higher administrative costs for new and more complex games and higher advertising costs to attract players, the amount of revenue available for government services may decline farther. Finally, lotteries appear to be generally regressive.

4. SUMMARY

This chapter shows that governmental, tax-financed activity in the United States represents a large share of our gross domestic product and consumes some 12 to 15 percent of personal income. This investment includes spending over $350 billion a year on public K–12 education. Raising the revenue to finance governmental operations is an important and complex issue.

There are five criteria on which taxes can be measured and compared. They include:

- the tax base,
- yield,
- equity,
- the economic effects of the tax, and
- administration and compliance issues.

Each is important in terms of assessing the impact of taxes on individuals and on the jurisdictions that rely on the revenues they generate.

In general, the federal government relies heavily on income (corporate and individual) taxes, while state revenues are composed approximately equally of sales and income taxes. Local school districts, like other local governments, are heavily dependent on the property tax.

Economists generally agree that the "best" taxes are those that have a broad base and low rate. That is, there are few exemptions to paying the tax and thus the base is relatively large, enabling the needed dollars to be collected with a low tax rate. In addition, most analysts support the notion that taxes should be progressive, consuming a larger proportion of wealthy individuals' income than of poor individuals' income. Income taxes tend to be the most progressive while sales taxes are generally the opposite, or regressive. While states have enacted many exemptions to the sales tax to make it less regressive, it remains a regressive form of taxation. Property taxes also tend to be regressive at the lowest income levels. As this chapter shows, there are two ways to think about the regressivity of the property tax. One makes the tax appear less regressive than the other, but both show substantial regressivity at the lowest income classes.

But for any individual or family unit, the ultimate impact or burden of taxes is the sum of all taxes at the local, state, and federal levels. Table 4.8 indicates the total tax burden by quintiles of income for 2001. And the results are quite interesting. First of all the taxes include all federal, state and local income, sales, and property taxes. The total also includes social security taxes. In addition, the total includes federal and state tobacco, alcohol, and gasoline taxes, so provide a pretty good estimate of total tax burden. What the numbers show is that the total tax burden is approximately equal across the five income classes! It is 18 percent for the lowest income quintile, reflecting the regressivity mentioned above, then drops to 14 percent for the second quintile, and rises to 19 percent for the top quintile. So although the federal income tax is very progressive, and most state income taxes are somewhat progressive, and while sales and property taxes are moderately regressive for the low-income categories, and the employee share of social security taxes is the same for incomes up to the cut-off point in the mid-$80,000s, the sum total average tax burden is between 14 and 19 percent of income, roughly more or less the same for all income categories.

Because different levels of government can collect different taxes more efficiently, and with fewer economic inefficiencies, a system of intergovernmental transfers, or grants, has developed in the United States. Intergovernmental grants are used by states and the federal government to provide incentives for local taxing jurisdictions (includ-

TABLE 4.8   Total Tax Burden by 2001 Income Quintiles

Income Quintile	Total Pretax Income	Total Taxes[a]	Taxes as a Percent of Income[b] (%)
First—bottom	$ 7,946	$ 1,449	18
Second	20,319	2,847	14
Third—middle	35,536	5,622	16
Fourth	56,891	9,835	17
Fifth—top	116,666	21,623	19

Source: Altman, 2002.

[a]Income includes income from all sources, including pensions and social security.

[b]Taxes include all federal and state income taxes; employee share of social security; property taxes; federal and state tobacco, alcohol, and gasoline taxes; and state sales taxes.

ing school districts) to implement programs that are a high priority for the granting government. Intergovernmental grants have also been used to reduce property tax burdens.

The major problem in school finance is the differential ability of school districts to gain equal access to property tax revenues. State and federal funding can help equalize tax burdens and ensure that a school district's spending level is based on the wealth of the state where it is located, and not on the basis of its individual property wealth. This important issue of finance equalization and the tools states use to meet district needs are the focus of Chapter 5.

Chapter 5 ─────────────────────────

School Finance Structures: Formula Options

School finance is concerned with the interrelated issues of raising, distributing, allocating, and using revenues for the purpose of educating children. This chapter moves from the issues of raising revenues, discussed in Chapter 4, to the issues involved in distributing revenues. The chapter has two sections.

Section 1 discusses intergovernmental grant theory because school finance equalization formulas represent one type of grant from one level of government—in this case the state—to another level of government—local school districts. Section 2 analyzes four types of formulas that states have and continue to use to distribute general education aid to local school districts: (1) flat grants; (2) foundation programs; (3) guaranteed tax base[1] programs; and (4) combination foundation and guaranteed tax base programs. Full-state funding and other types of state-determined spending programs are also discussed briefly. For each formula, three issues are discussed:

- intergovernmental aid properties,
- reflection of school finance values, and
- impact on fiscal equity.

School Finance Computer Simulation

The *School Finance* computer simulation that accompanies the text should be used when reading this chapter. The text includes some printouts from that simulation, but developing a more in-depth understanding of the different school finance formulas, how they work, and what impacts they have requires using the simulation to experiment with design variations of the different formulas.

---

[1]Guaranteed tax base programs are algebraically equivalent to district power equalization, percentage equalization, and guaranteed yield programs. These latter programs are not discussed individually in this chapter.

The appendix describes how to access the simulation on the World Wide Web, download it, and use it.

1. INTERGOVERNMENTAL FISCAL RELATIONS

Chapter 1 showed that financing education in the United States is achieved through the efforts of three levels of governments: local school districts, each of the 50 states, and the federal government. Indeed, the pattern for financing most public services in this country usually entails contributions from all three governments. This pattern of multiple levels of government finance is known as fiscal federalism.[2]

This section discusses two aspects of the fiscal federalism approach to school financing—first, the general advantages of this approach to financing K–12 educational services and second, intergovernmental grant theory, and its application to school financing. A full understanding of how school finance formulas work, which is the focus of Section 2 of this chapter, entails knowledge of the more general theories of public finance and intergovernmental grants.[3]

Advantages of a Federal Approach to Financing Education

Financing educational services through three levels of government—local school districts, states, and the federal government—offers four general advantages to governments in meeting public responsibilities: (1) fiscal capacity equalization; (2) equitable service distribution; (3) more economically efficient provision of the governmental service—education; and (4) decentralized decision-making authority (Musgrave and Musgrave, 1989; Rosen, 2001).

Each of these advantages is discussed here in terms of the state role in financing local school districts. While the state is the focus, the policy issue is the state fiscal role in a function that has been primarily financed at the local level. As discussed in Chapters 1–4, the problem with local financing that suggests a needed state role is the variation in the local ability to raise education funds. Ability to raise tax revenues is usually called a district's fiscal capacity and is usually measured by property value per pupil. Property value per pupil is used because, historically, most school districts have raised revenues by taxing property. Other measures of fiscal capacity, such as personal income, sales, or combined measures, could be used instead of, or in addition to, property wealth per pupil. But the discussion focuses on the most common measure of school district fiscal capacity—property wealth per pupil.

Fiscal Capacity Equalization.   The first and most important advantage of a fiscal federalism approach to financing schools is that a state, and only a state, can equalize the

[2]See also Musgrave and Musgrave (1989) for a more comprehensive discussion of fiscal federalism within the broader context of public finance.

[3]This chapter refers often to various specific school finance formulas. The reader might first quickly read the second section of the chapter to gain some familiarity with these formulas before reading this section.

fiscal capacity of its local school districts. As Chapter 1 showed, in most states there are substantial disparities among school districts in their ability to raise revenues through local property taxes. Some districts have a large per-pupil property tax base, and others have a much smaller per-pupil property tax base. Consequently, the same tax rate produces widely varying amounts of revenue per pupil. Local districts cannot compensate for these varying levels of fiscal capacity—that is a role for a higher level of government, such as the state.

Indeed, school finance has a long tradition of states providing assistance to offset local disparities through what are called fiscal capacity equalization formulas (see Cubberly, 1906, and the rest of this chapter). Fiscal capacity equalization mitigates inequalities in the financial ability of school districts by offering relatively larger amounts of aid to districts with less fiscal capacity (i.e., are less able to raise funds from their own sources). Fiscal capacity equalization has been the major focus of school finance for more than 150 years, and it is only possible because education is financed through a fiscal federalism system—that is, by all three levels of government.

Equity in Service Distribution.   A second advantage of a fiscal federalism approach to school financing is that states can create mandates or provide financial assistance to school districts to promote equity in service distribution. Fiscal equalization grants do not guarantee that districts will make the same decisions regarding the level of services they offer students. In fact, different approaches to providing the level and quality of education services (or any local government service for that matter) are one of the strengths of a fiscal federal system. However, if the state believes a minimum level of service must be provided, a federal structure offers a number of mechanisms (e.g., mandates, minimum expenditure levels, categorical programs) to ensure that minimum service levels—in today's terms, adequate service levels—are provided.

Efficiency in Service Production.   A third advantage for creating a multilevel school system concerns efficiency in producing educational services. Many schools or school districts can benefit from economies of scale. That is, as the size of the school grows, the unit costs of educating each child decline; a larger school or district organization might be more efficient than a very small one. The state may be able to use its influence to encourage very small school districts to consolidate and therefore promote efficiency in the local production of educational services. It is possible that if a school or school district grows beyond a certain size, it will no longer realize these efficiencies, and in fact, the unit cost of providing educational services may begin to increase. Indeed, large statewide school systems as well as large urban districts may suffer from such diseconomies of large scale. Therefore, a decentralized system of schools helps avoid the diseconomies that would exist if each state were simply one large school system. Andrews, Duncombe, and Yinger (2002) provide an excellent summary of current research findings on scale economies in education.

Decentralized Decision Making.   The fourth advantage of a fiscal federal system is that decentralized decision making provides individuals choices in selecting the mix of public services that match their personal preferences. Tiebout's (1956) classic theory of local expenditures describes this phenomenon as "voting with your feet." He suggests that when there are a number of jurisdictions located within close proximity, individuals choose to live in the area that offers a mix of public services most closely matching their preferences.

The nearly 15,000 school districts in the United States provide an example of Tiebout's theory. For example, realtors report that homebuyers frequently ask about the quality of local schools. Clearly, many people make decisions about where to live, at least in part, on the basis of their perception of the quality of local educational services. One would expect young families concerned about the education of their children to move into areas identified as having good schools, even if that required higher property tax payments. By contrast, a retired couple living on a fixed income might be less directly concerned with the quality of the local schools and more interested in an area with substantial senior citizen services and generally lower property taxes. This is not to imply that people without children in schools are not concerned about the quality of education, nor that good local schools is the only item that matters to young families with school-age children. The example merely suggests how individuals can make decisions about where to live on the basis of a number of factors, the quality of the local schools, and resulting tax payments, being only two of those factors.

Intergovernmental Grants and Their Objectives

In a fiscal federal system, there are two ways the central government can influence or coordinate the decisions of school districts in order to capitalize on these four advantages. The central government—states or the federal government—can mandate changes in the way local services are provided, or it can use intergovernmental grants to influence local behavior. While mandates offer the most direct way of achieving legislative goals, there are political and, in many states, financial problems with their use.

Thus, the most common approach taken by the states and the federal government to influence school district behavior is through intergovernmental grants. For example, when the federal government decided that more attention should be given to low-achieving students in districts with large numbers of students living in poverty environments, it created a program—The Elementary and Secondary Education Act of 1965—which provided funds to local school districts to design and implement new compensatory education programs. Similarly, state general-education-aid grants are designed to assist local school districts in implementing overall K–12 education programs.

Different designs of state or federal grants can have quite different local fiscal impacts. Some grants simply replace local funds with state or federal funds. Other grants produce higher education expenditures than would occur if only local districts provided revenues. Still other grants both increase educational expenditures and focus the new spending on services for specific students or for specific areas within education. A key issue in designing school finance grants is to specify the objective of the grant and then design it on the basis of intergovernmental grant principles to maximize those objectives.

Intergovernmental grants from states or the federal government to local school districts can take one of two main forms: (1) general or block grants and (2) categorical aid. In addition, both of these mechanisms can include or not include requirements for matching expenditures on the part of local school districts. Decisions on these dimensions (i.e., the specific design of the grant formula, together with programmatic requirements) affect how local districts respond to the state or federal grant initiative. Break (1980), Musgrave and Musgrave (1989), and Rosen (2001) provide more discussion on the theory of intergovernmental grants, and Tsang and Levin (1983) apply this theory to school district behavior.

Unrestricted General Aid. Unrestricted general aid or block grants, the form of school finance equalization grants, increase a school district's revenue, but do not place restrictions on the use of that revenue. General grants are most effective when the state's goal is fiscal capacity equalization (i.e., to provide districts with additional revenue to offset their varying ability to raise local education revenues). Flat grants are a school finance mechanism that provides an equal amount of per-pupil revenue to each school district based solely on the number of students. On the other hand, foundation and guaranteed tax-base programs provide general aid to districts in inverse proportion to their property wealth per pupil.[4]

General grants, however, are the least effective in getting school districts to change their behavior in line with state expectations, precisely because such grants carry no restrictions. Districts can use general aid to supplant local revenues and thus reduce tax rates, or to increase overall education spending and thus provide more or better educational services. Without restrictions, there likely will be no clear pattern to local district response. In particular, if the state provides general aid and hopes that the new funds will be used for specific purposes (e.g., to increase spending for mathematics and science education), the likelihood of such a uniform local response is low. This is because local governments attempt to maximize their local objectives, and in the process likely will make different spending decisions than the state might prefer.

Numerous studies of unrestricted or general state aid grants to school districts consistently have found that school districts use a portion of the grant for tax reductions and a portion for increased education spending (Adams, 1980; Black, Lewis, and Link, 1979; Bowman, 1974; Cohn, 1974; Grubb and Osman, 1977; Ladd, 1975; Miner, 1963; Park and Carroll, 1979; Stern, 1973; Vincent and Adams, 1978). In reviewing these studies, Tsang and Levin (1983) found that, on average, local school districts spend about half of increases in state general aid dollars on educational programs and about half to reduce local tax rates; this typical behavior is included in all simulations that accompany this text. However, as we discussed in Chapter 1, over the past decade and a half, many lower-wealth districts in several states appeared to have used a larger portion for property tax relief.

Generally, though, if the state's goal for general-aid programs is fiscal capacity equalization, unrestricted grants work quite well to meet that goal. Since districts low in property wealth per pupil generally have above-average tax rates and below-average expenditures per pupil, increases in general aid let them reduce their tax rates more to the

---

[4]Section 2 of this chapter provides a detailed description of how flat grants and foundation programs operate. It also provides the reader with examples of the effects of these programs using fiscal capacity equalization criteria.

average while also increasing education spending, thus addressing both disadvantages that exist with heavy reliance on local education financing.

If one accepts the notion that local districts are better able to determine the program needs of the local population (in this case, student educational needs), then unrestricted grants offer advantages in terms of economic efficiency. Unrestricted grants provide local districts with increased revenues and let each district decide how to use those revenues, drawing upon local needs and priorities. Unrestricted grants also are effective tools for maintaining an equitable but decentralized decision-making system.

Unrestricted general grants can be used to provide some equity in service distribution either to establish some kind of minimum level of service, or provide districts with at least some minimum level of funding. As Section 2 of this chapter shows, flat grants and foundation school finance programs were designed to accomplish these objectives. However, since unrestricted grants do not place limitations on district expenditures from local sources, there is no constraint on wealthy districts to increase education spending substantially above the minimum. One way to address these problems is to link a district's general aid to its willingness to spend local resources for education through a matching requirement.

Matching General Grants. The most common way to tie a district's general aid to its own willingness to spend is to use a matching grant. Matching grants link the level of state general-aid assistance at least in part to the level of effort made by the local school district, as well as to its fiscal capacity. In school finance, the most common general matching grant system is the guaranteed tax base (GTB) program.[5] Many state school finance programs are called percentage equalizing, guaranteed yield, or district power equalizing. Although the specific operating details of each of these systems vary, they are all designed to achieve the same goal, namely to equalize the revenue-raising ability of each school district, at least up to some point.

Intergovernmental grant theory analyzes matching grants in terms of how they change the relative tax prices[6] districts pay for educational services. A GTB program, for example, lowers the tax price of educational services for districts low in property wealth per pupil, because with the GTB they are able to levy a lower tax rate, and thus pay less, for a certain level of education services. Indeed, for the level of education services supported before a GTB program, property-poor districts are able to substantially lower their tax rates to provide the same level of services. In other words, the tax price to local citizens—taxpayers—is substantially decreased. Economic theory predicts that individuals faced with choices are price sensitive, and will purchase more of lower-priced items, all other things being equal.

---

[5]While a foundation program also requires a local match—the local required tax effort—it functions more like a flat grant than a more open-ended matching program, such as the GTB.

[6]The tax price generally is the tax rate a district must levy to purchase a given level and quality of school services. Poor districts generally have to levy a higher tax rate and thus pay a higher tax price to purchase such a given bundle of school services than a wealthy district because, at a given tax rate, the poor district would raise less per pupil than the wealthier district.

As it plays out in school finance, a GTB gives a district with low property value per pupil the ability to raise as much money at a given tax rate as the wealthier district that has a per-pupil property value equal to the tax-base guarantee. Thus, with the same tax rate or tax effort, the poor district will be able to raise substantially more revenue than it could before the GTB. As predicted from the preceding discussion, a district would be expected to use part of this new money to increase expenditures and use part of the money to reduce its tax rate. Thus, the impact of a general matching grant is similar to that of an unrestricted general grant. Again, as Chapter 1 showed, many school districts in several states have taken advantage of the property tax relief element of GTB programs at the expense of raising spending levels.

Categorical Grants.   In contrast to general unrestricted grants, categorical grants have restrictions on how they can be used, and have significant impacts on school district behavior. Categorical grants are provided to school districts for a specific reason or purpose, and often come with strict application, use, and reporting requirements. Categorical grants are used to ensure that school districts provide services deemed important by the state or federal governments. These services are often provided more efficiently locally, but without the grant, school districts might not choose to provide them, at least not at the state- or federal-desired level of such services.

A variety of categorical grant mechanisms are used by states and the federal government. Some categorical grants require local school districts to meet the needs of specified populations; for example, Title I assistance was created so districts could provide additional educational services to children from low-income backgrounds. Other categorical grant programs are designed to support specific district functions, such as pupil transportation. The manner in which a district receives categorical grant funds can also vary. Many categorical grant programs are designed so that they are available to recipient districts automatically—dollars flow by formula. Others have specific application rules and procedures; districts must write proposals in order to receive funds.

States can provide school districts with categorical grants using a variety of grant formula designs. Districts might receive categorical grants on the basis of some sociodemographic characteristic, such as incidence of poverty or degree of urbanization. Alternatively, districts might be eligible for categorical grants on the basis of the number of children meeting a specific criterion, such as a learning disability. Finally, districts could simply be reimbursed for expenditures devoted to a specific function. District fiscal response to a categorical program will depend on the specific nature of the grant's distribution mechanism.

Since one purpose of a categorical grant is to encourage specific actions on the part of local school districts, federal and most state categorical grants usually include rules and regulations that restrict district use of these resources for their intended purpose. A commonly used fiscal enforcement tool is the maintenance of effort provision. This provision requires districts to prove that spending on the supported program from its own funds does not decline as a result of the grant. The early Title I "supplement not supplant" requirement is an example of a maintenance-of-effort provision. Other enforcement provisions include audits and evaluations to ensure that recipient districts establish programs designed to meet the purpose or goals of the grant program. Many cat-

egorical grants have specific reporting requirements that help the contributing government monitor use of the funds.

Numerous studies have shown that categorical grants usually stimulate educational
expenditures by at least the level of the grant and sometimes by more than the amount of
the grant (Grubb and Michelson, 1974; Ladd, 1975; Tsang and Levin, 1983; and Vincent
and Adams, 1978). The primary explanation is that the strings and requirements attached
to categorical grants make it difficult for districts to spend the funds elsewhere and virtually force districts to increase spending by at least the amount of the grant. Another explanation is that categorical grants are provided for specialized programs on which local
districts would spend less, if anything at all, in the absence of the categorical grant.

Categorical grants present a different trade-off between equity and efficiency than
do general grants. Categorical programs encourage districts to treat needy students differently by making additional resources available to produce similar, or hopefully similar, achievement outcomes. Anytime resources are devoted to a needy student, it implies
a loss of what could have been produced if the resources were evenly distributed across
all students (Monk, 1990). As a result, categorical grants trade economic efficiency for
equity in the provision of services.

Categorical programs, by their nature, are more centralized than general grants
since it is the state or federal government that determines what population needs extra
services. Moreover, some federal programs, such as the program for disabled children,
include very specific requirements for identifying and serving eligible students. Although the final determination of what specific services to provide are left to local district and parental discretion, there are very detailed identification and service procedures identified in the law and accompanying regulations.

Finally, since categorical grants are designed to provide assistance to groups of
students or to districts on the basis of some characteristic (e.g., expensive transportation
needs in a small, sparsely populated rural district), they are not generally designed to
equalize fiscal capacity. Nevertheless, both special-service provision and fiscal capacity
equalization can be accomplished with well-designed grant schemes. These issues are
discussed in more depth in Chapter 6.

2. SCHOOL FINANCE FORMULAS

This section uses the equity and adequacy framework developed in Chapter 3 to analyze
how different school finance formulas affect the equity and adequacy of a representative
20-district sample of school districts. The text shows how various school finance objectives can be in conflict, as well as how politics might intervene to constrain the amount
of equity a state political system can produce. Thus, school finance formula design is
both a substantive and political task that seeks to balance many objectives—equity, educational, fiscal, and political. "Perfect equity" is generally not possible.

This section has six parts: discussion of the characteristics of the illustrative sample of districts included in the simulation, and then a discussion of flat grant programs,
foundation programs, guaranteed tax base (GTB) programs, combination foundation-
GTB programs, and full-state funding.

Equity and Adequacy of the Simulation Sample Districts

In designing new school finance structures today, analysts and policymakers begin with state education finance systems that have evolved over several years. Local districts have real property tax rates, and state general aid has been distributed according to some mechanism, usually with the goal of reducing spending disparities caused by unequal distribution of the local per-pupil property tax base.

Figure 5.1 displays data for a representative sample of 20 districts that will be used throughout the chapter to demonstrate the impact of various new school finance structures. The data have been taken from a state with school finance circumstances typical of the rest of the country. The numbers indicate several characteristics of the extant school finance system in the state from which the sample was selected.

First, there are large differences in property value per pupil. The richest district has $278,052 in property value per pupil, which is almost 16 times the value ($17,456) in the poorest district. The weighted average[7] property value per student is $97,831, which is about 5.6 times the value of the poorest district, and about half the value of the second-wealthiest district ($198,564).

The third column in Figure 5.1 shows that property tax rates also vary considerably, from a low of 25.5 mills to a high of 39.64 mills, a difference of over 50 percent. Notably, it is the lower-property-value districts that have the higher property tax rates and the higher-property-value districts that have the lower property tax rates. Because of differences in the tax base, the second-wealthiest district raises $199 per pupil for each mill levied and thus raises $5,445 per pupil in local revenues at its tax rate of 27.42 mills. On the other hand, the second-poorest district raises only $26 for each mill levied and thus raises just $996 for its 38.5 mill tax rate. Thus, even though the poorer district exerts a higher tax effort, it produces a much lower level of revenues because its tax base is so low. On the other hand, the wealthier district raises a much higher level of local revenues per pupil even though it exerts a lower tax effort because its tax base is so much larger.

State aid is distributed in an inverse relationship to property value per pupil (i.e., the poorest districts receive the largest amount of per-pupil state aid) and state aid per pupil declines as property value per pupil rises. In fact, the poorest district receives about 6.4 times the state aid of the wealthiest district on a per-pupil basis. Thus, state aid is distributed in a fiscal capacity equalizing pattern. But, even the wealthiest district receives some level of state general aid ($437 per pupil for this sample). This distribution of state aid is characteristic of most states. All states use some type of fiscal capacity equalizing school finance formula to distribute its general aid, and all districts receive some minimum level of general aid.

But the difference in state aid allocations, while providing higher amounts to property-poor districts, is not sufficient to offset the 16 to 1 difference in property value

---

[7]All statistics in the figure and in the computer simulation are calculated in a manner that statistically weights each district value by the number of students in the district. Thus, the values for district 17, with 30,256 students contributes more to the weighted average than the values for district 6, which has only 956 students. Using student-weighted statistics has become the more prominent way to present statistics in school finance analyses. The results, therefore, indicate the impact of the funding structure on students.

Base Data

Adequacy Level	$ 5,350.00
Pupil Weights	no
Disabled	—
Limited English	—
Low Income	—

District	Pupils	Property Value per Pupil ($)	Property Tax Rate (Mills)	Local Revenue per Pupil ($)	State Revenue per Pupil ($)	Total Revenue per Pupil ($)
1	1,290	17,456	39.64	692	2,788	3,480
2	5,648	25,879	38.50	996	2,623	3,620
3	1,678	31,569	37.15	1,173	2,535	3,708
4	256	35,698	36.20	1,292	2,460	3,752
5	10,256	40,258	35.91	1,446	2,401	3,847
6	956	43,621	35.74	1,559	2,393	3,952
7	4,689	49,875	34.89	1,740	2,358	4,099
8	1,656	55,556	34.17	1,898	2,273	4,171
9	8,954	61,254	33.73	2,066	2,218	4,284
10	1,488	70,569	33.44	2,360	2,091	4,450
11	2,416	78,952	33.23	2,624	2,081	4,704
12	5,891	86,321	32.89	2,839	2,031	4,870
13	2,600	94,387	32.10	3,030	1,969	4,999
14	15,489	102,687	31.32	3,216	1,937	5,154
15	2,308	112,358	30.85	3,466	1,908	5,374
16	2,712	125,897	30.50	3,840	1,724	5,564
17	30,256	136,527	30.05	4,102	1,527	5,630
18	2,056	156,325	28.63	4,476	1,424	5,899
19	3,121	198,564	27.42	5,445	1,130	6,575
20	1,523	278,052	25.50	7,090	437	7,527
Weighted Average		97,831	32.34	3,028	1,925	4,953
Weighted Std. Dev.		48,514	2.91	1,269	433	841
Median		102,687	31.32	3,216	1,937	5,154

Totals		
	Amount	Percent
Local Revenue	318,727,208	61.14%
State Revenue	202,540,166	38.86%
Total Revenue	521,267,374	
Pupils	105,243	

Equity Measures	
Horizontal Equity	
Range	$4,047
Restricted Range	2,955
Federal Range Ratio	0.816
Coef. of Variation	0.170
Gini Coefficient	0.094
McLoone Index	0.810
Verstegen Index	1.086
Fiscal Neutrality	
Correlation	0.991
Elasticity	0.324
Adequacy	
Odden-Picus	0.895

FIGURE 5.1   Base Data

per pupil among districts. Thus, the poorest district, receiving 6.4 times the aid of the wealthiest district and exerting 1.5 times the tax effort, still has revenues per child that total only 46 percent of total revenues in the highest-spending district. The figures illustrate a consistent pattern—the lower the property value per child, the lower the total revenues per pupil, even though per-pupil state aid and property tax rates are higher.

Figure 5.1 also includes statistical measures of the fiscal equity of this school finance system. In terms of horizontal equity for students, the coefficient of variation for total revenues per pupil is 17 percent, which means that roughly two-thirds of these districts have total revenues per pupil that are within 17 percent of the weighted average ($841 in this case), and if this were a normal distribution, 95 percent of districts would have total revenues per pupil within 34 percent of the average ($1,682 in this case). The value of the coefficient of variation indicates that the fiscal-capacity-equalizing distribution of state general aid is modest, offsetting just a portion of the differences in local ability to raise property taxes. To further understand the impact of state general aid, compare Figure 5.1 with the results of a "no-state-aid" situation, which can be determined by running a computer simulation and setting the "flat grant" equal to zero. Notice that the coefficient of variation more than doubles, showing that the state aid that was provided clearly helped to reduce but not eliminate differences in total revenues per pupil.

The McLoone Index in Figure 5.1 indicates that the average total revenue per pupil for the bottom 50 percent of students is just 81 percent of that of the student at the median, or 19 percent below the median. Again, state aid has helped push this statistic toward 1.00, which would indicate full equity for the bottom 50 percent, as compared with the McLoone Index of 0.582 in the no-state-aid case (again, run a "flat grant" at zero from the menu in the simulation).

The Verstegen Index shows that the average total revenues per pupil in the top 50 percent is just 8.6 percent above the median. This figure shows that for this sample the revenue-per-pupil figures for the higher spenders are closer to the median than the revenues per pupil for the lower spenders, which are just 19 percent shy of the median.

In terms of fiscal neutrality, or the degree to which total revenues per pupil are linked to property wealth per pupil, Figure 5.1 shows a high correlation at 0.991, as well as a healthy elasticity, at 0.324. This means that revenues are strongly related to wealth, and that increases in wealth produce substantial increases in revenues, specifically, that a 10 percent increase in wealth produces a 3.2 percent increase in revenues. For example, as wealth increases about 100 percent from about $50,000 to $100,000, revenues per pupil increase about 33 percent, which is slightly more than the actual total revenue per pupil increase from $4,099 to $5,154. To see this graphically, click on the "base chart" tab at the bottom of the simulation spreadsheet. It shows that as property wealth per pupil increases, so too do revenues per pupil, reflecting the positive value for elasticity.

We have used the figure of $5,350 as the revenue-per-pupil figure that represents an "adequate" amount in all subsequent simulations. We simply selected a figure somewhat above the median, although this was an arbitrary selection. As discussed in Chapter 3 and later in this chapter, sophisticated analysis is needed to identify an "adequate" expenditure figure. But we had to select some figure, and we use the $5,350 figure consistently in all simulations in this chapter. The Odden-Picus Adequacy Index shows that those districts spending below the "adequate level" spend on average just 89.5 percent of the "adequate" figure of $5,350.

Figure 5.2 shows graphically the relationship between revenues per pupil and property value per pupil for this sample, and Figure 5.3 shows the same data but with no state aid at all. For both, there is an almost linear relationship between the two variables, but the slope of the graph is much steeper for the no-state-aid case. Thus, state aid has reduced the magnitude but has not eliminated the role of property value per pupil in producing revenue-per-pupil disparities.

In sum, the sample of 20 districts reflects the current context of school finance in many states. There is wide disparity in the local per-pupil property tax base. State aid is distributed inversely to property wealth, and is somewhat fiscal-capacity equalizing, but not sufficiently equalizing to offset differences in property wealth, nor sufficient to produce an "adequate" spending level for all districts. As a result, the equity statistics reflect a system that needs further improvements to meet horizontal equity, fiscal-neutrality equity, or adequacy standards. This chapter discusses how different types of school finance formulas for general school aid produce equity improvements in the distribution of fiscal resources for this sample of districts.

All school finance general-aid programs are education block grants. They provide unrestricted revenues to be used by local districts and schools for any education purpose. Sometimes they require districts to spend a minimum percentage on teacher salaries or a maximum on administration, but generally they are completely unrestricted. Furthermore, they rarely carry restrictions for maintaining local effort, so districts can even use large increases in general-aid revenues to help reduce local property tax rates. Indeed, as discussed above, on average half of each general-aid dollar is used to increase local education spending, and half is used to reduce local property tax rates.

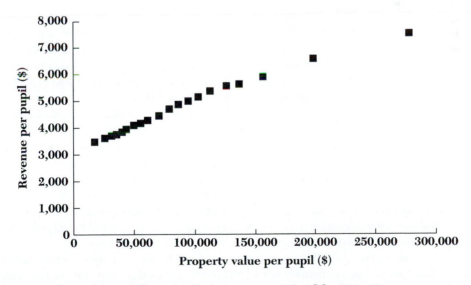

FIGURE 5.2   Scatter Plot of Total Revenue v. Wealth: Base Data

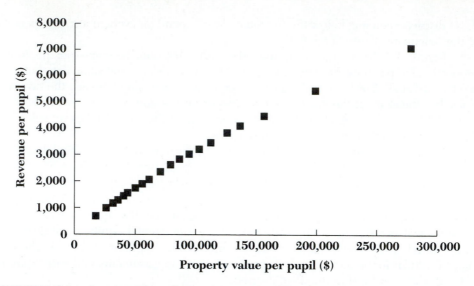

FIGURE 5.3   Scatter Plot of Revenue v. Wealth: Flat Grant

Although the history of education block grants is associated with attempts to deregulate and consolidate categorical programs for special students such as the disabled or low achievers, the idea of a block grant is attractive to local educators. Block grant funds give local school districts more autonomy since the money can be spent as the districts wish. Indeed, the history of school finance general-aid programs is a history of education block grants.

Flat Grant Programs

During the late eighteenth and early nineteenth centuries, there were few public schools in this country. Most schools were private, and churches ran many schools. Only a small proportion of the population attended formal schooling. As the country developed and interest emerged not only in formally educating its citizens but also in forging a common culture, local governments began to create public schools.

As discussed in Chapter 1, these schools were not part of state systems of education as exist today, but were independent creatures of local governments. Through various means, including taxation and "in kind" contributions, localities built schools (often one-room schools), hired teachers (who often lived in schools and were paid in terms of room and board rather than money), and educated increasing numbers of children.

From the beginning to at least the middle of the nineteenth century, the inequities associated with this laissez faire approach to creating and financing schools were recognized. Indeed, some localities were too poor to create any type of public school, while larger, wealthier localities were able to levy local taxes to finance them.

Recognizing these different circumstances, states began to require each locality to have at least one public elementary school and often provided a lump sum—a flat grant, usually on a per-school basis—to help support some type of local elementary school program. This approach remedied the problem of the poorest locality being unable to create a school on its own; in these communities, state funds often became the only fiscal support for the school.

But the flat grant approach also provided funds to localities that had been able to create a school with their own resources, thus providing them with even more education dollars. Though the overall impact was to expand education and boost the average level of schooling, and even perhaps education quality, the flat grant program benefited poor and rich districts alike.

Over time, states increased the level of flat grants in part to reflect rising costs of education. Growing numbers of students required shifts in the formula structure from flat grants per school to flat grants per classroom or per teacher to finance schools and classrooms that had outgrown the initial one-room-school context. As the education system continued to grow, it became clear that the level of the flat grant, always quite low, would need to be increased to finance the type of education system needed for an emerging industrial society. The response to these growing needs is described in the next section on foundation programs.

Today, states do not use flat grants as the major formula to apportion state general school aid. However, as recently as 1974, Connecticut's school-aid formula was a flat grant of $250 per pupil. Nevertheless, flat grant programs have several intriguing characteristics, some of which may be quite attractive to some districts. For example, some states, such as California, have constitutional requirements to provide a minimum amount of per-pupil state aid to local districts. These minimums function as flat grant programs for the very wealthy districts. California must provide a minimum $120 per pupil in state aid for all districts even if the formula calculation would provide for no state aid.

From an intergovernmental-grant design perspective, flat grants provide general-purpose operating funds. They are based solely on some measure of local education need, such as the number of schools, classrooms, teachers, or students. Flat grants have no local matching requirements. Flat grants also flow to local districts in equal amounts per unit of educational need regardless of differences in local fiscal capacity (i.e., regardless of local property wealth per pupil or household income). As such, they are unlikely to have a major impact on improving the fiscal neutrality of a school finance system, because they are unlikely to reduce the connections between local fiscal capacity and expenditures per pupil. Moreover, flat grants are not the most effective tool for raising local education spending, since districts could use the state funds to reduce the level of local dollars and thus to reduce local property tax rates.

The Flat Grant Formula.   However, one appealing aspect of flat grants is that they are easy to calculate. Algebraically, state aid per pupil for a flat grant is:

$$SAPP = FG$$

and, total state aid is defined as:

$$TSA = SAPP \times pupils$$

where

$$SAPP = \text{state aid per pupil},$$
$$FG = \text{the amount of the flat grant},$$
$$TSA = \text{total state aid, and}$$
$$\text{Pupils} = \text{the number of students in the school district.}[8]$$

Once the unit of need is identified, which today is typically pupils, a flat grant provides an equal number of dollars for each of those units of need—pupils—in all districts. Such a program is appealing because all education policy leaders, at both state and local levels can easily understand it. Furthermore, because a flat grant treats all districts equally, it seems fair on the surface. State education revenues are raised by taxing citizens across the state and then returning the money to localities in what appears to be a fair manner by providing an equal number of dollars for each unit of need.

Flat grants reflect the traditional American concern with the bottom half, or poorest segment, of the population. A flat grant implements the value of providing a bare-minimum level of support for those students and districts at the bottom in terms of relative spending or fiscal capacity. As the previous historical discussion indicates, education flat grants were created to ensure that even the poorest localities could offer some type of education program. And while they have been successful in doing so to some extent, the fact that flat grants were typically quite low has meant that they fall short of ensuring a minimum level of quality.

Figures 5.4 and 5.5 graphically depict the impact of a flat grant program on the ability of school districts to raise funds for education. Figure 5.4 represents the situation prior to a flat grant program. The solid lines show the revenues per pupil raised at different tax rates, 30 and 40 mills in this example, for districts with different levels of property value per pupil. For example, at 30 mills, the district with a property value per pupil of $50,000 raises just $1,500 per pupil, whereas the district with a property value of $100,000 raises $3,000. At 40 mills, the district with a property value per pupil of $50,000 raises more, $2,000 per pupil, and the district with a property value of $100,000 raises $4,000. The graph shows that revenues increase both as property value per pupil increases and as the local tax rate increases.

Figure 5.5 depicts the same districts under a flat grant program. The result is simply that the amount of the flat grant, $1,000 in this case, is added to local revenues per pupil. The slopes of the lines do not change. The district with a property value per pupil of $50,000 now has $3,000 ($2,000 of local revenues plus the $1,000 flat grant) at a 40 mill tax rate, and the district with a property value per pupil of $100,000 now has $5,000 ($4,000 of local money plus the $1,000 flat grant) at the same tax rate. Wealthier districts still raise more money, but with the flat grant all districts have at least $2,000 per pupil.

Fiscal Equity Impacts of Flat Grant Programs.   Figure 5.6 shows the result of replacing the current state-aid system for the sample of districts with a flat grant of $2,000

---

[8]In this book, pupils are the unit of need. But there are other measures of local need, such as teachers, classrooms, and schools, which could also be used with these formulas.

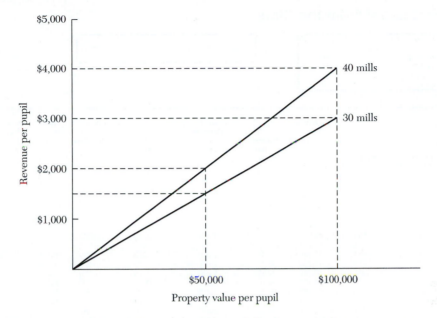

FIGURE 5.4   Graphical Representation of the Impact of No State Aid

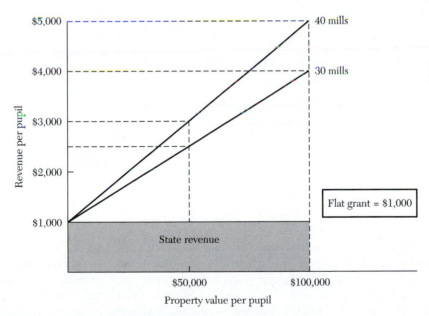

FIGURE 5.5   Graphical Representation of the Impact of a Flat Grant

Flat Grant from the State

Adequacy Level	$ 5,350.00
Pupil Weights	no
Disabled	—
Limited English	—
Low Income	—

Amount of Flat Grant	$ 2,000.00

District	Pupils	Property Value per Pupil ($)	Property Tax Rate (Mills)	Local Revenue per Pupil ($)	State Revenue per Pupil ($)	Change in State Revenue per Pupil ($)	Total Revenue per Pupil ($)	Change in Total Revenue per Pupil ($)
1	1,290	17,456	39.64	692	2000	(788)	2,692	(788)
2	5,648	25,879	38.50	996	2000	(623)	2,996	(623)
3	1,678	31,569	37.15	1,173	2000	(535)	3,173	(535)
4	256	35,698	36.20	1,292	2000	(460)	3,292	(460)
5	10,256	40,258	35.91	1,446	2000	(401)	3,446	(401)
6	956	43,621	35.74	1,559	2000	(393)	3,559	(393)
7	4,689	49,875	34.89	1,740	2000	(358)	3,740	(358)
8	1,656	55,556	34.17	1,898	2000	(273)	3,898	(273)
9	8,954	61,254	33.73	2,066	2000	(218)	4,066	(218)
10	1,488	70,569	33.44	2,360	2000	(91)	4,360	(91)
11	2,416	78,952	33.23	2,624	2000	(81)	4,624	(81)
12	5,891	86,321	32.89	2,839	2000	(31)	4,839	(31)
13	2,600	94,387	32.10	3,030	2000	31	5,030	31
14	15,489	102,687	31.32	3,216	2000	63	5,216	63
15	2,308	112,358	30.85	3,466	2000	92	5,466	92
16	2,712	125,897	30.50	3,840	2000	276	5,840	276
17	30,256	136,527	30.05	4,102	2000	473	6,102	473
18	2,056	156,325	28.63	4,476	2000	576	6,476	576
19	3,121	198,564	27.42	5,445	2000	870	7,445	870
20	1,523	278,052	25.50	7,090	2000	1563	9,090	1,563
Weighted Average		97,831	32.34	3,028	2,000	75	5,028	75
Weighted Std. Dev.		48,514	2.91	1,269	0	433	1,269	433
Median		102,687	31.32	3,216	2,000	63	5,216	63

Totals

Category	Amount	Percent	Change from Base Amount
Local Revenue	318,727,208	60.23%	(0)
State Revenue	210,486,000	39.77%	7,945,834
Total Revenue	529,213,208		7,945,834
Pupils	105,243		

Winners and Losers

Category	Winners	Losers	No Change
State Aid	8	12	0
Total Revenue	8	12	0

Equity Measures

Horizontal Equity	
Range	$6.398
Restricted Range	4.448
Federal Range Ratio	1.485
Coef. of Variation	0.252
Gini Coefficient	0.140
McLoone Index	0.742
Verstegen Index	1.149
Fiscal Neutrality	
Correlation	0.995
Elasticity	0.485
Adequacy	
Odden-Picus	0.871

FIGURE 5.6   Flat Grant from the State

per child. That amount is slightly higher than the average state aid in the original sample, and is about 40 percent of average total revenues per pupil, although there is no magic in the $2,000 figure. This flat grant increases state aid $7.9 million, from $202.5 million to $210.4 million. Note that there is no increase in local effort, and the total increase in funding from $521.3 million to $529.2 million is the result of the state's flat grant.

The flat grant completely erases the fiscal capacity equalizing impact of the original state aid, actually decreasing state aid in the poorest districts and increasing it in the wealthier eight districts. All the equity statistics indicate a less equal distribution: the range increases, the coefficient of variation increases, the McLoone Index decreases, the Verstegen Index rises, and the Adequacy Index falls. Further, both fiscal neutrality statistics increase, thus showing a stronger and more significant relationship between total revenues per pupil and property value per pupil. Indeed, the graph of this flat grant (use the simulation to view the graph by clicking on the "flat grant" tab) is very similar to the graph of the no-state-aid case (see Figure 5.4). The difference is that revenues per pupil are about $2,000 higher with the flat grant; the graph has been shifted upward by the level of the flat grant. In short, at low levels, a flat grant is not a viable option for enhancing the fiscal equity of a state's school finance system.

As the size of the flat grant increases, though, it begins to have a positive impact on the fiscal equity of the school finance system. For example, a flat grant of $4,000 per pupil reduces the coefficient of variation from 0.252 to 0.181, and the fiscal neutrality elasticity from 0.489 to 0.347. Use the simulation to confirm these figures. A flat grant of $5,000 further improves these statistics, lowering the coefficient of variation to 0.158 and the property wealth elasticity to 0.304. Again, use the simulation to confirm these figures. Note that when the flat grant is $5,000, no district spends less than the adequacy level of $5,350 so the Adequacy Index will be 1.0, as shown in the equity measures box.

If the flat grant were increased over time to $10,000 and local tax rates and property value per pupil stayed the same, the flat grant would be the major source of school revenues. At this level, both the coefficient of variation and the wealth elasticity also would be negligible. Put a different way, though a low-level flat grant would have a deleterious impact on the fiscal equity of the sample districts, a very high flat grant would swamp the current inequities and produce a highly equalized system.[9]

Of course, as the level of the flat grant rises, so also does the total or state cost of the program. The positive impacts on fiscal equity, in other words, are achieved only at significant cost. Nevertheless, the point of this example is that while low-level flat grants are unattractive except on simplicity grounds, higher-level flat grants can improve the fiscal inequities characteristic of most state school finance structures.

Finally, reviewing the equity measures and means and standard deviations of the major variables can make a few technical statistical points. First, the standard deviation ($433) stays the same irrespective of the level of the flat grant. Thus, adding a constant amount to all variables in a sample does change the standard deviation. This phenomenon helps explain why the coefficient of variation decreases as the flat grant increases. Since the coefficient of variation is the standard deviation divided by the mean, the numerator (standard deviation) remains constant while the denominator (mean or average revenues per pupil) increases. Second, the correlation coefficient also stays the same irrespective of the level of the flat grant. Again, adding a constant amount to all variables

---

[9]Readers are encouraged to run these flat grant amounts on the computer simulation and to review the results on the computer screen as well as perhaps to print them out. In addition, the reader should view the scatter plots for each run. The scatter plot for the flat grant at $10,000 shows that the graph of total revenues per pupil v. property wealth per pupil is almost a straight, horizontal line.

in a sample does not change the correlation. This suggests that the equity gains are achieved with substantial state expenditures, and the wealthy districts still receive more than poor districts. Also note that the range and restricted range remain the same as you run increasingly larger flat grants. Equity is achieved because the differences caused by variation in property wealth per pupil is a smaller portion of total district revenue as the flat grant increases.

Flat grants were early attempts to involve the state in redressing local differences in the ability to support public schools. Flat grants are easy to understand intergovernmental-aid programs. But they provide assistance to poor and rich districts alike. They are expensive, even at relatively low values. And at the affordable low values, they tend to worsen measures of school finance equity. For these reasons, they are not used as general-aid policy instruments today.

Foundation Programs

As the shortcomings of flat grant programs became increasingly obvious at the turn of this century, there was a search for a new and more powerful formula. At about that time, New York State created a commission to study its school finance system with the specific charge to create a new school finance structure that went beyond the flat grant approach. George Strayer and Roger Haig, professors at Columbia University, were hired as the consultants to this commission. Their new creation was a formula that would come to dominate school finance during the rest of the century. Today, most states use some variation of the Strayer-Haig foundation, or minimum foundation program as it originally was called. Indeed, in many states, the synonym for "school finance formula" is "minimum foundation program"; the state role in school finance is defined, as it were, as providing a minimum foundation program.

Strayer and Haig ingeniously incorporated several school finance issues into their new foundation program school finance formula. First, the foundation program addresses the issue of a minimum quality-education program. Though flat grants provided financial assistance for localities to provide some level of local school funding, the low level of the flat grant was rarely sufficient to finance what could be called even a minimum quality-education program. A goal of the minimum foundation program, however, was to set an expenditure per pupil—the minimum foundation—at a level that would provide at least a minimum quality-education program. The idea was to put a fiscal "foundation" under every local school program that was sufficient to provide an education program that met minimum standards. Thus, the foundation program was designed to remedy the first major defect of the low-level flat grant.

But what about the cost? The reason flat grants remained low was that to raise them to higher levels required more funds than the state could afford. The foundation program resolved this dilemma by financing the foundation expenditure per-pupil level with a combination of state and local revenues. A foundation program requires a minimum local tax effort as a condition of receiving state aid. The required local tax effort is applied to the local property tax base. State aid per pupil is the difference between the foundation per-pupil expenditure level and the per-pupil revenues raised by the required local tax rate. State aid is inversely related to local property wealth.

The Foundation Formula.   Algebraically, state aid per pupil for a foundation program is:

$$SAPP = FRPP - (RTR \times PVPP)$$

where

$$SAPP = \text{state aid per pupil,}$$
$$FRPP = \text{foundation expenditure revenue per pupil,}$$
$$RTR = \text{the local required tax rate, and}$$
$$PVPP = \text{local property value per pupil.}$$

A district's total state aid would be:

$$TSA = SAPP \times \text{Pupils,}$$

where

$$TSA = \text{total state aid,}$$
$$SAPP = \text{state aid per pupil, and}$$
$$\text{Pupils} = \text{the number of students in the school district.[10]}$$

Thus, the state and local school district share the total cost of the foundation program. A state could afford to enact such a program, and therefore substantially raise the minimum expenditure per pupil, because local tax revenues financed a large portion of the increase. Indeed, the advent of foundation school-aid formulas formally underscored the joint and interrelated state and local roles in financing public elementary and secondary schools.

Foundation Policy Issues.   From an intergovernmental-aid design perspective, the foundation program has several attractive features. First, it links local school districts to the state in a sophisticated structure of intergovernmental fiscal relationships. Second, it continues to provide large sources of general aid to local school districts but through a mechanism by which local and state revenues are formally combined in the general-aid "pot." Third, it formally requires a local match in order to receive state aid; the district must levy the required local tax rate as a condition of receiving state foundation aid.[11]

---

[10]Again, teachers, classrooms, or schools could be used as the need measure. Several states have used a foundation program with teachers as the need measure; Texas used such a program up to 1984.
[11]Historically, states have "hedged" on this requirement. Though most districts levy a tax rate above the minimum required local tax rate, a few do not. The policy issue for most states is whether to force these districts to raise their tax rate to the minimum level. The dilemma is that most of these low tax effort districts are districts lowest in property wealth and household income (i.e., the poorest of the poor). States usually have not ultimately required these districts to raise their tax rates. Sometimes, as in New York State, the districts receive state aid as if they were levying that minimum tax rate. Other states, such as Texas, reduced state aid by a factor equal to the ratio of the actual local property tax rate to the foundation-required tax rate. In the school finance simulation, there is no option to force districts to levy the required minimum tax rate, or to have state aid reduced in the preceding proportionate manner. All simulations discussed in the text used force districts to levy the minimum in order to receive state general aid.

Fourth, per-pupil state aid is related to fiscal capacity. Since the required local tax rate produces less money in a district with low property value than in a district with high property value, state aid becomes higher in the poor district. In fact, there is nearly a linear relationship between the level of state aid and the level of local property value per pupil: as property value decreases, state aid increases. Thus, a foundation program finances a minimum base education program in each school district, provides general aid in a manner that is fiscal capacity equalizing (i.e., increases as property value per pupil decreases), and requires a local contribution as well. These are all attractive features of intergovernmental-aid formulas.

The foundation program takes one or two steps beyond the flat grant, reflecting the American concern with the less well-off, and reflects the value of providing at least a minimum quality-education program. Foundation programs were designed, in fact, to ensure that there would be sufficient revenues from state and local sources to provide a minimum quality-education program in each school district. Viewed from today's education objectives, especially educational adequacy, which seek to have all students achieve to some high minimum level, this does not seem to be a very lofty goal. But viewed from the perspective of the beginning of the twentieth century, it was a bold step forward. The foundation program allowed states to implement an education finance structure that substantially upgraded the education systems in the lowest-spending schools to a level that at least passed a standard of minimum adequacy. In 1986–87, 30 states had such a foundation program or a foundation program as a component of their school-aid program (Salmon et al., 1988); the number had changed to 40 in 1993–94 (Gold, Smith, and Lawton, 1995) and is about that number today (see Sielke et al., 2001).

Three major shortcomings of foundation programs emerged over the years. The first is that a foundation program typically allows districts to spend above the minimum foundation level. This fiscal leeway, or local add-on, generally is financed entirely by local revenues, though sometimes it is aided by a GTB program (see p. 295 for discussion of combination foundation-GTB programs). Without the GTB, districts with a high property value per pupil can levy a small tax rate above the required local effort and take in large amounts of supplemental revenues, while districts with a low property value per pupil can levy a substantial extra tax rate and still see only a small amount of additional revenue per pupil. In fact, this feature of foundation programs ultimately led to the court cases discussed in Chapter 2. This is because over time, the local add-on component of education revenues far surpassed the foundation program revenues, producing a system that, while more equitable than a system with no state aid, still left education revenues per pupil strongly linked to local property wealth per pupil. Further, this local add-on feature is viewed by some as the "Achilles heel" of the finance structure in all states that today have a foundation program as their system for providing general school aid.

Second, though minimum foundation programs initially boosted the minimum level of local school spending, often the minimum dollar amount increased very slowly over time and quickly ceased being high enough to meet minimum standards. Put another way, after the initial years, minimum foundation programs often did not provide sufficient revenues per pupil for an education program that would meet even the lowest acceptable standards. The low foundation expenditure level was maintained in part by technical problems (the law specified a specific dollar amount as the foundation expenditure and required a legislative action each year for it to increase) and in part by fiscal constraints (the state could not afford to raise it significantly). Over time, the low level forced districts that wanted to provide a higher-quality program to expand their local add-on, which gradually moved the overall system into one based more and more on local add-ons, and thus on local property value per pupil.

Third, while foundation programs usually increased total education revenues in property-poor districts and thus helped them to enhance their education program, strict state-aid formula calculations for wealthier districts yielded a negative number. This result meant that these districts could raise more than the minimum foundation expenditure at the required tax rate. In a world of perfect fiscal equity, the state would have required such districts to send a check in the amount of the negative aid to the state, which the state would have put it in the general fund for redistribution to poorer districts. But states did not enact this "recapture" component. If state-aid calculations produced a negative-aid figure, the state simply provided no aid to that district.

This meant that even under a minimum foundation program, districts high in property value per pupil were able to raise more funds at the given required tax rate just with local funds than other districts had with a combination of state and local funds. The fiscal advantage for districts high in property value per pupil was further enhanced by prior receipt of flat grant state aid, which had been distributed to all districts, irrespective of their level of property wealth per pupil. For these districts, the state faced a dual-policy dilemma: whether under the foundation-aid calculation to require them to send negative aid checks to the state, which was rarely if ever invoked, and whether to take away the flat grant aid and thereby reduce their state aid to zero. Most states took a political route to this dilemma and distributed an amount that was the larger of the new amount under the foundation formula or the previous level of aid (i.e., they did not take away the old flat grant aid). This "hold harmless" approach has typified school finance structures (as well as most other intergovernmental-aid structures) for years. So, not only were the wealthiest districts not forced to revert negative aid to the state but also they kept some minimum level of per pupil state aid. Indeed, states often gradually increased the minimum amount over the years.

Such policy dilemmas and ultimate policy decisions substantially blunted the ability of minimum foundation programs to impact the fiscal equity of a state's school finance structure. While new minimum foundation programs boosted the fiscal resources of the lowest-spending districts, which was a clear objective and a definite positive feature, their shortcomings, especially over time, severely limited their role as an adequate school finance mechanism.

The base sample of districts shows the residue of these incremental approaches to school finance (see Figure 5.1); even the districts highest in property value per pupil receive some state aid. Thus, the school finance policy question is what type of a foundation program can enhance the fiscal equity of the school finance condition of the sample districts? In addressing this question, there are two policy decisions that have to be made:

- the foundation expenditure level, and
- the required local tax rate.

Three policy issues then have to be considered:

- the impact on the fiscal equity of the sample,
- the total costs (usually in state revenues but also considering changes in local revenues), and
- the number of "winners" and "losers" (i.e., the number of districts with increases and decreases in state aid).

And a politically viable combination of these policy issues needs to be produced in order for a specific foundation formula to be enacted into law. Generally, equity must improve, the cost must be affordable, and there needs to be more winner than loser districts. Accomplishing these goals simultaneously, however, is usually difficult.

Setting the Foundation Level.   There are no magic solutions to setting the foundation expenditure level. Usually, states set a level that, combined with the amount raised locally by the required tax rate, equals the amount of state appropriations available. This is a politically grounded but substantively vacuous approach since it is decided on availability rather than on a needs basis, but it is probably the norm. During the past 30 years, most states simply determined a particular spending level, deemed sufficiently high enough by the appropriate cross-section of political and education leaders, and sought to fund that spending level over time. To ensure that the level stayed "current" or increased with inflation, states often legislated a mechanism that automatically increased the foundation expenditure per pupil level each year. Inflating it by the increase in the consumer price index, or the deflator for state and local governmental services, is a common approach.

A second approach is to set a specific policy target such as 50 or 100 percent of the statewide average expenditure. The policy target could even be to bring the foundation level up to the spending in some district above the average; a late 1970s bill in California set the expenditure of the district at the 75th percentile as the foundation expenditure target. Whatever the level, this approach provides a clear policy target as to what the foundation base spending level will be. Odden and Clune (1998) recommend the use of such policy targets in order to give the school finance system a specific and clear equalization goal. Setting the foundation expenditure level at the median will eliminate all "savage" fiscal inequalities (Kozol, 1992) because it would raise the expenditures of all low-spending districts up to at least the median.

Today, the challenge to calculating a foundation expenditure level is to determine an "adequate" level (i.e., an amount of money per pupil that would be sufficient to teach students to some high minimum standard). Odden and Clune (1998) and Verstegen (2002) argue that this is one of the most pressing, as well as complex, tasks for linking the school finance structure to the goals and strategies of standards- and school-based education reform.

Determining an Adequate Foundation Spending Level.   Chapter 3 identified the four methods that have been used to identify an adequate foundation level of expenditure: (1) the successful district approach, (2) the professional judgment approach, (3) the cost function approach, and (4) the evidence-based approach. Further research is needed for all of these methods, as the findings about the adequate expenditure level vary both across as well as within states, depending on the method used (see for example, Augenblick and Myers, Inc., 2001a, 2001b). Verstegen (2002) raises several other issues related to identifying an adequate expenditure level in education.

Finally, when running simulations, a rationale needs to be provided for any specified adequate expenditure level, or the results for the Odden-Picus Adequacy Index should be ignored. The figure that might be in the simulation does not necessarily have any substantive rationale; it simply might be the figure used by the individual who last used the simulation program. A figure derived from an explicit adequacy study gives a much stronger meaning to the Adequacy Index.

Setting the Foundation Tax Rate. After the foundation expenditure level is determined, setting the required tax rate raises another set of interrelated issues. First, if the required tax rate is above the tax rate in any poor school district, it will require that district to raise its tax rate. That often is a politically difficult requirement to enact. Second, and related, the level of the required tax rate determines the state cost of the program: the higher the required local effort, the less the state cost (but the greater the local cost).

Third, the foundation expenditure level and required tax rate are connected in a way that determines which districts are eligible for at least some aid, and which districts receive zero (or even negative) aid. The zero-aid district is defined as:

$$SAPP = FRPP - (RTR \times PVPP) = 0.$$

Solving this equation for PVPP identifies the property value per pupil below which districts will receive some foundation aid and above which they will not. The solution becomes:

$$FRPP = RTR \times PVPP, \text{ or transposing and dividing by RTR,}$$
$$PVPP \text{ (the zero aid district)} = FRPP/RTR,$$

where

$$FRPP = \text{the foundation expenditure revenue per pupil level,}$$
$$RTR = \text{the required tax rate, and}$$
$$PVPP = \text{the property value of the zero-aid district in thousands}$$
$$\text{of dollars of assessed valuation.}$$

Thus, if the foundation level is $3,000, and the required tax rate is 30 mills, the zero-aid district has a property value per pupil of $100,000.

The zero-aid district is an important policy variable to consider. Districts with property value above this level will not be eligible for any state aid (or at best be "held harmless" with their previous level of state aid), and their legislative representatives might vote against the proposal if self-interest is the only motivating variable. Another policy aspect of the zero-aid district is that it identifies a level up to which the state provides some fiscal capacity equalization. The policy issue is the level to which the state wants to equalize fiscal capacity: to the statewide average, or the 75th percentile, or the 90th percentile, or the property value per pupil of the wealthiest district, or any other level it chooses.

In other words, setting the foundation expenditure level and the required tax rate simultaneously determines the level of education program that becomes the base, the state and local cost, the zero-aid district, the level up to which the state seeks to equalize fiscal capacity, and the numbers of state aid gainers and losers. In short, it determines several key aspects of the political economy of the foundation program itself.

All of these characteristics of a foundation program are depicted in Figure 5.7 for a foundation program with an expenditure per pupil of $2,000 and a required tax rate of 20 mills. For the first 20 mills, all districts with a property wealth less than $100,000 (the zero-aid district) receive a total of $2,000 per child; districts with a property value per pupil above $100,000 raise more than the foundation level, as the slope of the 20-mill line shows. If districts decide to levy a tax rate above the required rate, as most districts do, the additional funds are raised solely from the local property tax base. So at 30 mills, the district with a property wealth per pupil of $50,000 would produce $2,000 per pupil for the first 20 mills and only $500 per pupil for the next 10 mills, or $2,500 per pupil in total, whereas the district with a property wealth per pupil of $100,000 also would produce $2,000 per pupil for the first 20 mills but would produce $1,000 for the next 10 mills, or $3,000 per pupil in total.

Fiscal Equity Impacts of Foundation Programs.   Setting these parameters determines how the new foundation program will impact the fiscal equity of the finance struc-

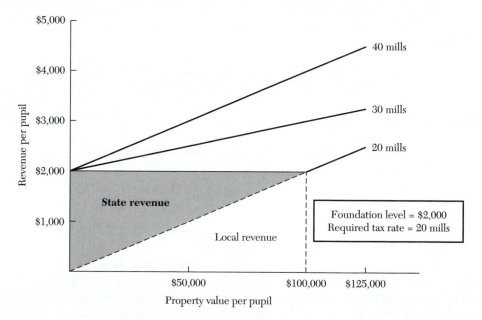

FIGURE 5.7   Graphical Representative of the Effect of a Foundation Program

ture. Figure 5.8 shows several figures for a foundation program with the foundation expenditure level set at $5,154, the median level for the base sample, and a required tax effort of 31.32 mills (also the median).[12] This means that the zero-aid district has a property value per pupil of $164,559, which is between districts 18 and 19 in the sample.

This also means that this program will provide fiscal capacity equalization for districts that enroll 95.6 percent of the students (which is the cumulative enrollment of districts 1–18). The program increases state aid by 9.7 percent—$50.6 million. It also positively impacts fiscal equity, reducing the coefficient from 17 percent for the base sample to 7.1 percent, reduces the wealth elasticity from 0.324 to 0.146, and raises the Adequacy Index from 0.895 to 0.985. It raises spending above the foundation level in the poorest and lowest-spending 13 districts. This impact can be seen by using the simulation to view the graph of the results; the left-hand portion of the graph from Figure 5.2 (the base data) has been rotated up (clockwise) at about the wealth of the zero-aid district to form a horizontal line at the foundation expenditure level of $5,154. But, this foundation program also reduces aid to six districts; even districts 15–18, which receive some foundation aid, have a net loss of aid from their base context.

A foundation program with the expenditure level set at $4,000 and the required tax rate at 39 mills, which thus provides for fiscal capacity equalization up to just $102,500, the statewide average property value per pupil, produces a net drop in state aid and also a reduction of state aid for 15 of the 20 districts. (Use the simulation to assess the broader impacts of this set of parameters.) On the other hand, a foundation at $5,154 with a required tax rate of 25 mills, which provides for fiscal capacity equalization up to $206,160, provides at least some state general aid for 19 of the 20 districts, further enhances fiscal equity (the coefficient of variation drops to 5.8 percent, the wealth elasticity declines to 0.131 and the Adequacy Index becomes 1) but the state cost rises by $64 million. (Again, use the simulation to assess the broader impacts of this set of parameters.)

These results indicate that the foundation expenditure level, required tax effort, level of fiscal capacity equalization, state costs, numbers of winners and losers, and school finance fiscal equity and adequacy all are interrelated. These interrelations suggest why getting legislatures to enact a complicated school finance reform is not an easy task; several variables—educational, political, and fiscal—need to be balanced simultaneously.

As found in some research (Odden and Busch, 1998), a school finance system that required all districts to spend at least at the median of state spending per pupil reflects a strategy that might begin to move the system toward adequacy (see also Rubenstein, 2002). Yes, research in every state would be needed to determine more explicitly what an adequate spending level would be. But ensuring that districts spent at least as much

[12]For the Foundation, Guaranteed Tax Base and Combination simulations, state aid has been set equal to zero if the calculation produces a negative figure, but districts are not "held harmless" (i.e., they lose state aid if the calculation produces a zero-aid figure). Further, a local tax response has been built into the simulation under which districts increase their local property tax rate to cover the lost aid. For these districts, the last column of the results show no total revenue loss, but this is a result of a loss of state aid and an equal increase in local revenues. There is also a response model for districts that have state aid increases. These districts use half the state aid increase to raise spending, and half to reduce local property tax rates. For the foundation part of the program, though, tax rates cannot be reduced to below the required tax rate.

Foundation Program

Adequacy Level	$	5,350.00
Pupil Weights		no
Disabled		—
Limited English		—
Low Income		—

Foundation Level	$5,154.00
Required Tax Rate	31.32

District	Pupils	Property Value per Pupil ($)	Old Property Tax Rate (Mills)	New Property Tax Rate (Mills)	Change in Property Tax Rate (Mills)	Old Local Revenue per Pupil ($)	New Local Revenue per Pupil ($)	Change in Local Revenue per Pupil ($)	New State Revenue per Pupil ($)	Change in State Revenue per Pupil ($)	Total Revenue per Pupil ($)	Change in Total Revenue per Pupil ($)
1	1,290	17,456	39.64	35.48	(4.16)	692	619	(73)	4,607	1,819	5,227	1,747
2	5,648	25,879	38.50	34.91	(3.59)	996	903	(93)	4,343	1,720	5,247	1,627
3	1,678	31,569	37.15	34.23	(2.91)	1,173	1,081	(92)	4,165	1,630	5,246	1,538
4	256	35,698	36.20	33.76	(2.44)	1,292	1,205	(87)	4,036	1,576	5,241	1,489
5	10,256	40,258	35.91	33.62	(2.30)	1,446	1,353	(92)	3,893	1,492	5,246	1,400
6	956	43,621	35.74	33.53	(2.21)	1,559	1,463	(96)	3,788	1,395	5,250	1,298
7	4,689	49,875	34.89	33.11	(1.79)	1,740	1,651	(89)	3,592	1,233	5,243	1,144
8	1,656	55,556	34.17	32.75	(1.43)	1,898	1,819	(79)	3,414	1,141	5,233	1,062
9	8,954	61,254	33.73	32.53	(1.21)	2,066	1,992	(74)	3,236	1,017	5,228	944
10	1,488	70,569	33.44	32.38	(1.06)	2,360	2,285	(75)	2,944	853	5,229	778
11	2,416	78,952	33.23	32.28	(0.95)	2,624	2,548	(75)	2,681	601	5,229	525
12	5,891	86,321	32.89	32.11	(0.78)	2,839	2,771	(68)	2,450	419	5,222	352
13	2,600	94,387	32.10	31.71	(0.39)	3,030	2,993	(37)	2,198	228	5,191	192
14	15,489	102,687	31.32	31.32	0	3,216	3,216	0	1,938	0	5,154	0
15	2,308	112,358	30.85	33.28	2.43	3,466	3,739	273	1,635	(273)	5,374	0
16	2,712	125,897	30.50	34.57	4.07	3,840	4,353	513	1,211	(513)	5,564	0
17	30,256	136,527	30.05	34.80	4.76	4,102	4,752	650	878	(650)	5,630	0
18	2,056	156,325	28.63	36.09	7.46	4,476	5,641	1,166	258	(1,166)	5,899	0
19	3,121	198,564	27.42	33.11	5.69	5,445	6,575	1,130	0	(1,130)	6,575	0
20	1,523	278,052	25.50	27.07	1.57	7,090	7,527	437	0	(437)	7,527	0
Weighted Average		97,831	32.34	33.37	1.03	3,028	3,261	232	2,173	248	5,434	481
Weighted Std. Dev.		48,514	2.91	1.56	3.17	1,269	1,598	382	1,318	907	384	610
Median		102,687	31.32	31.32	0	3,216	3,216	0	1,938	0	5,246	0

150

	Totals		
Category	Amount	Percent	Change from Base Amount
Local Revenue	343,155,687	60.01%	24,428,479
State Revenue	228,688,560	39.99%	26,148,394
Total Revenue	571,844,247		50,576,873
Pupils	105,243		

Winners and Losers			
Category	Winners	Losers	No change
State Aid	14	6	0
Total Revenue	14	0	6

FIGURE 5.8 Foundation Program

Equity Measures	
Horizontal Equity	
Range	$2,373
Restricted Range	1,384
Federal Range Ratio	0.267
Coef. of Variation	0.071
Gini Coefficient	0.030
McLoone Index	0.992
Verstegen Index	1.070
Fiscal Neutrality	
Correlation	0.900
Elasticity	0.146
Adequacy	
Odden-Picus	0.985

as the median would be a way for states to move immediately forward on the adequacy school finance agenda. Odden (1998) shows the results of such a school finance system for the three states with the "new" school finance problem discussed in Chapter 1: Illinois, Missouri, and Wisconsin. He simulated a foundation program set at the median spending level in each state. Not only would such a program represent progress in providing an adequate level of funding, but also the programs produce substantial improvements in fiscal equity. In all three states, both the statistical measures of spending disparities (coefficient of variation and McLoone Index) and the statistical measures of the linkage between spending and wealth (correlation and wealth elasticity) improve, as would the Adequacy Index. To work over time, the spending level would need to be inflation-adjusted each year to continue to provide an adequate spending base.

In summary, foundation programs have several attractive features. They began as programs designed to provide a minimum quality-education program but, today, can be used to guarantee a higher-quality program, perhaps one sufficient to meet the needs of an adequate education system, one in which students learn to high minimum standards. They are unique in having this base program guarantee as a critical variable. Second, they are funded by a combination of state and local funds that link states and school districts inextricably in a fiscal federalism partnership for funding public schools. Third, they are fiscal-capacity equalizing (i.e., they provide state aid in an inverse relationship to local property value per pupil), and thus also address the key structural problem of school finance—the disparity in the local property tax base. Their key defect may be that they allow local spending above the foundation program, and if the base program is low, these local fiscal add-ons—financed entirely with local property tax revenues—increase the linkages between property wealth and education spending, the major weakness of previous school-aid formulas and an issue targeted in school finance litigation.

On the other hand, it could be argued that if the state actually determined and fully funded an adequate foundation base, together with appropriate adjustments for special student, district, and school needs, then the state's interest in education and its funding contribution would have been fulfilled. Such a position would allow districts to spend more if they wish, but only by using local money. Although this position could be criticized, a state could defend it assuming that it truly had determined and funded an adequate spending base.

Guaranteed Tax Base Programs

Guaranteed tax base (GTB) programs, surprisingly, are late-twentieth-century phenomena in school finance structures. The first guaranteed tax base programs were enacted in the early 1970s after the initial rounds of school finance litigation. The late arrival of guaranteed tax base programs is perplexing because, as the name suggests, this type of school finance program addresses the traditional structural flaw in traditional approaches to local financing of public schools, namely the unequal distribution of the local property tax base. A GTB program simply erases this inequality by guaranteeing, through state aid allocations, that each local district can function as if it had an equal property tax base per pupil. The details of how this program works will be described here. Conceptually, it is simple, and in terms of school finance policy, it addresses a basic inequity in school finance: unequal access to a local property tax base.

This simple and straightforward program took a somewhat complicated course in evolving to its current state. The early forms of GTB programs actually were called percentage-equalizing programs and were first introduced in the 1920s. They were proposed for two major reasons. First, foundation program levels remained low, and most districts enacted local add-ons that were financed entirely from their local property tax base. Local add-ons came to dominate the level of total revenues, and there was a search for a school finance mechanism that went beyond foundation programs and provided state fiscal-capacity equalizing aid for the overall spending levels in local school districts.

Second, because the state fiscal role remained small as the level of the minimum foundation programs remained low, policy pressure grew to increase the state role in the financing of education. Over time, in fact, many states sought to increase the state role to some fixed target, usually 50 percent. Since most state aid was distributed in a fiscal-capacity equalizing manner, the assumption was that the fiscal equity of the school finance system would improve as the state role increased toward, or even surpassed, 50 percent.

The percentage equalizing formula was designed to address both of these policy concerns. First, the state share (in percentage terms) of total costs was directly included in the formula. The formula was designed to provide a larger state role in low-property-wealth districts and a smaller state role in higher-property-wealth districts, thus providing a fiscal-capacity equalizing thrust to the program. The formula calculated a state-aid ratio for each district. The ratio was higher in property-poor districts and lower in property-wealthy districts. The state role policy target, say 50 percent of total dollars spent on education, was usually set for the district with statewide average property value per pupil.[13]

To determine state aid, the state-aid ratio was applied to the local spending level, which was a local policy decision of each district. The aid ratio times the spending level produced the amount of state aid per pupil for each district. State aid, therefore, varied with both the level of wealth and the level of locally determined spending. During 1986–87, five states had percentage equalizing programs, a number that went down to four in 1993–94 (Gold, Smith, and Lawton, 1995). The percentage equalizing formula is both more complicated and algebraically equivalent to a guaranteed tax base program.

As previously stated, guaranteed tax base programs were enacted beginning in the early 1970s, at the time of the first successful school finance court cases. These court cases

[13]State aid per pupil for a percentage-equalizing program is equal to:

$$SAPP = [1 - LR(PVPPd/PVPPk)]TREVPP,$$

where

$$SAPP = \text{state aid per pupil,}$$
$$LR = \text{local role in percent terms [the state role is } (1 - LR)],$$
$$PVPPd = \text{property value per pupil for each district,}$$
$$PVPPk = \text{property wealth per pupil in the comparative district, usually}$$
but not necessarily the statewide average, and
$$TREVPP = \text{total (state and local) revenue per pupil.}$$

The zero aid district is PVPPk/LR. The aid ratio is $1 - LR(PVPPd/PVPPk)$.

had directly challenged the relationship between expenditures and wealth caused by the unequal distribution of the local tax base per pupil. The book that developed the "fiscal neutrality" legal theory for these cases (Coons, Clune, and Sugarman, 1970) also discussed the design and operation of a new district power-equalizing school finance structure. Power equalizing was a system that would equalize the power of local districts to raise funds through the property tax. The mechanism was for the state to guarantee a tax base that all districts would use in deciding upon school tax rate and expenditure levels. Subsequently, these approaches became known as guaranteed tax base programs. Guaranteed tax base programs are also called guaranteed yield, or resource-equalizing programs in some states.

The GTB Formula.   The formula for calculating state aid for a guaranteed tax base programs is:

$$SAPP = DTR \times (GTB - PVPP),$$

where

$$SAPP = \text{state aid per pupil,}$$
$$DTR = \text{the local district property tax rate,}$$
$$GTB = \text{the tax rate guaranteed by the state, in thousands}$$
$$\text{of dollars of property value per pupil, and}$$
$$PVPP = \text{the local district property value per pupil.}$$

Total GTB state aid, therefore, is:

$$TSA = SAPP \times Pupils,$$

where

$$TSA = \text{total state aid,}$$
$$SAPP = \text{state aid per pupil from the GTB formula, and}$$
$$Pupils = \text{the number of students in the school district.}$$

Several interesting features of the GTB state aid formula should be mentioned. First, the amount of state aid a district receives varies with the size of the local tax base; the greater the local tax base (PVPP), the smaller the factor (GTB – PVPP) and thus the smaller the amount of per-pupil state aid. In other words, like with the foundation program, state aid varies inversely with property wealth per child.

A second feature is that the local expenditure (or revenues) per pupil is equal to the tax rate times the GTB. This can be shown algebraically:

$$\text{local revenue} = DTR \times PVPP, \text{ and}$$
$$\text{state aid} = DTR \times (GTB - PVPP), \text{ so}$$
$$\text{total revenues} = \text{local revenue} + \text{state aid, or substituting,}$$
$$\text{total revenues} = (DTR \times PVPP) + (DTR \times (GTB - PVPP)).$$

Combining terms on the right hand side and factoring out DTR:

$$\text{total revenues} = DTR \times (PVPP + GTB - PVPP), \text{ which is:}$$
$$\text{total revenues} = DTR \times GTB$$

In other words, the GTB operates just exactly as it is designed.[14] Districts can function as if they have the GTB as their local tax base. Once they determine their desired spending level, they divide it by the GTB to determine the local tax rate they must levy. Or conversely, by multiplying their local property tax rate by the GTB, they identify their per-pupil spending level. As a corollary, by multiplying their local property tax rate times the local property tax base, they also identify the amount of local revenues they must raise.

A final feature is that state aid is a function of the local school tax rate; the higher the tax rate, the greater the state aid. This feature has two implications. First, if local districts increase their property tax rate, they not only raise more funds locally, but also become eligible for more state aid. This can be an attractive component for a campaign to increase the local school property tax rate. Second, and related, the total amount of revenues the state needs to appropriate is, in part, determined by local action. Put differently, the state is not in complete control of the level of revenues needed to finance the general-aid school finance formula; if districts increase local tax rates more than anticipated, additional state funds are needed to fully fund the GTB formula.

This feature has been troublesome when the GTB formula has been considered by many legislatures, which themselves want to be in complete control of the level of funding needed for the general-aid program. Many states reject the GTB because of this feature. But, over time, local tax rates usually settle into fairly predictable patterns, and states can fairly easily predict the level of appropriation needed to fund the formula. Michigan, for example, had a GTB program for over a decade in the 1970s and 1980s and had no more difficulty predicting the level of appropriations needed than did other states that used different school-aid distribution mechanisms. Many other factors complicate estimation of state aid, including for example, enrollment projections, property value projections, and estimates of state tax revenues. Many factors beyond the design of the general aid formula itself make state-aid predictions an imperfect art.

GTB Policy Issues.   Guaranteed tax base programs have several attractive features as an intergovernmental-grant mechanism. First, a GTB requires a local match, which is equal to the district tax rate times its property value per pupil. Indeed, while GTB aid increases as the local tax rate increases, thus requiring more state funds, the local tax rate applied to the local tax base increases local revenues as well. In other words, more GTB aid does not come without a local cost; it also requires an increase in local revenues. Indeed, the local match feature of the GTB formula structure helps keep both local tax rates and state aid at acceptable levels over time.

Second, the GTB program equalizes fiscal capacity. As local property wealth decreases, GTB aid as a percent of local expenditure increases, and vice versa. This is generally a desired feature for school finance formulas. But, the GTB program goes further than that by directly addressing the disparity in the local property tax base per child. The

---

[14]Strictly speaking, this holds for all districts only if the state has a total recapture plan. In the absence of such recapture, this applies only to districts with property wealth at or below the GTB level.

GTB program simply makes the GTB tax base equal for all districts, at least for those districts with a property value per pupil less than the GTB. If the primary school finance problem is the unequal distribution of the property tax base, the GTB program is precisely the school finance structure that remedies the problem.

In terms of values, the GTB program reflects the American values of choice, local control, and equal education opportunity as defined by equal access to a tax base. For districts with a property value per pupil less than the GTB, it provides for equal dollars per pupil from state and local sources for equal school tax rates. A pure GTB program, moreover, implements the value of local control since it allows local districts to decide on the level of tax rate they want to levy for schools, and thus the level of per-pupil school spending. If localities want a higher-quality program, they are free to exert a higher school tax rate. The GTB ensures that all districts levying that tax rate will have the same spending per pupil from the general fund, and thus provides ex ante equity. If districts want a program that is funded at a level comparable to the average, they need only levy the average school tax rate.

Because a GTB program allows different local decisions on education per-pupil spending levels, equality of spending is not its focus. Indeed, without a requirement for a minimum school tax rate, GTB programs do not even require a minimum education expenditure per-pupil level. Still, in most situations where GTB programs have been enacted, they increase expenditures in all but the lowest tax-rate school districts. However, it should be emphasized that a GTB program is incompatible with the horizontal equity principal for students because it does not require equal spending per child.

Figure 5.9 indicates graphically some of these characteristics of a GTB program, for a GTB set at $100,000. The graph shows that for districts with a property value per pupil below the GTB, revenues differ according to the tax rate, but that all districts have the same revenues per pupil (from state and local sources) if they levy the same tax rate. As the 20-mill line shows, the higher a district's property wealth per pupil, the greater the share of total revenue provided from local sources. If the tax rate is raised to 30 mills, all districts get $3,000 per pupil, and the proportion of state aid is inversely related to the district's property wealth. The graph also shows that districts above the GTB raise higher revenues per pupil at any given tax rate but receive no state aid.

In implementing a GTB program, there is one primary policy issue to resolve: the tax base level that the state wants to guarantee. While there are no absolute standards by which to assess this policy issue, there are several benchmarks. The state could seek to guarantee the tax base up to the 50th percentile of students, the statewide average, or to a higher percentile, such as the 75th, 90th, or even higher. A GTB program in response to a typical fiscal neutrality court suit would need to hit at least the 75th percentile, and probably the 90th percentile. The legal question would be: What constitutes substantial equal access to raising education dollars? The answer would be: At least the 75th percentile, and probably higher, but how much higher varies by state and court. Rather than just identifying a value for the GTB, Odden and Clune (1998) argue for selecting a specific target that provides a clear equalization goal, such as the wealth at some high level (the 90th percentile).

There are two secondary policy issues. One is whether a minimum tax rate is required. A minimum tax rate translates into a minimum expenditure per pupil (which

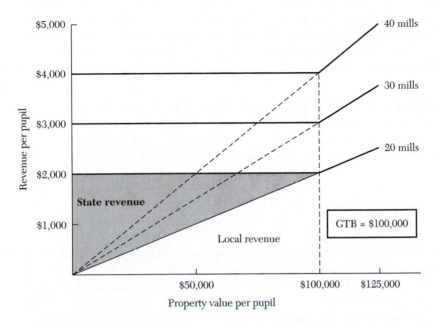

FIGURE 5.9 Graphical Representation of the Effect of a Guaranteed Tax Base Program

equals the minimum tax rate × the GTB). Requiring a minimum would make a smoother transition from a minimum foundation program, for which the state policy goal includes a minimum base program, to a GTB program that in its pure form does not have a minimum expenditure requirement. Odden and Busch (1995) show that such a minimum tax rate would have eliminated all the very low spending per-pupil districts in Wisconsin, which simultaneously would have provided all districts with sufficient dollars to fund the expensive, comprehensive, Modern Red Schoolhouse school design (Odden, Archibald, and Tychsen, 1998; Odden and Busch, 1998).

A second issue is whether to cap GTB aid at some tax rate, or whether to cap local school tax rates at some level. Under the first type of cap, GTB aid would be available only up to a set tax rate. As tax rates rise above the set level, the state would no longer participate, leaving the districts with only local funds from the extra tax effort. This would give the GTB an unequalized local add-on element, as exists for all foundation programs. Over time, a tax rate cap could turn the GTB program into a structure in which non fiscal-capacity-equalized add-ons dominate the structure and produce a system, as exists in many states, in which expenditures per pupil are strongly related to the level of local property value per child.

The second type of cap is an absolute cap on the local tax rate. Not only would GTB aid not be available above this tax rate, but also districts would not be allowed to levy a tax rate above the cap. This tax-rate cap would have the effect of an expenditure cap, since the maximum expenditure would be the tax-rate cap times the GTB. This type of cap certainly puts a major constraint on local control, but it also limits the variation in expenditures per pupil that would be allowed by a GTB program. The Kentucky school finance reform enacted in 1990 adopted both of these options (see discussion beginning on p. 295 in the combination foundation-GTB section, and Picus, Odden, and Fermanich, 2001).

Fiscal Equity Impacts of GTB Programs. Figure 5.10 displays the simulation results for a GTB program where the GTB is set at $138,000, which is about the 94th percentile for the sample of districts. Interestingly, this level of GTB would require a decrease in state aid, and would leave the state role at much less than 50 percent of the total at only 29 percent ($155.8 million divided by $538.7 million).

This level of GTB has positive impacts on fiscal equity and adequacy. It reduces revenue-per-pupil disparities. In terms of horizontal equity for students, the coefficient of variation drops to 12.5 percent and the McLoone Index increases to 0.866. It also increases the Adequacy Index to 92.6.

In terms of fiscal neutrality, it reduces the correlation between total revenues per pupil and property value per pupil but more importantly reduces the wealth elasticity to 0.246. The latter is to be expected since the GTB provides equal access to a tax base for districts with 94 percent of all students. This simulation shows the impact that a GTB at the 90th or so percentile can have on the equity of the school finance structure. Use the simulation to view the graph of the GTB results.

Although the GTB is focused on providing equal tax bases and not equal spending, it is nevertheless effective in helping to reduce overall revenue-per-pupil disparities, as the horizontal equity statistics indicate. This impact on closing spending gaps occurs because the GTB raises the effective tax base in low-wealth districts that in the sample have above-average tax rates. Therefore, when a GTB program is implemented, these districts qualify for substantial new amounts of state aid—due both to their low wealth and their high tax rates—and enables them to both increase their school spending (thus reducing expenditure per-pupil disparities) and reduce their tax rates to more average levels. In short, while a GTB allows for differences in spending based on tax effort, when implemented in many states, it also reduces overall revenue-per-pupil disparities.

The data in Figure 5.10 reveal several other aspects of this GTB as well as of the sample districts before application of the GTB. First, though the GTB covers 94 percent of the students, it only increases aid for 10 of the 20 districts (i.e., districts 1–10).[15] In the real world, enacting such a school finance program that at best would provide "hold harmless" aid for 50 percent of all districts would be very difficult to enact politically.

Put another way, even though 7 of the 10 districts are eligible for some state aid, only 10 districts would be eligible for greater amounts of state aid, or put differently, 7 of the districts eligible for at least some GTB aid would receive less state aid than under the old structure used by the sample state. Thus, fully half the districts would lose some or all of their state aid.

---

[15]Recall that the fiscal response model built into the simulation increases the local property tax rate to a level where local funds replace lost state funds for state-aid "losers," and increases expenditures and reduces the tax rate each by half the amount of the state-aid increase for state-aid "winners."

Guaranteed Tax Base (GTB)

Adequacy Level	$	5,350.00
	Guaranteed Tax Base	$138,000.00
Pupil Weights	no	
Disabled	—	
Limited English	—	
Low Income	—	

District	Pupils	Property Value per Pupil ($)	Old Property Tax Rate (Mills)	New Property Tax Rate (Mills)	Change in Property Tax Rate (Mills)	Old Local Revenue per Pupil ($)	New Local Revenue per Pupil ($)	Change in Local Revenue per Pupil ($)	New State Revenue per Pupil ($)	Change in State Revenue per Pupil ($)	Total Revenue per Pupil ($)	Change in Total Revenue per Pupil ($)
1	1,290	17,456	39.64	32.43	(7.21)	692	566	(126)	3,909	1,121	4,475	995
2	5,648	25,879	38.50	32.37	(6.13)	996	838	(159)	3,629	1,005	4,466	847
3	1,678	31,569	37.15	32.01	(5.14)	1,173	1,010	(162)	3,407	871	4,417	709
4	256	35,698	36.20	31.69	(4.51)	1,292	1,131	(161)	3,242	783	4,374	622
5	10,256	40,258	35.91	31.89	(4.02)	1,446	1,284	(162)	3,117	716	4,401	554
6	956	43,621	35.74	32.19	(3.55)	1,559	1,404	(155)	3,038	645	4,442	490
7	4,689	49,875	34.89	32.29	(2.60)	1,740	1,611	(129)	2,846	488	4,457	358
8	1,656	55,556	34.17	32.20	(1.97)	1,898	1,789	(110)	2,655	382	4,443	272
9	8,954	61,254	33.73	32.39	(1.34)	2,066	1,984	(82)	2,486	267	4,470	185
10	1,488	70,569	33.44	32.84	(0.59)	2,360	2,318	(42)	2,215	124	4,532	82
11	2,416	78,952	33.23	34.09	0.86	2,624	2,691	68	2,013	(68)	4,704	0
12	5,891	86,321	32.89	35.29	2.40	2,839	3,046	207	1,824	(207)	4,870	0
13	2,600	94,387	32.10	36.23	4.13	3,030	3,419	390	1,580	(390)	4,999	0
14	15,489	102,687	31.32	37.34	6.02	3,216	3,835	619	1,319	(619)	5,154	0
15	2,308	112,358	30.85	38.94	8.09	3,466	4,375	909	999	(909)	5,374	0
16	2,712	125,897	30.50	40.32	9.82	3,840	5,076	1,236	488	(1,236)	5,564	0
17	30,256	136,527	30.05	40.79	10.75	4,102	5,570	1,467	60	(1,467)	5,630	0
18	2,056	156,325	28.63	37.74	9.11	4,476	5,899	1,424	0	(1,424)	5,899	0
19	3,121	198,564	27.42	33.11	5.69	5,445	6,575	1,130	0	(1,130)	6,575	0
20	1,523	278,052	25.50	27.07	1.57	7,090	7,527	437	0	(437)	7,527	0
Weighted Average		97,831	32.34	36.17	3.83	3,028	3,638	610	1,481	-444	5,119	166
Weighted Std. Dev.		48,514	2.91	3.76	6.04	1,269	1,871	674	1,279	882	638	272
Median		102,687	31.32	37.34	6.02	3,216	3,835	619	1,319	-619	5,154	0

(continued)

FIGURE 5.10 Guaranteed Tax Base (GTB)

Equity Measures	
Horizontal Equity	
Range	$3,153
Restricted Range	2,173
Federal Range Ratio	0.494
Coef. of Variation	0.125
Gini Coefficient	0.066
McLoone Index	0.866
Verstegen Index	1.086
Fiscal Neutrality	
Correlation	0.984
Elasticity	0.246
Adequacy	
Odden-Picus	0.926

Totals			
Category	**Amount**	**Percent**	**Change from Base Amount**
Local Revenue	382,907,400	71.07%	64,180,192
State Revenue	155,839,458	28.93%	(46,700,708)
Total Revenue	538,746,858		17,479,484
Pupils	105,243		

Winners and Losers			
Category	Winners	Losers	No change
State Aid	10	10	0
Total Revenue	10	0	10

FIGURE 5.10 Guaranteed Tax Base (GTB) (*continued*)

These realities would reduce the political chances of having such a program legislatively enacted. Though the old school finance program arguably allocated too much aid to districts high in property wealth per pupil, and a GTB at the 94th percentile would seemingly be good enough on an ex ante basis, these actual results suggest that the politics of enactment in the sample state would be difficult.

These features of the impact of a relatively high GTB are not dissimilar to the impact of such a GTB in many states today. The reason is that most states allocate some general state aid in sufficiently large amounts to even the wealthiest districts, so that a transition to a GTB—even at a reasonably high level—becomes problematic politically. Though a "hold harmless" provision would blunt the loss of state aid, such an overall program would mean that for most districts their general state aid would not increase in the short to medium run, an unappealing scenario. These realities also mean that unless states that want to enact a GTB program enact one soon, the transition problems of the level of state general aid provided to the highest-wealth districts could worsen over time, making it more complicated to enact a high-level GTB program.

These dilemmas for a GTB are portrayed more drastically for a GTB at $98,000, roughly the statewide average property value per pupil and just above the wealth of district 13, and the wealth of the district that includes 45 percent of the students. (Readers should run this GTB on the simulation and review the results.) Under this program, 18 of the 20 districts will lose state aid, and state aid itself will drop by almost two-thirds. This level of GTB, which is higher than the GTB component of the general aid formula in most states,[16] would not likely be politically feasible in the sample state.

A GTB of $160,000, on the other hand, which guarantees a per-pupil property value higher than 18 of the 20 districts, and districts that enroll over 95 percent of the students, would push the state role to 39 percent, would lower the coefficient of variation to just 0.094 and the wealth elasticity to only 0.194, and would increase the Adequacy Index to 0.955. These are substantial impacts.

For such a high-level GTB, however, the simulation probably indicates a higher expenditure per-pupil level for the lower-wealth districts than might occur in practice. It would be unlikely for districts to increase local spending by nearly 50 percent, as the current simulation response model assumes. With a GTB at this high a level, such districts probably would use more than half their state-aid increase to reduce property tax rates; moreover, as discussed in Chapter 1, some low-wealth districts might use most of their state-aid increases for property tax relief rather than expenditure increases. Again, readers should run this GTB using the simulation and review the results, as well as the scatter plot. Indeed, readers should run GTB programs in between $98,000 and $160,000 to find a level that reduces some of the political minuses of the former, but is less costly than the latter.

In summary, guaranteed tax base school finance formulas are relatively simple school finance structures that address a primary structural problem of local financing of schools: unequal access to a school tax base. The GTB remedies this defect by making the tax base equal to the GTB for all districts with a property value per pupil below the

---

[16]Most state GTB programs guarantee the wealth of the district for which the cumulative percent of students is at some level below the 66th percentile.

GTB. The primary policy question for a GTB is the level at which to set the GTB; courts likely would require the GTB to be set at a level to provide "substantial" equal access to a school property tax base. This would equal the level of the district for which the cumulative percentage of students in that district (and all districts with lower property value per pupil) is at or close to the 90th percentile.

GTB programs reflect the value of choice and local control. Thus, GTB programs allow for differences in per-pupil spending. While spending differences are allowed, they are caused not by differences in property value per pupil but by differences in tax effort: The higher the tax effort, the higher the expenditure per pupil. For policymakers and educators who hold the horizontal equity principle for students above local choice, the GTB program is not the appropriate school finance program.

Further, although GTB programs are fiscal-capacity equalizing, the level of state aid is determined both by the GTB level, set by state policy, and by local property tax rates, set by local policy. Thus, the amount of state aid is not under the complete control of state policymakers. This feature has made several states skittish about enacting a GTB program, even though they may prefer it as the general-aid structure. States that have enacted GTB programs, however, have devised several phase-in mechanisms that allow them to control the level of state aid, and have found that over time, local tax rates settle into a predictable pattern that makes forecasting the level of state-aid appropriations no more difficult than for other types of formulas, all of which have variables that require both art and science for predicting and thus determining state-aid needs.

Finally, although guaranteed tax base programs are the most straightforward form of school-aid formulas designed to equalize the tax base, they often do not accomplish their objective of eliminating the link between spending and wealth, especially for the "new" type of school finance program. Because of the vagaries of local behavior, moreover, they often lead to overall rising education expenditures (because they lower the local cost of spending on education) and lead to the new type of school finance problem: high expenditures, high tax rates, and high property wealth per pupil versus low expenditures, low tax rates, and low property wealth per pupil.

It should be noted that many economists predicted these impacts (Feldstein, 1975; Ladd, 1975, and more recently, Reschovsky, 1994). GTB programs lower the local cost, or "price" of spending on education. Rather than just tapping the local tax base at a high tax rate to spend an extra $100 per pupil, the district can tap the GTB and increase that amount of spending at a much lower tax rate. When prices are lowered for desired commodities, such as education, people usually buy more of that commodity. So economic theory would predict higher overall education spending with a high-level GTB program. Secondly, research showed that the demand elasticity for education was often low in low-property-wealth districts, which were also typically low in average household income, and high in higher-property-wealth, higher-household-income districts, such as metropolitan suburban districts. Thus, these economists predicted that lower-wealth districts would decide not to raise relative spending very much while the higher-wealth districts would decide just the opposite.

To verify these ostensibly deleterious elements of GTB programs, Odden (1998) simulated pure forms of GTB programs for the three "new" school finance problem states discussed in Chapter 1—Illinois, Missouri, and Wisconsin—by setting the GTB at the 95th percentile of property wealth per pupil and providing GTB aid for all levels of spending. All of the equity statistics worsened; spending disparities widened and the relationship between spending and property wealth strengthened. More-generous GTB programs were not what these states needed to improve fiscal equity. We discuss this issue further in Chapter 7.

Combination Foundation and Guaranteed Tax Base Programs

States also have enacted combination school finance formulas. These two-tier plans usually include two different school finance formulas in the overall approach to providing general education aid through a fiscal-capacity equalizing program. One type of formula is used for the base, or tier-one program, and another type of formula is used for spending above the base, or tier-two program.

Missouri has had a two-tiered, combination foundation and guaranteed tax base program since the late 1970s. Similar to many states, Missouri had a minimum foundation program before it underwent a school finance reform in 1977. The program, which was enacted in 1977 and then updated in 1993, retained the foundation program to ensure a base spending level, a key feature of a foundation approach. The 1993 bill set the foundation expenditure level at just below the previous year's statewide average expenditure per pupil. For the second tier, the legislature put a GTB program on top, so that districts wanting to spend above the foundation level could have equal extra spending for equal extra tax rates. The 1993 bill set the GTB at the wealth of the district for which, after rank ordering all districts on the basis of property value per pupil, the cumulative percentage of students was 95 percent (i.e., the 95th percentile). The bill was technically written as a GTB at the 95th percentile, with a minimum tax rate that determined the foundation expenditure base (i.e., the GTB was also the "zero-aid" district for the foundation portion of the formula). GTB aid was provided for spending up to the 95th percentile of expenditures per pupil.

The combination approach was used for other new school finance formulas established during the early months of 1990. Both Texas and Kentucky, under court order to revise their school finance structures, enacted combination foundation and guaranteed tax base programs. In Texas, the 1989–90 foundation program provided a base spending level of $1,477, equal to about 42 percent of the statewide average expenditure per pupil. The guaranteed tax base program was set at $182,500, the wealth of the district just below the statewide average of $191,300. Texas placed a tax rate cap on the GTB component of the formula, providing GTB aid for just an extra 3.6 mills above the foundation required tax rate, or for an extra $657 per pupil. Districts were also allowed to levy higher tax rates, for which revenues were derived solely from the local tax base.

Kentucky enacted a similar type of combination program (see Picus, Odden, and Fermanich, 2001). The 1989–90 foundation base was set at $2,305, which was about 77 percent of the statewide average. Kentucky also put a GTB on top of the foundation program, setting it at about 150 percent of the statewide average. This GTB program, however, included two tiers, each with its own type of tax rate cap. The first tier limited the additional tax rate beyond which districts could not receive GTB aid, but it gave school boards the flexibility to increase spending (and thus the local tax rate) by 15 percent over the foundation base and still receive GTB aid. In addition, taxpayers could increase spending by a local vote (and thus the local tax rate) by another 15 percent but would not be eligible for GTB aid for this second 15 percent spending boost. Thus, expenditures above the foundation base are limited to an additional 30 percent, half of which is fiscal-capacity equalized by a GTB.

This combination approach merges the best features of the foundation and GTB programs and simultaneously remedies a major defect of each. The foundation portion of the combined program first ensures a base spending level, usually above what had been a minimum level. This base spending level, a key feature of foundation programs, is financed with a combination of local and state funds. The spending base remedies a possible shortcoming of pure GTB programs that do not require a minimum spending level.

The GTB portion of the combined program ensures equal education spending per pupil for equal tax rates above the foundation-required tax rate. This component remedies a defect of a minimum foundation program: unequalized spending above the foundation base.

The Combination Foundation and GTB Formula.   The formula for calculating the foundation portion of the combination program is the same as that for the regular foundation program:

$$SFAPP = FRPP - (RTR \times PVPP),$$

where

$$SFAPP = \text{state foundation aid per pupil,}$$
$$FRPP = \text{foundation expenditure revenue per pupil,}$$
$$RTR = \text{the local required tax rate, and}$$
$$PVPP = \text{local property value per pupil.}$$

Total foundation state aid would be:

$$TFSA = SFAPP \times Pupils,$$

where

$$TFSA = \text{total foundation state aid,}$$
$$SFAPP = \text{state foundation aid per pupil, and}$$
$$Pupils = \text{the number of students in the school district.}$$

For the GTB portion, state aid would be:

$$SGTBAPP = (DTR - RTR) \times (GTB - PVPP),$$

where

$$SGTBAPP = \text{state guaranteed tax base aid per pupil,}$$
$$DTR = \text{the local district property tax rate,}$$

RTR = the required tax base for the foundation program
(GTB aid is provided only for tax rates above the foundation required tax rate),
GTB = the tax rate guaranteed by the state,
in thousand dollars of property value per pupil, and
PVPP = the local district property value per pupil.

Total GTB state aid, therefore, is:

$$TGTBSA = SGTBAPP \text{ x Pupils}$$

where

TGTBSA = total guaranteed tax base state aid,
SGTBAPP = state-guaranteed tax base aid per pupil from the above formula, and
Pupils = the number of students in the school district.

Total state general aid for the combination program, therefore, would be:

$$TSA = TFSA + TGTBSA.$$

Combination Foundation and GTB Program Policy Issues.   A combination foundation and GTB program can be a fairly attractive package. Both components of the program require local matching funds and provide for fiscal capacity equalization. A base spending level is guaranteed. The ability to spend above the base is possible on an equal basis for rich and poor districts alike, thus providing a fiscally neutral system, at least on an ex ante basis. And two American values—concern for the bottom half and local choice—are tied together in a single general aid program.

The downside of the GTB portion of the combination program is that it allows for different spending levels and thus does not conform to the horizontal equity principle for students. But the fact is that this value conflicts with the value of local choice, so that both values cannot be satisfied by any one formula. The combination foundation-GTB program is about the closest a school finance formula can come to adhering to both of these values. There is an expenditure equality dimension, in terms of a base program that is mandated for all students. But there is local choice to spend above this base. If a state enacted a cap on the level of extra expenditures, such as the 30 percent cap in Kentucky, the program might be more appealing to those who champion horizontal equity for children.

At the same time, as just discussed, the second-tier GTB has turned out to function as an incentive to spend more, and primarily by above-average-wealth, suburban districts. As a result, the two-tier system, just like an unbridled GTB program, creates a system that generally produces the "new" school finance problem: low-spending, low-tax-rate and low-wealth districts versus high-spending, high-tax-rate, and high (or above-average) wealth districts, which some would not consider to be a fair system.

Figure 5.11 depicts graphically how a combination foundation-GTB program works. The lowest horizontal line shows that the minimum revenues per pupil are the

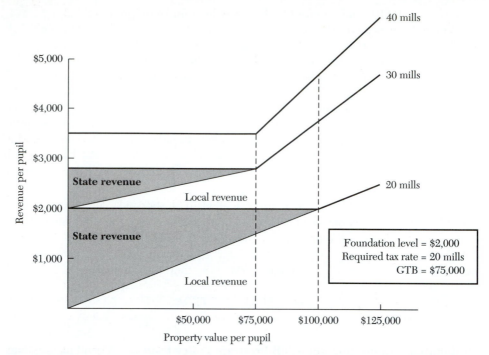

FIGURE 5.11   Graphical Representation of the Impact of a Combination Foundation and Guaranteed Tax Base Program

foundation expenditure level of $2,000. The upper two horizontal lines reflect the impact of a GTB at $75,000 for total tax rates of 30 and 40 mills (with 20 mills being the required tax rate for the foundation portion of the program). Note that the zero-aid district level for the foundation portion of the program is $100,000 and, obviously, $75,000 for the GTB portion of the program. For each tax-rate level, the revenue-per-pupil line is initially horizontal and then slopes upward only beyond the level of the zero-aid district, indicating that districts with a property value per pupil above this level will raise more per pupil than is provided even by the GTB.

There are several issues that need to be addressed with a combination foundation-GTB program. The first two are the general policy targets of:

1. The level of base spending in the foundation program, and
2. The level of the GTB.

The same considerations raised here for each program individually can be applied to the combination program. States might set the base expenditure at a level sufficiently high for districts, on average, to provide an adequate education program. This type of policy target could become a new rationale for how high the base spending in state foundation programs should be in the future. Though not exactly stated in its new legislation, Kentucky sought to take this approach in its 1990 school finance reform.

For ex ante fiscal neutrality, the GTB also needs to be set at a relatively high level, such as the 90th percentile or property wealth per pupil. On the other hand, there may be some flexibility for the GTB level. For example, if the base spending level is set high enough for the average student to meet ambitious student-achievement objectives, the state might want to limit local add-ons, to 30 percent as Kentucky has done, or even to a smaller amount. At this point, since all students on average have been funded for an education program designed to meet some new high-performance level, one could argue that local add-ons are merely an element of local choice on how to spend discretionary income. Thus, a GTB at just the statewide average, or the 50th percentile, which would focus the GTB on equal access to a tax base just for the bottom half, might be viewed as sufficient. How these policy dilemmas will play out in different states remains to be seen.

The key conceptual point in the preceding two paragraphs is that there is potentially an implicit trade-off between the level of the foundation base spending and the level of the GTB. If the base spending level is high enough to teach most students to meet bold new achievement levels, the base level will in itself require new education funds and substantially raise school spending for all students. Fewer districts will feel they need to spend above the base. Thus, because GTB-aided spending becomes much more a matter of discretionary spending, the GTB level can be focused on districts with below-average spending. Extra spending could even be capped, since spending levels would already be at much higher levels.

On the other hand, if the base spending level is much lower, then the GTB component becomes a much larger portion of the overall program, and its level becomes much more critical to the fiscal equity impact of the system. If the base spending level is low, more districts—undoubtedly more than half the districts—would want to spend more. Thus, local add-ons become a larger part of the overall system. In order to make the system fiscally neutral, the GTB would have to be set at a high level, such as the 90th percentile.

There is a plausible, substantive rationale for having a lower foundation base spending level and a higher GTB level. The substantive argument concerns differences in educational needs and costs between metropolitan (urban and suburban) and non-metropolitan (rural) districts. In most states, foundation expenditure per-pupil levels are too low for most districts to provide an adequate education program. But often, a modest increase in the foundation level would be sufficient to allow most nonmetropolitan school districts to provide an adequate education program.

But raising the foundation expenditure to a level that would be sufficient for metropolitan districts, which usually face educational prices that are from 10 to 20 percent higher than those in nonmetropolitan districts, is usually too expensive for the state. Moreover, raising the foundation expenditure to a level that would allow metropolitan districts to provide an adequate program could, then, also allow nonmetropolitan districts to provide a higher-level quality program than they need. Indeed, it might provide so much money for rural districts that some local education leaders and their legislatures would argue that excessive funds were being allocated to schools.

Though the divergence between the resource needs of urban and rural districts should not be overstated, this is an issue that arises in nearly all states that seek to raise the foundation base to a level sufficient to provide an adequate education program. In states with the most ambitious policymakers, the level usually becomes more than rural districts need for adequacy and less than urban districts need, a compromise that is not efficient for either.

However, this dilemma could be remedied by setting the base at an adequate level for the lowest cost districts and then adjusting it by a price index (Chambers, 1981, 1995; Fowler and Monk, 2001; McMahon, 1994; Monk and Walker, 1991) for districts facing higher costs. But, an education price index, though technically straightforward to develop, has only been enacted in a few states, such as Texas and Ohio. Education price indices are discussed further in Chapter 6.

Fiscal Equity Impacts of Combination Foundation and GTB Programs.   Figure 5.12 shows a combination program with the foundation set at the median, the required tax rate at the median, and the GTB add-on at about the 94th percentile. This is a fairly generous combination, two-tier school finance system.

For this simulated program, both local and state revenues increase. Local revenues increase in the wealthier districts and decrease in the poorer districts. The state role rises to nearly 41 percent. The impact on equity and adequacy is quite impressive: The coefficient of variation is below 10 percent, the McLoone Index is above 95 percent, the Verstegen Index is just 104.4 percent, and the Adequacy Index is 99 percent. These positive impacts are a result in part of the generous parameters of the program, simulated as well as the fact that the base data represent the typical school finance problem. Readers should run additional combination simulations that are somewhat less generous than the one depicted in Figure 5.12.

At the same time, combination foundation-GTB programs might not be a desired approach for states that represent the "new" school finance problem such as Illinois, Missouri, New York, and Wisconsin. Odden (1998) analyzed the results of adding a second-tier, 90/90 GTB to the adequate foundation program that was defined as the median expenditure level. The GTB was set at the 90th percentile of district wealth and provided aid to districts spending up to the 90th percentile of expenditures per pupil. He found that nearly all of the equity statistics worsen. Moreover, the extra state cost was considerable. Because these states represent the newer version of fiscal disparities (higher spending associated with higher tax rates, both attributes associated with higher wealth), the equity results are not surprising.

For states with these types of problems, the results show that GTB programs, even on top of adequate foundation spending levels, simply worsen fiscal equity. The results suggest that GTB school finance elements should probably not be a primary part of school finance systems for such states. Nevertheless, many school finance experts, including these authors in the first edition of this book (Odden and Picus, 1992) for years recommended second-tier GTB programs on top of foundation programs. Given the negative impact on fiscal equity as well as the considerable costs of such additions, such recommendations should be viewed skeptically in the future. Indeed, since a GTB simply assists districts in spending above an adequate level, one could argue that such a program, whatever its effects on fiscal equity, is beyond the state interest in school finance. The adequate spending base and the adjustments for special needs discussed in the next chapter largely fulfill the state interest.

Combination Program

Adequacy Level	$	5,350.00

Foundation Level	$5,154.00
Required Tax Rate	31.32

Pupil Weights	
Disabled	no
Limited English	—
Low Income	—

GTB	—
GTB Rate Cap Above	$138,000.00
Foundation Tax Rate	99

District	Pupils	Property Value per Pupil ($)	Old Property Tax Rate (Mills)	New Property Tax Rate (Mills)	Change in Property Tax Rate (Mills)	Old Local Revenue per Pupil ($)	New Local Revenue per Pupil ($)	Change in Local Revenue per Pupil ($)	New State Foundation Revenue per Pupil ($)	New State GTB Revenue per Pupil ($)	Change in State Revenue per Pupil ($)	Total Revenue per Pupil ($)	Change in Total Revenue per Pupil ($)
1	1,290	17,456	39.64	35.48	(4.16)	692	619	(73)	4,607	501	2,321	5,728	2,248
2	5,648	25,879	38.50	34.91	(3.59)	996	903	(93)	4,343	403	2,123	5,649	2,030
3	1,678	31,569	37.15	34.23	(2.91)	1,173	1,081	(92)	4,165	310	1,940	5,556	1,848
4	256	35,698	36.20	33.76	(2.44)	1,292	1,205	(87)	4,036	250	1,826	5,491	1,739
5	10,256	40,258	35.91	33.62	(2.30)	1,446	1,353	(92)	3,893	224	1,716	5,471	1,624
6	956	43,621	35.74	33.53	(2.21)	1,559	1,463	(96)	3,788	209	1,603	5,459	1,507
7	4,689	49,875	34.89	33.11	(1.79)	1,740	1,651	(89)	3,592	157	1,391	5,400	1,302
8	1,656	55,556	34.17	32.75	(1.43)	1,898	1,819	(79)	3,414	118	1,259	5,351	1,179
9	8,954	61,254	33.73	32.53	(1.21)	2,066	1,992	(74)	3,236	92	1,110	5,320	1,036
10	1,488	70,569	33.44	32.38	(1.06)	2,360	2,285	(75)	2,944	71	924	5,300	850
11	2,416	78,952	33.23	32.28	(0.95)	2,624	2,548	(75)	2,681	56	657	5,286	582
12	5,891	86,321	32.89	32.11	(0.78)	2,839	2,771	(68)	2,450	41	460	5,262	392
13	2,600	94,387	32.10	31.71	(0.39)	3,030	2,993	(37)	2,198	17	245	5,208	209
14	15,489	102,687	31.32	31.32	0.00	3,216	3,216	0	1,938	0	0	5,154	0
15	2,308	112,358	30.85	32.91	2.06	3,466	3,698	232	1,635	41	(232)	5,374	0
16	2,712	125,897	30.50	34.29	3.79	3,840	4,317	477	1,211	36	(477)	5,564	0
17	30,256	136,527	30.05	34.77	4.72	4,102	4,747	644	878	5	(644)	5,630	0
18	2,056	156,325	28.63	36.09	7.46	4,476	5,641	1,166	258	0	(1,166)	5,899	0
19	3,121	198,564	27.42	33.11	5.69	5,445	6,575	1,130	0	0	(1,130)	6,575	0
20	1,523	278,052	25.50	27.07	1.57	7,090	7,527	437	0	0	(437)	7,527	0
Weighted Average		97,831	32.34	33.34	1.00	3,028	3,257	229	2,173	82	331	5,512	559
Weighted Std. Dev.		48,514	2.91	1.55	3.15	1,269	1,596	380	1,318	120	1,011	363	478
Median		102,687	31.32	31.32	0.00	3,216	3,216	0	1,938	0	0	5,471	0

(continued)

FIGURE 5.12 Combination Program

Totals

Category	Amount	Percent	Change from Base Amount
Local Revenue	342,810,303	59.09%	24,083,095
State Revenue	237,324,515	40.91%	34,784,349
Total Revenue	580,134,818		58,867,444
Pupils	105,243		

Winners and Losers

Category	Winners	Losers	No change
State Aid	14	6	0
Total Revenue	14	6	0

Equity Measures

Horizontal Equity	
Range	$2,373
Restricted Range	1,367
Federal Range Ratio	0.262
Coef. of Variation	0.066
Gini Coefficient	0.029
McLoone Index	0.962
Verstegen Index	1.044
Fiscal Neutrality	
Correlation	0.768
Elasticity	0.115
Adequacy	
Odden-Picus	0.992

FIGURE 5.12   Combination Program (*continued*)

Full-State-Funding and State-Determined Spending Programs

The final category of school funding programs has generally been referred to as full state funding. A full-state-funding program implements the equality value, or horizontal equity, for students by simply setting an equal expenditure per-pupil level for all districts. Districts cannot spend less than this amount nor can they spend more. For this reason, if a state wants to implement the horizontal equity principle for students (i.e., a program that provides for equal spending), a full-state-funding program is the only choice.

As the name of the program connotes, in the pure form, such a program is fully funded by state revenues, which is the case in Hawaii. But that is not a necessary characteristic of such a program. The key characteristic is that a "full-state-funding" program requires equal spending per pupil in all districts. The revenues, however, could be derived from a combination of state revenues and local property tax revenues. The state could require a uniform statewide property tax rate for schools and set state aid as the difference between what that would raise and the total revenues needed to provide the equal spending level. This has been the approach taken by New Mexico for years and also the approach of the 1998 school finance reform in Vermont. California has a version of full state funding called a revenue limit program. The state sets a base spending per-pupil level for each district and finances it with a combination of state and local property tax revenues. It is conceptually equivalent to a full-state-funding program.

Likewise, Florida has a different approach that makes the system function almost like a full-state-funding program, financed with a combination of state and local revenues. Florida has a combination foundation and GTB program, but the GTB program has an absolute maximum tax-rate cap. Since most districts are at the cap, and since the GTB is higher than the wealth of most districts, the structure comes close to being the equivalent of a full-state-funding program.

In this book, full state funding is used to indicate a school finance program that requires equal per-pupil spending across all school districts. The program can be financed solely with state funds, but also can be financed with a combination of state and local funds, usually property tax revenues. For our purposes, the defining element of a full-state-funding program is that districts cannot spend less or more than the level set by the state, thereby satisfying the horizontal equity principle.

3. SUMMARY

This chapter first showed that school financing in the United States represents a fiscal federalism approach: all three levels of government fund schools—local school districts as well as states and the federal government. This approach to funding public K–12 education provides several advantages: fiscal capacity equalization, equity in the provision of educational services, efficiency in producing educational results, and local choice for the level and quality of school services.

The second part of the chapter identified five different types of school funding formulas—flat grants, foundation, guaranteed tax base, combination foundation-GTB, and full-state-funding programs. For each of the first four, the chapter explained how the formula worked, the values it represented, the decisions that must be made in designing the formula, and provided examples of the effects of various designs for each formula. The discussion showed that for most formulas, educational, equity, fiscal, and political goals must be balanced in designing viable school finance formulas in order to get them enacted into law. Although equity and adequacy are prime goals, their costs and fiscal impacts play crucial roles in whether they can be accepted politically.

4. SUGGESTED PROBLEMS

Study Group Exercises

Problems 5.1, 5.2, and 5.3 should be considered as study group exercises using the 20-district simulation sample (see www.mhhe.com/odden3e). These problems raise the interrelated issues of school finance equity goals; state, local, and total costs; and the particular interests of districts with below-average and above-average property wealth per pupil.

Problem 5.1   Divide yourselves into groups of one, two, or three so that each group represents one of the school districts in the 20-district sample. With your group, do the following:

First, design a foundation program with an increased state cost of $25 million that gives your district the greatest increase in state aid. Discuss why your plan should be the one proposed to the legislature, and argue on the basis of the impacts of your program on school finance equity and adequacy.

Second, design a foundation program with an increased state cost of $25 million that you feel is best for your particular district *and* that you think would garner two-thirds support of your classmates, or of the legislature that would be deliberating such a proposed change.

Compare the different foundation programs.

Problem 5.2   Divide yourselves into two groups. Members of group 1 represent superintendents from districts low in property value per pupil (i.e., districts 1–10). Members of group 2 represent superintendents from districts high in property value per pupil (i.e., districts 11–20). You could vary the districts in the different groups; there does not have to be 10 districts in each group. With your group, do the following:

Simulate a combination foundation-GTB program with total extra costs at $45 million (i.e., the sum of increased state and local revenues).

For this exercise, you will need to consider school finance equity and adequacy as well as political feasibility. You must decide whether your interest is better served by a relatively low foundation program with a relatively high GTB or a relatively high foundation program and a modest GTB, or something in between, and must explain why.

Compare the different designs. Some should have large increases in state aid combined with large decreases in local revenues for a total revenue increase of $45 million. Others should have increased state costs much closer to the $45 million and much less property tax relief.

Problem 5.3   Again divide yourselves into groups—of two, three, or four depending on the size of the study group—representing different types of districts, below-average wealth, average wealth, and above-average wealth. With your group, do the following:

Design a school finance program—foundation, GTB, or combination foundation-GTB—that improves both horizontal equity and adequacy. Be sure to identify all the key formula and policy parameters, and have clear equity goals.

Be sure to argue the merits of your proposals on equity, adequacy, and cost grounds. At the end, the entire study group votes on the different proposals presented, keeping in mind that the collective group represents taxpayers as well as the education community. The vote should be on one proposal.

Individual Exercises

Problem 5.4   Assume that the base data for the 20-district sample on the *School Finance* simulation represents the condition of school finance in your state. A taxpayer rights group has conducted an analysis of that system, and based on that analysis have sued in state court arguing that school spending levels are a function of district wealth. They have asked the court to invalidate the state's funding structure. You are the chief of staff of the state legislature's school finance committee. In analyzing a printout of the base data from the simulation, you see that per-pupil revenue ranges from $3,480 to $7,527, with a tax rate in the lowest revenue district of 39.64 mills and 25.5 mills in the highest revenue district. The state share of total educational revenue is under 40 percent. Moreover, you note that the correlation of revenue and wealth per pupil is 0.991, and the wealth elasticity is far above 0.10. Looking carefully at a graph of revenue versus wealth per pupil for the base data, you conclude there is substantial likelihood the court will invalidate the state finance structure.

Additionally, a number of years ago, the state's voters approved an expenditure limitation. As a result, the state is unlikely to have more than $50 million in additional funds to devote to education next year.

Using the *School Finance* simulation, design a school finance foundation program that reduces the correlation between wealth and revenue, without increasing state spending by more than $50 million. Experiment with different combinations of foundation level and required levy effort. Experiment with combinations of high and low foundation levels and high and low RTRs. Find more than one foundation level/RTR combination that costs the state $50 million. Identify different foundation programs at this state cost that benefit poorer districts more than wealthy districts, and then identify foundation programs that spread the additional $50 million to most districts. Once you have three or four possible options, answer each of these questions:

1. How do each of these combinations meet the fiscal neutrality criteria that might be used in the lawsuit?
2. What impact does each of these options have on the horizontal equity of the system?
3. How does total revenue for education change under each of these options? How does the state's share of total revenue change?

4. Which foundation program option would you recommend to the legislature? Why?
5. How will you address legislative questions about districts that gained and lost state aid?
6. If the state suddenly found that it could devote $60 million to education next year rather than $50 million, how would you change your recommendations?

Problem 5.5   Using the same information as presented in Problem 5.4, relax the restriction that you must use a foundation program to design a new school finance system. Experiment with the GTB option, and find a model that meets the $50 million state spending-increase limitation. How does this model compare with the foundation program you recommended to the legislature in Problem 5.1? Specifically:

1. How does total state spending change under the GTB compared with the foundation program?
2. How do local district tax rates compare?
3. Are there more winners or losers under the GTB? How does the magnitude of each district's gain or loss in state aid vary between the two options?
4. Which model, the GTB or foundation program, does a better job of minimizing the relationship between wealth and revenue?
5. Which of the two models better meets horizontal equity standards?
6. How does the state's share of total educational revenue compare between the two models?
7. Which model would you recommend to the legislature? Describe the trade-offs that policymakers will have to make in choosing one option over the other.
8. How does your analysis change if there is $60 million available for education instead of $50 million?

Problem 5.6   A number of states have opted to use a two-tier program, relying on a foundation program to provide a base level of revenue for all districts, and a GTB to equalize district decisions to supplement that base. Using the same $50 million limitation, design a combination (two-tier) school finance system for your state. How does this model compare to the two preceding models? What would you now recommend to the legislature? Why? What happens if the state is willing to increase its commitment to $60 million?

Summary Tables

For all proposals, have students create summary tables to display the results of your various simulations. For foundation programs, rank them from lowest to highest foundation level (or highest to lowest). The following indicates the type of data to include:

Simulation	Flat Grant	Foundation Level	Required Tax Rate	Zero Aid District	GTB	Adequacy Expenditure Level	Number of State Aid Winners/Losers
Base Data							
1	4,000	—	—	—	—	$5,350	20/0
2	—	$5,154	31.32	$164,559	—	5,350	14/6
3	—	—	—	138,000	$138,000	5,350	10/10
4	—	5,154	31.32	164,559	138,000	5,350	16/0

Simulation	Change in Local $ (in Millions)	Change in State $ (in Millions)	Change in Total $ (in Millions)	Coefficient of Variation	McLoone/Verstegen Index	Wealth Elasticity	Odden-Picus Adequacy Index
Base Data	—	—	—	0.170	0.810/1.086	0.324	0.895
1	0	$218.4	$218.4	0.181	0.814/1.107	0.347	0.994
2	$24.4	26.1	50.6	0.030	0.992/1.070	0.146	0.985
3	64.2	−46.7	17.5	0.125	0.881/1.086	0.246	0.926
4	24.1	34.8	58.9	0.066	0.962/1.044	0.115	0.99

Adjustments for Student Needs, Education Level, Scale Economies, and Price

The discussion of the various school finance formulas in Chapter 5 implicitly assumed uniformity along several dimensions that, in the real world, do not hold. For example, some students have special needs and require additional educational services above those provided through state equalization aid and local, general-fund resources. Further, some argue that it is wise to spend more on students at different education levels. Traditionally, many states have spent more on secondary students, although there is an increasing trend to spend more on students in kindergarten through grade 3. Many states still have small schools that experience diseconomies of scale, such as those located in isolated rural areas. Finally, the price of purchasing educational goods varies across districts in a state, especially in large, diverse states such as California, Florida, New York, and Texas.

The next four sections of this chapter discuss each of the preceding four types of vertical equity adjustments to basic school finance formulas that reflect legitimate reasons for providing unequal resources: special student needs, education level (elementary and secondary), scale economies/diseconomies, and geographic price indices. There are many different ways of determining just how much adjustment is necessary, as well as many different methods of providing those adjustments. The following explores several of these possibilities, raising a number of policy questions in the process.

1. ADJUSTMENTS FOR DIFFERENT PUPIL NEEDS

If different pupil needs that require extra educational resources were evenly distributed across all school districts in a given state, neither special adjustments to regular school finance formulas nor separate categorical programs would be needed. The extra amounts could be included in the spending levels set for the regular program. But, the incidence of different pupil needs is not distributed evenly across all school districts. Students from homes with incomes below the poverty level tend to be concentrated in large, urban districts and in small, typically rural, isolated school districts. Low-income students are much less prevalent in suburban school districts, though numbers are increasing in urban-ring suburbs. Similarly, students for whom English is not the primary language are also not found in equal percentages in all types of school districts; these students also tend to enroll in greater percentages in urban and rural school districts. Nor are students with physical or mental disabilities found in equal concentrations in all school districts; indeed, some suburban school districts that have developed especially effective programs for disabled children see the percentage of such students rise as parents move to that district in order for their child to have access to the outstanding program.

In short, the demographics of students with different types of special educational needs vary from school district to school district. Some districts have a higher concentration of such students than others do. Indeed, some of the largest metropolitan school districts have extraordinarily high percentages of students who need supplemental educational services, approaching 50 percent in the largest districts in the country, such as Chicago, Dallas, Los Angeles, and New York City.

Furthermore, the prices districts face in providing these additional services vary considerably, further intensifying the fiscal burden of appropriately educating students with special needs. Large central cities face the highest prices and usually have the highest concentration of special-needs students. Many rural districts, which generally have lower prices, tend to face high costs for special-needs students because the low incidence dramatically increases the per-pupil costs of the necessary services. For example, if there is only one blind student in a rural school, the cost for providing appropriate services is spread over just that one student, while in more populated areas, the incidence of blindness is typically higher, so that the costs of providing the additional services can be spread over more children.

If states required local districts to provide the necessary supplemental services solely from local funds, they would be placing an extra financial burden on districts that would vary substantially by district. Further, since the incidence of special-needs students is not necessarily related to local fiscal capacity, such a state requirement could worsen school finance inequities. In short, because of demographics and price differences, a state role is necessary to make the provision of extra services for special-needs students fair across all school districts. This section discusses school finance programs to accommodate these vertical equity adjustments that recognize how differences among students require providing more services to meet their special needs.

Development of Special-Needs Programs

There is a rich developmental history associated with the major special-needs programs: (1) compensatory education programs for low-income students (Borman, Stringfield, and Slavin, 2001); (2) language acquisition programs for limited-English-proficient (LEP) students (Hodge, 1981; Slavin and Calderon, 2001); and (3) special-education programs for physical and mentally disabled students (Verstegen, 1999). Both the federal government and the states have been major actors in this history.

Compensatory Education.   The federal involvement in compensatory education began in 1965 with passage of the Elementary and Secondary Education Act (ESEA); Title I provided grants to local school districts on the basis of the number of students from families with incomes below the poverty level. Within districts, schools use the funds to provide extra educational services for low-achieving students. While there is a long history of implementation of this federal compensatory education program, by the early 1980s the program was firmly in place across the country (Odden, 1991).

Further, while in the early years a substantial portion of Title I dollars supplanted, or replaced, local dollars, by the end of the 1970s each Title I dollar produced a minimum of an extra dollar of expenditures on compensatory education programs (Odden, 1988). A series of rules and regulations developed during the 1970s, focused primarily on funds allocation and use, helped produce those fiscal outcomes. "Comparability" required districts to allocate district and state funds equally across schools before allocating Title I dollars. "Supplement and not supplant" required districts to ensure that Title I dollars provided extra educational services and did not merely replace local funds. And "children in greatest need" requirements ensured that only the children with the lowest student achievement were eligible to receive extra educational services, once Title I funds reached the school level.

In 1981, ESEA was replaced with the Education Consolidation and Improvement Act (ECIA), and Title I was replaced by Chapter 1. In 1988, the Hawkins-Stafford School Improvement Amendments made several changes to Chapter 1 with the intent of improving compensatory education programs across the country. During the 1990–91 school year, Chapter 1 provided approximately $5.4 billion to serve close to 5 million children. In 1994, the Improving America's Schools Act was passed, which reauthorized Title I of the ESEA, and changed the name of the program back to Title I. This act represented a shift in federal aid to education, giving new responsibilities to states, districts, and the federal government to ensure quality education for low-income children.

In 2001, the program was again reauthorized by the U.S. Congress and given the name "No Child Left Behind (NCLB)," which was a campaign theme of President George W. Bush. Though funding levels were increased to $13.5 billion for 2001–02, the distribution and funding requirements remained essentially the same. NCLB has become known largely for its new accountability requirements (Linn, Baker, and Betebenner, 2002). The legislation requires states to test all Title I students in grades 3–8 every year, and to document that each child makes "adequate yearly progress" in their academic achievement. Not doing so subjects failing schools to a series of intervention programs and ultimately allows students not making such progress to choose to attend another school or to use their Title I funds to seek private tutoring. Title II of NCLB also consolidated several other federal programs into a single "pot" to be used for a wide array of strategies to improve teacher quality, including professional development and performance pay.

Over the years, Title I stimulated many states to enact their own compensatory education programs. Most state programs were designed to complement the federal program. California and New York were among the first states to enact compensatory education programs. In the early 1980s, nearly 20 states had compensatory education programs in their general-aid formula, with about 10 states distributing the funds on the basis of pupil weights (McGuire, 1982). A mixture of poverty and student-achievement measures determined student eligibility. In 1993–94, the number of states with compensatory education programs and/or compensatory education pupil weights increased to 28, and the number rose to 34 by 1998–99. Table 6.1 shows states' approaches to funding compensatory education.

It is important to keep in mind that while both federal and state compensatory programs provide opportunities for low-achieving students to receive additional educational services, the programs do not establish a legal right to such extra services. The services are available solely because of the federal and state programs.

Bilingual Education. Services for students with limited English proficiency emerged in the mid-1970s primarily after the 1974 *Lau v. Nicholas*[1] case in California. This case was brought in San Francisco where students who did not speak English were immersed in classes taught in English. While the case was filed as an equal protection case, it was decided on the basis of federal antidiscrimination laws. The court held that it was discriminatory to place non-English-speaking students in classes where the language of instruction was English. As a result, districts created bilingual programs that provided instruction in English as a second language and instruction in subject matter classes in the student's native language until they learned enough English to be instructed in English only.

While debates have surrounded various approaches to bilingual education, the key finding of *Lau* is that the language capability of students must be considered in designing an appropriate instructional environment. Today, for example, when one class might have students with many different native languages, bilingual instruction is not possible and a "sheltered English" instructional approach may be an acceptable option (Krashen and Biber, 1988; Slavin and Calderon, 2001). In all instructional approaches, lessons have dual objectives: development of English language as well as content knowledge. The *Lau* decision made access to a language-appropriate classroom environment a legal right of all LEP students.

In 1967, just prior to the *Lau* ruling, Title VII was added to the federal ESEA program. Title VII provided funds for districts to design and implement bilingual education programs. Funds were available on a proposal basis only; districts wrote proposals, and a review process determined which proposals received funding. In 1990, the federal government provided about $189 million for bilingual education. In 1998, the amount of federal monies allocated to bilingual education in the form of instructional services, support services, professional development, and foreign language assistance was approximately $204 million.

The population of LEP students in this country continues to grow. Some estimates say that there are now 50 percent more LEP students than there were in 1990 (Pompa, 1998). Three states—New York, California, and Texas—continue to enroll the majority of LEP students, but populations are growing in Arizona, Florida, Illinois, New Mexico, Oklahoma, and Washington as well.

States began to provide bilingual education programs in part as a response to *Lau,* and many more are finding it necessary today due to the growing numbers just cited. In

[1] 414 U.S. 653.

TABLE 6.1   State Funding Levels of Compensatory Education

State	Statutory Poverty Weight (%)	Total Poverty-Based Funding (in Millions)	Poverty Funding per Low-Income Student	Implicit Poverty Weight (%)
Alabama	N/A	$ 29.0	$ 197	3.1
Alaska	None	0	0	0.0
Arizona	N/A	19.5	121	2.0
Arkansas	N/A	10.0	111	2.0
California	N/A	465.6	403	5.5
Colorado	11.5–30	129.7	1,739	25.8
Connecticut	25	230.3	4,206	37.1
Delaware	None	0	0	0.0
Florida	None	0	0	0.0
Georgia	N/A	34.8	146	1.9
Idaho	None	0	0	0.0
Illinois	7.8–45.6	458.0	1,658	22.3
Indiana	N/A	182.2	1,728	20.1
Iowa	N/A	9.1	196	2.6
Kansas	10	56.5	1,164	15.8
Kentucky	15	200.6	1,642	25.5
Louisiana	17	228.1	1,232	19.7
Maine	None	0	0	0.0
Maryland	25	170.9	2,033	23.5
Massachusetts	34.3–42.4	578.6	5,199	52.5
Michigan	11.5	394.0	1,792	20.3
Minnesota	1–60	225.2	3,075	35.8
Mississippi	5	30.4	237	4.9
Missouri	22	346.2	2,700	36.0
Montana	None	0	0	0.0
Nebraska	1–24.75	38.5	1,215	15.0
Nevada	None	0	0	0.0
New Hampshire	50–100	50.0	3,529	42.6
New Jersey	N/A	543.4	3,732	31.9
New Mexico	9.15	68.6	919	13.8
New York	N/A	1,247.0	2,240	19.6
North Carolina	N/A	176.7	910	14.6
North Dakota	None	0	0	0.0
Ohio	N/A	336.2	1,444	17.2
Oklahoma	25	206.3	1,876	32.1
Oregon	25	97.6	1,380	17.1
Pennsylvania	None	0	0	0.0
Rhode Island	N/A	61.8	2,516	25.4
South Carolina	26	128.7	1,111	16.3

TABLE 6.1   State Funding Levels of Compensatory Education *(continued)*

State	Statutory Poverty Weight (%)	Total Poverty-Based Funding (in Millions)	Poverty Funding per Low-Income Student	Implicit Poverty Weight (%)
South Dakota	None	$ 0	$ 0	0.0
Tennessee	N/A	24.1	155	2.7
Texas	20	1,579.0	1,979	27.7
Utah	N/A	10.5	247	4.6
Vermont	25	3.8	387	3.7
Virginia	2–12	156.0	1,174	15.1
Washington	N/A	70.6	574	7.7
West Virginia	None	0	0	0.0
Wisconsin	N/A	83.4	947	10.0
Wyoming	N/A	2.8	252	3.0
Total		$8,683.6	$1,191	15.1

Source: Carey, 2002.

1975, 13 states had bilingual education programs. By 1993–94, 30 states had bilingual education programs, many of which were allocated on the basis of pupil weights. In 1998–99, 34 states had programs for students whose native language was other than English. Table 6.2 lists states' approaches to funding bilingual education programs.

Special Education.   For years, most states have supported special-education programs for physically and mentally disabled students, at least to some degree (Verstegen, 1999). But during the late 1960s and early 1970s, it became apparent that many disabled students were being prohibited from attending local public schools. Whether because certain disabilities were so severe they required very costly services, or because of blatant discrimination against disabled individuals, these exclusions were challenged on equal protection grounds. One of the first court decisions occurred in the *Pennsylvania Association of Retarded Children* v. *Pennsylvania* (PARC) case in 1972, in which a Pennsylvania court held that district actions prohibiting disabled students from attending local public schools violated the equal protection clause of the U.S. Constitution. This decision spawned several other court cases as well as a spate of new federal and state policy initiatives.

    In 1975, Congress enacted the federal Education for all Handicapped Children Act, P.L. 94-142, now known as the Individuals with Disabilities Education Act (IDEA). This sweeping new federal program essentially made access to a free, appropriate, public education program a *legal right* of all children. In order to receive any federal education dollars, states have to demonstrate that they are providing appropriate special-education services to all disabled children. The services have to meet a series of detailed

TABLE 6.2   States' Approaches to Funding Education for Limited-English-Speaking Children

State	LEP Program Description	State Funding
Alabama	No program or aid reported.	
Alaska	Bilingual programs are included in special needs funding—part of the 20% proportional increment available to all districts that file a special needs plan with the state.	
Arizona	*Extra Weight:* 0.6	
Arkansas	State aid appropriated for students with limited-English-speaking proficiency.	$2,100,000 in 1998–99
California	Proposition 227, passed in 1998, dramatically changed the way schools provide bilingual education in California. It requires that all children be taught in English and eliminates most bilingual classes.	$1,500,000 in 1998–1999
Colorado	The English Language Proficiency Act pays for up to 2 years of additional service to children whose dominant language is not English. Seventy-five percent of the appropriation is to be used for this purpose; the remainder of the appropriation is to be used for bilingual or multilingual students whose dominant language is difficult to determine. These students are to be funded at the greater of $200 or 10% of the statewide average per-pupil operating revenues for the prior year. State funding is not sufficient to meet formula costs; therefore payments to districts are prorated.	$2,600,000 in 1998–1999
Connecticut	State funds to help pay for the bilingual education programs that districts are required to provide in schools with 20 or more limited-English-proficiency pupils. *Extra Weight:* 0.10	$2,000,000 in 1998–1999
Delaware	No program or aid reported.	
District of Columbia	Uniform Funding Formula (UFF) requires bilingual services and provides funding intended to cover the reasonable cost of required services. Any shortfall in actual costs must be absorbed by general education funding. *Extra Weight:* 0.40	$10,900,000 in 1998–99 (included in UFF formula funding).

TABLE 6.2 States' Approaches to Funding Education for Limited-English-Speaking Children *(continued)*

State	LEP Program Description	State Funding
Florida	*Extra Weight:* 0.201	
Georgia	Funding is on a cost reimbursement basis, based on the students served the previous year. In 1998–99 the funding was $854.38 per itinerant segment and $640.78 per nonitinerant segment, both of which were then adjusted for the training and experience factor of the local school district. Students in K–3 could be counted for only one segment; those in grades 4–8 could be counted for no more than two segments; and those in grades 9–12 could be counted for no more than 5 segments.	$22,500,000 in 1998–99
Hawaii	No program or aid reported.	
Idaho	Funded as part of regular program with additional $3.0 million for 1998–99 to satisfy requirements of legal action brought against the state.	$3,000,000 in 1998–99
Illinois	The state reimburses school districts for transitional bilingual education and transitional programs of instruction for children of limited English proficiency. Transitional bilingual education programs are required in school districts with 20 or more students with the same native language. Transitional programs of instruction apply to school districts with less than 20 students of the same language background, and are optional.	$56,200,000 in 1998–99
Indiana	No program or aid reported.	
Iowa	*Extra Weight:* 0.19 for up to 3 years	$5,400,000 in 1998–99
Kansas	*Extra Weight:* 0.2	
Kentucky	No program or aid reported.	
Louisiana	Funding is included in the basic support formula and is not distinguishable.	
Maine	Bilingual education programs are subsidized as part of the operating costs allocation.	
Maryland	Annually legislated amount per pupil provided by the state.	$23,600,000 or $1,350 per ESL pupil in 1998–99

(continued)

TABLE 6.2   States' Approaches to Funding Education for Limited-English-Speaking Children *(continued)*

State	LEP Program Description	State Funding
Massachusetts	Funding for the transitional bilingual education (TBE) is a component of the foundation budget. In FY98, 29,300 FTE pupils participated in a TBE program.	$214,000,000 in 1998–99
Michigan	Reimbursements to districts on basis of number of LEP students.	$4,200,000 in 1998–99
Minnesota	LEP revenue = Regular LEP revenue [LEP base revenue (68% of one LEP teacher salary for every 40 LEP students, plus 47% of the cost of supplies and equipment, up to $47 per LEP pupil) times the ratio of the LEP enrollment in the current year to the LEP enrollment in the base year] plus LEP concentration revenue ($190 times the lesser of 1 or the ratio of district LEP concentration [LEP enrollment / total enrollment] to 11.5%). However, the state total regular LEP revenue is capped at $16.1 million, which has resulted in actual funding being prorated.	$22,000,000 for 168 school districts in 1998–99
Mississippi	No program or aid reported.	
Missouri	No program or aid reported.	
Montana	No program or aid reported.	
Nebraska	No program or aid reported.	
Nevada	No program or aid reported.	
New Hampshire	No program or aid reported.	
New Jersey	Bilingual education aid is allocated on the basis of $1,102 for each bilingual education pupil enrolled in the district.	$53,200,000 in 1998–99
New Mexico	*Extra Weight:* 0.50	$36,900,000 in 1998–99
New York	*Extra Weight:* 0.16	$58,600,000 in 1998–99
North Carolina	Funding for students identified as LEP through a language proficiency test. Each eligible school system receives a base of half a teacher assistant or $9,490. School systems also receive an additional 50% of allocated funds based on the number of LEP students and 50% based on a concentration of LEP students.	$5,000,000 in 1998–99
North Dakota	Funding appropriated per year for approved programs for LEP students.	$150,000 or $300 per pupil in 1998–99

TABLE 6.2   States' Approaches to Funding Education for Limited-English-Speaking Children *(continued)*

State	LEP Program Description	State Funding
Ohio	Funding for bilingual education can be derived from other basic aid and categorical grants in state aid as well as federal grants-in-aid.	
Oklahoma	*Extra Weight:* 0.25	$20,500,000 in 1998–99
Oregon	*Extra Weight:* 0.50	
Pennsylvania	No program or aid reported.	
Rhode Island	One of the new investment funds, the language assistance fund, has as its purpose to assist students that require additional language educational services. The program distributes an annual state allocation determined as part of the state budget process based on the number of full-time equivalent limited-English-proficient students reported by the school districts.	$1,300,000 in 1998–99
South Carolina	No program or aid reported.	
South Dakota	No program or aid reported.	
Tennessee	No program or aid reported.	
Texas	*Extra Weight:* 0.10	$115,100,000 in 1998–99
Utah	Funding for bilingual education subsumed under Alternative Language Services, a composite of program funding considered to be a special-purpose district-optional program under the basic support formula.	$2,800,000 in 1998–99
Vermont	*Extra Weight:* 0.2	
Virginia	Aid provided to local school divisions for ESL programs.	$3,200,000 in 1998–99
Washington	State aid for funding a transitional bilingual program.	$33,300,000 or $664.91 per ESL pupil in 1998–99
West Virginia	Allocation for alternative language services for LEP students.	$0.1 million in 1998–99
Wisconsin	State reimburses a percentage of costs based on the ratio of appropriation to eligibility.	State contribution was 21% or $8,300,000 in 1998–99
Wyoming	Commencing July 1, 1999, resources are to be available under the finance model for limited-English-proficient students.	

Source: Data extracted from Dayton et al., 2001.

federal requirements, many of which were initially written into IDEA. While several states initially responded negatively to the detailed federal requirements and some states refused all federal education aid for a few years, today all states comply with the mandates of this federal law.

IDEA authorized the federal government to fund up to 40 percent of nationwide costs for special-education services. In the year it was enacted, Congress appropriated $300 million or about $74 per disabled student, much less than the 40 percent that had been authorized. In 1990, federal outlays for special education were $2 billion (in constant FY 1998 dollars; National Center for Education Statistics, 1998); and by 1999–2000 that figure climbed to $3.7 billion (Chambers, Parrish, and Harr, 2002). According to the most recent data collected by Center for Special Education Finance, approximately 6.2 million children between the ages of 0 and 22 qualified for special-education services in the 1999–00 school year, representing about 13 percent of the total enrollment. Of all the dollars spent on special education in this country, the most up-to-date estimate of the federal portion is 7.5 percent (Chambers, Parrish, and Harr, 2002).

Federal funds are allocated on a per-pupil flat grant basis. The federal law requires that states identify students in these 12 special-education categories:

1. deaf,
2. deaf and blind,
3. hard of hearing,
4. mentally retarded,
5. multihandicapped,
6. orthopedically impaired,
7. other health impaired,
8. seriously emotionally disturbed,
9. learning disabled,
10. speech impaired,
11. visually impaired, and
12. autistic.

During the 2001–02 school year, the percentage of the estimated enrollment (ages 6–17) of each state that received special-education services ranged from approximately 9 to 18 percent (U.S. Department of Education, Office of Special Education Programs, 2002). As will be discussed, many states use the federal student categories to structure their state programs for the handicapped. Even though the per-pupil costs of providing services varies substantially by category, the federal program allocates the same flat grant amount for each identified student, regardless of category.

In the late 1980s, a regular-education initiative was begun by a diverse group of individuals who believed that a focus on labeling disabled students into a number of special categories and often pulling students out of regular classrooms for instruction was doing more harm than good for many of these students. This initiative reinforced the earlier views of many that labeling students was not the best approach to providing extra services for these students. Instead, many argued that all students had particular needs, and that schools should identify the different types of services necessary to serve their student population. The service levels needed could then determine funding. States such as Iowa and Massachusetts, in fact, restructured their state programs for the disabled on this basis.

In the 1990s, the regular-education initiative transformed into a more "inclusive" initiative. The goal, generally consistent with the original intent of IDEA, was to include disabled students in regular-education classrooms as much as possible. Although there has been controversy over how best to implement inclusive practices, this remains the dominant service delivery focus for disabled students today (McDonnell, McLaughlin, and Morison, 1997). All states now have programs to serve disabled students. The funding strategies and state program and service strategies vary a great deal. Table 6.3 shows the states that used a pupil-weighting approach to funding in the 1998–99 school year.

Issues in Determining Costs of Special-Needs Programs

Four major issues must be addressed in assessing and calculating costs for special-needs programs; these issues cut across all special-needs programs. They are: (1) defining student eligibility; (2) identifying appropriate services; (3) determining the appropriate placement; and (4) calculating state and local cost shares.

Student Eligibility.   Since most states allocate special-needs funds on the basis of the number of eligible students, regulations on student eligibility become very important. As just mentioned, compensatory education program guidelines usually define "eligibility" in two ways: (1) poverty measures such as household income, eligibility for free or reduced-price lunch, or some other measure of poverty; or (2) achievement measures including the type of tests used, the content areas to be tested, and degree of divergence from the average or grade norm. Traditionally, states used the number of students from families eligible for Aid to Families with Dependent Children, the federal welfare program, but with the changes in welfare policy, that practice is declining, and most use counts of students eligible for federal free and reduced-price lunch. Special-education programs need guidelines on the number of discrete handicapping categories, assessment procedures, and whether there are "caps" on eligibility in any one category, such as the federal 2 percent cap on funding for students with learning disabilities (Chambers, Parrish, and Guarino, 1999; Moore et al., 1988). Bilingual education programs need to identify the types of language examinations that can be used and criteria for determining partial or full English proficiency (i.e., criteria for determining the transition into "sheltered English" instruction or into the regular classroom). In each area, these issues become quite complex. Finally, there is pressure to move away from narrow categories of student eligibility to broader categories, such as simply needing a low, medium, or high level of extra services.

Further, eligible age ranges need to be identified. In many states, disabled children from birth to 21 are eligible for public education services; other states limit eligibility to conventional school age. Mainly school-age children are eligible for compensatory and bilingual education services, although most of the money for these programs is spent at the elementary level. A service and policy issue is whether secondary students

TABLE 6.3   States Using a Form of Pupil Weighting for Special Education

State		Extra Student Weight
Alabama	*Special education*	1.5
Arizona	Hearing handicapped	3.341
	Multiple disabilities, autism, and severe mental retardation (resource program)	1.995
	Multiple disabilities, autism, and severe mental retardation (self-contained)	5.015
	Multiple disabilities with severe sensory impairment	6.025
	Orthopedic impairments (resource program)	1.744
	Orthopedic impairments (self-contained)	5.641
	Preschool severe delay	4.979
	Emotional disabilities, mild mental retardation, specific learning disability, speech/language impairment, and other health impairments	0.003
	Emotional disability (private)	2.633
	Moderate mental retardation	2.808
	Visual impairment	4.832
California	Special Education Local Program Agencies (SELPAs) receive a flat amount of state aid for each special education ADA. The amount was determined by dividing the 1997–98 SELPA special education funding by the 1997–98 SELPA K–12 ADA. The resulting figure is the special education allotment per K–12 ADA each SELPA receives. The amount is adjusted annually by a cost-of-living adjustment and by the change in SELPA total ADA. A provision of the formula provides extra funding for SELPAs with above average number of high-cost special-education students.	
Delaware	Weighting occurs in the formula allocating pupil-unit ratios.	
	Educable mentally handicapped	15 pupils per unit
	Seriously emotionally disturbed	10 pupils per unit
	Learning disabled	8.0 pupils per unit
	Intensive learning center	8.0 pupils per unit
	Blind	8.6 pupils per unit
	Partially sighted	10 pupils per unit
	Trainable mentally handicapped	6.0 pupils per unit
	Severely mentally handicapped	6.0 pupils per unit plus aide
	Physically impaired	6.0 pupils per unit plus aide
	Hearing impaired	6.0 pupils per unit
	Deaf/blind	4.0 pupils per unit plus aide
	Autistic	4.0 pupils per unit plus aide

TABLE 6.3   States Using a Form of Pupil Weighting for Special Education *(continued)*

State		Extra Student Weight
District of Columbia	*Special Education*	
	Level 1 (services <6 hours/school week)	0.22
	Level 2 (services 7–15 hours/school week)	0.80
	Level 3 (services >15 hours/school week)	1.73
	Level 4 (separate school or program)	1.72
Florida	*Exceptional Student Programs*	
	Support level 1	0.341
	Support level 2	1.072
	Support level 3	2.287
	Support level 4	3.101
	Support level 5	5.860
Georgia	*Special Education—Category I* (Self-contained specific learning disabled and self-contained speech-language disordered)	1.3561
	Special Education—Category II (Mildly mentally disabled)	1.7406
	Special Education—Category III (Behavior disordered, moderately mentally disabled, severely mentally disabled, resourced specific learning disabled, resourced speech-language disordered, self-contained hearing impaired and deaf self-contained orthopedically disabled, and self-contained other health impaired)	2.4857
	Special Education—Category IV (Deaf-blind, profoundly mentally disabled, visually impaired and blind, resourced hearing impaired and deaf, resourced orthopedically disabled, and resourced other health impaired)	4.6338
	Special Education—Category V (Special education pupils in the above categories whose IEPs specify specially designed instruction or supplementary aids or services in alternative placements, in the least restrictive environment, including the regular classroom and who receive such services from personnel such as paraprofessionals, interpreters, job coaches, and other assistive personnel)	1.4473
Indiana	*Severely Disabled Students* (Multiple handicapped, orthopedic handicapped, visually impaired, hearing impaired, emotionally handicapped [FT], severely/profoundly mentally handicapped, dual sensory impaired, autism, and traumatic brain injury)	$7,285 per student

(continued)

TABLE 6.3   States Using a Form of Pupil Weighting for Special Education *(continued)*

State		Extra Student Weight
	Nonduplicated Moderately Disabled Students (Emotionally handicapped [all other], learning disabled, mildly/moderately mentally handicapped, and other health impaired)	$1,977 per student
	Duplicated Students with a Communication Disorder (Communication disordered and homebound)	$469 per student
Iowa	Students receiving special education are assigned an extra weight of .68, 1.35, or 2.74. These weights are calculated to generate sufficient funds to cover the excess cost of special education.	
Kentucky	Severely handicapped children	2.35
	Moderately handicapped children	1.17
	Speech	0.24
Louisiana	Students identified with exceptionalities	1.5
New Hampshire	Special-education catastrophic aid addresses the cost of severely handicapped students. After spending 3.5 times the estimated state average cost per pupil for the preceding school year, districts are entitled to receive in state aid 80% of subsequent costs up to a maximum of 10 times the state average cost per pupil. All remaining costs after this expenditure level is exceeded are reimbursed in full by the state.	
New Jersey	Tier I pupils—occupational therapy, physical therapy, speech, and counseling.	$154 per pupil
	Tier II pupils are residents in the district not receiving Tier IV intensive services and meeting the criteria for specific learning disability or perceptually impaired, traumatic brain injury or neurologically impaired, cognitive impairment, mild or educable mentally retarded and preschool disabled and some vocational programs.	$3,024 per pupil
	Tier III pupils are residents in the district not receiving Tier IV intensive services meeting the criteria for cognitive impairment—moderate or trainable mentally retarded, orthopedically impaired, auditorily impaired, communication impaired, emotionally disturbed, multiply disabled, other health impaired or chronically ill, and visually impaired.	$6,104 per pupil
	Tier IV pupils are the number of pupils classified as eligible for special-education resident in the district receiving intensive services.	$8,420 per pupil

TABLE 6.3   States Using a Form of Pupil Weighting for Special Education *(continued)*

State		Extra Student Weight
New Mexico	Students enrolled in special-education programs are classified as A, B, C, or D depending upon the type and extent of services needed.	
	A/B-level membership	0.700
	C/D-level membership	1.000
	D-level membership	2.000
	3- and 4-year-old DD membership	2.000
New York	*Time in Special Education Programs or Services Weight*	
	At least 60% of the day	1.70
	At least 20% of the week or 5 periods	.90
	Direct/indirect consultant teacher	.90
North Carolina	State cap at 12.5	
North Dakota	State pays $134 per pupil	
Ohio	*Special Education Supplement*	
	Mildest category of condition	0.22
	Middle category of condition	3.01
	Most severe category of condition	3.01 but allows for the further provision of aid to subsidize more expensive IEP costs.
Oklahoma	Learning disabilities	0.40
	Hearing impaired	2.90
	Visually impaired	3.80
	Multiple handicapped	2.40
	Speech impaired	0.05
	TBI	2.40
	Autism	2.40
	MR	1.30
	Emotionally disturbed	2.50
	Physically handicapped	1.20
	Deaf and blind	3.80
	Special education summer program	1.20
Oregon	Special education (students with an IEP)	2.0
South Carolina	Educable mentally handicapped	0.74
	Learning disabilities	0.74
	Trainable mentally handicapped	1.04
	Emotionally handicapped	1.04
	Autism	1.57
	Orthopedically handicapped	1.04

(continued)

TABLE 6.3   States Using a Form of Pupil Weighting for Special Education *(continued)*

State		Extra Student Weight
	Visually handicapped	1.57
	Hearing handicapped	1.57
	Speech handicapped	0.90
South Dakota	Level 1 (8.9% of ADM): speech and language, learning disabled, other health impaired, preschool	$3,504 per child
	Level 2: mental retardation, emotionally disturbed	$7,914 per child
	Level 3: deaf-blind, hearing impaired, orthopedic impairment, deaf, traumatic brain injury, visually impaired	$10,116 per child
	Level 4: autism	$14,705 per child
	Level 5: multiple disabilities	$15,808 per child
Texas	Speech therapy	4.0
	Resource room	2.0
	Self-contained, mild/moderate	2.0
	Self-contained, severe	2.0
	Off home campus	1.7
	Nonpublic day school	0.7
	Vocational adjustment class	1.3
	Mainstream special education	0.1
Utah	Special education	1.53
Washington	The allocation for students with disabilities aged 3–21 sets an overall spending cap equal to 12.7% of the total student population. The formula for 1998–99 is as follows: (a) the annual average headcount of birth through age 2 special-education enrollment, times the district's 1998–99 basic education allocation, times 1.15, plus (b) the annual average FTE basic education enrollment, times the district's enrollment percent, times the district's 1998–99 basic education allocation rate per student, times 0.9309.	
West Virginia	Special education	2.0

Source: Data extracted from Dayton et al., 2001.

should also have these extra services. Finally, the incidence of special-needs students varies widely overall and by program.

Appropriate Services.   Program guidelines also need to identify the range of services on which funds can be spent. Some programs restrict spending to current operating activities, while others allow capital expenditures such as buildings and equipment as well. Within operating expenditures, some programs allow only instructional expenditures, whereas others permit spending on other functional categories, such as transportation, which is generally costly. Within instructional expenditures, some programs limit spending to certain subject areas, such as reading and mathematics, while others allow spending on all academic content areas, including art, music, and physical education. Some programs allow funds to be used for professional development, such as Title II of No Child Left Behind.

Another issue is the degree to which program funds can be spent on administration. Because many categorical programs need special management and have reporting requirements—to ensure that only eligible students are served and that funds are spent as intended—many districts have created special categorical program administration staff to manage the program and meet reporting and compliance requirements. Many programs specify a maximum portion of program funds that can be spent on administration.

Other service issues include the diagnostic activities necessary to determine placement, class-size policies, and length of school day and year for special programs. Also at issue are the "related services" such as counseling, medical services, occupational therapy, and parent counseling that may be required for disabled students. It has been difficult to determine the level of need for these services; the guideline has been that related services are required if they are related to educational need. Related services can become costly for students with multiple physical disabilities, so these guidelines can have a substantial impact on special-education costs.

Another issue is the comprehensiveness and level of quality of special services. The *Rowley* U.S. Supreme Court decision held that disabled students were required to have access to an *adequate* educational program, but not the highest-quality educational program that would optimize their intellectual growth. In this case, a blind individual sued a district to force employment of a teacher to read materials in a one-to-one tutoring situation, arguing that such a service was needed to maximize her learning. The district refused, and the court upheld the district's action, stating that the federal law required only adequate educational services, not services to maximize student performance. Of course, standards-based education reform has set a high bar for what can be considered adequate, even for disabled children (Goertz et al., 1999).

Educational Placement. The method by which educational services are provided to students with special needs can produce substantial cost variations for students at the same grade level and with the same special-education need. There are six basic placement categories: (1) preschool; (2) resource program; (3) self-contained classroom; (4) individual tutoring; (5) home or hospital program; and (6) residential care. Most compensatory education and bilingual education programs are provided in regular classrooms or through resource programs, as are special-education services for disabled students who are mainstreamed in the regular-education program. Unfortunately, while this strategy serves the appropriate students, achievement impacts are modest (Borman and D'Agostino, 2001; Reynolds and Wolfe, 1999).

Moore and colleagues (1988), Chambers and Parrish (1983), and most recently Chambers, Parrish, and Harr (2002) show how costs vary widely—by a factor of 2 to 1—across different educational placements. In the 1990s, individual tutoring also became a service strategy; this clearly is a costly service approach but it also is the most effective and could be the most cost effective as short-term tutoring could reduce or eliminate the need for longer-term assistance (Shanahan, 1998; Slavin, Karweit, and Wasik, 1994).

Costs.   Once decisions are made about student eligibility, types of services required or eligibility for reimbursement, and educational placement, program costs are relatively easy to calculate. One of the most sophisticated mechanisms for determining special-needs program costs is the Resource Cost Model (RCM), developed by Chambers and Parrish in 1994. Using groups of professional educator experts, the RCM first identified base staffing levels for the regular-education program, and then identified effective program practices and their staffing and resource needs for compensatory, special, and bilingual education. All ingredients were costed out using average price figures but, in determining the foundation base dollar amount for each district, the totals were adjusted by an education price index. Such a program could be used by a state to determine the level of cost associated with numerous local special-needs programs, but no state has yet adopted such a model. Nevertheless, it is a robust analytic tool that can be used to determine costs for special-needs programs.

Of course, after total costs have been determined, the next task is to identify the state and local shares of those costs. Those issues are discussed next.

General Approaches to Formula Adjustments for Special-Needs Students

States use categorical and not general-aid grants to finance programs for special-needs students. These strategies can be divided into two general approaches: full-state funding and state-local cost sharing.

Full-state Funding.   The first is for the state to cover the entire cost of providing the additional services. This approach certainly has strong appeal to local districts and eliminates fiscal inequities caused by requiring local districts to finance these services by raising local revenues. Under this approach, local districts document the extra costs and submit a reimbursement claim to the state each year. Alternatively, if the program costs are "forward-funded," districts submit an application for reimbursement of estimated costs. The state then needs a reconciliation mechanism to ensure that payments equal actual costs. Modifying the next year's payment by the difference between predicted and actual costs is a straightforward example of such an adjustment.

A full-state-funded approach to programs for special-needs students requires rigorous state oversight or an audit mechanism to ensure that only legitimate local costs are reimbursed. With the state paying the full cost of the extra services, local districts would have a fiscal incentive to develop and implement comprehensive, high-quality programs. If the state had neither cost controls nor regulatory guidelines that monitored local programs, state costs could soar. While any state reimbursement program for special-needs students requires some regulatory and program guidelines, such mechanisms are an absolute requirement for a state program that reimburses 100 percent of local costs.

Over the long term, it is difficult for states to fully fund all special services. When service provision is mandated, as is the case for special education, a drop in state funding forces districts to encroach on the general fund for dollars to cover the full costs of the special programs (Murphy and Picus, 1996; Parrish and Wolman, 1999).

State-local Cost Sharing.   Over the years, most states have devised different strate-gies for sharing the costs of special needs programs with local school districts. States have created several types of specific grant structures for implementing the state-local sharing approach.

Categorical flat grant.   The simplest approach has been to provide a flat grant per eli-gible pupil. Sometimes the flat grant is based on the number of teachers or classroom units instead of pupils. Very few states currently use this approach, but it is the mecha-nism the federal government uses to distribute both Title I funds and funds for disabled students.[2] The drawback to this approach is that it provides the same per-pupil level of financial assistance to rich and poor districts alike and, if the amount does not cover all costs, districts low in property value per pupil need to levy a higher incremental tax rate to make up the difference.

Excess-cost reimbursement.   A second state-local cost-sharing strategy is "excess-cost reimbursement," in which the state reimburses a percentage (less than 100) of excess local costs. This ensures that local districts finance at least some portion of the costs of the programs they create and implement. The local match is, in part, a fiscal incentive for local districts to control costs; if program costs soar, the local match puts a direct strain on the local budget as well as the state budget. However, the fact that the local share is raised by increasing the local tax rate or encroaching on the general-fund budget may result in a disadvantage for property-poor districts, which have to exert a higher in-cremental local tax rate to make up the difference between full program costs and the costs shared by the state. These districts may also have less ability to use general-fund dollars to make up the difference.

Fiscal capacity equalization.   A third state-local sharing strategy includes a fiscal-capacity equalizing component in the state reimbursement program. For example, using this strategy, the state could turn a flat grant into a foundation grant with a required local effort, thereby inserting an element of need into the distribution formula. Alternatively, the state could use a separate guaranteed tax base program for the marginal tax rate to raise the extra revenues needed to finance the total costs of a special-needs program.

Pupil weights.   The most prevalent method of state and local cost sharing that includes a fiscal-capacity equalizing element emerged in the 1970s and is called pupil weighting. Under this strategy, each classification of special-needs pupil is given an extra weight that indicates, relative to some norm expenditure (usually the statewide average), how much additional services cost. Thus, for example, if the extra weight for a compensatory education student is 0.25, indicating services cost 25 percent more, that student would be counted as 1.25 students in determining state aid. The advantage of a pupil-

[2]However, under the 1997 Amendments to the Individuals with Disabilities Act, when appropriations to states exceed $4.92 billion, a new formula will take effect. States will receive a base level of funding in the amount of the previous year, but 85 percent of the funds above that amount will be distributed based on the state's relative share of the national school-age population, and 15 percent based on the state's relative share of the national low-income school-age population (Verstegen, Parrish, and Wolman, 1998.)

weighting approach is its simplicity in incorporating the level of need for each student into the school-aid formula. This approach also ensures that the state share of such extra costs is higher in low-wealth than in high-wealth districts. Another advantage is that only one school finance formula is used to provide all state aid to local districts; in a weighted-pupil approach, the weighted-pupil count is used for all state-aid calculations.

A weighted-pupil approach also directly indicates the degree of vertical equity adjustment included in the school finance system; the weights are the vertical adjustments. The adequacy of the vertical equity adjustments turns on whether the specific pupil weights are set at the right level. In calculating the fiscal equity of the resultant distribution of educational resources, equity statistics are calculated using the number of weighted pupils. For this reason, pupil weights are often viewed as among the most equitable policy for distributing the additional resources needed to educate students with special needs. (Again, see Table 6.3 for states that use pupil weights to fund extra programs for disabled students.)

Although a pupil-weighting system can be used with any type of school finance formula, technical issues do arise in the following three ways. First, if the weight for any particular type of student is determined by comparing the excess costs required to the statewide average expenditure per pupil, this expenditure must then be included in the state-aid program, such as the foundation expenditure level, in order for the weight to be accurate. However, states with foundation programs often set the foundation expenditure at a level below the statewide average expenditure per pupil, but use a pupil weight that has been calculated using the statewide average. This method inevitably leads to less additional resources provided than are required.

The second technical issue arises when a state has a guaranteed tax base program with a pupil-weighting system. In this case, districts that tax at an above-average level will have expenditures above the statewide average and thus the pupil weight might generate more additional revenues than are needed to cover excess costs. The reverse would be true for districts spending below the state average.

Third, some feel that there are problems with labeling students as needing extra resources. Some argue that this practice creates a stigma, instead suggesting use of systems that identify the service levels schools need to educate the whole student body.

Despite the advantages of pupil weights, one reason some states do not adopt a weighted-pupil approach is political: districts above the zero-aid district would receive no special-needs assistance under a pupil-weighting system. Most policymakers believe that even wealthy districts should receive some assistance for their special-needs students. Thus, a categorical program approach that uses a separate program formula for distributing financial support for special-needs students would make all districts, rich or poor, eligible for such state aid. While at first blush this might seem inequitable, the politics of state-aid distribution often requires this approach. It is often the property-wealthy districts that have the stronger political voices.

Moreover, it is difficult to maintain political support for any strongly redistributive programs, such as general school finance formulas that equalize fiscal capacity. Thus, providing at least some state aid for all districts, even if it is just for special-needs students, helps legislators maintain political support for a general aid program that provides aid inversely to property value per pupil.

Despite these technical and political concerns, pupil-weighting programs are rising in popularity (see Sielke et al., 2001).

Census funding.   Another approach for a state contributing to the additional resources needed for special education is called "census-based" funding, a strategy that emerged in the 1990s. This is done through the use of a formula based on total district enrollment rather than counts of special-education students. A fixed dollar amount is provided for a fixed percentage of students, and districts are required to provide appropriate services for all disabled students. Sometimes, the low-incidence, high-need students, such as the multiply handicapped, are funded separately and fully by the state, as these students are not found proportionately in all districts. California approved a census-funding system, in part because many felt the old system created too many fiscal incentives to identify students as needing special education, and in part to improve the equity of the distribution of state aid for special education. Other reasons included the desire to give the local districts more flexibility while holding them accountable, and having a system that was easy to understand. By the end of 1998, Massachusetts, Montana, North Dakota, Pennsylvania, Alabama, and Vermont all used census-based special-education funding systems as well. And as just noted, most new federal money under the IDEA program is distributed on a census basis.

As with all of the other state-local cost-sharing models, census-based funding has both advantages and disadvantages. The major advantages are all the reasons California decided to adopt it: simplicity, flexibility, equity, and built-in cost-controls. The major disadvantage is that the equity depends on the distribution of special-education students across all the districts in a state; if they are concentrated in a few districts, those districts will have to make up the difference between the state aid distributed on the basis of total district enrollment and the actual count of students with special needs. This is an especially important issue with the incidence of students with severe disabilities, who are sometimes extremely expensive to educate.

Another potential disadvantage involves the potential for districts to lose funding under a census-based system. In California, the phase-in process ensured that no district received less aid than they received under the previous system, but the possibility exists that in the future, some districts may receive less funding under a true census-based system. While this may not result in a true loss of equity, it may be difficult politically to convince school districts if they are receiving less money than the amount to which they were accustomed.

Poverty adjustment.   Still another method of providing adjustments for students with special needs is the poverty adjustment. With this method, poverty is used as a proxy for all special-education needs in any given district based on the assumption that districts with higher percentages of students in poverty also require more special-education funds. According to the Center for Education Finance, only three states use such an adjustment: Louisiana, Oregon, and Connecticut (Parrish, 1997). One of the most compelling arguments in favor of poverty adjustments is that while it may not be a perfect proxy for special-education needs, it is the best available indicator that can be determined without district involvement, eliminating all of the complications associated with the identification of students with special needs. On the other hand, because the link between poverty and special-education need is unclear and has not been statistically significant in a number of studies, use of poverty adjustments to allocate special-education funds may be a poor way of targeting special-education dollars.

Summary.   In short, there are two general approaches states can use to assist local districts in providing extra educational services for students with special-education needs: full-state funding and state-local cost sharing. For reasons already described, the more popular approach is some form of state and local cost sharing. Of the many methods of sharing the cost with localities, pupil-weighting programs have become the most popular; in 1998–99, 20 states used pupil weights in their state special-education funding system. Pupil weights provide a way to directly identify the degree of additional services the state wants to provide as well as a method of sharing the cost by allocating state aid through the general-aid formula using a weighted count of pupils. This strategy also conditions the level of extra aid received on local fiscal capacity; even if the number of special-needs students is the same, districts with a low property value per pupil will receive more money for special education than districts with a high property value per pupil.

Finally, the interaction of the specific funding formulas and the rules and regulations accompanying them provide incentives and disincentives for student identification, program placement, and dollar use. At the local level, districts sometimes identify students in higher reimbursement categories and place them in lower-cost instructional programs to increase revenues and reduce costs. While some of these interactions are desired, the limits of such flexibility need to be understood and addressed. Hartman (1980) discusses such issues for special education.

As discussed previously, census-based funding addresses the incentive problem as well. Further, after years of experience, local educators have become quite sophisticated at "pooling" dollars for special-needs students and creatively providing services (McLaughlin, 1999). Today, the push for comprehensive school reform programs (e.g., see Stringfield, Ross, and Smith, 1996), under the federal Obey-Porter Comprehensive School Reform program, actively encourages schools to include special-needs students in all aspects of the regular-education program.

Distribution Formulas for and Costs of Compensatory Education Programs

The federal and most state compensatory distribution formulas are based on measures of the number of students from low-income backgrounds. There are attempts to concentrate funds in the most poverty-impacted schools and districts. Policymakers also seek to set funding at a level that will fully fund a needed service. But accomplishing these objectives has been difficult.

Distribution Formulas.   The federal government has provided funds to local school districts for compensatory programs since the 1965 passage of the Elementary and Secondary Education Act (ESEA). The 1994 ESEA reauthorization made several changes to the Title I allocation formula, which were largely retained by the 2001 No Child Left Behind reauthorization as well. Before the reauthorization, the federal government allocated funds to states on the basis of the number of low-income children in each county and the state's per-pupil expenditures for elementary and secondary education (with an upper and lower limit on the amount that the state expenditure could deviate from the national average). The funds were then suballocated to counties and then to districts and schools within counties.

The reauthorized act made two major changes. The first involved the data by which the number of low-income children is counted. Previously, the number of low-income children was calculated using decennial census data. But because the numbers of children in need change more than once every 10 years, there was concern about using census data that are only updated once a decade. The reauthorized act required data on low-income children to be updated every two years using biennial census data that was collected beginning in 1996. In FY 1997, these data were used for the first time.

The second change involved the federal government's practice of distributing money to states on the basis of county-level poverty data. Under the old law, Title I dollars were distributed to states on the basis of county-level data and then suballocated to districts. If the county and school district boundaries were not coterminous (which is the case in most states), the state used a subcounty allocation formula to distribute funds to local school districts based on the number of low-income students in each district. Under the new law, allocations continued in this manner until FY 1999, when grants began to be calculated on the basis of the poor-child population in each district.

Once the funds have been allocated to the district, districts must distribute them among the schools in that district. Initially, the idea was to concentrate the funds in the highest-poverty schools and then to the lowest-achieving students in those schools. Though districts had always had some discretion over school distribution, more restrictive requirements were added over the years. Today, in determining school allocations, districts must first rank all of their schools in terms of poverty levels. The poverty measure employed must be one of the five specified by Title I, including: (1) children aged 5–17 in poverty as counted by the most recent census; (2) children eligible for free *and* reduced-price lunches under the National Free School Lunch Act; (3) children in families receiving income assistance; (4) children eligible to receive medical assistance under the Medicaid program; and (5) a composite of any of the preceding measures.

Once all the schools in a given district are ranked according to poverty level, the district is required to serve all schools with 75 percent poverty and higher. After serving all of those areas, the district may serve the lower-poverty schools using the rank that has already been determined, or by creating grade-level groupings. Since the law does not specify what a service is, the requirements still provide districts with considerable discretion in funds allocation. The lower cost a district specifies for a service, the more possible it is to distribute at least some dollars to more schools. Higher-cost programs would drive most funds to the highest-poverty schools.

Compensatory Education Program Costs.   Because school districts have substantial latitude in determining the kind of compensatory programs they offer, determining compensatory education program costs is a difficult task. By contrast, programs for other

special-needs students are more specified. Law requires districts, for example, to provide appropriate services to all disabled children. Once a child's disability has been identified, and an appropriate level of service agreed upon, it is relatively straightforward to
determine the costs of that service. While there may be variations in costs and instructional techniques across districts, it is possible to estimate an average cost for each special service provided within a region or state.

The problem of determining compensatory education program costs, however, is
more complex. Although Title I and most state compensatory programs require that program funds be expended on low-income and/or low-achieving students, neither generally specifies the types or levels of services that should be provided. As a result, districts
have considerable flexibility in determining the breadth and intensity of services provided. This flexibility was enhanced in the 1990s by allowing schools with 50 percent or
more poverty students to use Title I funds for *schoolwide* programs serving all students.

As a result, one district may choose to offer intensive services to a subgroup of eligible low-income students (e.g., one-to-one tutoring for low-achieving students in
grades 1–3), while another district may elect to serve all of the eligible student population with a less-intense program (e.g., pull-out, resource-room, remedial services). In
fact, a number of program options and thus program costs are possible, all of which can
impact the final distribution of compensatory education dollars. In the late 1980s, Goertz (1988) found that among 17 large districts, allocation rules included:

- uniform allocation to each eligible building,
- allocations based on the number of low-achieving students in a building, and
- allocations based on the relative size and/or poverty of the building's student body.

It is likely that these procedures increased in variability in the 1990s, with the trend towards more schoolwide programs.

In part as a result of these allocation and service variations, Goertz's (1988) study
found considerable differences in instructional expenditures per pupil within and
among Chapter 1 (Title I, as it was known in 1988) programs. Across different schools,
one district had a Chapter 1 expenditure range of $300 to $2,500 per pupil, while in another district, expenditures ranged from $450 to $625. The lowest per-pupil Chapter 1
expenditures identified in the 17 districts was $175 (in a district with an expenditure
range of $175 to $1,070), and the highest was the $2,500 per pupil identified here. It is
probably the case that similar program cost variations exist today.

At the state level, the Texas State Board of Education (1986) reviewed the costs of
compensatory education and recommended an extra weight of 0.2 for all eligible compensatory education students—implying that compensatory education cost 20 percent
more than the state's foundation expenditure level. Although subsequent studies suggested that many districts did not spend that much extra for compensatory education, in
part because compensatory education services within the regular school day were provided in lieu of other services, the legislature retained the 0.2 extra weighting.

Another problem in identifying the costs of compensatory education programs
today is the fact that many programs are schoolwide. This makes it extremely hard, if not

impossible, to determine how much money is spent on low-income children in a school, since the compensatory education money is being used to fund a program for all children. Furthermore, because schools with high poverty levels are the ones who are eligible and therefore likely to apply their Title I allocation to schoolwide programs, it is no longer easy to discern where the more-intensive services for low-income children are offered. Nor is it clear that "intensive services" are the ones bringing the best results; hence, the move in the direction of schoolwide programs.

A final challenge in identifying the costs of compensatory education programs has arisen in this era of standards-based reform. Many more states now fund programs, in addition to the Title I funds they receive, in order to raise the achievement of low-income students. A survey of the states conducted by the Center on Budget and Policy Priorities (Carey, 2002) found that 83 percent of existing programs for low-income students have only been implemented in their current form since 1990. Where states once had one overarching compensatory education program under Title I, many states now have several programs targeted toward students from disadvantaged backgrounds. In part as a result of this increase, programs for low-income students today are more diverse in terms of size, focus, and method of funding (Carey, 2002). This Center on Budget and Policy Priorities (Carey, 2002) reports that 13 states adjust their basic state-aid formulas in order to fund additional programs for disadvantaged students, while 18 states have separate categorical grants for this purpose. This change in the breadth and nature of programs for low-income students makes it more difficult to estimate costs because the definition of a compensatory education program is evolving as additional programs are being funded by states and because the funding mechanisms for them vary by state and program.

Given all of the complications, finding the answer to the long-standing question of how much extra funding needs to be provided per pupil for compensatory programs is difficult. The answer requires specifying the level of achievement desired, the additional programmatic strategies needed to produce this achievement, and the costs of those programmatic strategies.

One program for which this type of analysis can be approximated is the Success for All/Roots and Wings program (Slavin et al., 1996). It includes a core curriculum designed to teach students to proficiency standards in reading, writing, mathematics, science, and social studies. There is considerable evidence of the effectiveness of this program, and it has been shown to be replicable across a wide range of schools and education systems (Borman et al., 2002; Slavin and Fashola, 1998). For purposes of discussion, let us assume that this program provides the types of additional services and strategies students from low-income backgrounds need to achieve to rigorous proficiency standards.

The costs of this program have been identified (Odden, 1997a). In addition to all of the elements associated with a traditional school, the minimum elements of this program for an elementary school of 500 students, with nearly all from poverty backgrounds, are:

1. one to two schoolwide instructional facilitator(s),
2. four to five reading tutors,
3. family liaison professional,
4. $30,000 for materials, and

5. $30,000 for professional development provided by the national network associated with this school design.

These ingredients include six to eight (an average of seven) professional staff positions and $60,000 for training and materials. Using national average prices, this would require the school to have an additional $410,000 (7 positions times $50,000 in salary and benefits for each, plus $60,000 for training and materials). This would be above the core staffing of one principal, one teacher for every 25 students, appropriate additional teachers for preparation time, and art, music, and physical education. Also, the program strongly recommends a full-day kindergarten program, which, if not already in place at the school implementing the design, would require two additional teachers, raising the costs to $510,000. Roots and Wings/Success for All also strongly suggests that each student receive a preschool education, which could further increase the costs. Finally, some schools find that an additional tutor or two enhances the ability of the program to teach all students to high-proficiency standards.

For illustrative purposes, assume a program slightly above the minimum requirements is needed, and that the additional costs of that version of the Roots and Wings/Success for All program is about $500,000. That would amount to $1,000 for every student in the school, which in this case would be every low-income student in the school. If the state average expenditure were $5000, this would represent a 20 percent addition, or a 0.20 weight; the weight would rise (drop) as the expenditure were lower (higher). This would mean that in addition to the "adequate" foundation program, the state would need to provide an additional $1,000 for every low-income student, assuming that those extra dollars would be used to finance a strategy or set of strategies to teach all students to state-set proficiency standards (i.e., a schoolwide program such as Success for All/Roots and Wings). Districts should be able to pool the funds from both Title I and state compensatory education programs to provide this level of extra funding to each school.

In summary, compensatory education funds are distributed to school districts on the basis of the number of eligible pupils. For the federal Title I program, the number of low-income students in a district determines eligibility. Many state programs use income measures for eligibility, while others offer compensatory aid for low-achieving students. Table 6.1 summarizes the eligibility requirements for state-operated compensatory education programs. Compensatory education programs generally include requirements to ensure that districts do not use the money to replace local funds, but do not delineate how services should be provided, or how many of the eligible students must be served. Consequently some districts attempt to provide compensatory services to all eligible schools and students, others focus their resources at specific populations, and still others use their Title I resources to fund schoolwide programs. This results in a tremendous range in the breadth and intensity of the compensatory education services provided across the United States.

Costs and Formulas for Financing Bilingual Education Programs

Studies of the costs of providing bilingual education have produced widely varying results, from less than an extra 5 percent (Carpenter-Huffman and Samulon, 1981; Gonzalez, 1996) to an extra 100 percent (Chambers and Parrish, 1983). There are several reasons for these variations, and they speak to what a bilingual education program is and how it should be structured.

Five specific issues determine the costs of bilingual education programs: (1) student eligibility; (2) minimum number of LEP students required to trigger provision of a bilingual education program; (3) instructional approach used; (4) transition into the regular program; and (5) class size.

A score on some type of English language proficiency test usually determines student eligibility. States use different tests and have selected different cut-off points for eligibility, from below the 23rd percentile in one state, to much higher levels in other states. Clearly, the higher the threshold, the more students eligible, and the fewer the number of low-incidence programs.

Most states also require a school or district to have a minimum number of students in a grade level in order to provide a bilingual education program. Minimums have ranged widely, from 10 students in a grade in a school in California, to 20 students in a district in Texas (Nelson, 1984). The lower the minimum number of children and the larger the unit for that minimum, the more students will qualify.

Class size in many states also is limited, sometimes to as low as 10 students in a class. Other states do not set lower limits on class size for bilingual or English as a second language classes. Small class-size requirements boost per-pupil costs.

The instructional approach and transition policies also affect the level of services provided. Most state bilingual education policy assumes that students classified as limited-English-proficient will be able to transition into regular classes, taught in English, within a three-year period. A longer transition period (i.e., providing extra services to students who need more than three years to transition and perform well in English-only classrooms) would boost per-pupil costs.

Finally, the instructional approach used is a major determinant of program costs. A few comments on bilingual education program goals and characteristics of instructional strategies that work will help provide some background for assessing the nature of the instructional approach and thus the results of cost studies based on different instructional approaches.

Students who are eligible for bilingual education programs usually live in families where a language other than English is spoken, so that English is not the student's native language. The key issue is the degree to which the student is proficient in English as a language for learning. Literacy (i.e., the ability to read, write, do mathematics, and think) can be developed in any language; literacy is neutral with respect to language (Office of Bilingual Education, 1984). Once literacy is developed in one language, it is easily transferred to another language once the second language is learned. Students diagnosed as limited-English-proficient are students who do not have sufficient English language proficiency to learn in English. Research shows that the most effective approach for such students is to teach them regular subjects in their native language, as well as an English as a second-language class (Krashen and Biber, 1988; Slavin and Calderon, 2001). The goal of such a program is to have the students learn English while simultaneously learning regular academic subject matter.

The same research shows that students (adults, too, for that matter) learn conversational English first; this English proficiency is sufficient for conversing on the playground, playing with friends, talking about the weather, etc., but it is not sufficient for academic learning (see also Cummins, 1980). When this conversational level of English proficiency is learned, the student is ready for "sheltered English" instruction in subjects that have some language and terminology of their own, such as mathematics and science (Krashen and Biber, 1988), but still need instruction in their native language for history and language arts, and continuation of ESL classes. This intermediate approach helps the student gain the level of English proficiency needed to learn academic subjects. History/social science is the next subject for sheltered English instruction; the last such class is language arts. In other words, the most effective program is to begin instruction in the native language, transition sequentially to sheltered English instruction in mathematics, science, history/social science, and language arts, and only then transition to regular classroom instruction. ESL instruction also should continue until the full transition to the regular classroom.[3]

The Krashen and Biber (1988) report does not make recommendations for major class size reductions. Nor does this report recommend the common school practice of having an English-only instructor assisted by a bilingual education aide. This configuration is quite common across the country because there are insufficient numbers of bilingual teachers to teach students in their native language. In this circumstance, Krashen and Biber recommend ESL with a sheltered English instruction approach.

Thus, the major extra costs of bilingual education for the most effective instructional approach are threefold:

- An ESL teacher. If the class has a normal number of students and is used for six periods a day, the extra cost is about 1/6 (i.e., the cost of the extra period of instruction).
- Intensive staff development in sheltered English instruction. This is professional expertise that can and should be learned by all teachers. Knowledge of a second language is not required. Sheltered English instruction is instruction mediated by a variety of mechanisms and with a conscious English-language-development component.
- Additional materials both in the native language of the student and for mediating the sheltered English instructional approach. These extras would seem to add to a maximum of an extra 20 to 25 percent. Note that regular classes are taught by either bilingual teachers, teachers using a sheltered English approach, or in a regular classroom; other than staff development, these classes entail no additional costs.[4]

Most studies of bilingual education program costs reflect these levels of costs. Garcia (1977) found the add-on costs for bilingual education in New Mexico to be about

---

[3]We are aware that bilingual programs are somewhat controversial, and indeed, California by initiative eliminated bilingual education programs. Nevertheless, schools need to adopt some strategy to ensure that students who do not have English proficiency learn English and learn other academic content as well.
[4]Some states and districts pay bilingual teachers a bonus of up to $5,000. This clearly is an extra cost. The bonus is rationalized on the basis that bilingual teachers are in short supply and have an area of expertise—proficiency in a second language—that other teachers do not have.

27 percent. Three studies by the Intercultural Development Research Association found bilingual education to cost an extra 30 to 35 percent in Texas (Cardenas, Bernal, and Kean, 1976), an extra 17 to 25 percent in Utah (Guss-Zamora et al., 1979), and an extra 15 to 22 percent in Colorado (Robledo et al., 1978). An early 1990s study of such programs in California found the marginal cost of LEP services to be $361 in 1990–91 (Parrish, 1994); when compared with the total education revenues per pupil in California in the same year, the cost of LEP services amounts to an additional 8 percent. Parrish (1994) also found a broad range of costs depending on the instructional approach, which he attributes to the range in the resource-teacher services needed for the different approaches. The costs in his study ranged from $131 per student in a sheltered English program to $1,066 for an ESL program, or from 3 to 22 percent above regular education costs.[5] While some of these studies analyzed program configurations quite different from that just described, the findings provide a range of cost estimates that are nevertheless comparable.

Finally, though districts have typically reported higher costs for bilingual education programs than most studies have found (Carpenter-Huffman and Samulon, 1981), there have been studies that also report considerably higher costs for bilingual education programs than those just cited. The Chambers and Parrish (1983) study in Illinois found that these additional costs ranged from $848 per pupil to $5,113 per pupil, or between 33 and 100 percent for different program structures in Illinois school districts. The highest cost figure assumed both a low incidence and a very low class size, the latter a characteristic absent from some of the other studies, including the Krashen and Biber (1988) studies of effective California programs.

Bilingual education continues to be controversial. In California, Proposition 227, which took effect in the summer of 1998, sharply curtailed bilingual classes, instead encouraging immersion for LEP students. In 2002, Massachusetts voters approved a similar initiative while Colorado voters turned one down. In spite of the controversy, the key ingredients for an effective program structure are an ESL program to teach English, regular teachers who either teach in the native language or in a sheltered English format, neither of which entails extra costs, supplementary materials, and staff development. Moreover, as the diversity of the student's native language increases, as is increasingly the case, sheltered English instruction inevitably becomes the dominant instructional mode in addition to ESL; the many languages within each classroom preclude a bilingual teaching strategy. Additional costs for this program structure, as well as those found in several research reports, range between 25 and 35 percent.

Costs and Formulas for Financing Special-Education Programs

Identifying the costs of special-education programs for physically, mentally, and learning-disabled students has been a major focus of study for the past three decades. Initially, studies sought to identify different costs by disability, taking into account how that cost

[5]If the base revenue limit ($3,331), rather than total revenues per pupil ($4,743), are used to calculate these percentages, the estimate for LEP services would be 11 percent above regular education costs; sheltered English instruction would be 4 percent; and the more expensive ESL program would be 32 percent above regular education costs (Gold et al., 1992).

varied by the size of the district. Then, special-education cost research focused more on excess costs as a function of educational placement (Moore et al., 1988; Rossmiller and Frohreich, 1979).

Rossmiller conducted some of the earliest work under the auspices of the early 1970s' National Education Finance Project, or NEFP (Johns, Alexander, and Jordan, 1971; Rossmiller et al., 1970). This work was probably the first analysis of special education costs that produced results that could be used to create pupil-weighting programs. Indeed, in 1973, Florida enacted one of the first special-education pupil-weighting programs as a new approach for financing special education, a program that became a model for other states. Florida adopted these weights for 1976–77, based in large part on the Rossmiller and NEFP analyses:

Educable mentally retarded	2.3
Trainable mentally retarded	3.0
Physically handicapped	3.5
Physical and occupational therapy, part-time	6.0
Speech and hearing therapy, part-time	10.0
Deaf	4.0
Visually handicapped, part-time	10.0
Visually handicapped	3.5
Emotionally disturbed, part-time	7.5
Emotionally disturbed	3.7
Socially maladjusted	2.3
Specific learning disability, part-time	7.5
Specific learning disability	2.3
Hospital and homebound, part-time	15.0

In addition to the general points made previously on factors that determine program costs, there are three key issues related to determining special-education program costs. The first is the level of program quality. Most of the early studies sought to identify good special-education programs and based special-education cost estimates on the expenditure patterns of those programs. Few studies set a priori standards for program quality. Thus, studies have been plagued over the years by various definitions of program quality.

The second issue is identification of services included in the study. The most controversial aspect of this issue is whether to include administrative services, such as general district administration, as well as noneducational related services.

A third issue, especially for determining per-pupil costs, is how the number of students is determined—whether by head count or full-time equivalents. The importance of this issue, and resultant program structures, is shown by the high weights for students receiving part-time services in the early Florida program. Kakalik (1979) provides an overview of issues in determining special education costs. Parrish (1996) also discusses costs in his recent article on special-education finance.

Three large studies of nationwide special education costs have been conducted: one by Kakalik and colleagues (1981) using data from the mid-1970s; one by Moore and colleagues (1988) using data from the mid-1980s; and the most recent by Chambers, Parrish, and Harr (2002), using data from the late 1990s. All three used a representative national sample, thus providing a picture of actual special-education expenditures across all programs in the country. The results in terms of excess costs for special education programs for the first two studies were quite similar. Kakalik and colleagues presented results as ratios of special-education expenditures to regular-education expenditures in 1977–78 for 13 categories of disabling conditions; the weights ranged from 1.37 for speech-impaired children to 5.86 for the blind. The overall weight across all categories was 2.17. Kakalik and colleagues also presented data comparing special-education expenditures with regular-education expenditures by 10 categories of educational placement. For the in-school program, the ratios or weights ranged from 1.37 for regular classroom plus related services to 3.24 for special all-day school. The regular classroom plus part-time special classroom arrangement had a weight of 2.85.

Moore and colleagues (1988) presented no pupil weights or ratios in their report, tending rather to emphasize the linkage between type of educational program or educational placement, and disabling condition. These figures are summary findings of 1985–86 special education program costs:

Handicapping Condition	Preschool	Self-Contained	Resource Room
Speech impaired	$3,062	$ 7,140	$ 647
Mentally retarded	3,983	4,754	2,290
Orthopedically impaired	4,702	5,248	3,999
Multihandicapped	5,400	6,674	NA
Learning disabled	3,708	3,083	1,643
Seriously emotionally disturbed	4,297	4,857	2,620
Deaf	5,771	7,988	NA
Deaf-blind	NA	20,416	NA
Hard of hearing	4,583	6,058	3,372
Other health impaired	3,243	4,782	NA
Autistic	6,265	7,582	NA
Visually impaired	4,068	6,181	3,395

These results can be transformed into pupil weights by comparing these costs with 1985–86 expenditures per pupil for regular students, which was $2,780. Since these figures are costs just for the special-education services, the $2,780 figure would have to be added to them in order to calculate the weight. Moore and colleagues found that the overall average expenditure for special education across all programs and placements was $3,649. Thus, their study produced an overall weight of 2.3 [($3,649 + $2,780)/$2,780], close to the Kakalik and colleagues (1981) finding of 2.17 (see also Chaikind, Danielson, and Braven, 1993).

As recently as 1996, Parrish (1996), a leading expert on special-education expenditures and costs, called 2.3 "the generally accepted cost figure" (i.e., that on average, educating special-education students required 2.3 times the amount for "regular" students, or that it required an additional 130 percent to provide appropriate additional educational services to all disabled students). Though actual additional costs were difficult to capture because of lack of uniform accounting for both expenditures and service strategies, demographic trends suggesting a higher rate of needy students and more complex disabilities, consolidation of funding sources and inclusion, the extra 1.3 figure was generally accepted with the caveat that it was increasingly difficult to sort out the cost of educating special-needs students (Chambers, Parrish, and Guarino, 1999; National Research Council, 1999).

In March 2002, however, Chambers and colleagues reported the results of the largest and most sophisticated study of special education costs ever conducted. The Special Education Expenditure Project (SEEP) collected data for the 1999–00 school year from more than 9,000 students with disabilities who attended more than 1,000 schools in over 300 local education agencies. The major new finding from the study was that the 1.3 extra weight had declined to 0.9. This amounts to $5,918 per pupil over the base expenditure of $6,556. This does not mean, however, that overall special education expenditures dropped, because the actual number of students classified as disabled has been increasing for years. It simply means that both because of changes in service delivery (with considerable inclusion) and student demographics (with an increase in students identified with less intensive service needs, such as learning disabilities), the overall weight reflecting the need for extra revenues had dropped from 1.3 to 0.9.

Simulation of Adjustments for Special-Needs Students

Adding adjustments for special-needs students to a state school finance structure clearly improves the vertical equity of the system, but also improves both horizontal equity and fiscal neutrality. The improvements, however, require additional revenues. Figure 6.1 shows the base data simulated with these weights representing additional student educational need:

- compensatory education students (i.e., students from a low-income family usually represented by the number of students eligible for free and reduced-price lunch) weighted an extra 0.20,
- limited-English-proficient students weighted an extra 0.20, and
- disabled students weighted an extra 0.9.

It takes some analysis to fully understand the results in Figure 6.1, relative to those in Figure 5.1, the base data without pupil weights. First, as indicated near the bottom, left-hand side of Figure 6.1, these weights produce an additional 14,905 pupil units (120,148 minus 105,243). The number of additional student units in each district can be determined by comparing the "Weighted Pupils" column in Figure 6.1 with those in Figure 5.1.

Second, the simulation shows that the 20-district sample needed an additional $103.5 million in revenues to fund these extra needs, which is shown as additional state revenue (again in comparison to Figure 5.1). This additional amount represents the full cost of the extra weights, and for the 20-district sample, it is assumed that the state provides all these additional dollars. In the state simulations that accompany Chapter 7, the

Adequacy Level	$	5,350
Pupil Weights		**yes**
Disabled		0.9
Limited English		0.2
Low Income		0.2

District	Weighted Pupils	Property Value per Weighted Pupil ($)	Property Tax Rate (Mills)	Local Revenue per Weighted Pupil ($)	State Revenue pe Weighted Pupil ($)	Total Revenue per Weighted Pupil ($)
1	1,703	13,224	39.64	524	3,173	3,697
2	7,286	20,255	38.50	772	3,145	3,918
3	2,098	25,255	37.15	938	3,091	4,029
4	312	29,261	36.20	1,059	3,014	4,073
5	12,205	33,830	35.91	1,215	2,943	4,158
6	1,128	36,967	35.74	1,321	2,946	4,267
7	5,458	42,848	34.89	1,495	2,915	4,410
8	1,911	48,142	34.17	1,645	2,834	4,480
9	10,243	53,544	33.73	1,806	2,776	4,582
10	1,702	61,686	33.44	2,063	2,728	4,791
11	2,764	69,014	33.23	2,293	2,789	5,083
12	6,669	76,255	32.89	2,508	2,703	5,211
13	2,933	83,676	32.10	2,686	2,651	5,337
14	17,317	91,849	31.32	2,877	2,560	5,437
15	2,576	100,679	30.85	3,106	2,556	5,662
16	3,010	113,421	30.50	3,459	2,364	5,823
17	33,463	123,442	30.05	3,709	2,153	5,862
18	2,266	141,856	28.63	4,061	2,041	6,102
19	3,433	180,513	27.42	4,950	1,840	6,790
20	1,672	253,235	25.50	6,457	1,308	7,765
Weighted Average		85,694	32.46	2,653	2,548	5,201
Weighted Std. Dev.		45,280	2.97	1,199	388	821
Median		83,676	32.10	2,686	2,651	5,337

Totals		
	Amount	**Percent**
Local Revenue	318,727,208	51.01%
State Revenue	306,112,115	48.99%
Total Revenue	624,839,323	
Weighted Pupils	120,148	

Equity Measures	
Horizontal Equity	
Range	$4,068
Restricted Range	2,872
Federal Range Ratio	0.733
Coef. of Variation	0.158
Gini Coefficient	0.087
McLoone Index	0.838
Verstegen Index	1.095
Fiscal Neutrality	
Correlation	0.990
Elasticity	0.285
Adequacy	
Odden-Picus	0.923

Additional state revenue for weighted pupil categorical programs	103,571,949

FIGURE 6.1   Base Data with Pupil Weights

additional amount would be the increment above what the state actually provides for special student needs, as most states already provide some level of assistance for low-income, LEP, and disabled students, but generally not a sufficient amount. Nevertheless, the $105.6 million figure identified in Figure 6.1 is the amount required to fully fund the identified pupil weights.

It should be noted that the bulk of the extra costs is for disabled students. Readers should run a series of simulations, each time giving a weight to just one of the three categories of special-needs students. The results will show that the incidence of bilingual students is quite low, which is the case in most states (with the notable exceptions of California, Arizona, New Mexico, Texas, Florida, and New York). Since the extra cost for each bilingual student is just 20 percent, the total additional costs for just this student group are minimal. Extra costs for compensatory education alone is higher because the incidence of low-income students is about 20 percent of all students. The incidence of disabled students is about 10 percent which, when combined with an extra cost of 90 percent for each student, produces the largest extra cost for a special-needs student category.

The equity statistics for the base data with pupil weights (Figure 6.1) are also somewhat better than those for the same districts without the extra costs of special needs students recognized and funded (see Figure 5.1). All equity and adequacy statistics for this simulation are based on the number of need-weighted pupils. The coefficient of variation and wealth elasticity are somewhat smaller, and the McLoone and Odden-Picus Adequacy Index are somewhat larger. Of course, costs also rise; horizontal, vertical, and fiscal-neutrality equity, as well as adequacy gains emerge at a price—but this time the price of fully funding programs for special-needs students.

Figure 6.2 uses these weights for a foundation program simulated at the new median expenditure per weighted pupil of $5,337, and at a required tax rate of 32.10 mills, the new state median. All equity and adequacy statistics for this simulation are also based on the number of weighted pupils. First, the total state cost of the program increases by an additional $10.9 million, compared with the weighted-pupil base data. These increased costs should be expected because the foundation level raises spending in many of the low-expenditure districts. Local revenues rise too, largely because of state-aid losses for the high-wealth districts.

Second, in part as a result, the equity statistics improve substantially, just as they did for a similar foundation program without weights. The coefficient of variation drops from 0.158 to 0.070, the McLoone Index rises from 0.838 to 0.991, the wealth elasticity drops from 0.285 to 0.141, and the Adequacy Index rises from 0.92 to 1.00. In short, vertical adjustments for special-needs students produce equity on all fronts, with this level foundation program.

2. ADJUSTMENTS FOR DIFFERENT GRADE LEVELS

For years, the primary grade-level adjustment in school finance formulas was for secondary students, who typically were provided an additional 25 percent of resources, or weighted 1.25. The rationale for this practice was that, given current patterns of elementary and secondary school organization, costs were higher for secondary students. More specialized classes were provided, more expensive educational programs (such as vocational education) were provided, and often class sizes were smaller, at least for several types of classes.

Table 6.4 shows the adjustments by grade level states made during the 1998–99 school year. As expected, most states, but largely those states in the Midwest and East,

Foundation Program

Adequacy Level	$ 5,350		Foundation Level	$5,337
			Required Tax Rate	32.1
Pupil Weights	yes			
Disabled	0.9			
Limited English	0.2			
Low Income	0.2			

District	Weighted Pupils	Property Value per Weighted Pupil ($)	Old Property Tax Rate (Mills)	New Property Tax Rate (Mills)	Change in Property Tax Rate (Mills)	Old Local Revenue per Weighted Pupil ($)	New Local Revenue per Weighted Pupil ($)	Change in Local Revenue per Weighted Pupil ($)	New State Revenue per Weighted Pupil ($)	Change in State Revenue per Weighted Pupil ($)	Total Revenue per Weighted Pupil ($)	Change in Total Revenue per Weighted Pupil ($)
1	1,703	13,224	39.64	35.87	(3.77)	524	474	(50)	4,913	1,740	5,387	1,690
2	7,286	20,255	38.50	35.30	(3.20)	772	708	(64)	4,693	1,548	5,401	1,484
3	2,098	25,255	37.15	34.62	(2.52)	938	874	(64)	4,526	1,435	5,401	1,372
4	312	29,261	36.20	34.15	(2.05)	1,059	999	(60)	4,398	1,384	5,397	1,324
5	12,205	33,830	35.91	34.01	(1.91)	1,215	1,150	(64)	4,251	1,308	5,401	1,243
6	1,128	36,967	35.74	33.92	(1.82)	1,321	1,254	(67)	4,150	1,204	5,404	1,137
7	5,458	42,848	34.89	33.50	(1.40)	1,495	1,435	(60)	3,962	1,047	5,397	987
8	1,911	48,142	34.17	33.14	(1.04)	1,645	1,595	(50)	3,792	957	5,387	907
9	10,243	53,544	33.73	32.92	(0.82)	1,806	1,762	(44)	3,618	842	5,381	798
10	1,702	61,686	33.44	32.77	(0.67)	2,063	2,021	(41)	3,357	629	5,378	588
11	2,764	69,014	33.23	32.67	(0.56)	2,293	2,254	(39)	3,122	332	5,376	293
12	6,669	76,255	32.89	32.50	(0.39)	2,508	2,478	(30)	2,889	186	5,367	156
13	2,933	83,676	32.10	32.10	—	2,686	2,686	—	2,651	0	5,337	0
14	17,317	91,849	31.32	33.18	1.86	2,877	3,048	171	2,389	(171)	5,437	—
15	2,576	100,679	30.85	35.33	4.48	3,106	3,557	451	2,105	(451)	5,662	—
16	3,010	113,421	30.50	36.39	5.89	3,459	4,127	668	1,696	(668)	5,823	—
17	33,463	123,442	30.05	36.35	6.31	3,709	4,488	779	1,375	(779)	5,862	—
18	2,266	141,856	28.63	37.49	8.86	4,061	5,319	1,257	783	(1,257)	6,102	—
19	3,433	180,513	27.42	37.61	10.19	4,905	6,790	1,840	—	(1,840)	6,790	—
20	1,672	253,235	25.50	30.66	5.16	6,457	7,765	1,308	—	(1,308)	7,765	—
Weighted Average		85,694	32.46	34.56	2.10	2,653	2,992	339	2,638	90	5,630	429
Weighted Std. Dev.		45,280	2.97	1.68	3.85	1,199	1,635	475	1,314	939	394	562
Median		83,676	32.10	32.10	—	2,686	2,686	—	2,651	0	5,437	0

FIGURE 6.2 Foundation Program with Weights

(continued)

Totals

Category	Amount	Percent	Change from Base Amount	Change from Weighted Pupil Base Amount
Local Revenue	359,459,562	0.53%	40,732,354	40,732,355
State Revenue	316,967,753	0.47%	114,427,587	10,855,638
Total Revenue	676,427,315		155,159,941	51,587,993
Weighted Pupils	120,148			

Winners and Losers

Category	Winners	Losers	No change
State Aid	13	7	0
Total Revenue	13	0	7

Equity Measures

Horizontal Equity	
Range	$2,428
Restricted Range	1,423
Federal Range Ratio	0.265
Coef. of Variation	0.070
Gini Coefficient	0.030
McLoone Index	0.991
Verstegen Index	1.075
Fiscal Neutrality	
Correlation	0.916
Elasticity	0.141
Adequacy	
Odden-Picus	1.000

FIGURE 6.2 Foundation Program with Weights (*continued*)

TABLE 6.4   States Using a Form of Pupil Weighting for Grade-Level Differences, 1998–99

State	Pupil-Weighting Program Description	
Alabama	K–3	1.57
	4–6	1.00
	7–8	1.05
	9–12	1.22
Arizona	K–8	1.158
	9–12	1.268
Colorado	Pre-K and K	0.5
Delaware	Grade-level weighting occurs in the formula allocating staff-teacher ratios:	
	Half-day K	34.8 pupils per unit
	1–3	17.4 pupils per unit
	4–12	20.0 pupils per unit
District of Columbia	Preschool and pre-K	1.16
	K–5	1.05
	6–8	1.00
	9–12	1.20
Florida	K–3	1.057
	4–8	1.000
	9–12	1.138
Georgia	K	1.3210
	1–3	1.2424
	4–5	1.0067
	6–8	1.0122
	9–12	1.0000
Indiana	Half-day K	0.5
Kansas	K and special education pre-school students regardless of whether they attend a full-day or half-day program.	0.5
Maryland	K	0.5
Massachusetts	Elementary	1.00
	Middle	1.05
	High school	1.09
Michigan	K	0.5
Minnesota	Disabled pre-K and K	1.00
	Regular K	0.53
	1–6	1.06
	7–12	1.30
Nebraska	K (except K programs providing 1,032 or more hours of instruction)	0.5

(continued)

TABLE 6.4   States Using a Form of Pupil Weighting for Grade-Level Differences, 1998–99 *(continued)*

State	Pupil-Weighting Program Description	
	1–6 1.0	
	7–8 1.2	
	9–12	1.4
Nevada	K	0.6
New Jersey	K	0.5
	Elementary	1.0
	Middle	1.12
	High school	1.2
New Mexico	K and 3- and 4-year-olds	1.440
	1	1.200
	2–3	1.180
	4–6	1.045
	7–12	1.250
New York	Half-day K	0.5
	Full-day K–6	1.00
	7–12	1.5
North Carolina	Grade-level weighting occurs in the formula allocating pupil-teacher ratios:	
	K–2	1 per 20
	3	1 per 22.23
	4–6	1 per 22
	7–8	1 per 21
	9	1 per 24.5
	10–12	1 per 26.64
North Dakota	Approved preschool	1.2924
	K (all districts)	0.5720
	Rural elementary (1–8)	1.3198
	1–6 (<100 ADM)	1.2012
	1–6 (100–999)	0.9477
	1–6 (1,000 +)	0.9706
	7–8 (all districts)	0.9832
	9–12 (< 75 ADM)	1.4905
	9–12 (75–149)	1.1981
	9–12 (150–549)	1.0917
	9–12 (550 +)	1.0473
Ohio	K	0.5
Oklahoma	K (full or half day)	1.3
	1–2	1.351
	3	1.051
	4–6	1.0
	7–12	1.2

TABLE 6.4   States Using a Form of Pupil Weighting for Grade-Level Differences, 1998–99 *(continued)*

State	Pupil-Weighting Program Description	
Oregon	K	0.5
Pennsylvania	Half-day K	0.5
	Full-day K and Elementary	1.0
	Secondary	1.36
South Carolina	K	1.30
	Primary	1.24
	Elementary	1.00
	High school	1.25
Tennessee	Grade-level weighting occurs in the formula allocating pupil-teacher ratios:	
	K–3	1 per 20
	4–6	1 per 25
	7–9	1 per 30
	10–12	1 per 26.5
Utah	K	0.55
Vermont	Elementary	1.0
	Secondary	1.25
Washington	Grade-level weighting occurs in the formula allocating staff-teacher ratios:	
	K–3	1 staff unit per 18.42 students maximum (depends on ratio maintained by the district)
	4–12	1 staff unit per 21.74 students
Wisconsin	5-year-olds enrolled in half-day K	0.5
	5-year-olds enrolled in full-day K five days a week	1.0
	4-year-olds in a K program, regardless of the length of time in school	0.5
	4-year-olds in a K program providing at least 87.5 additional hours of outreach activities	0.6
Wyoming	K	0.5

Source: Data extracted from Dayton et al., 2001.

provide more revenues for secondary students, ranging from less than one, to 50 percent more than is allocated to lower grades. Interestingly, several states also weight kindergarten students up to an additional 57 percent and students in grades 1–3 up to an additional 57 percent. This practice began in the 1970s; the rationale was that if students learned successfully in the early years, compensatory or remedial programs in the later years would not be needed, at least not at current levels.

There are strong arguments for concentrating educational investments in the early years. Indeed, preschool programs provide long-term achievement and other benefits (Barnett, 1995, 2000). Further, extended-day kindergarten programs for low-income children help boost performance in later grades (Puelo, 1988). One-to-one tutoring in the early grades produces achievement gains on the order of a half to a full standard deviation (Shanahan, 1998; Slavin, Karweit, and Wasik, 1994). Finally, small class sizes of about 15 also improve achievement for kindergarten and first-grade students (Achilles, 1999; Grismer, 1999).

Such research results firmly support investing more at the early grades, perhaps even weighting K–3 students an extra 25–30 percent. As educational productivity (i.e., the link between resources and student achievement) assumes greater importance in the twenty-first century, extra investments for the early years should expand.

3. ADJUSTMENTS FOR SIZE

There is substantial controversy over size adjustments in state school finance formulas. There are several possible conditions that could produce higher costs that might qualify for a size adjustment in the state-aid program: (1) small school size; (2) small district size; (3) large school size; and (4) large district size. The general policy issue is whether small (or large) schools or districts experience diseconomies of scale (i.e., whether it costs more per pupil to run a small [or large] school or district). If size affects school operational costs, the policy question is whether those costs should be recognized in the state-aid formula through a special adjustment or whether the school or district should be urged or required to consolidate (or separate) into a larger (or smaller) entity, thereby reducing costs and avoiding the need to spend extra money.

The major focus for size adjustments has been on small schools and districts. The general perception in the policymaking community is that small schools or districts are inefficient and should consolidate into larger entities. Indeed, as the data in Chapter 1 showed, school and district consolidation has been a common occurrence over the past 50 years. Both districts and schools have consolidated into larger entities. Many states have had incentive programs that rewarded small districts that consolidated into larger ones (Salmon et al., 1988).

Analysts, however, argue that the expected cost savings from the massive school and district consolidation have not been realized (Guthrie, 1979; O'Neill, 1996; Ornstein, 1990) and that consolidation might actually harm student performance in rural schools (Sher and Tompkins, 1977) as well as have broad negative effects on rural communities (Coeyman, 1998; Seal and Harmon, 1995). If small schools or districts indeed cost more, but consolidation reduces performance and disrupts communities, the better policy choice might be to resist consolidation and provide special adjustments to compensate for the higher costs.

The research on diseconomies of small and large scale generally does not support a consolidation policy. From an economic perspective, the concept of diseconomies of scale includes both costs and outputs. The issue is whether costs per unit of output are higher in small schools or districts, or put differently, whether costs can be reduced while maintaining output as size rises. In an extensive review of the literature, Fox (1981) concluded that little research had analyzed output in combination with input and size variables, and Monk (1990) concluded after assessing the meager extant research that there was little support for either school or district consolidation.

For elementary schools, research knowledge is thin, but data suggest that size economies that reduce costs by more than one dollar per pupil exist up to but not beyond 200 pupils (Riew, 1986). Thus, very small schools experience diseconomies of small size and, except in isolated rural areas, potentially could be merged into larger ones. But the real opportunities for cost savings from school consolidation from these small sizes are not great, precisely because many such schools are located in isolated rural areas and there are no other schools nearby with which to consolidate.

At the secondary level, the data are more mixed. Few studies exist that simultaneously assess both size and output, so scale diseconomies have not been adequately studied. Riew (1986) found that there were cost savings, below one dollar per pupil, for middle schools with enrollments above 500; again, many middle schools already enroll more than this number. In analyzing whether larger secondary schools actually provided more comprehensive programs, an argument for larger size, Monk (1987) concluded in a study of New York that program comprehensiveness increased consistently in secondary schools only for size increases up to but not beyond about 400 students. In subsequent research, Haller and colleagues (1990) found that while larger schools offered more comprehensive programs, there was wide variation among both smaller and larger schools, and there was no clear point that guarantees program comprehensiveness. Further, Hamilton (1983) shows that social development is better in small high schools.

Studies of district size generally analyze expenditures per pupil as a function of size without an output variable, such as student achievement (Fox, 1981). To document diseconomies of district size, however, expenditures, size, and output need to be analyzed simultaneously, since the goal is to determine if costs per unit of output decrease as the number of students in the district increases. Again, in reviewing the literature, Monk (1990) concluded that definitive statements could not be made about district consolidation.

In the most recent review of scale economies and diseconomies, Andrews, Duncombe, and Yinger (2002) assessed both cost function (an approach to determining educational adequacy discussed in Chapters 3 and 5) and production function research. The studies reviewed generally assessed costs in tandem with student achievement outputs. The authors concluded that there were potential but modest cost savings that could be realized by consolidating districts smaller than 500 students into districts with 2,000 to 4,000 students; of course this would be an option only for small districts a short distance from each other and not for rural, isolated small districts. The authors also found that the optimum size for elementary schools was in the 300 to 500 pupil range, and for high schools was in the 600 to 900 range (see also, Lee and Smith, 1997, on high school size). Both findings suggest that our very large urban districts and schools are far beyond the optimum size and need to be somehow downsized.

4. ADJUSTMENTS FOR PRICE DIFFERENCES

An issue that gained prominence in school finance during the 1970s and 1980s was the difference in prices that school districts faced in purchasing educational resources. Districts not only purchase a different market basket of educational goods (just as individuals purchase a different market basket of goods), but they also pay different prices for the goods they purchase. Today, because some schools manage their budget on site and do all of their own purchasing, schools can also be included in this discussion. District (and/or school) expenditures determine quantity issues (numbers of different types of educational goods purchased, such as teachers, books, buildings, etc.), the level of quality of those goods, and cost of or price paid for each good. The variety, number, quality, and price of all educational goods purchased determines school district (and/or school) expenditures. While "expenditures" are often referred to as "costs" in school finance parlance, there is a difference between these two economic terms. "Expenditure" refers to the money spent on school resources; "cost" refers to the money spent on school resources to receive a certain level of output or to provide a certain quality of service.

Prices that school districts (and/or schools) face in purchasing educational resources differ across school districts, and many states have taken an interest in trying to adjust school-aid allocations to compensate for geographic cost or price differences. For example, a teacher of a certain quality will probably cost more in an urban area where general costs of living are higher than in nonurban areas where general costs of living are lower. But prices or cost variations that districts must pay for teachers also differ among school districts because of variations in the nature of the work required, the quality of the working environment, and the local community. Teachers might accept marginally lower salaries if, for example, they teach four rather than five periods a day, or have smaller classes. Teachers might accept marginally smaller salaries if there are numerous opportunities for staff development (McLaughlin and Yee, 1988). Or teachers might want marginally higher salaries if there are few cultural opportunities in the surrounding community. The combination of differences in general cost of living, working conditions, and the surrounding community produces differences in prices that districts must pay for teachers of a given quality.

Similarly, districts within the same state might have to allocate more or less general revenues for such noneducational activities such as transportation and heating/cooling. Districts in sparsely populated rural areas face higher-than-average transportation costs because their students are spread over a wider geographical region, and because fuel and repair costs may also be higher. Districts in especially cold or unusually warm environments must spend more for heating or air conditioning. These higher-than-average expenditures are beyond the control of the district and, holding both quality constant and assuming similar technical efficiency, impose higher costs on district budgets.

These are just a few examples of factors that constrain the ability of school districts, even those with the same total general revenue per pupil, to provide the same level and quality of educational services to their students. States have recognized these price and cost variations but only recently have begun to make adjustments for them in state-aid formulas.

While there are several different approaches that can be taken in constructing cost-of-education indices (Berne and Stiefel, 1984; Brazer, 1974; Chambers, 1981; Kenny, Denslow, and Goffmann, 1975), there is substantial correlation among price indices constructed with different methodologies (Chambers, 1981). Whatever methodology is used, price differences can vary substantially across districts. In studies of California (Chambers, 1978, 1980), Florida (Kenny, Denslow, and Goffman, 1975), Missouri (Chambers, Odden, and Vincent, 1976), New York (Wendling, 1981b), and Texas (Augenblick and Adams, 1979; Monk and Walker, 1991) within-state price variations ranged from 20 percent (10 percent above and below the average) in California, to 40 percent (20 percent above and below the average) in Texas. These are substantial differences. These results mean that high-cost districts in California must pay 20 percent more for the same educational goods as low-cost districts; thus, with equal per-pupil revenues, high-cost districts are able to purchase only 75 percent of what low-cost districts can purchase. The differences in Texas are even greater. Such price differences, caused by circumstances and conditions essentially outside the control of district decision makers, qualify as a target for adjustments in some state-aid formulas. For a primer on education price indices in education, see Fowler and Monk (2001).

There are two different approaches states can take in using a price or cost-of-education index. First, state aid could be multiplied by the price index, thus ensuring that equal amounts of state aid could purchase equal amounts of educational goods. But this approach leaves local revenues unadjusted by price indices. A better method would be to multiply the major elements of a school-aid formula by the price index to ensure that total education revenues could purchase the same level of resources. Thus, the price index would be applied to the foundation expenditure level in a foundation program, the tax base guaranteed by the state in a guaranteed tax base program, the state-determined spending level in a full-state-funding program, or total current operating expenditures for a percentage equalizing formula.

As such, including a price index in a school finance formula is relatively simple. In addition, the fact that price indices tend to remain stable over time (Chambers, 1981) suggests that states would need to develop price indices only periodically, once every three to five years, if they were used as part of a state-aid formula. Furthermore, the National Center of Education Statistics (NCES) has already developed different versions of such education price adjustments for all school districts in the country (Chambers, 1995; McMahon, 1994), which any state could use (http://nces.ed.gov/pubs/96068ica.html). States have been reluctant to add education price adjustments to their school-aid formulas, in part because developing them requires some complex econometric analyses and manipulations and in part because they have the potential of changing allocations considerably.

While the existence of the NCES price indices would alleviate the need for analysis, price indices do alter the distribution of state aid. In general, education price indices are higher in urban and metropolitan areas than in rural areas. Thus, with a given amount of state aid, use of a price index would shift the shares of state aid at the margin from rural to urban school districts. This distributional characteristic injects an additional political dimension to constructing a state-aid mechanism that is politically viable. Nevertheless, prices vary across school districts and affect the real levels of education goods and services that can be purchased. Including an education price index in the school-aid formula is a direct way to adjust for these circumstances that are outside the control of school district policymakers.

Summary

This section discussed adjustments for price differences, one of the many important adjustments that must be made to a school finance formula if it is to be equitable. The next two sections outline ways to make these important adjustments to school finance formulas.

A New School Finance Formula.   Given all of the necessary adjustments for students with special needs as well as all of the other adjustments just discussed, as well as the push for educational adequacy rather than just educational equity, a particular type of school finance formula may be in order. This new formula, one which would provide an adequate fiscal base that enables schools to deliver an education program that teaches students to high-achievement standards, would consist of six elements:

1. a base spending level that would be considered adequate for the average child,
2. an extra amount of money for each child from a low-income background,
3. an extra amount for each disabled student,
4. an extra amount for each student who needs to learn English,
5. adjustments for education level and scale diseconomies, and
6. a price adjustment for all dollar figures to ensure comparable spending power.

With such a school finance system, a state could reasonably say it had financed the state's core interests in education. In addition, if states were allowed to pool categorical money from federal and state sources, such a school finance system could also be said to finance a large portion of the federal government's interests in education as well.

An Econometric Approach to Adjustments for Different Needs.   But an even simpler type of school finance system might be possible in the future, if quite complex research is successful in quantifying how much money it takes to teach different students to standards, as discussed in Chapter 3. Economists such as Reschovsky and Imazeki (1998, 2001), Downes and Pogue (1994), Duncombe, Ruggiero, and Yinger (1996), Ladd and Yinger (1994), and Ruggiero (1996) have been pursuing the cost function approach that simultaneously determines an average, foundation spending level and adjustments for all of the special needs just listed, including student needs, issues of scale, education level, or geographic price differences. The results can be used for a somewhat simpler school finance structure—a foundation expenditure per pupil with one overall "cost" adjustment.

In the work being conducted with Wisconsin data, Reschovsky determined how much money a district, with the average demographic characteristics, must spend to teach students to state average-performance levels. In his analysis, he focused on average achievement levels, although he could have set the performance target at a higher level, say the 70th percentile. This amount of money would reflect the "adequate" foundation base, "adequate" being defined by the performance level that the state chooses. From the results of the cost function, he then constructed one overall cost adjustment that accounts for:

1. different characteristics of students, specifically the percentage from a low-income background (as measured by eligibility for free and reduced-price lunch), the percentage disabled, and the percentage with limited English proficiency,
2. different prices across school districts and labor market regions, and
3. economies and diseconomies of scale, as measured by the number of students.

Put differently, this research constructed an overall cost index that adjusts for student need differences, price differences, and scale economies/diseconomies. Related work by others attempts also to adjust for efficiency differences (see, for example, Duncombe, Ruggiero, and Yinger, 1996).

Although the research is state-of-the-art and uses complex econometric statistical analyses, the primary benefit of the research is that two important numbers are produced: the expenditure level needed in the average or typical district/school, and a cost adjustment that accounts for all other factors: student need, price, scale, and at some level, efficiency. Thus, the school finance formula would be a cost-adjusted foundation program. The program would provide a base spending level, which for the Wisconsin data was $6,333 for the 1996–97 school year. The cost factor varied widely, from a low of 0.59 percent to a high of 2.00. The amount of money guaranteed to each district would be the foundation amount, $6,333, times the cost factor. This means that given the preceding characteristics of schools/students/districts, the average district required $6,333 to teach its students to average achievement levels, while the least needy districts/schools required only 59 percent of that, or $3,736 (lower than any district actually spent), and the most needy district required $12,666 (higher than the neediest district actually spent). And these amounts would be sufficient to produce the average achievement level. If Reschovsky had set the achievement level desired above the current average, the dollar figures would have been higher.

Though more research of this type is needed, the goal of the cost-function approach is to create a simplified but adequate school finance formula. When research on this subject becomes more definitive, school finance systems can be more tightly linked to education goals. In turn, the state would know how much money is needed in each school to educate students to state-set achievement standards.

Results from the cost-function research also can be disaggregated to produce different student weights, a scale-economy adjustment, an education-level adjustment, and a geographic price adjustment. When this disaggregation was conducted in a study in Kansas, the state's pupil weights for special needs were quite close to the weights calculated from the cost-function analysis (Johnston and Duncombe, 1998).

5. SUMMARY

There are many legitimate reasons for states to allocate more revenues for certain student or district characteristics. These vertical equity adjustments are not only justified, but also may be required as a matter of equity and adequacy. While specific levels of adjustments can be refined and changed based on new research findings, there is strong consensus that states should share in funding services for low-achieving poor children, limited-English-proficient children, and children with physical and mental disabilities. There also is consensus that price adjustments are warranted, although states have been reluctant to use price indices that are developed using standard (and quite sophisticated) econometric methods. When pupil weights are used to recognize the additional costs associated with special-needs students and a price index is added to the formula, equity analyses should use both a weighted-pupil count and price-adjusted dollars.

There is less consensus surrounding adjustments for secondary and early elementary students and for small (or large) size. While many states weight high school students an extra 25 to 30 percent, this weight reflects current expenditure patterns more than productivity findings. Indeed, the research base is stronger for investing more in the K–3 grades; K–3 weightings, including extended-day kindergarten and even preschool programs for low-income four-year olds, are increasing policy choices.

Controversy still surrounds the costs associated with small districts and schools. Although policymakers generally support school and district consolidation, research undergirding that policy option is thin. In general, research does not support incentives to create larger schools and districts, but state policies providing extra resources for small schools and districts in isolated rural areas make sense. The same research suggests that very large urban districts and very large schools suffer from diseconomies of large size, and need to somehow be made smaller.

States still use many different general-aid formulas and have many different methods of adjusting for the additional costs associated with students with special needs. Some of these include full-state funding, census-based funding, and pupil weights. In the years to come, policymakers will continue to grapple with the question of which of these methods is the most feasible, comprehensible, politically viable, and equitable. And while that question can be answered differently in different states, it is clear that there is no longer any question that such adjustments are needed. Using one of the methods outlined at the end of this chapter for designing a school finance formula that is adjusted for different student needs, including an econometric approach to such an adjustment, is necessary to ensure that the educational needs of all pupils are met.

Chapter 7

Improving State School Finance Systems

Chapter 5 described a variety of formulas and strategies for improving state school finance systems. In this chapter, we use those formulas and strategies to "fix" the school finance systems in four different states. The states present different types of school finance problems, so this chapter shows how one needs to tailor a school finance formula or structural change to the specific nature of the school finance problem being addressed. As the chapter will demonstrate, a school finance structure that improves the equity or adequacy of a school finance system in one state might exacerbate it in another, and vice versa.

The chapter has five sections. Section 1 describes the overall framework that will be used to determine the nature of the school finance problem in each state, as well as to identify the goals to be attained by any proposed improvement. Sections 2, 3, 4, and 5 then use the framework to analyze the school finance systems in Vermont, Wisconsin, Illinois, and Kentucky, respectively.

1. A FRAMEWORK FOR ANALYSIS

When assessing the degree of equity or adequacy in a state's school finance system, one needs some type of framework to structure that analysis. We provided such a framework in Chapter 3. In this section of this chapter, we use the concepts developed in Chapter 3 to structure our analysis of the finance systems in each of four states.

Students are the group of concern for these analyses. Our discussions will assess equity and adequacy from the perspective of students.

The unit of analysis will be the district, as the information in the state files on this text's website (www.mhhe.com/odden3e) includes fiscal data only on a district-by-district basis. When computing all statistics, each district's value will be statistically weighted by the number of students in the district. This means the values of large districts will affect the statistical results more than the values of smaller districts. Finally,

State Database
Simulation

the data include information only for the K–12 districts in Wisconsin and Illinois. This excludes a small number of districts in Wisconsin, but a larger number in Illinois. In these two states, there are both elementary-only and high school–only districts, in addition to districts that serve all grades from kindergarten to grade 12. But we analyze only the data for the K–12 districts. Vermont is more complex. Many "districts" in Vermont are individual schools with locally elected boards. These schools are generally part of a Supervisory Union, which provides many district-level services to the school. The taxing authority for the school, however, remains in the local community, and for the purposes of this analysis, they are treated as individual districts. All districts in Kentucky are K–12 districts.

In most cases, the analysis will use an ex post versus an ex ante analysis (i.e., will assess results using fiscal data on actual behavior). In some instances, though, there will be ex ante comments on the nature of the current state formula. As this discussion will show, sometimes when systems appear highly equitable from an ex ante perspective, they produce a system that is quite inequitable from an ex post perspective.

The object of analysis will be state plus local revenues per pupil. This fiscal object essentially includes all local revenues as well as state equalization aid, which often is called state general aid. This revenue total comprises the fiscal resources for the "regular" education program. Although the state data on this text's website for the state simulation exercises also contain categorical program data for state compensatory education, bilingual education, and handicapped programs, we do not use those data in the analyses in this chapter. Thus, this chapter only addresses issues related to the "regular" education program, and not any programs for extra student needs. In other words, the analysis here ignores the issue of vertical equity, or adjustments for special student (or district) needs. We urge readers to address vertical equity and to identify differences in results when issues of special-needs students are included in the analyses.

Each analysis will assess issues of both horizontal and fiscal neutrality equity, as well as adequacy. For horizontal equity, the coefficient of variation will be the key disparity statistic, but the analyses also will incorporate the McLoone Index, to make comments on the equity of the bottom half of the distribution. The analysis will use a 0.10 standard for the coefficient of variation (CV); CVs less than or equal to 0.10 will indicate an equitable distribution. The analysis will use a 0.95 standard for the McLoone Index, labeling a distribution with a McLoone Index equal to or higher than 0.95 as providing equity for the bottom half of the distribution.

For fiscal neutrality, the analyses will focus on the wealth elasticity, using a standard of 0.10, thus concluding that a wealth elasticity less than or equal to 0.10 would indicate a negligible link between the resource variable and property wealth per pupil. The discussion will mention the correlation coefficient, particularly noting when it is below 0.5, but will use the elasticity statistic to draw conclusions about the connection between state and local revenues per pupil and property wealth per pupil.

Finally, the Odden-Picus Adequacy Index will be used to draw conclusions about the adequacy of each state's school finance system. For two states, this part of the analysis will reference studies that have suggested an adequate revenue-per-pupil figure for the regular-education program. But for the other two states, the specification of the adequate amount per pupil will have less research support, and therefore this chapter will only be able to make comments on the adequacy issue. Our standard will be an Adequacy Index of 1.0 on the assumption that there are or are not "adequate" revenues per pupil in all districts.

Following the Odden and Clune (1998) call to set "policy targets" for improving state school finance structures, we will assess the impact of two general strategies in all states for improving the equity and adequacy of their school finance structure. First, we will simulate a GTB at or above the 90th percentile, a level that provides ex ante fiscal neutrality. Second, we will simulate a foundation at least at the median, which could be a rough approximation of adequacy and find a preferred solution.

Before beginning the analysis, we would like to note several aspects of decision rules programmed within the simulation. First, "winners" and "losers" are defined as those gaining or losing state aid. Second, politically we assume that representatives of "winner" districts would vote for the program, with the reverse true for representatives of "loser" districts. Third, as discussed elsewhere, we assume a "fifty-fifty" use of new state-aid dollars for increased spending and local property tax relief (i.e., the simulation has districts using half of state aid increases to hike spending, and half to lower local property tax rates). This latter assumption, however, is constrained by foundation program parameters which first require a district to spend at least at the foundation expenditure level and, if below the zero-aid district, to tax at least at the required foundation tax rate.

2. SCHOOL FINANCE IN VERMONT

The Vermont data are for the 1996–97 school year, the year Vermont's school finance system was declared unconstitutional in the *Brigham* v. *Vermont* court case (*Brigham* v. *State of Vermont*, No. 96-502) (Vt. filed Feb. 5, 1997). The data were downloaded from the Vermont Department of Education's website and adjusted to include only public school districts that raised and spent public tax dollars. There were a total of 201 districts with some 73,000 students and regular-education expenditures of $450.2 million that year from state and local sources. Property wealth is equalized to 100 percent of market value.

Prior to the enactment of Act 60, the 1997 school-funding law enacted in response to the Vermont Supreme Court's ruling in Brigham, the Vermont school finance system relied primarily on a foundation program. The major problem with the foundation program, as pointed out in the court decision, was that average school-funding levels substantially exceeded the foundation level. Moreover, most funds raised and spent above the foundation level were raised through unequalized property tax levies. This led to the "traditional" school finance problem previously identified, low-wealth districts with high tax rates and low per-pupil revenues.

To address the problems identified by the court, the Vermont legislature passed Act 60, which established a block grant program guaranteeing each district essentially $5,000 per pupil at a uniform statewide tax rate of $1.10 per $100 of assessed valuation, or 11.1 mills. Although called a block grant, it is clearly a foundation program.

A second-tier GTB was also included in Act 60. Rather than provide state funding to help districts reach their revenue goals, however, the second tier is funded entirely through property taxes in the districts that elect to participate in the second tier. The system, frequently referred to as the "shark tank" by the Vermont media, creates a system where districts that elect to raise revenues beyond the $5,000 level don't know what their tax rate will be until all districts have determined how much revenue they will collect through the guaranteed yield. A uniform tax rate is then established across the state. Chapter 5 pointed out that one of the potential problems with a GTB is that the cost to the state can't be predicted with certainty. In Vermont, the state has shifted the risk to school districts, with wealthy districts absorbing higher levels of risk—if they choose to participate in the second tier.

To mitigate against high property taxes, homeowner property taxes in the first tier are limited to a maximum of 2 percent of income for taxpayers with incomes below $75,000. Total property taxes including the second tier and other municipal property taxes are limited to no more than 5 percent of household income for those earning less than $75,000 a year (there is a sliding scale based on income). The impact of this is to shift more of the property tax burden to out-of-state property owners (who constitute a substantial proportion of taxpayers) and to nonresidential property.

The Vermont School Finance Problem

Figure 7.1 displays the base data for Vermont. The data from the 201 districts are displayed by deciles. Each decile has approximately 10 percent of the students in the state. Consequently, the number of districts in each decile (reported in the last column of the figure) varies from a low of 9 in the sixth decile to a high of 29 in the lowest revenue decile. The figure shows total state plus local spending of $450,185,325, with local districts raising over 72 percent of this total.

Across the deciles, average total revenue per pupil ranged from $4,659 to $8,191, a ratio of 1 to 1.75. Property wealth generally increases as spending increases. Across the deciles, property wealth per pupil ranges from a low of $236,776 per pupil to a high of $777,284 per pupil, a factor of 3.25 to 1. State aid per pupil declines as revenues and wealth increase, while locally raised revenues climb with wealth and spending level.

The coefficient of variation is 0.147, above the 0.10 standard identified in Chapter 3. The McLoone Index is estimated at 0.90, below the 0.95 standard we also established in Chapter 3. The Verstegen Index stands at 1.016 showing that there is some but not substantial variation in spending per pupil for districts above the median.

Determining a reasonable revenue level for the adequacy calculation was difficult. For Vermont, we have used a very low figure—the $5,000 per pupil, the block grant level established by the legislature in Act 60. With that figure, the Odden-Picus Adequacy Index is 0.994. That means that to bring those districts with revenues per pupil below $5,000 to that spending level, revenues would have to increase by 0.006 percent relative to $5,000 or only by about $30 per pupil. Others might choose to set the adequacy level higher, in which case the Adequacy Index would be lower.

The adequacy calculation may be a predictor of the problems Vermont is likely to encounter as Act 60 is implemented. Recall that the second tier is equalized entirely by local property taxes levied on districts that participate in that pool. Since most districts are spending above the level of the $5,000 block grant, most would be expected to par-

Adequacy Level	$	5,000
Pupil Weights		no
Disabled		—
Limited English		—
Low Income		—

Decile	Average Number of Pupils per District in Decile	Average Property Value per Pupil ($)	Average Property Tax Rate (Mills)	Average Local Revenue per Pupil ($)	Average State Revenue per Pupil ($)	Average Total Revenue per Pupil ($)	Number of Districts in Decile
1	252	239,362	11.51	2,719	1,940	4,659	29
2	385	242,444	12.79	3,107	2,177	5,284	18
3	368	249,748	14.02	3,475	2,056	5,531	21
4	432	236,776	14.33	3,402	2,342	5,744	17
5	371	507,437	12.86	4,392	1,536	5,928	19
6	821	317,844	13.73	4,269	1,831	6,100	9
7	391	350,994	14.60	4,805	1,540	6,345	18
8	214	432,737	14.05	5,517	1,160	6,677	27
9	466	509,522	15.09	5,699	1,436	7,136	18
10	335	777,284	13.09	7,392	800	8,191	25
Weighted Average		338,713	14.05	4,452	1,691	6,142	
Weighted Std. Dev.		223,080	2.88	1,645	1,059	905	
Median		214,200	10.91	2,337	3,699	6,037	

Totals		
	Amount	Percent
Local Revenue	326,279,231	72.48%
State Revenue	123,906,094	27.52%
Total Revenue	450,185,325	
Pupils	73,294	

Equity Measures	
Horizontal Equity	
Range	$6,712
Restricted Range	2,851
Federal Range Ratio	0.597
Coef. of Variation	0.147
Gini Coefficient	0.094
McLoone Index	0.900
Verstegen Index	1.016
Fiscal Neutrality	
Correlation	0.482
Elasticity	0.072
Adequacy	
Odden-Picus	0.994

FIGURE 7.1   Base Data (Vermont), 1996–97

ticipate in the second-tier GTB. In this case, property taxes on the wealthy districts are likely to go up dramatically. The alternative is substantial declines in the level of per-pupil revenue, and hence spending. But if $5,000 is an appropriate adequacy level, then the argument for higher spending would be less forceful. On the other hand, if $5,000 is below an adequate expenditure level, then there could be pressures to increase the $5,000 base to a higher level, and reduce "forced" spending above the base.

In terms of fiscal neutrality, Figure 7.1 shows that the correlation between revenue and wealth is 0.482, and the elasticity is a relatively low 0.072. However, if you download the simulation from this text's website and analyze the Vermont data, you will see that the graph of the base data shows the presence of a few high-wealth, medium-revenue-level districts. These outliers have the effect of lowering the elasticity. Eliminate those outliers from the model, and there is a very strong relationship between wealth and revenue.

Improving the Vermont School Finance System

Since the Vermont legislature has already taken steps to improve the equity of the Vermont school finance system, we will begin our analysis with the changes made in Act 60. First we will consider a simple foundation program using the parameters of the state's block grant. That will be followed by the promised GTB at the 90th percentile of wealth, and finally a combination program with similar characteristics.

First, we simulated a foundation program with a foundation level of $5,000 and a required local effort (RLE) of 11.1 mills, which reflects the first tier of the reform Vermont enacted. The result increased total spending by just $3.1 million, with the state share falling by just over $3.2 million, and local taxes increasing by $6.3 million. A total of 108 districts experienced a loss of state aid and were forced to make it up through increased property taxes, which occurred in all but the second and third deciles. Only districts in the two lowest-revenue deciles experienced increases in revenue. Both the horizontal equity and fiscal-neutrality measures showed very small improvements, while the Odden-Picus Adequacy Index improved to 1.0, meaning all of the districts received at least $5,000 per pupil in total revenue. Again, if a higher adequacy level were set, the Adequacy Index would have been less than 1.0.

Figure 7.2 shows the results of a GTB program using a per-pupil property wealth level of $510,800 representing the district at the 90th percentile of wealth. The figure shows immediately why the legislature was unwilling to fund a high-level GTB program. A GTB at this level would raise an additional $48.5 million for schools, provide taxpayers with $19.7 million in property tax relief, and cost the state an additional $68.2 million. Finding those revenues would have been difficult. Recall that additional revenues would be collected from a statewide property tax under Act 60. If this simulation is indicative of what would have happened after Act 60 was implemented, at an average property wealth of $338,713, property tax rates would have to increase an average of 2.75 mills across the state, thus offsetting the modest property tax relief shown on Figure 7.2.

Interestingly, although the GTB increased spending dramatically, it did little to change the horizontal equity statistics, which remain roughly the same as in the base data. Correlation and elasticity do decline, however.

Figure 7.3 displays the results of a combination program using the block grant parameters and a GTB level of $510,800. This compromise appears to be the best option of those presented, but is more generous than the program Vermont enacted. Total revenue increased by just over $30.2 million, with a drop of $4.2 million in local taxes and an increase in state funding of $34.5 million. While the horizontal equity figures show very small improvements, the elasticity declined to 0.001. The correlation is higher than under the GTB, but this is in large part due to the very low elasticity observed, and highlights the policy problem identified in Chapter 5 when using both figures. The state share of total revenue increases to almost 33 percent, and while 71 districts lose state revenue, all districts have as much total revenues, or more than before. Nevertheless,

Adequacy Level $ 5,000.00   **Guaranteed Tax Base** $510,800.00

Pupil Weights
Disabled   no
Limited English   —
Low Income

Decile	Average No. of Pupils	Average Property Value per Pupil ($)	Average Old Property Tax Rate (Mills)	Average New Property Tax Rate (Mills)	Average Change in Property Tax Rate (Mills)	Average Old Local Revenue per Pupil ($)	Average New Local Revenue per Pupil ($)	Average Change in Local Revenue per Pupil ($)	Average New State Revenue per Pupil ($)	Average Change in State Revenue per pupil ($)	Average Total Revenue per Pupil ($)	Average Change in Total Revenue per Pupil ($)	Number of Districts in Decile
1	252	247,425	10.70	10.15	(0.54)	2,624	2,494	(130)	2,693	539	5,187	409	28
2	328	433,400	11.80	10.88	(0.92)	3,572	3,388	(184)	2,482	696	5,870	511	23
3	329	330,077	12.40	11.88	(0.52)	3,922	3,873	(49)	2,312	514	6,185	466	22
4	382	305,800	13.70	12.51	(1.19)	4,036	3,759	(277)	2,749	917	6,507	640	18
5	338	361,016	13.53	12.44	(1.08)	4,456	4,242	(213)	2,428	831	6,671	618	19
6	616	370,771	14.02	12.89	(1.12)	4,752	4,466	(285)	2,419	886	6,886	601	14
7	593	293,217	15.26	13.82	(1.44)	4,453	4,052	(402)	3,006	1,207	7,058	805	12
8	423	488,250	14.26	12.85	(1.41)	5,069	4,727	(342)	2,554	1,095	7,282	753	16
9	390	461,014	14.56	13.53	(1.03)	5,965	5,738	(226)	1,920	846	7,658	620	21
10	266	605,657	16.08	14.49	(1.59)	6,598	6,230	(368)	2,517	1,259	8,747	871	28
Weighted Average		338,713	14.05	12.90	(1.14)	4,452	4,183	(269)	2,621	931	6,804	662	
Weighted Std. Dev.		223,080	2.88	2.07	1.26	1,645	1,734	407	1,417	862	923	489	
Median		347,600	15.27	13.28	(1.99)	5,306	4,616	(690)	2,167	1,705	6,783	1,014	

Totals

	Amount	Percent	Change From Base Amount
Local Revenue	306,579,415	61.48%	(19,699,816)
State Revenue	192,126,350	38.52%	68,220,255
Total Revenue	498,705,765		48,520,440
Pupils	73,294		

Winners and Losers

Category	Winners	Losers	No Change
State Aid	155	46	0
Total Revenue	155	0	46

Equity Measures

Horizontal Equity	
Range	$6,407
Restricted Range	3,416
Federal Range Ratio	0.639
Coef. of Variation	0.136
Gini Coefficient	0.065
McLoone Index	0.897
Verstegen Index	1.101
Fiscal Neutrality	
Correlation	0.292
Elasticity	0.029
Adequacy	
Odden-Picus	0.999

FIGURE 7.2 Guaranteed Tax Base (GTB) (Vermont)

Adequacy Level	$	5,000.00
Pupil Weights		
Disabled	no	
Limited English	—	
Low Income	—	

Foundation Level	$5,000.00
Required Tax Rate	11.10
GTB	$510,800.00
GTB rate cap above foundation tax rate	99.00

Decile	Pupils	Property Value per Pupil ($)	Old Property Tax Rate (Mills)	New Property Tax Rate (Mills)	Change In Property Tax Rate (Mills)	Old Local Revenue per Pupil ($)	New Local Revenue per Pupil ($)	Change in Local Revenue per Pupil ($)	New State Foundation Revenue per Pupil ($)	New State GTB Revenue per Pupil ($)	Change in State Revenue per Pupil ($)	Total Revenue per Pupil ($)	Change in Total Revenue per Pupil ($)	Number of Districts in Decile
1	251	235,630	10.82	11.45	0.63	2,518	2,689	170	2,385	99	210	5,173	410	27
2	408	247,653	12.87	12.18	(0.68)	3,154	3,005	(149)	2,268	285	613	5,558	458	19
3	300	446,483	11.62	12.03	0.40	3,699	3,893	194	1,676	343	18	5,912	459	24
4	377	286,265	14.21	13.47	(0.74)	4,026	3,854	(172)	1,834	511	593	6,198	552	20
5	431	336,381	13.97	13.19	(0.79)	4,400	4,254	(147)	1,627	515	612	6,395	439	16
6	461	398,325	13.36	13.18	(0.18)	4,860	4,880	19	1,247	474	208	6,600	246	16
7	590	332,077	15.23	14.18	(1.05)	4,827	4,592	(234)	1,528	627	827	6,748	389	13
8	443	392,846	14.25	14.12	(0.13)	5,119	5,119	0	1,219	598	299	6,936	311	13
9	302	515,566	14.34	13.78	(0.56)	5,848	5,773	(75)	1,069	616	480	7,458	350	29
10	315	668,483	15.62	14.62	(0.99)	6,918	6,749	(169)	1,031	850	754	8,630	376	24
Weighted Average		338,713	14.05	13.62	(0.42)	4,452	4,394	(58)	1,647	514	470	6,555	413	
Weighted Std. Dev.		223,080	2.88	2.14	1.33	1,645	1,756	447	1,080	418	781	900	398	
Median		516,700	12.24	12.60	0.37	6,324	6,513	189	—	—	(189)	6,513	—	

Totals	Amount	Percent	Change From Base Amount
Local Revenue	322,063,154	67.04%	(4,216,076)
State Revenue	158,370,429	32.96%	34,464,335
Total Revenue	480,433,584		30,248,259
Pupils	73,294		

Winners and Losers			
Category	Winners	Losers	No Change
State Aid	130	71	0
Total Revenue	106	0	95

Equity Measures	
Horizontal Equity	
Range	$5,365
Restricted Range	3,182
Federal Range Ratio	0.613
Coef. of Variation	0.137
Gini Coefficient	0.076
McLoone Index	0.900
Verstegen Index	1.110
Fiscal Neutrality	
Correlation	0.371
Elasticity	0.051
Adequacy	
Odden-Picus	1.000

FIGURE 7.3   Combination Program (Vermont)

the number of state-aid-loser districts represents about one-third of all districts, which diminishes the political attractiveness of even this program.

In short, the Vermont school finance system is difficult to improve without spending more state money. The reform that was enacted, Act 60, has been controversial because of its burden on out-of-state property owners and the redistributive nature of the second tier. Only time will tell how this reform will ultimately be implemented.

Data for the 2000–01 school year are now on the text website, so readers can analyze the impact of Act 60 for that school year, as well as simulate the impact of different types of school finance formulas to perhaps improve equity and adequacy even more than Act 60. For such simulations, the adequacy level of $5,000 should be substantially hiked. Visit this text's website for a link to a fairly recent description of the Vermont school finance system, the result of a major project of the American Education Finance Association.

Vermont School Finance System

3. SCHOOL FINANCE IN WISCONSIN

The Wisconsin data are for the 1995–96 school year. Property wealth is equalized to 100 percent of market value. For 1995–96, Wisconsin had a three-tiered, GTB school finance structure, which was enacted in 1995, though the formula parameters changed each year. For tier one, the state guaranteed a tax base of $2 million per pupil, up to the first $1,000 of spending. Since the GTB for this tier exceeded that of all school districts, tier one provided some state aid to all 379 school districts. There were two reasons for this "generous" nature of tier one. First, this transformed what had been termed "minimum" or "hold harmless" aid for the wealthy districts into a "bona fide" state-aid allotment. To be sure, this shift was in part simply political, but it did eliminate the use of "minimum" aid, a phrase that indicated an inequitable allocation of state support. Second, because this state-aid formula was enacted primarily to provide property tax relief, the provision of at least some aid ensured that even the wealthiest districts would experience some property tax relief (see subsequent discussion of cost controls). Although many Wisconsin policymakers and education leaders criticized this element of the formula, it nevertheless was enacted as a part of the new structure.

Tier two provided the bulk of state aid. The GTB for tier two was $406,592, which covered districts that enrolled 95 percent of all students. Tier-two GTB aid was provided for spending from $1,000 up to $5,786, which was the expenditure per pupil of the district that enrolled the 56th percentile student.

Tier three had a straightforward and a unique element. The GTB was set at the statewide average. Districts with a property wealth below that level could use tier three for any amount of spending above the tier-two ceiling of $5,786. This was the straightforward element of tier two.

The unique element of tier two pertained to those districts with a property wealth per pupil above the state average, or the tier-three GTB. For these districts, there was a "negative-aid" calculation. When these districts decided to spend above the tier-two expenditure ceiling of $5,786, a negative value for tier-three aid was determined. This negative amount was then subtracted from the tier-two aid but only until and if it reduced tier-two aid to zero. Since a previous court decision in Wisconsin had determined that it was unconstitutional for the state actually to "recapture" local property tax revenue through a negative-aid calculation, the tier-three factor never required districts to send funds to the state for redistribution to other districts. But tier-three calculations could potentially reduce tier-two aid amounts to zero. Tier-three negative calculations primarily affected higher-spending metropolitan school districts, those surrounding Milwaukee and Madison. Districts also always retained their tier-one aid, which politically was intended as an amount that all districts would receive.

Finally, when the state enacted this program, it also imposed "cost controls" on local school districts. Previously, school boards had the power to raise local property tax rates to increase school spending. The cost controls continued that authority but only for an inflationary expenditure increase, which has been a little above $200 per pupil for several years. Districts could exceed this expenditure-per-pupil increase limit, but they needed voter approval to do so. When enacted in 1995, the $200 per-pupil cost increase limit combined with the $1,000 per pupil of aid for tier one meant that the bulk of that additional revenue, even for the wealthiest districts, had to be used for decreasing the property tax rate, absent a local vote to use it for increased spending.[1]

The overall goal of the Wisconsin school finance structure was to set the state role in financing schools at two-thirds of all revenues.

The Wisconsin School Finance Problem

Figure 7.4 shows the base data for Wisconsin for 1995–96. The data are grouped into deciles ranked by total revenues per pupil; the simulation attempts to have approximately the same number of students in each decile. Since the data are ranked by total revenues per pupil, the averages in all columns show the average of that variable for their decile of spending. So the average property wealth per pupil in the first decile is the average of property wealth per pupil for the first decile of spending, not the first decile of property wealth. Nevertheless, in our discussion, we will refer to the property wealth figure as a rough indicator of the average of the respective decile as if the data had been ranked by property wealth per pupil. But readers should know that this is a rough approximation.

The data show there was a wide variation in property wealth per pupil: the average was $218,605, but it was only $165,734 in the lowest decile and fully $331,347 in the wealthiest decile. Without substantial state equalization aid, districts would have great difficulty raising equivalent amounts of money per child at the same tax rate. Note, however, that the GTB in Wisconsin's second tier ($406,592) exceeded the average property wealth per pupil of the tenth and wealthiest decile, so it was above the 90th percentile.

---

[1]The Wisconsin system also includes limits on teacher salary increases to help districts keep overall spending increases within the expenditure cap. If, during collective bargaining, districts provide a "qualified economic offer (QEO)," that offer can be imposed for a negotiation settlement and teachers are unable to go to arbitration or strike. Further, a QEO is defined as at least a 3.8 percent increase in salaries *and* benefits. As benefits have increased at far above that rate, the effect of the QEO over the years has been to hold teacher salaries to insignificant increases.

Adequacy Level	$ 6,030.00
Pupil Weights	no
Disabled	—
Limited English	—
Low Income	—

Decile	Average Number of Pupils per District in Decile	Average Property Value per Pupil ($)	Average Property Tax Rate (Mills)	Average Local Revenue per Pupil ($)	Average State Revenue per Pupil ($)	Average Total Revenue per Pupil ($)	Number of Districts in Decile
1	1,701	165,734	12.56	2,084	3,025	5,108	47
2	1,959	168,277	13.23	2,228	3,153	5,381	41
3	2,697	186,804	13.53	2,528	2,975	5,502	30
4	1,811	167,573	13.78	2,309	3,294	5,602	32
5	34,060	151,904	13.96	2,121	3,557	5,678	3
6	2,911	183,485	14.15	2,598	3,153	5,751	28
7	1,476	169,609	14.84	2,514	3,415	5,929	54
8	1,919	188,730	15.72	2,971	3,173	6,145	38
9	1,904	204,424	17.03	3,444	3,016	6,460	47
10	1,723	331,347	17.73	5,146	2,008	7,154	47
Weighted Average		211,438	14.67	3,137	2,726	5,862	
Weighted Std. Dev.		93,728	1.85	1,487	1,154	547	
Median		218,605	13.97	3,054	2,627	5,681	

Totals		
	Amount	Percent
Local Revenue	2,527,836,576	53.50%
State Revenue	2,196,748,542	46.50%
Total Revenue	4,724,585,118	
Pupils	805,908	

Equity Measures	
Horizontal Equity	
	$4,694
Restricted Range	1,715
Federal Range Ratio	0.331
Coef. of Variation	0.093
Gini Coefficient	0.107
McLoone Index	0.961
Verstegen Index	1.033
Fiscal Neutrality	
Correlation	0.454
Elasticity	0.090
Odden-Picus	0.947

FIGURE 7.4   Base Data (Wisconsin)

This shows that the second tier of the Wisconsin system provided property wealth equalization up to a very high level (i.e., provided substantial ex ante fiscal neutrality equity).

Tax rates also varied but within a small range, with an average tax rate of 12.56 mills in decile 1 to 17.73 mills in decile 10.

The figure also shows that revenues per pupil varied, but by a much smaller percentage than property wealth per pupil. Spending per pupil from state, general, and local sources varied from $5,108 in the lowest-spending decile, to just $5,678 in the fifth decile, and then to $7,154 in the tenth decile.

One of the most interesting features of Figure 7.4 is that it reveals a state with the "new" school finance problem. As property wealth per pupil rises, so also does spending per pupil. But local property tax rates also rise with property wealth. So Figure 7.4 shows that in Wisconsin, lower-wealth districts have lower tax rates and also lower spending levels, while higher-wealth districts have higher tax rates and thus higher spending levels. It appears that it is the link between tax rates and property wealth that drives the spending–property wealth connection in Wisconsin. Further, recall that for a GTB, the higher the tax rate, the higher the spending-per-pupil level. In Wisconsin, most districts apply their tax rate to the GTB for spending at least up to $5,786; since the GTB is higher than the average for even the tenth decile, tax rates are more a determinant of spending levels than are property values.

Despite this phenomenon, the equity statistics show a fairly equitable distribution of education revenues. The CV is 0.093 and thus meets the equity standard for that statistic. The McLoone Index is 0.961, which also meets the standard of 0.95 for this statistic. Thus, in terms of horizontal equity, the Wisconsin school finance system in 1995–96 for K–12 districts met tough standards for an equitable distribution.

This finding is important for two reasons. First, the Wisconsin constitution requires a school finance system that is as equitable as "practical," which these statistics show has been accomplished. The distribution was not perfectly equal, and even the wealthiest districts received some amount of state general aid. But the system nevertheless meets our horizontal equity standards. Second, though, Wisconsin used a GTB-type school finance structure, which defers spending levels to local districts and thus was not focused on providing equality of spending per pupil. Nevertheless, the structure provided a high degree of spending-per-pupil equality.

In terms of fiscal neutrality, the Wisconsin system also received good but not superlative marks. The correlation coefficient was just 0.454, and the wealth elasticity was 0.090, both just meeting the equity standard for this statistic. Though some improvements could be made in reducing the linkage between spending and property wealth, the data already showed a remarkable degree of fiscal neutrality equity. The problem in making improvements on this front will be the tax-rate–property wealth link. Because higher-wealth districts have higher tax rates, they also have higher spending levels; the spending differences are caused mainly by tax effort differences not tax base differences.

Finally, the Odden-Picus Adequacy Index is 0.947, with the adequacy expenditure level set at $6,030; this is the 1997 adequacy figure of $6,333 found by Reschovsky and Imazeki (1998) but deflated by 5 percent to a 1995–96 figure. The relatively high Adequacy Index suggests that Wisconsin may not be far from providing an "adequate" amount of money for the average child in all districts. It would need to increase the funding for those districts below the adequate level by an average of 0.053 percent relative to the adequacy level, or by an average of about $320 to produce adequacy for all K–12 districts for the average student.

Improving the Wisconsin School Finance System

A key question for Wisconsin school finance is: What needs to be improved? From an ex ante perspective, those who filed a court case in the late-1990s argued that districts with a wealth above that in the second-tier GTB should not receive any state support. They proposed eliminating tier one, which provides some aid to all districts, and either reducing state aid to zero for any district with a wealth above the tier-two GTB level or actually changing the constitution to allow for recapture. Others might take issue with that perspective, but it would produce a school finance structure with a "purer" version of ex ante fiscal equity.

In the summer of 2000, the Wisconsin Supreme Court[2] ruled that Wisconsin's school finance system was "as uniform as practicable," and found the system constitutional on equity grounds. However, the court suggested that an adequacy case could be brought and even identified an adequacy standard—the funding would need to be adequate for all students to achieve to proficiency standards in core subjects tested (reading and writing, mathematics, science, geography, and history) and to receive instruction in the arts, music, vocational training, physical education, social sciences, health, and foreign languages, in accordance with their age and aptitude. An adequacy case has not yet been brought, but a proposal for what would constitute adequate funding has been made (Norman, 2002).

A second approach is to determine whether a high-level GTB program, which provides ex ante fiscal neutrality, can in fact reduce the link between spending and property wealth per pupil. This task is difficult because of the tax-rate–property wealth link. To assess the efficacy of this strategy, we ran simulations of a one-tier GTB set at $350,000, $400,000, and $500,000, all guaranteeing property wealth per pupil greater than the 90th percentile. The horizontal equity statistics worsened under each one of these programs, though the simulation results portray a "rosier" picture because all state aid losses are made up with greater local taxes to ensure that spending does not decline if aid is lost. And the lower of these GTB levels also produced many state-aid "losers," which diminished their political viability as well.

This result occurs because this state represents the "new" school finance situation. Since tax rates rise with property wealth per pupil, a higher GTB simply widens the spending-per-pupil difference between lower-wealth and higher-wealth districts. This result increases the coefficient of variation, reduces the McLoone Index, and increases the wealth elasticity between total revenues per pupil and property wealth per pupil. A GTB program, even a combination foundation-GTB program, with the GTB set at a high level, simply worsens fiscal equity statistics in a state like Wisconsin with the "new" school finance problem. Readers should simulate these programs on their own and view the results to confirm these statements.

As an alternative, Figure 7.5 shows the results of simulating a foundation program at $6,000 per pupil with a required tax rate of 14 mills. Even though it is above the median, the $6,000 foundation expenditure figure was chosen because it had been suggested by many education and political leaders as an expenditure level and a school finance structure that might be more suitable for the state. The 14-mill tax rate was the median tax rate for this simulated program, and just above the median in the base data. Further, these two figures produce a "zero-aid" district of $428,571, which is slightly above the extant tier-two GTB level. Another way of interpreting this program is that it turns the extant system from a GTB of around $428,571 with local decision-making on the level of a tax rate, to one with a required tax rate of 14 mills; this requirement raises the spending in all districts now spending below $6,000 to the $6,000 per-pupil level.

---

[2]*Vincent v. Voight*, 614 N.W.2d 388 (Wis., 2000).

Adequacy Level	$	6,030.00
Pupil Weights	no	
Disabled	—	
Limited English	—	
Low Income	—	

Foundation Level	$6,000.00
Required Tax Rate	14.00

Decile	Pupils	Property Value per Pupil ($)	Old Property Tax Rate (Mills)	New Property Tax Rate (Mills)	Change In Property Tax Rate (Mills)	Old Local Revenue per Pupil ($)	New Local Revenue per Pupil ($)	Change in Local Revenue per Pupil ($)	New State Revenue per Pupil ($)	Change in State Revenue per Pupil ($)	Total Revenue per Pupil ($)	Change in Total Revenue per Pupil ($)	Number of Districts in Decile
1	1,741	163,524	13.12	14.00	0.88	2,146	2,289	143	3,711	522	6,000	665	46
2	2,447	165,838	13.24	14.00	0.76	2,197	2,322	125	3,678	490	6,000	615	32
3	3,197	180,497	13.63	14.00	0.37	2,452	2,527	75	3,473	381	6,000	456	3
4	4,621	172,210	13.26	14.00	0.74	2,290	2,411	121	3,589	487	6,000	608	33
5	2,196	183,647	13.23	14.00	0.77	2,431	2,571	141	3,429	481	6,000	622	37
6	2,043	168,550	14.35	14.10	(0.25)	2,413	2,374	(39)	3,640	258	6,014	218	40
7	1,660	170,404	14.90	14.35	(0.55)	2,537	2,442	(95)	3,614	211	6,056	116	48
8	2,126	200,279	15.66	14.90	(0.76)	3,134	2,969	(166)	3,196	197	6,165	31	34
9	1,904	204,424	17.03	16.71	(0.33)	3,444	3,298	(146)	3,162	146	6,460	0	47
10	1,723	331,347	17.73	17.95	0.21	5,146	5,062	(84)	2,092	84	7,154	0	47
Weighted Average		211,438	14.67	14.61	(0.06)	3,137	3,086	(50)	3,085	359	6,171	309	
Weighted Std. Dev.		93,728	1.85	1.39	1.01	1,487	1,326	254	1,105	209	334	291	
Median		115,963	13.48	14.00	0.52	1,555	1,615	60	4,385	460	6,000	520	

	Totals		Change From
	Amount	Percent	Base Amount
Local Revenue	2,487,224,527	50.01%	(40,612,049)
State Revenue	2,486,126,518	49.99%	289,377,976
Total Revenue	4,973,351,045		248,765,927
Pupils	805,908		

Winners and Losers

Category	Winners	Losers	No Change
State Aid	322	32	13
Total Revenue	224	0	143

Equity Measures	
Horizontal Equity	
Range	$3,032
Restricted Range	902
Federal Range Ratio	0.150
Coef. of Variation	0.054
Gini Coefficient	0.118
McLoone Index	1.000
Verstegen Index	1.057
Fiscal Neutrality	
Correlation	0.529
Elasticity	0.065
Adequacy	
Odden-Picus	0.997

FIGURE 7.5 Foundation Program (Wisconsin)

As just mentioned, all Wisconsin simulations use $6,030 as the adequacy level, a figure slightly above the foundation level and the median because that was the figure determined by Reschovsky and Imazeki (1998) as sufficient for the average district to teach the average student to the average-performance level on Wisconsin standards. Actually, Reschovsky and Imazeki identified a figure of $6,333 but for the 1996–97 school year; we deflated that figure by 5 percent to $6,030 for 1995–96. Although we could have set the foundation level at the adequacy level, we decided to set it just below that level simply to show it produces an Adequacy Index less than 1. If adequacy were the primary goal, we would have set the foundation expenditure level at the adequacy figure.

Figure 7.5 shows that the simulated foundation program improves equity on both fronts as well as improves the adequacy of the Wisconsin school finance system. The coefficient of variation drops from 0.093 to 0.054, the McLoone Index increases to a perfect 1.0, the wealth elasticity drops to 0.065, and the Adequacy Index improves to 0.997.

The cost is modest, about a 13 percent increase in state funds but a decline of about 3.5 percent in local funds. At the required tax rate of 14 mills, local school districts previously levying a school tax rate below 14 mills (mostly lower-wealth districts) increased their local effort, while the middle-wealth districts previously levying above 14 mills had modest local tax-rate declines. The highest-wealth districts also had modest tax-rate hikes. This foundation program could be simulated with a lower required tax rate; the equity statistics would remain about the same, and the total increased cost would be about the same, but the local portion of the increase would drop and the state portion would rise. Where to set the required tax rate would need to be determined through the political process. At the 14 mill rate, the program increased aid to 322 districts, and not surprisingly, reduced aid to 32 districts, largely those districts that had received some aid from the first tier.

In sum, a school finance system such as that in Wisconsin, which already produces a fairly equitable school finance system but with differences in spending and wealth reflecting the "new" school finance problem, can be enhanced with high-level foundation programs. The simulations showed that GTB programs simply worsened equity measures. Further, in a state such as Wisconsin, which already spends far above the national average, the simulations show that adequacy can be approached with only modest increases in spending, however split between local districts and the state.

We should note, however, that these results do not address the issue of providing extra funds for special-student needs, particularly those students who have disabilities, speak a native language other than English, or come from low-income families and thus need additional education supports. Busch, Kucharz, and Odden (1996) show that insufficient aid for special-needs students was a shortcoming of the Wisconsin finance system that needed enhancement. Reschovsky and Imazeki (1998) found that a 2.0 weight was needed for each low-income child (i.e., that twice as much money was required to teach a low-income child to state standards). The Wisconsin database on this text's website (www.mhhe.com/odden3e) includes these additional data, and readers are encouraged to experiment with alternative ways to address these special-education needs and assess their costs as well as their impacts on fiscal equity and adequacy.

In addition, the text's website also includes Wisconsin data for the 1998–99 and 2000–01 school years so readers can analyze equity and adequacy impacts over several years as well as select a more recent year to simulate alternative ways to make even more improvements in equity and adequacy. Visit this text's website for links to more information about the Wisconsin school finance system.

4. SCHOOL FINANCE IN ILLINOIS

The Illinois data are for the 1994–95 school year, and again, include only the "unit districts" (i.e., the districts that serve all grades from kindergarten through grade 12). Property wealth per pupil in Illinois is equalized to only about 33⅓ percent of market value (i.e., lower than Wisconsin). Thus, to compare the property wealth and tax rates in Illinois with those in Wisconsin, one would need to multiply the Illinois wealth figures by 3 and divide the tax rates by 3 to provide information relative to full market value.

In 1994–95, Illinois had a two-pronged school finance structure. Most districts operated under a typical foundation-type school finance formula. The foundation expenditure level was set at $2,900 with a required local property tax rate of 19 mills. Readers might conclude that the foundation level was quite low. For that year, the average expenditure per pupil for operating purposes in Illinois was $6,136 (National Center for Education Statistics, 1998), so the foundation expenditure level was just 47 percent of the average. The zero-aid district had a property wealth per pupil of $105,072, which was below that of many districts.

On the other hand, the state also used a weighted-pupil count to determine and allocate state aid; weights were provided by education level, counting students in kindergarten through grade 6 as 1.0, in grades 7 through 8 as 1.05, and grades 9 through 12 as 1.25. Using a weighted-pupil count as the denominator generally decreases the expenditure figure when compared with a figure without weighted-pupil counts. The database in the simulation includes weighted-pupil counts.

The data also exclude the Chicago school district; this large, urban district actually enrolls about one-third of all students in K–12 districts and thus would cover three deciles in a simulation. Such a district usually is identified separately in a school finance analysis, but the simulation data used exclude this district altogether.

The Illinois School Finance Problem

For years, Illinois struggled with proposals to enhance the state role in public school financing. As Figure 7.6 shows, the state role in 1994–95 for these K–12 districts was just 43.5 percent; when Chicago is included, the state role for K–12 districts was below 40 percent. For the decade prior to 1994–95, the state experienced school finance legal challenges, votes on constitutional changes to increase the state role, and proposals for school reform from both the governor and various members of the legislature.

Figure 7.6 shows there was a good case to be made for shortcomings in the Illinois school finance system. The data are grouped into deciles ranked by total revenues per pupil; the simulation attempts to have approximately the same number of students in each decile.

The data show there was a wide variation in property wealth per pupil: the average was $57,107, but it was close to $30,000 in the lowest deciles and $182,744 in the

Adequacy Level	$ 4,500
Pupil Weights	no
Disabled	—
Limited English	—
Low Income	—

Decile	Average Number of Pupils per District in Decile	Average Property Value per Pupil ($)	Average Property Tax Rate (Mills)	Average Local Revenue per Pupil ($)	Average State Revenue per Pupil ($)	Average Total Revenue per Pupil ($)	Number of Districts in Decile
1	1,834	51,825	22.79	1,056	1,552	2,607	45
2	1,645	31,555	28.88	905	1,992	2,897	51
3	1,919	31,120	30.87	942	2,004	2,946	43
4	1,261	31,768	32.53	1,020	1,986	3,007	62
5	2,161	42,664	33.63	1,412	1,685	3,098	41
6	1,940	44,988	35.24	1,565	1,621	3,187	43
7	2,427	50,658	36.71	1,832	1,465	3,296	34
8	2,269	54,741	38.57	2,077	1,352	3,429	37
9	2,392	63,644	41.15	2,564	1,129	3,693	32
10	4,304	182,744	35.21	4,994	359	5,353	21
Weighted Average		57,107	33.45	1,881	1,450	3,330	
Weighted Std. Dev.		51,377	5.38	1,260	634	763	
Median		43,365	34.02	1,475	1,665	3,140	

Totals		
	Amount	Percent
Local Revenue	1,565,784,916	56.47%
State Revenue	1,206,982,693	43.53%
Total Revenue	2,772,767,609	
Pupils	832,553	

Equity Measures	
Horizontal Equity	
Range	$10,883
Restricted Range	1,806
Federal Range Ratio	0.646
Coef. of Variation	0.229
Gini Coefficient	0.034
McLoone Index	0.931
Verstegen Index	1.161
Fiscal Neutrality	
Correlation	0.821
Elasticity	0.190
Adequacy	
Odden-Picus	0.726

FIGURE 7.6   Base Data (Illinois)

wealthiest decile. The wealthiest decile had just over six times the property wealth per pupil, and thus six times the ability to raise local revenues for public schools, than the poorest deciles have. Even the average district had about twice the wealth as the poorest deciles. Without substantial state equalization aid, districts would have great difficulty raising equivalent amounts of money per child at the same tax rate. Though not shown, the property wealth per pupil in Chicago was substantially above the state average.

Tax rates also varied but within a smaller range, with an average tax rate of 33.45 mills, and ranging from at or below 22.79 mills in the lowest-spending decile to 35.21 mills in the highest-spending decile and 41.15 in the ninth decile.

The figure also shows that revenues per pupil varied, but by a much smaller percentage than property wealth per pupil. Spending per pupil from state general and local sources varied from $2,607 in the lowest-spending decile, to just $3,098 in the fifth decile, and then to $5,353 in the tenth decile. The average was just $3,330, far below the Wisconsin average of close to $6,000, though the Wisconsin data use unweighted-pupil counts compared with the weighted counts in the Illinois database.

The data in Figure 7.6 also show that Illinois was another state with the "new" school finance problem. As property wealth per pupil rises, so also did spending per pupil. But local property tax rates also rose with property wealth. Just as in Wisconsin, lower-wealth districts in Illinois had lower tax rates and also lower spending levels, while higher-wealth districts had higher tax rates and thus higher spending levels. It appears that it is the link between tax rates and property wealth as well as a wealth advantage that drove the spending–property wealth connection in Illinois. Although it is unlike in Wisconsin, where local tax rates apply to a relatively high GTB state program, for spending above the foundation in Illinois, local tax rates applied to local wealth only. The result, nevertheless, is that wealth, tax rates, and spending levels all rose in tandem.

The data also show that there are anomalies in the connections among property wealth, tax rates, and spending in Illinois. For example, the lowest-spending decile actually had a wealth of $51,825, close to the state average but a very low tax rate of 22.79 mills. These are mainly rural and agricultural districts in southern Illinois. If these districts had levied just average tax rates, their expenditures per pupil would have been significantly higher. They simply did not tap their wealth advantage. Conversely, the property wealth per pupil of the tenth decile was over double that of the nearest (ninth) decile. This dramatic wealth advantage allowed these districts to enjoy very high spending with tax rates just a small bit above the state average. Thus, although there was a general, positive connection between wealth, tax rates, and spending, the bottom- and top-spending deciles represented differences from the general overall pattern.

The larger role of local wealth in driving spending disparities in Illinois is reflected in the equity and adequacy statistics, all of which are "worse" than those in Wisconsin. The coefficient of variation is 0.229, far above the standard of 0.10. The McLoone Index is below 0.95 at 0.931. The wealth elasticity is a high 0.190, and the correlation between spending per pupil and property wealth per pupil is high at 0.821. But again, since the state presents the "new" type of school finance problem, a high-level GTB, which provides ex ante fiscal neutrality equity, will unlikely improve these equity statistics by much.

Finally, the low level of spending is reflected in the Odden-Picus Adequacy Index, which is just 72.6 percent. As is indicated in the figure, we set the adequate spending level at $4,500. This was a level somewhat higher than that identified by an Illinois study of the level of state and local revenues per pupil needed to have 70 percent or more of students achieve at or above state standards on the Illinois state testing system (Hinrichs and Laine, 1996).

In sum, Illinois presents several types of school finance problems. These data for 1994–95 showed wide disparities in spending per pupil, a large local role in financing schools, a "new" school finance problem in which higher-wealth districts have higher spending but also higher tax rates, and a system that fell far short of providing adequate revenues.

Improving the Illinois School Finance System

Though a state could focus on simply reducing expenditure-per-pupil disparities, or just decreasing the link between spending and wealth, or providing more adequate levels of revenues, this analysis will assess the progress various new school finance strategies make on all three of these fronts.

We simulated a GTB program at $100,000, a figure that is at the lower-end approximation of the 90th percentile and close to the zero-aid district in the extant foundation program (Figure 7.7). We can somewhat predict the effect of this program. For a $100,000 GTB, a tax rate of 30 mills is needed to produce spending at the $3,000 per-pupil level. Higher tax rates are needed to produce higher spending levels. Because of this, even this relatively high-level GTB might require most districts to increase tax rates just to maintain former spending levels.

That is precisely what we found. A GTB of $100,000 required both local and state revenues to rise. Local revenues rose in the lower-decile districts because even this high-level GTB provided them less state aid. State revenues rose in the mid-wealth deciles because the GTB provided both more money for higher spending and for local property tax relief. Local revenues also rose for the higher-wealth districts.

Perhaps not surprisingly, this GTB did not make significant gains on equity and adequacy statistics. The coefficient of variation was still high at 0.22, the McLoone Index dropped to 0.90, the fiscal neutrality statistics improved modestly, and the Adequacy Index rose from 0.726 to 0.747. Though this program cost only an extra total of $79.5 million, it had almost no positive equity or adequacy impact on the system. The program also produced over 100 state-aid "losers," rendering the program politically problematic as well.

Thus, we ran a GTB at a much higher level—$150,000—thus ensuring some substantial property tax relief at the risk of not making sufficient equity gains in this state with the "new" school finance problem. Figure 7.7 presents the results. First, the state cost rose substantially, which might make such a program unaffordable. Though there was some local tax relief, which was one of the goals, it was not very high.

Though the equity and adequacy statistics improved, there is not sufficient progress to declare the system sound. The coefficient of variation at 0.178 is still far above the standard of 0.10. The McLoone Index is just 0.885. But both the fiscal neutrality and adequacy statistics are much better, with the wealth elasticity at 0.112 and the Adequacy Index at 90.2 percent.

The problem with a GTB program for a state with the "new" school finance problem is that a very high, and thus very expensive, GTB must be used, and then only modest gains on some equity and adequacy fronts are produced. Thus, we tried a foundation program to ensure that the lower-spending districts actually had to raise spending, which allowed spending above the foundation level but only with local wealth. Figure 7.8 shows a foundation program with a foundation expenditure of $4,300 and a required tax

Adequacy Level	$	4,500

Guaranteed Tax Base	$150,000.00

Pupil Weights	no
Disabled	—
Limited English	—
Low Income	—

Decile	Average No. Of Pupils	Average Property Value per Pupil ($)	Average Old Property Tax Rate (Mills)	Average New Property Tax Rate (Mills)	Average Change in Property Tax Rate (Mills)	Average Old Local Revenue per Pupil ($)	Average New Local Revenue per Pupil ($)	Average Change in Local Revenue per Pupil ($)	Average New State Revenue per Pupil ($)	Average Change in State Revenue per Pupil ($)	Average Total Revenue per Pupil ($)	Average Change in Total Revenue per Pupil ($)	Number of Districts in Decile
1	1,844	52,702	22.78	20.08	(2.70)	1,080	968	(112)	2,054	527	3,022	415	45
2	1,678	35,774	28.67	24.00	(4.66)	1,025	859	(166)	2,741	866	3,600	700	49
3	1,731	34,331	30.33	25.01	(5.32)	1,039	859	(180)	2,893	977	3,752	797	44
4	1,733	33,926	32.02	26.04	(5.98)	1,082	884	(198)	3,022	1,095	3,906	897	52
5	1,390	41,204	33.50	27.08	(6.42)	1,374	1,117	(257)	2,945	1,220	4,062	963	53
6	2,764	43,183	35.16	28.19	(6.97)	1,511	1,217	(294)	3,012	1,340	4,228	1,046	34
7	2,657	50,237	36.11	28.99	(7.12)	1,789	1,456	(332)	2,893	1,400	4,349	1,068	31
8	2,343	56,761	37.34	29.98	(7.37)	2,041	1,668	(373)	2,864	1,482	4,532	1,109	36
9	2,515	54,468	40.16	31.91	(8.26)	2,153	1,740	(413)	3,046	1,652	4,786	1,239	31
10	2,608	123,955	39.98	33.51	(6.47)	3,766	3,404	(361)	2,246	1,352	5,650	991	34
Weighted Average		57,107	33.45	27.66	(5.79)	1,881	1,599	(282)	2,604	1,155	4,203	872	
Weighted Std. Dev.		51,377	5.38	4.18	2.06	1,260	1,219	165	768	408	749	298	
Median		51,477	34.22	27.79	(6.43)	1,762	1,431	(331)	2,738	1,296	4,168	965	

Totals	Amount	Percent	Change from Base Amount
Local Revenue	1,330,981,501	38.04%	(234,803,415)
State Revenue	2,168,176,978	61.96%	961,194,285
Total Revenue	3,499,158,480		726,390,871
Pupils	832,553		

Winners and Losers			
Category	Winners	Losers	No Change
State Aid	398	11	0
Total Revenue	398	0	11

Equity Measures	
Horizontal Equity	
Range	$10,883
Restricted Range	1,895
Federal Range Ratio	0.564
Coef. of Variation	0.178
Gini Coefficient	0.005
McLoone Index	0.885
Verstegen Index	1.125
Fiscal Neutrality	
Correlation	0.612
Elasticity	0.112
Adequacy	
Odden-Picus	0.902

FIGURE 7.7 Guaranteed Tax Base (GTB) (Illinois)

Adequacy Level	$ 4,500.00
Pupil Weights	no
Disabled	—
Limited English	—
Low Income	—

Foundation Level	$4,300.00
Required Tax Rate	35.00

Decile	Pupils	Property Value per Pupil ($)	Old Property Tax Rate (Mills)	New Property Tax Rate (Mills)	Change in Property Tax Rate (Mills)	Old Local Revenue per Pupil ($)	New Local Revenue per Pupil ($)	Change in Local Revenue per Pupil ($)	New State Revenue per Pupil ($)	Change in State Revenue per Pupil ($)	Total Revenue per Pupil ($)	Change in Total Revenue per Pupil ($)	Number of Districts in Decile
1	1,665	38,308	25.85	34.07	8.22	869	1,176	308	3,033	1,139	4,209	1,447	49
2	1,587	28,626	29.42	35.00	5.58	824	1,002	177	3,298	1,225	4,300	1,402	53
3	1,265	36,557	30.63	35.00	4.37	1,078	1,279	201	3,021	1,160	4,300	1,361	63
4	1,941	44,736	31.52	35.00	3.48	1,372	1,566	194	2,734	1,094	4,300	1,288	45
5	2,294	57,029	31.59	35.00	3.41	1,782	1,996	214	2,304	1,013	4,300	1,226	30
6	3,355	55,841	33.92	35.04	1.12	1,879	1,956	77	2,346	1,006	4,301	1,083	29
7	2,009	43,754	36.30	35.59	(0.71)	1,585	1,552	(33)	2,769	1,095	4,321	1,063	40
8	1,951	51,579	38.18	36.55	(1.63)	1,951	1,874	(77)	2,495	1,039	4,369	963	40
9	3,384	51,440	40.32	37.66	(2.66)	2,055	1,928	(127)	2,500	1,049	4,427	922	25
10	2,591	126,140	39.30	36.53	(2.77)	3,771	3,647	(124)	1,468	601	5,115	477	35
Weighted Average		57,107	33.45	35.48	2.02	1,881	1,960	79	2,440	990	4,400	1,070	
Weighted Std. Dev.		51,377	5.38	2.53	4.14	1,260	1,218	233	946	342	482	424	
Median		63,337	34.00	35.00	1.00	2,153	2,217	63	2,083	968	4,300	1,032	

Totals

	Amount	Percent		Change from Base Amount
Local Revenue	1,631,873,444	44.55%		66,088,528
State Revenue	2,031,483,579	55.45%		824,500,886
Total Revenue	3,663,357,023			890,589,414
Pupils	728,146			

Winners and Losers

Category	Winners	Losers	No Change
State Aid	397	12	0
Total Revenue	393	0	16

Equity Measures

Horizontal Equity	
Range	$10,883
Restricted Range	359
Federal Range Ratio	0.083
Coef. of Variation	0.110
Gini Coefficient	0.977
McLoone Index	0.997
Verstegen Index	1.048
Fiscal Neutrality	
Correlation	0.785
Elasticity	0.098
Adequacy	
Odden-Picus	0.964

FIGURE 7.8 Foundation Program (Illinois)

rate of 35 mills, which is 1 mill above the median. We simulated foundation programs at lower tax-rate levels but the costs seemed too high, though as Figure 5.8 shows, this program is not low cost either.

Such a foundation program, which is similar to the reform enacted by Illinois in late 1997, does accomplish the goal of raising the state percentage and lowering the local percentage role in financing schools. And it also makes larger gains on all equity and adequacy fronts. The coefficient of variation at 0.110 is just above the 0.10 standard, the McLoone Index is 0.997, which indicates that nearly all districts are spending at the median. The wealth elasticity is below 0.10 at 0.098, and the Adequacy Index is 0.964. But the program required an extra $891 million in state revenues and $66 million more in local revenues, the latter produced by setting the required minimum local tax effort at 35 mills.

The dilemma in "fixing" the Illinois school finance system was that lower foundation levels produced less progress on equity and adequacy. Higher foundation levels could not be accompanied by a required local tax effort that exceeded 35 mills, which is still quite high, and thus required large infusions of state dollars. The bottom line was that the only way significant equity and adequacy gains could be made was by raising the foundation level, as the state ultimately did. But the "cost" of doing so was a substantially enhanced state fiscal role, close to an increase of $1 billion, which represented an 68 percent increase from the base of $1.2 billion.

The high state cost was one reason the state had struggled for years to enact a school finance reform. The only option was a much larger state role; that either required a state tax hike, which was not politically feasible, or a very healthy economy that produced increased in-state revenues that could be devoted to school finance. That was the scenario that finally prevailed. The fact that such a program also raised state aid in nearly all districts added to the political acceptability of the program.

Illinois School Finance System

This text's website now includes data for the 2000–01 school year. Readers are encouraged to analyze the equity impacts of this system, as compared with that in 1994–95. Visit the text website for links to more information about the Illinois school finance system.

5. SCHOOL FINANCE IN KENTUCKY

In response to the landmark ruling of the Kentucky Supreme Court in *Rose* v. *Council for Better Education*[3] in June 1989, the Kentucky General Assembly dramatically changed the system of public K–12 education in that state. Among the many components of that ruling, the Kentucky Supreme Court upheld an earlier circuit court ruling[4] holding that the state's school finance system violated the Kentucky constitution's education clause, which requires the general assembly "to provide an efficient system of common schools throughout the Commonwealth."[5] In assessing the constitutionality of the Kentucky school finance system, the circuit court had found that (Augenblick, 1991):

[3]*Rose* v. *Council for Better Education, Inc.*, 88-SC-804-TG (Ky. 1989).
[4]*Council for Better Education, Inc.* v. *Wilkinson*, 85-CI-1759 (Franklin Cir. Ct., Div. I, Ky. May 31, 1933).
[5]Kentucky Constitution Sec. 183.

1. there was marked variation in property wealth of school districts,
2. the allocation of state aid did not compensate for the variation in wealth,
3. there was a wide disparity in the per-pupil revenue of schools districts, and
4. the quality of education was contingent on available revenue.

The circuit court concluded that an efficient school finance system required *substantial uniformity* and *substantial equality* of financial resources.

In response to the ruling in Rose, the Kentucky General Assembly completely overhauled the organization and structure of K–12 education, and created a new school finance system. The new system, called Support Education Excellence in Kentucky, or SEEK, was designed to dramatically improve the equity of Kentucky's school finance system.

Various analyses of the SEEK formula concluded that the equity of the system improved substantially between 1989–90 and the implementation of SEEK in 1990–91 (see Augenblick, 1991, and Adams, 1994). Further, Picus, Odden, and Fermanich (2001) concluded that equity had consistently improved throughout the 1990s, using a common equity framework (see Chapter 3 in this book) and data over a 10 year-period from 1991 to 2000. Further, Picus, Odden, and Fermanich also used pupil weights and a geographic price adjustment, finding that need and price-adjusted dollars showed the most equity for the system.

Developed a decade ago as part of Kentucky's wide-ranging school reform, the SEEK formula has not been substantially revised since its inception. For 2000–01, the SEEK formula relied on three levels of funding for school districts as described next.

Adjusted Base Guarantee

This is a foundation program that provided each district with $2,994 per pupil (2000–01) through a combination of local taxes and state aid. The number of pupils is adjusted by a series of factors or "add-ons" that affect the cost of providing services to students including:

- A pupil-weighting system for exceptional children with special needs. This includes weights of 2.35 for severely handicapped children, 1.17 for moderately handicapped children, and 0.24 for children requiring speech programs. In addition, home and hospital students are multiplied by the base guarantee less the capital outlay allotment of $100.
- A transportation adjustment based on the population density of a school district.
- A weight of 0.15 for students participating in the free lunch program.
- An adjustment for students unable to attend regular school due to short-term health problems.

Each district levies a property tax of 30 cents per hundred dollars of assessed value, or an equivalent amount through a combination of taxes for school purposes on utilities, motor vehicles, occupational license receipts, or as an excise tax on income. The difference between the foundation guarantee and the district's locally raised revenue is provided by the state. The amount of the unadjusted per-pupil basic allotment for each of the 10 years from 1991–00 is displayed in Table 7.1.

- **Tier I:** This is an optional component that allows a district to raise up to an additional 15 percent of the adjusted base guarantee through an equalized property tax or property tax equivalent. Districts with property wealth less than 150 percent of the state average receive state equalization aid that makes up for the difference between the local tax base and equalization level. For 1999–00, the Tier I equalization level was $410,000, and it grew to $470,000 for 2000–01. Table 7.1 shows the equalization level for Tier I for each year from 1991 to 2000. It should be noted that fiscal year 1994–95 was the first year in which a uniform system of valuing property at 100 percent of real value was required across Kentucky.
- **Tier II:** Another optional component of the system allows school districts to generate additional revenue up to 30 percent of the total of the adjusted base guarantee plus the revenue generated in Tier I. This revenue is not equalized by the state. Thus, a district taking full advantage of both Tier I and Tier II authority could raise a total of $4,371 per ADA before the add-ons are computed. This is 49.5 percent higher than the adjusted base guarantee. Obviously, the add-ons for special education, compensatory education, transportation, and home/hospital children establish a unique (and slightly higher) adjusted base guarantee for each individual district. However, the formula still allows each district to raise nearly half again as much as the adjusted base guarantee.

In addition to the funding in the SEEK formula, the state provides limited funding to school districts through a number of categorical programs including programs for state agency children, gifted and talented, early childhood education, vocational education,

TABLE 7.1   Adjusted Base Guarantee and Tier I Equalization Level in Kentucky: 1990–91 through 1999–2000

Year	Adjusted Base Guarantee ($ per ADA)	Tier I Equalization Level ($ per ADA)
1990–91	2,305	225,000
1991–92	2,420	225,000
1992–93	2,420	280,000
1993–94	2,495	280,000
1994–95	2,517	295,000
1995–96	2,593	295,000
1996–97	2,673	365,000
1997–98	2,756	365,000
1998–99	2,839	410,000
1999–00	2,924	410,000

textbooks, teacher testing and internships, staff development, family resource/youth service centers, and regional service centers. These programs are relatively small, and according to Murray (2001) represented less than 9 percent of total state aid in 1998–99. Visit the text website for links to fairly recent and more detailed descriptions of the Kentucky school finance system.

Kentucky School Finance System

The Kentucky School Finance Problem and Simulated Improvements

Kentucky data for three school years—1990–91, 1995–96, and 1999–00—are available on this text's website. Readers are encouraged to select one, two, or all three years of these data and first analyze the nature of the school finance problem in that year, and then simulate alternative school finance systems to make improvements beyond that which the SEEK program has produced. Readers can also use the data to assess the degree to which Kentucky school finance equity changed over that 10-year period.

6. SUMMARY

Fixing state school finance problems is no easy task. It requires balancing equity and adequacy goals with the political economy of education—producing sufficient winners at a cost the state can afford. Though not discussed at length here, all of the final programs simulated produced many more school districts that had their state-aid amounts increased than those that did not.

These examples also show that the nature of the school finance problem varied dramatically across the four states, thus requiring different kinds of solutions. The Vermont system was somewhat easier to improve as it represented a more "traditional" school finance situation; a high GTB worked in this state, though the best structure was a two-tier system. But high GTBs did not work in either Wisconsin or Illinois, as both states represented "new" school finance problems. In these states, high-level GTBs were expensive and produced only modest equity and adequacy gains. The resolution in both states required a higher-level foundation program; such a program could be funded with quite small increases in state aid in Wisconsin but required large increases in Illinois. And the SEEK program in Kentucky was a high foundation program.

Other states will require even different solutions, some perhaps requiring more of a two-tiered school finance structure as in Vermont, which we favored more in the first edition (Odden and Picus, 1992). Others will require still different mixes of state and local revenues. The bottom line in improving state school finance systems requires some combination of these:

1. getting a clear understanding of the nature of the problems—too much local revenue, inadequate spending, wide spending disparities, significant connections between spending and wealth, or etc.,
2. determining which type of school finance structure—GTB, foundation, or two-tiered, foundation-GTB programs—likely will work,

3. determining a level of spending adequacy, and
4. simulating alternative forms of the formula structures that might resolve the problems and assessing the gains in equity and adequacy in light of both local and state costs as well as political impacts (state aid winners and losers and numbers of districts that have to raise local taxes).

Judging which program might be the one to try in a state will depend on answers to these school finance, public finance, and political effects questions, answers that will vary by state, and probably vary by time within any individual state.

7. SUGGESTED PROBLEMS

State Database
Simulation

1. From this text's website, select a state with newer data. Analyze the degree of equity and adequacy of that state's school finance system. Compare what you find with that for earlier years discussed in this chapter.
    a. Use the simulation to find alternative school finance programs that improve both equity and adequacy. Require viable programs to have at least 60 percent of districts be "winner" districts and limit state-aid increases to 20 percent.
    b. Discuss the cost and the impacts on equity and adequacy.
    c. Use the preferred program in "part a" to address vertical equity as well, by including pupil weights for students from low-income backgrounds, ESL students, and disabled students.
        i. What is the additional cost?
        ii. What is the impact on equity?
2. Select a second state and conduct the same analyses as for Problem 1.
3. Briefly compare and contrast:
    a. The nature of the school finance problem in the two states.
    b. The nature of the school finance reform to remedy the problem.
    c. The effect that pupil weights have on the preferred school finance reform in terms of cost and impacts on equity.

— Chapter 8

School District Budgeting

The first seven chapters of this book focused on how money is raised and then distributed to school districts. But, once the money is distributed, districts need a plan for using those funds. This is typically revealed in a district's budget. In this chapter, we discuss the process of school district budgeting. Our focus here is mostly on the mechanics of building a budget, estimating the expenditures needed to provide the educational program developed by the district, and estimating the revenues the district will receive to fund those expenditures. Revenues need to be greater than, or at least equal to, expenditures for the budget to be in balance. This is critical because all 50 states require local governments to submit balanced budgets every year.

This chapter includes four sections. The first provides a detailed definition of budgets and budgeting, explaining why budgets are necessary and what role they play in the management of a school system. In the second section, we consider the different approaches that exist for building a budget, focusing on how those models can be used in an educational setting. The third section of this chapter provides a detailed discussion of budgeting specifics, describing the step-by-step process of creating a school district's budget and using the budget to manage the district's fiscal status. Finally, in the fourth section, we review some recent approaches to budgeting in large urban school systems.

The budget document reflects the priorities and decisions of a school district's leadership. Therefore it should be thought of as a supporting document rather than a controlling document. Once decision makers have established their priorities and determined what programs they want to implement, it is through the budget that the necessary resources are allocated to the objects and functions necessary to implement those priorities. The process of building a budget also helps the district leadership understand whether or not sufficient resources exist for particular programs and helps them make decisions across competing needs when revenues are not sufficient to meet all proposed programmatic functions. The purpose of this chapter is to provide readers with the ability to review and understand the budget document prepared by his or her school district, and to understand how resources are being allocated to the different functions of the district.

1. DEFINING BUDGETS

At first glance, a school district's budget appears to be a large collection of seemingly incomprehensible numbers, prepared by an obscure office somewhere in the district's central administration. In reality, that document provides a great deal of information about the school district, its educational philosophy, and its management style. The budget also provides information on the priorities of the school district and indicates how they will be carried out. Because of these diffuse functions—all of which can be attributed to a budget—it is hard to define exactly what a budget is and what it is supposed to do.

In the first edition of his book, *School District Budgeting*, Hartman (1988b, p. 2) defined a budget as:

> . . . a document which specifies the planned expenditures and anticipated revenues of a school district in a given fiscal year, along with other data and information relating the fiscal elements to the educational philosophy, programs, and needs of the district.

There are three major components of a budget that can be depicted as a triangle. Shown in Figure 8.1, these elements are the educational program of the school district, revenues, and expenditures. In our view, a description of the district's educational program should form the base of the triangle. This is because—absent a clear description of the district's educational priorities—there is no foundation on which to base decisions about the level of expenditures needed to operate the district. Expenditures and revenues are represented on the sides of the triangle to reflect the reality that expenditures must be less than or equal to revenues if the budget is to remain in balance.

At a more specific level of detail, Woods and colleagues (1995, p. 12-22) suggest that a budget serves six different functions including:

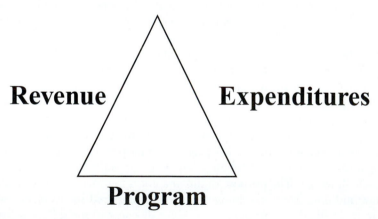

FIGURE 8.1   The Budget Triangle

- *A record of the past.* It reflects bargains and compromises that have been made in the past, reflects including priorities of earlier administrations, provides a record of earlier budget decisions, and by inference indicates what has been eliminated in the past.
- *A statement about the future.* It links proposed expenditures with desired future events. As such, it represents a plan to determine future events through current actions.
- *Predictions of future actions.* Budgets specify connections between words and numbers in a budget document and future human behavior. Whether the behavior intended by the makers of the budget occurs is not a given, but rather a matter of observation.
- *A mechanism for allocating resources.* Funds are almost always more scarce than desireds. As a result, a budget is a mechanism for allocating resources across competing demands, and if the intent were to reach certain objectives at the lowest possible cost, then a budget can also serve as an instrument for pursuing efficiency.
- *A form of power.* Budgets are mechanisms through which individuals or subunits bargain over conflicting goals, make side-payments, and attempt to motivate each other to achieve their own specific goals.
- *Signals.* Budgets serve as signals of the preferences of others, and provide a way for each group in an organization to communicate their priorities and desires.

Budgeting is not a static activity. In fact, it is a continuous process that includes developing, approving, and implementing a spending plan for the district. Budget documents take many forms. Often the format of school district budgets is mandated by the state, leaving local districts with little opportunity to vary the information or the look of the budget document from the information required by the state. Where more local options are possible, budget documents themselves take on a variety of appearances. Throughout this chapter, we will argue that a budget document should be both comprehensive in terms of describing the expenditure plan of the school district, but easy to read and understand. This is, as we will see, a difficult task.

Developing a budget is a complex process. The first step is to determine what is needed and how much it will cost. Once determined, iterations and adjustments may be needed if revenues are insufficient to meet all identified needs. At that point those responsible for the budget must either reduce the costs of providing services, or find additional revenue sources.

2. APPROACHES TO BUDGETING[1]

Given the large sums of money appropriated to school districts, it is not surprising that they play a central role in district management and are the focus of considerable

[1]Much of this section draws heavily from Chapter 12, also on budgeting, in Wood and colleagues (1995).

attention. In fact, most school district budgets are remarkably similar in both appearance and content. There are six features common to any good budget (Wood et al., 1995):

- *Unity.* The budget document should describe all of the programs and services of the school district. The budget document should include detailed revenue and expenditure forecasts for the general fund as well as for all other budgetary funds used by the school district, including capital funds.

- *Regularity.* Budgets must be prepared on a regular basis. In the United States, virtually all government agencies, including school districts, prepare annual budgets. Some states use biennial budgets, but the norm is the 12-month or annual budget. More importantly, the budget should reflect the same 12-month period each year. Most school districts use a fiscal year that runs from July 1 of one year to June 30 of the following year. The determination of a fiscal year is generally a state requirement, and several states rely on a calendar year, and at least one, Texas, requires school districts to use a fiscal year beginning on September 1 and ending on August 31.

- *Clarity.* A well-designed budget document makes it clearer how the district's revenue is collected and spent. It will identify all sources of revenue and indicate not only how much is spent, but in general, what those funds will be used to purchase. Particularly important are personnel counts by function or program, and separate breakdowns of expenditures for supplies and materials, travel, and other goods and services. The budget should be displayed in a manner that is understandable to the average citizen and provide aids to its review, such as descriptions of the budget process and a comprehensive table of contents.

- *Balance.* The budget must be balanced. This means that revenue should equal or exceed expenditures plus any amount budgeted for contingencies. If a district's end-of-year actual revenue exceeds expenditures, the difference can be added, where legally permissible, to the district's financial reserves. In years where revenue is tight, districts may choose to draw down these reserves rather than make larger reductions in the upcoming year's operational budget. If this is done, the budget document should make it clear that the year's expenditures are expected to exceed that year's revenue and indicate what plans exist to correct the imbalance before the reserves are exhausted.

- *Publicity.* School district budgets are public documents that describe how the district plans to use the tax revenue it collects to provide educational services to the children attending school in the district. As such, it is the right of every citizen in the district to review and comment on that budget. The budget development process (described in this chapter) should provide ample opportunity for comment by the public, and all budget hearings should be open to the public. Often, state law prescribes the number and time of public hearings. Many districts make copies of their budget publicly available through local libraries and the school district offices.

- *Operational adequacy.* The expenditures detailed in the budget should be adequate to provide the services required to meet the district's mission and goals.

All budgets should have these six components. They ensure that the budget document will provide sufficient information on the programs of the school district. But, within the context of these six components, there are still a number of different approaches to developing the budget and providing the information it contains. Three common approaches are (1) line-item budgets, (2) program budgeting, and (3) zero-based budgeting.

Line-Item Budgets

The line-item budget is a technique where individual lines describe allocations for various objects of expenditure, such as personnel salaries, textbooks, supplies, contractual services, and capital outlay. It is these individual line items that are the focus of analysis, authorization, and control. It is the most common form of budgeting in use in school districts today, and prior to the 1960s was used almost exclusively in all public sector budgets.

Line-item budgets are particularly useful for educational agencies because they focus on identifiable items and offer information that is straightforward and easy to understand. Moreover, line-item budgets provide an excellent way to monitor and control expenditures by comparing actual expenditures with the budget for any and all line items. The level of detail contained in a line-item budget is limited only by the amount of detail school district managers and decision makers wish to see.

Typically, the focus of a line-item budget is on what is purchased, not the purpose of those expenditures. As a result, it is hard to use line-item budgets for sophisticated planning or for management functions. Since similar items, such as teacher salaries, are budgeted under the same line item, absent incredible levels of detail and disaggregation, it is difficult to ascertain how much is spent for teachers in different programs, different schools, or for different programs within individual schools.

For example, if one wanted to assess a school district's progress in meeting the requirements of the Federal No Child Left Behind (NCLB) law, it would be difficult to identify specific expenditures focused on such things as ensuring a high-quality teaching force, or meeting state standards for proficiency. It is generally hard to ascertain how much a school is spending on its math or science programs, and to determine if teaching resources are being shifted to math and science from other subjects to meet a goal of improved performance in these two areas.

While increasing the number of line items in the budget and creating more detail can ameliorate these shortcomings, that action has the effect of increasing the size of the district's budget, making it less accessible to both the public and to most employees of the school district. Similarly, if teacher salaries are in one line item, benefits in another location, and supplies and materials in a third, it is hard to get a clear picture of the resources allocated to an individual program.

Such program knowledge is important to strong school management. If a school has determined that a priority is to improve reading comprehension among the students, it most likely will need to focus additional resources toward its reading program. A line-item budget often makes it difficult to ascertain what resources are being directed toward a particular subject, like reading, and makes it difficult to tell at that micro level if resource allocation patterns have changed over time.

There are alternatives to the line-item budget. However, at the core of each alternative is still some form of line items describing the revenues and expenditures of an individual program. So in reality, line items are both necessary and a critical component of any budget. What other budget approaches offer is different ways to combine line items to facilitate understanding of the budget and to improve management practice.

Program Budgeting

Program budgeting, also known as Planning, Programming, and Budgeting System (PPBS) or the Planning, Programming, Budgeting, and Evaluation System (PPBES), is an approach to budgeting developed from a special study of resource allocation in the United States Department of Defense conducted by the RAND Corporation in the 1950s. Many federal programs of the mid-1960s required school districts to implement program budgeting to receive federal funds (Brackett, Chambers, and Parrish, 1983). Dade County, Florida, was the first district to implement program budgeting concepts in the nation. This provided a stimulus for national dissemination, and a number of other large school districts developed their own versions of program budgeting by the early 1970s. Unfortunately, program budgeting did not live up to the early hype. Its use was eventually discontinued at the federal level, and program budgeting systems in New York and California were abandoned in 1970s.

There are seven major steps to program budgeting:

1. The school district identifies and defines its mission, goals, and objectives, and clarifies its desired outcomes.
2. Alternative approaches or programs for achieving these outcomes are specified.
3. The alterative programs are translated into fiscal and nonfiscal requirements. This includes planned expenditures and proposed revenue sources for a program. Ideally, this is done for a multiyear period and not for a single budget cycle.
4. Each alternative approach is analyzed to determine its cost effectiveness.
5. With this information, it is possible to select the best combination of programs and establish the optimum course of action for the district.
6. Once implemented, each program is reviewed and an assessment of the degree to which desired outcomes were achieved is made.
7. The evaluations are cycled back into the system at the beginning of a new budget cycle.

This is a very "top-down" decision-making approach. In addition, specifying alternative program options and costing them out in detail is very labor intensive, requiring additional budget staff. These two factors have limited the acceptance of program budgeting in school districts.

While many larger school districts were able to absorb the costs of additional personnel, smaller districts that tried to implement program budgets generally relied on existing staff, often will little success. One reason program budgeting did not gain widespread acceptance in schools may have been the tremendous amount of work required. In systems that were able to employ new budget analysts, there was often conflict between the program budget staff and the other budget and accounting staff. In systems where the existing staff was given this additional responsibility they did not have the time, energy, or even training to implement program budgeting methods adequately. This conflict between the new program budgeting system and the old way of doing things may be partially responsible for the lack of widespread acceptance of program budgeting in school districts. Moreover, where it is used in schools, modified and simplified versions of the system have been put into place rather than increase staff to fully implement a true "program budget." There is little research on the effectiveness of such modified approaches.

Despite its lack of use in public schools, program budgeting offers a number of improvements over traditional line-item budgets. Its primary strength is that it requires the school district to improve its planning capabilities. Districts that have given up on pure program budgeting have sometimes continued the long-term planning process. Such planning efforts will no doubt pay off as districts work to meet NCLB proficiency standards by 2014.

A second strength of program budgeting is its focus on accountability, performance, and achievement of objectives. Program budgeting requires establishment of clear goals and objectives, and forces planners to determine what resources are necessary to achieve those goals. When properly implemented, spending decisions are made on the basis of what is needed to achieve the district's goals, and not on some other basis such as "that's the way we have always done it in the past." It also helps decision makers consider the full range of available options, and requires the evaluation of several options before selecting the one that appears to be the best for meeting the district's needs.

One of the major weaknesses or problems with program budgeting is its cost. Allan Schick (1971) has estimated that to fully implement a program budgeting system takes as long as five years. During that time, regular budget staff are often required to do their regular job as well as complete all of the required documentation for a program budget. For example, reaching agreement on the goals of a program can be a difficult task, further complicated by the need to garner public input. Once agreement on the goals has been reached, a number of alternative strategies might be developed. If seven such options exist, the staff has to analyze the costs and potential outcome of all seven, which potentially is seven times as much work as if only one option is considered. Schick found that as budget deadlines approached, staff often set these analyses aside in favor of getting the job done using the familiar tools of the past. As a result, program budgeting made little headway in gaining acceptance in school district finance offices.

Another feature of program budgeting that has limited its effectiveness in education is the bias toward centralized planning. This is contradictory to the current trend in education to shift responsibility for decision making—and sometimes—budget authority to school sites.

In the past, identification of clear and quantifiable goals has been problematic. Today, there is more agreement that school performance should be measured through the results of standardized tests. Although controversial, and not the topic of this chapter, the use of these tests to measure school results helps solidify the discussion on outcomes. It does not necessarily resolve the more complex issue of what resources are needed to achieve those goals—something for which program budgeting might be useful. Wood and colleagues (1995) suggested that the inability to specify the resources needed to achieve educational goals was a weakness of program budgeting. Today, with much more consensus on outcomes and goals, and greater effort toward defining the resources needed to reach those goals (see the discussion of adequacy in Chapter 3), program budgeting may be a powerful tool that districts can use to estimate the costs of educational programs and assess the relative trade-offs between programs.

Zero-Based Budgeting

Zero-based budgeting (ZBB) is a popular budget reform introduced in the 1970s. Peter Pyhrr first described it in an article in the *Harvard Business Review* in 1970. ZBB was instituted in Georgia for state government budgeting purposes in 1971, and was used in a number of other states as well as the federal government when former Georgia governor Jimmy Carter became president. ZBB is used in many school districts as well. Unlike program budgeting, which is rarely used today, ZBB is still in use in some places.

The generic form of ZBB has five basic steps:

- *Identification of decision units.* A decision unit is a program that consumes the resources of the government agency. They should be the lowest-level entities for which budgets are prepared, which in a school district generally means the school level. Since the decision units are generally based on existing organizational structures, school districts have no need to change their organizational structure to implement ZBB.
- *Analysis of each decision package.* Managers are asked to reassess and justify the operation of each program. Answers to these questions are part of this process: (1) Does the decision package support and contribute to the goals of the district? (2) What is the impact on the district if the decision package is eliminated? (3) Is there a way to accomplish the goals and objectives of the decision package in a more cost-effective manner?
- *Rank the decision packages.* All of the decision packages are ranked from the highest priority to the lowest priority. ZBB does not specify how the packages should be ranked, or what process should be used; this is up to the organization. In a school district it is assumed that the Board of Education would make the final ranking.
- *Acceptance of packages and allocation of funds.* In Pyhrr's (1971) model, once the decision packages have been ranked, and the costs of each specified, they are funded in order until funds run out. The higher a package's priority, the more likely it is to be funded. Those with lower priority will not be funded and thus are eliminated. In reality, school districts that use this process tend to use

the rankings to establish priorities for how well each program is funded. Those high on the priority list are fully funded, those lower on the list may only receive partial funding.

- *Preparation of the budget.* Once the decision packages are selected, the final budget is prepared and submitted for approval.

The term "zero based" comes from the practice of requiring all programs to be subject to this ranking process on an annual basis. For each budget cycle, all programs start with a base budget of zero and are only funded if they remain important to achieving the goals and objectives of the organization. This is a very "bottom-up" process where the manager responsible for that package specifies each decision package's outcomes and costs. Funding of each package is based on the relative importance of that package compared with all others in the school district.

ZBB was developed for business, and it assumes that low-priority packages are expendable. This is not always the case in a school district where many programs and services must be maintained regardless of their priority within the organization. As a result, governments that use this system have modified ZBB so that rather than accepting or rejecting a decision package outright, the rankings are used to allocate new funding to programs or determine which programs will absorb the largest share of budget reductions. As a result, few districts use ZBB in its pure form, and few really conduct annual reviews of decision packages.

One of the strengths of ZBB is that it requires better information concerning the activities of each department within an organization than do traditional budgeting processes. Unlike program budgeting, the ZBB process does not attempt to alter the program structure used by organizations. Rather, it requires participatory management in decision making, and allows all parties to review the goals and objectives of other parts of the organization. By requiring each department to build its program from zero each year, it provides an excellent way to make judgments about the true value of that program.

There are a number of weaknesses with the application of ZBB to public schools, however. It is hard to rank packages with diverse goals. District managers need to establish the criteria on which decision packages will be ranked choosing, for example, between effectiveness, efficiency, equity, or the extensiveness of each program. This is difficult in a situation where goals are diverse and programs are provided because of legal requirements outside of the control of the local school board and superintendent.

It is also improbable for a school district—or any public agency for that matter—to use a cutoff point for decision packages. In a declining budgetary period, how could district decision makers decide, for example, to eliminate all science programs, or the twelfth grade, or special education? In all three examples, there are important and legal reasons why such actions would be impossible. As a result, when funds are limited, rather than eliminate departments or programs, each department is typically asked to make marginal reductions. Departments are often asked to indicate what they would do with reductions of 10 percent, 20 percent, or some other number, and then reductions are required based on each program's individual priority resulting from the prioritization process. In other words, few programs are subject to a true "zero"-based analysis each year.

Summary

This section shows that despite attempts to implement major reforms in the process, school district budgeting has remained relatively stable over the years. Efforts to implement program budgeting or ZBB in school systems have been largely unsuccessful in the past. One of the reasons for this is the incremental nature of all public agency budgets, in particular those of school districts. Wildavsky (1988) argues that major changes to public agency budgets are hard to make and slow to be implemented because of what he terms incrementalism. In most public agencies, the first step in building the budget is to fund existing services at the same level in the next year. Once this is accomplished, new programs and services are possible only to the extent that revenues for the next year provide more resources than needed to fund existing programs. Public agencies are slow to eliminate or reduce programs that are not viewed as effective or efficient, and even slower to reduce personnel in those programs. As a result, changes in the structure of an organization as reflected in the budget are incremental.

This incremental process is not necessarily a bad thing. There are many functions of a school district that should be continued from year to year. However, traditional budgeting processes make adoption of new programs, and elimination of old programs, difficult in most school district budget processes. In Section 3 of this chapter, we review the steps taken by school districts to build their budgets.

3. BUDGET PREPARATION

There are five basic steps in developing a school district's budget. These include development of budget guidelines, preparation of the budget document, making modifications to the original budget, obtaining approval of the budget and administering or managing the budget. Each step is described in detail here.

Development of Budget Guidelines

The chief business officer of a school district is typically responsible for managing the budget process. As just described, the budget should reflect the district's educational plans and provide an estimate of the revenues and expenditures needed to put that plan in place, with a specific focus on one fiscal year. Building that budget is a complex task that takes substantially longer than a year and requires participation of district staff at many levels throughout the organization. By establishing annual budget guidelines, all participants have knowledge of the district's priorities, their role in the budget process, and what timelines must be observed to have a budget in place when the fiscal year begins. Hartman (2002) notes these items that should be included in the budget guidelines:

- A message from the superintendent describing the fiscal context for the year. This would include available funding, increases or reductions in revenue for the year, and any important changes in priorities from one year to the next.

- A budget calendar with a timeline for important steps in the process. This calendar includes the time to prepare, implement, and evaluate the budget and as a result starts nine to twelve months before the fiscal year and ends as much as six months after the fiscal year for which the budget is being prepared.
- Guidelines for staff and community participation at the district and school level, including procedures for public hearings as required by law, and as desired as part of an individual district's budget process.
- Budget forms that need to be filled out and submitted by schools and district departments.
- Information on the district's accounting structure or code that is to be used in preparation of the budget and in tracking revenues and expenditures during the fiscal year.
- Other information needed to prepare an accurate and timely budget submission to the district's business office.

Once the guidelines have been established, work on the budget document itself can begin.

Budget Preparation

The heart of the budget process is to estimate revenues and expenditures and ensure that the budget is in balance—that expenditures do not exceed revenue for the year. This discussion begins with estimating revenues followed by a discussion of expenditures.

Revenue Projection. We begin with estimates of school district revenue. This includes money the district receives from local property taxes, state aid, and federal programs. The first step is to project student enrollments, followed by estimates of property tax receipts, state funding, and revenues of categorical programs, both state and federal. Finally other sources of revenue must also be estimated.

Enrollment projections. As we have described in earlier chapters in this book, most school district revenue is accumulated on the basis of student enrollment, and districts receive a large portion of their funds on a per-pupil basis. Thus, the first step in estimating revenues is to make an accurate enrollment projection for the school year. More importantly, as part of any good long-range planning process, projections of enrollments into future years should be made as well. Methodologies for estimating enrollments are provided elsewhere (see, for example, Hartman, 2002; Wood et al., 1995). It is essential, however, to recognize the importance of accurate estimates of student enrollment as the basis of any school district budget.

First, state funding is typically based on some measure of the number of students in each school district. Whether the enrollment number used in state computations is actual enrollment (head count), or some more limited measure such as average daily membership (ADM) or average daily attendance (ADA), a district's basic revenue is determined by its number of students. Moreover, in state-funding systems that equalize revenues on the basis of per-pupil property wealth, the student count is a critical component of the wealth calculation and determines how much state funding the district will receive.[2]

In states with weighted-pupil funding systems, appropriate weights must be applied to each student before total "enrollment" for funding purposes is computed. For example, if a district has 1,000 students, and 10 percent of them are eligible for a special education weight of 0.9, then the enrollment of the district for state-funding purposes would be 1,090.[3]

Local revenues. Local revenues are generated primarily from property tax collections. The state finance formula may dictate the level of property taxation that is required. In many states, local districts have the authority to enact additional property taxes, either with approval of the school board, or approval of the district's voters. In states with a GTB or combination some portion of these property taxes will be equalized as described in Chapter 5. An important part of the budget process is to estimate total local revenues for general operating purposes.

Estimation of property taxes requires knowledge of the total assessed valuation of the property in the school district, and the tax rate the district is legally allowed to apply to the taxable property. In some states, districts are granted authority to levy a tax rate and revenues are dependent on the assessed value of the property in the district. In other states, districts have authority to raise a fixed sum of money through property taxes, making the tax rate dependent on the assessed valuation of the property in the district. In either case, the property tax collections are generally used as part of the computation of state aid to the district as well.

Each state has specific rules for levying property taxes that must be followed by school districts. An important component of estimating property tax revenues is to include a contingency for delinquent tax payments, which has the effect of reducing current year tax receipts. Recall that districts must not only balance their budget, but must also end the fiscal year in balance. Therefore, if revenues fall below predictions, expenditures must also be reduced. Thus, based on historical experience, districts need to be certain to allow for the nonpayment of some property taxes in their budget estimates. Historical trends are generally the best way to make this estimate, although current economic conditions should be factored into the estimate as well.

State revenue. Once enrollment has been estimated, this figure can be applied to state guidelines for funding. For example, the district can multiply its projected enrollment

---

[2]If this concept is not clear, readers can refer to the simulation that accompanies this text. By changing to a weighted-pupil count, each district's "enrollment" increases, and its property wealth per pupil declines. The same effect would occur if a district's actual enrollment count were to increase while property wealth remained constant; it would be relatively poorer in the state's finance system and thus eligible for more state funding.

[3]This is computed as follows:

    900 regular-education students

    190 special-education students (100 or 10 percent of the 1,000 students × 1.9)

   1,090 total weighted students

by the expected foundation level for the fiscal year to get an estimate of its general revenues funded through property taxes and state aid. This figure should provide the largest share of total revenues for the district.

The different models of state aid were discussed in detail in Chapters 5, 6, and 7 of this book. At the budget level, it is important for school administrators to estimate their state revenues as accurately as possible based on the mechanics of their individual state system. Understanding how the distribution formula works in a particular state is essential for managing a district's budget estimates.

In addition to general state aid, there may be a number of categorical programs for which the district is eligible. Common programs include special education, compensatory education, and bilingual education—programs that may also be funded through the general-aid formula with a pupil-weighting program. In addition, many states provide aid for pupil transportation (both regular home-to-school and special education) as well as for capital construction (see Chapter 11), and other priorities as established by the state legislature.

Successful school district business officers need to be aware of state categorical aid programs and how their district might qualify for funding to ensure that the children they serve receive all of the services for which they qualify. Moreover, once the funds are received, the district's financial managers must be sure that they are expended in conjunction with any rules that accompany the categorical funds. Keeping track of large numbers of individual categorical grants can be a demanding and complex task, particularly in states with a large number of such programs. For example, researchers in California have identified as many as 100 different categorical programs in recent years (Finkelstein, Furry, and Huerta, 2000).

Federal funds. The federal government provides resources for a number of categorical programs. The largest are Title I, which offers assistance to school districts with a high incidence of children from low-income families, and the school nutrition program, which subsidizes school food programs. There are many other federal programs for which school districts may qualify. Understanding the qualification requirements of federal programs and ensuring that the district receives funds for which it is eligible is a major undertaking in most school districts today.

Other revenues. Following the estimation of general revenues, the district must also estimate revenue from special programs and grants. If the state system uses weighted pupils, much of this may be included in the general-aid system. If not, funding from programs for such things as special education, transportation, compensatory education, bilingual education, and others must also be estimated using state rules, regulations, and guidelines. Again, at the heart of this estimate is the number of pupils who qualify for each program.

Estimating Expenditures

Parallel to the estimation of district revenue for the fiscal year, the district must also estimate total expenditure needs. There are many different approaches that can be used to estimate how much money will be needed. The most common approach is to determine how much it will cost to provide the same level of services to students in the district in the next year by adjusting current staffing and material needs by changes in the costs of those items. While this method provides a relatively accurate way to estimate expenditures, as described here in the discussion of approaches to budgeting, it does very little to relate those expenditures to the changing needs of the district.

Regardless of the sophistication with which estimates for future spending are made, there are some common spending categories that need to be included in any school district budget. The largest single item of expenditure for a school district is personnel. That is the primary focus of this discussion.

Personnel Costs. Accurate estimates of the number of personnel required across the school district are essential to the development of an accurate budget. Determination of the number and type of personnel needed is typically done through the use of staffing ratios.

Certificated staff. For teachers, the most common metric is to allocate teachers to school sites on the basis of the number of students at each school. If the district determines that there should be one teacher at each school for every 20 children, then the number of teachers needed at any school can be easily determined by dividing enrollment by 20. Many states have established legal guidelines for class sizes. For example, in Texas, class size in all K–4 classrooms must not exceed 22 students, and in California, there are strong financial incentives to encourage all K–3 classes to have 20 or fewer students. These requirements will also dictate to some extent how many teachers are needed at each school in the district.

Absent state policy guidelines for class size, staffing ratios are typically set either by the school board as a matter of policy, or as part of the district's collective bargaining agreement with the professional staff. In many districts, different ratios are established for different programs—so, for example, there may be lower staffing ratios for high schools than for elementary schools, and programs for children with disabilities may require substantially smaller classes for success.

The advantage to simple allocation rules for teachers is that in addition to making it easier to calculate teacher allocations to school sites, the rules provide more flexibility to the school-level decision makers. Some schools may elect to use all possible certificated staff in instructional programs to minimize class size, while others may choose to have slightly larger classes and use one or more of the certificated personnel for another purpose, such as counselors (see Chapter 10 on resource reallocation, for example). Other certificated staff are often allocated on the basis of staffing ratios as well.

School-site administrators. School-site administration typically includes the principal and any assistant principals assigned to the school. The number of administrators is often a function of the enrollment of a school, with additional administrators being assigned to a school at certain thresholds of enrollment. The thresholds are typically determined by the district's administration or the school board and may vary considerably from district to district or from state to state.

Some districts assign administrators on the basis of the number of teachers in a school, assuming that in carrying out the functions of instructional leader and providing evaluations of the teachers, it is the number of teachers that drive the workload of a principal more than the number of students. In theory, it is even possible to allocate such positions on the basis of both number of teachers and number of students—although if teachers are allocated to schools on the basis of consistent pupil-teacher ratios, the results should be roughly the same using any of these strategies.

Central office administrators. Staffing ratios for central office administrators are more difficult to establish. Some districts establish an overall pupil-administrator ratio for the central office and strive to keep within the bounds established. If necessary, they assign individuals to multiple functions. In other school districts, certain administrative positions are filled regardless of the ratio. It is common for all districts to have a superintendent and a business official. The number of other central office administrators depends largely on the size and complexity of the district. Curriculum and instructional specialists are often employed at the central level, as are specialists in human resources, transportation, legal affairs, and food services. The size and scope of the central office staff is largely determined by the size of the district and the extent to which district functions are managed centrally or assigned to school sites.

Other certificated staff. There are a number of other certificated staff at most schools. They include librarians/media specialists, counselors, instructional leaders/teacher coaches, mentors, student advisors, and nurses to name a few. A district can allocate these resources to schools on the basis of staffing ratios, or a district can be less specific and allocate positions for the school to use as it sees fit. The key in the budget process is to know how many individuals are allocated to each site, what they cost (salary and benefits), and what the total personnel commitment is at each location. Some of this may be determined by state guidelines, accrediting standards, on the basis of the number of students or some other rational basis such as the number of teachers in the school. Districts implementing one of the whole school reform models in their schools would want to allocate personnel to meet the specific needs of the reform model chosen.

In many instances, the standard ratios used by a school district to assign these certificated staff to schools may result in partial allocations, or in the worst case, a school may not have enough students to qualify for one or more of the positions. In some instances, such as nurses and counselors, it may be valuable to have individuals with these qualifications available all day, regardless of the number of students they serve. Consequently, many allocation rules provide that each school receive a minimum of one such professional. In instances where such allocations are made, it is important to budget for those positions appropriately.

Classified staff. In addition to the certificated staff, school districts employ large numbers of classified personnel. These individuals include teacher aides in classrooms, as well as people who are responsible for keeping school facilities clean and repaired, maintaining the grounds and buildings, driving school busses, doing clerical work, operating and repairing the district's computers, and other functions necessary to the operation of a complex organization.

Classified personnel are typically assigned to district cost centers on the basis of some staffing ratio. These ratios can be based on the number of students, the number of teachers at the site, or some other relevant factor. For example, it might make sense to assign school-site office personnel on the basis of the number of students and/or teachers at the school. However, custodians and grounds keepers may be assigned on the basis of a school facility's square footage, or the number of classrooms at the site. Similarly, bus drivers are needed on the basis of the number of pupils transported to and from school each day as well as needs for field trips and athletic contests. It is essential to consider all of these functions in determining the number of classified staff employed by the district when preparing the budget.

Total staff estimates. Once the number of positions to be filled has been estimated, they are typically reported in terms of full-time equivalents (FTEs). FTEs provide a measure of the number of full-time employees needed by the district. While many individuals in a school district may only work part of a day, for budget purposes, the number of FTEs is computed. Thus for example, if a district were to hire two individuals to work as librarians for a half day each, it has two employees, but only one FTE. A district's budget may report that school A has 4.5 FTE custodians. If a typical work day is considered to be 8 hours, 4.5 FTE translates into 36 hours a day of custodial time (i.e., 8 hours × 4.5 FTE = 36 hours). This does not necessarily mean that the school employs four fill-time custodians and one half-time custodian. It is just as likely that the school has one full-time head custodian, and seven individuals working half-time in that position. The school and the district would determine the exact distribution of personnel.

Budget documents should report the number of FTE personnel employed by program. Since personnel costs (salaries and benefits) often represent as much as 80 to 85 percent of a district's budget or more, accurate estimation of personnel requirements is essential to accurate budget development.

Other expenditures. Once the number of employees has been determined, it is much easier to estimate the expenditures necessary for carrying out the district's educational plan. At this point there are three general steps a district can take to estimate total expenditures:

1. identify the specific programs and/or functions around which the budget is to be constructed,
2. ascertain what resources are needed to operationalize the tasks essential to each of the programs or functions identified in the previous step, and
3. estimate the costs of the resources needed to implement each program or function.

Accounting for Expenditures and Revenues

After the budget is developed, districts then need mechanisms for tracking expenditures. They do this through fiscal accounting systems that have various elements, including funds, objects, functions, etc.

Fund Accounting. Like other public agencies, school district budgets rely on fund accounting. A fund is a self-balancing set of accounts related to a common topic. While the number of allowable funds varies across the 50 states, all school districts have a general fund. The general fund sometimes has a different name such as the operations and maintenance fund, or the operating fund, but its purpose is the same: to account for the general revenues and expenditures of a school system. As such, the general fund accounts for between 75 and 90 percent of total resources in the average school district, and expenditures made through the general fund include provision of instructional services (salaries, benefits, and supplies), general administration, maintenance of school buildings, utilities, and other expenses associated with the day-to-day operation of a school district.

Additional funds are used by school districts as needed. Table 8.1 displays a list of potential account funds as provided by the federal government (National Center for Education Statistics, 1990). Note that these descriptions may change as the National Center for Education Statistics was considering revisions to its accounting handbook as this book went to press. Updated information is available at the NCES website.

National Center for Education Statistics

Objects of Expenditure. The basic unit of accounting for a budget relies on objects of expenditure. Objects represent actual items that can be purchased. Object-oriented budget systems can be very basic, or very specific. Table 8.2 provides a simplified hypothetical accounting code for expenditures by object for a school district. The figure is not based on the actual accounting system of any particular state or school district and is only meant to be representative of what an object-level accounting system might look like. In a large, complex organization, all four of the digits in the code column might be used to fully identify the objects of expenditure in more detail. Moreover, the particular codes combinations displayed here are only an example and not necessarily reflective of how codes are actually assigned to expenditures and revenues. Most school systems would have a more sophisticated set of object codes to fully track their expenditures.

The problem with budgets that only provide object-level data is that they do not give the reviewer any sense of the purpose for which the resources are being used. For

TABLE 8.1   Federal Fund Classifications

Fund	Description
01	General fund
02	Special revenue funds (i.e., special education or federal projects)
03	Capital project funds
04	Debt service funds
05	Enterprise funds
06	Internal service funds
07	Trust and agency funds
08	General fixed assets
09	General long-term debt

Source: National Center for Education Statistics, 1990.

example, an object-level budget might contain a line item summarizing total certificated salaries for teachers (e.g., the 1100 category in Table 8.2). This would give the reviewer a concept of how much is spent on teacher salaries by the school district, but no sense of how those teachers are allocated among elementary, middle, or senior high schools or of the amount paid to substitute versus regular teachers. Moreover, a line item for teacher salaries at an individual school provides little information as to how those teacher resources are used by educational programs. To answer these questions, budgets can also be aggregated by function or program.

Function Classifications.   Functions describe general areas of expenditure such as instruction, administration, operations and maintenance, pupil transportation, and instructional support. Functional definitions vary across state accounting systems. How-

TABLE 8.2   Hypothetical Object-Level Accounting Classifications

Code	Classification
1000	Professional certificated salaries
1100	Teachers' salaries
1200	School administrators' salaries
1300	Supervisors' salaries
1400	Central office salaries
1900	Other certificated salaries
2000	Classified salaries
2100	Instructional aides' salaries
2200	Administrators' salaries
2300	Clerical and office worker salaries
2400	Maintenance and operations salaries
2500	Food services salaries
2600	Transportation salaries
2900	Other classified salaries
3000	Employee benefits
3100	Retirement
3200	Health
3300	Workers' compensation
3400	Unemployment insurance
3900	Other benefits
4000	Books and supplies
4100	Textbooks
4200	Books other than textbooks
4300	Instructional materials and supplies
4400	Other supplies
4600	Pupil transportation supplies
4700	Food services supplies

TABLE 8.2   Hypothetical Object-Level Accounting Classifications *(continued)*

Code	Classification
5000	Services and other operating expenditures
5100	Consultants
5200	Travel
5300	Insurance
5400	Utilities
5500	Rentals and leases
5900	Other services
6000	Capital outlay
6100	Sites and improvement of sites
6200	Buildings and improvement of buildings
6300	Books and media for new school libraries or major expansions
6400	Equipment
6500	Equipment replacement
7000	Other outgo
7100	Tuition
7200	Transfers out
7300	Interfund transfers
8000	Revenue
8100	Local revenue
8200	State revenue
8300	Federal revenue

Note: Classifications displayed here are examples of codes that are typically found in object-level accounting systems for public schools. Individual states and districts may use different definitions, and provide greater detail through the use of the 3rd and 4th digits in each code.

ever, the federal government has attempted to standardize functional definitions. Table 8.3 displays sample school district function classifications as developed by the federal government in *Handbook II,* Revised, 2nd edition (National Center for Education Statistics, 1990).

Program Classifications.   Expenditures can also be classified by programs. Table 8.4 provides a list of the programs used in Florida's accounting system. The more detailed the programmatic distinctions, the more complex the budget process becomes, and the bigger the budget document. The advantage of a program budget is that it gives managers, as well as school board members and the general public, a better picture of what the funds are actually being used to purchase. One of the difficulties with program budgets is that many services are hard to assign to a single program. Custodial services, for example, serve all programs at the school. If classified separately as a function, there is a great deal of information that it is possible to obtain about custodial services, but how those costs could—or should—be allocated to individual programs is not always a

TABLE 8.3   School District Function Classifications

Code	Function
1000	Instruction
2000	Support services
2100	Students
2200	Instructional staff
2300	General administration
2400	School administration
2500	Business
2600	Operations and maintenance of plant services
2700	Student transportation services
2800	Central
2900	Other support services
3000	Operation of noninstructional services
3100	Food services operations
3200	Other enterprise operations
3300	Community support operations
4000	Facilities acquisition and construction services
5000	Other uses
5100	Debt services
5200	Fund transfers

Source: National Center for Education Statistics, 1990.

Note: Functional codes and descriptions can be broken into smaller units using the 3rd and 4th digits of the code as desired by local districts.

simple task since some programs such as science labs and home economics require larger spaces and more cleaning resources than do traditional language arts and math classes.

Accounting Codes.   In reality, it is helpful to be able to track an individual expenditure by all three of these methods—object, function, and program. In addition, it is often helpful to track expenditures by the location where the expenditure is made. Locations usually include the schools in the district, the central office, and other areas and subareas as determined by the district. A generic accounting code might look something like that shown in Figure 8.2.

Additional sets of digits could be added to this account code structure to provide additional detail about every expenditure as well. The important factor to keep in mind in designing accounting code structures is that the greater the level of detail (i.e., more digits in the code) the greater the potential for error in coding expenditures. Thus there is always a trade-off between the complexity of the code and the potential accuracy of the data entered into the code. In Oregon, when a new accounting system was instituted, the system designers realized early on that if decision makers were to have useful data at

TABLE 8.4 Florida Program Classifications

Code	Program Description
Basic programs	
101	K–3 Basic education
102	4–8 Basic education
103	9–12 Basic education
Special programs for at-risk students	
120	Dropout prevention
131	Intensive English/ESOL K–3
132	Intensive English/ESOL 4–8
133	Intensive English/ESOL 9–12
Special programs for exceptional children	
210	Educable mentally handicapped
202	Trainable mentally handicapped
203	Physically handicapped
204	Physical and occupational therapy (part-time)
205	Speech, language, and hearing (part-time)
206	Speech, language, and hearing
207	Visually handicapped (part-time)
208	Visually handicapped
209	Emotionally handicapped (part time)
210	Emotionally handicapped
211	Specific learning disability (part-time)
212	Specific learning disability
213	Gifted (part-time)
214	Hospital and home-bed (part-time)
215	Profoundly handicapped
K–12 vocational programs	
301	Agriculture
302	Office
303	Distributive
304	Diversified
305	Health
306	Public service
307	Home economics
308	Technical trade and industry
309	Exploratory
316	Vocational education mainstream

(continued)

TABLE 8.4   Florida Program Classifications (*continued*)

Code	Program Description
Adult job preparatory vocational-education programs	
331	Agriculture
332	Office
333	Distributive
334	Diversified
335	Health
336	Public service
337	Home economics
338	Technical trade and industry
Adult supplemental vocational programs	
361	Agriculture
362	Office
364	Health
365	Public service
366	Home economics
367	Technical trade and industry
Adult general education program	
401	Adult basic skills
402	Adult secondary education
403	Lifelong learning
404	Adult handicapped

Source: Wood et al., 1995.

the school level as promised, a significant portion of the resources for implementation of the system would need to go to training staff at all of the schools and school districts.

Budget Preparation Summary

This section has described the many steps required to prepare a school district's budget. Typically, a budget presents information on the expected revenues and expenditures of

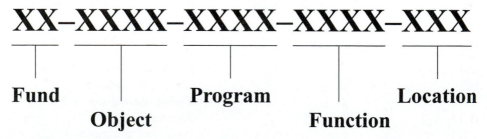

FIGURE 8.2   Sample Accounting Code Structure for a School District

TABLE 8.5   Sample Budget Presentation

Code	Actual 2002–03	Estimated 2003–04	Projected 2004–05
General fund			
1000 (Certificated salaries)	xxx,xxx.xx	xxx,xxx.xx	xxx,xxx.xx
2000 (Classified salaries)			
3000 (Benefits)			
4000 (Books and supplies)			
5000 (Services and other operating expenditures)			
6000 (Capital outlay)			
7000 (Other outgo)			
8000 (Revenue)			
Other funds			

the school district, along with information on the number of students served and the number of FTE employees who will be employed in the provision of educational services for those students. This information can be displayed by object of expenditure, function, or program, and can be provided at an aggregate district level, or disaggregated to specific locations such as school sites and other logical locations including the central office, the transportation department, and others as determined either by the district or as mandated by state policy.

The typical budget provides all of this information for at least three years. The most common presentation is to show actual revenues and expenditures for the year most recently completed, estimated revenues for the current year, and projected revenues and expenditures for the budget year. For example, if a district uses a July 1 to June 30 fiscal year, then as it prepares its budget for the 2004–05 fiscal year, the budget display would include actual expenditure and revenue data from 2002–03, estimated data for 2003–04, and projected data for 2004–05. An example of a very simplified budget document is shown in Table 8.5. This is provided only as an example of what a budget might look like. Obviously a district's budget would have many more entries, and each fund would be displayed separately. In addition, this example focuses on objects of expenditure, other displays by function and program could also be provided. Examples of budget documents can also be found in Bolton and Harmer (2000).

Budget Modification

If expenditure estimates exceed revenue projections, the district's administrators must make adjustments in one or both sides of the equation. Typically, it is easier to reduce expenditures than it is to increase revenue. Most state and federal programs have fixed revenue levels, and it is not likely that a school district will be able to seek additional funding from these sources over the short term. Local property taxes offer somewhat more hope, depending on the tax statues in the particular state. In many states it is possible to seek voter approval for higher property taxes. However, tax limitations in many states have curtailed this option. Additionally, there are often state restrictions on how much property taxes can be raised to maintain the equity of the system as discussed in Chapters 5, 6, and 7.

Reductions in expenditures often mean limited compensation for employees, or elimination of some positions or programs. Personnel reductions are never easy, and most districts attempt to make those cuts as far from instructional personnel as possible, although in times of severe budget reductions, reductions in the number of teachers— with the resultant increase in average class size—may not be avoidable.

Budget Approval

Once a balanced budget has been developed, the district's school board must approve it. The timing of this process, along with the required documents that must be submitted, and the time in which the general public may comment on the budget are generally prescribed by state law. In general, however, the superintendent submits the budget to the school board, makes copies available to the public, and helps the board schedule public hearings on the budget document. At this time, the board may further modify the budget to reflect its policies and goals (although superintendents typically work closely with either the board or a budget committee of the board to develop the budget, so there are generally few board-directed changes at this point).

Administering the Budget

The adopted budget serves as a guide for expenditure allocations throughout the year. Since it is impossible to estimate all expenditure needs perfectly during the budget process, it is important to continually monitor revenues and expenditures to make sure they are in line with budget projections. If there are changes either in the revenue available to the district, or in the expenditure needs of the district, modifications to the budget document must be approved by the school board. Such modifications may be the result of an unexpected influx of students, requiring more teachers and classroom space, or a change in the revenue receipts for one or more programs. At all times, the district administration and school board must strive to keep the budget in balance, reducing expenditures if revenue projections fall short, and increasing expenditures to meet the needs of a growing student population— provided the revenues to support those students are available. In short, the budget becomes an important management tool to help ensure that educational resources are focused on the priorities established at the beginning of the budget cycle.

4. BUDGET IMPLEMENTATION

In this section, we first discuss how school districts might consider developing a budget while attempting to give school sites more autonomy. Then we provide a brief description of budget implementation in two large cities, San Francisco and Seattle.

Distribution of Funds to the School Site

School districts in the United States typically use a set of formulaic ratios to direct resources to school sites. For instructional personnel, teachers are typically provided to a school site based on the number of students at the school, for example, one teaching position for every 25 students. Other personnel are generated on a variety of similar formulaic ratios based on numbers of students, other staff, or school characteristics.

The difficulty with using formulaic ratios for staff is they use *numbers* of personnel, not *cost* of the individual personnel assigned to the school site. Individual teacher salaries, for example, can vary by as much as 2 to 1, depending on an individual's previous teaching experience and educational attainment. Thus, if a school site were to receive a dollar distribution (e.g., based on the number of students in the school), the composition of its teaching staff would affect how well it could stay within its budget.

As a result of the differential costs of staff, most districts allocate positions to schools on the basis of average cost. That is, a school site generates its staff positions without regard to the cost of the individuals employed at the site, and essentially pays the average cost for each type of individual. Whether this model leads to school-site control depends on the way it is implemented at the district level. For example, can a school site change the mix of personnel it wants to employ, trading an assistant principal for one-and-a-half or two teaching positions? If so, are there district employment rules that limit this flexibility, even if it is provided for in theory? More important, what flexibility does a school have to change the mix of professionals? If it is unlimited, the district must absorb the risk of suddenly having surplus teachers, assistant principals, or counselors, if different trade-offs are made by the school sites. If the district absorbs the risk, the effect is likely to be a higher average cost for each position and potentially fewer staff at each school site in total.

On the other hand, giving each school a fixed budget based on enrollments and letting the site allocate the funds across staff has its own problems. What happens to schools where the average cost of a teacher is above the district average? With a fixed per-pupil budget, these schools will not be able to hire all the teachers they need, whereas a school with a relatively young teaching staff may be able to hire more teachers and reduce class size. Adding to this complexity is the effect of time, which will eventually lead to the retirement of experienced and expensive teachers and increased salaries of currently inexperienced teachers. Thus, a school that is advantaged today may be at a disadvantage in a few years.

Districts that want to use dollar formulas to allocate funds to schools must take these factors into account in distributing funds. One possibility is to adopt a model similar to that used by the Los Angeles Unified School District (LAUSD) under its consent decree for the *Rodriguez* v. *LAUSD*[4] lawsuit. Plaintiffs seeking to equalize general-fund per-pupil expenditures across all the district's schools sued the district. The settlement recognized that a large component of the differences in per-pupil expenditures are differential salaries of teachers due to variances in experience and education. The settlement calls for equalizing per-pupil expenditures on teacher salaries over time by requiring school sites to hire

---

[4]*Rodriguez* v. *LAUSD,* C611-358 (1992).

teachers such that the average cost of a teacher is approximately the same as the average cost of teachers across the district. Thus, a school with a relatively expensive teaching staff must hire additional teachers with relatively low salaries (and consequently less education and experience), and a school with a relatively inexpensive teaching staff must hire new teachers who are relatively expensive (and thus have more education and experience). The goal is to equalize the educational and experience characteristics of teachers at each school site.

Rather than provide school sites more control over the characteristics of their teaching staff, the Los Angeles system seems to have put more constraints on school decision makers, forcing them to consider the price of a teacher as well as his or her qualifications. Similar pressures would exist in any system that gave school sites a fixed dollar amount per pupil for budget purposes. This may or may not be a good thing.

On one hand, principals and school-based decision-making councils feel that some of their hiring flexibility has been eliminated. On the other hand, forcing schools to have a teaching staff with mixed levels of education and experience may have long-term benefits in terms of consistent school leadership and instructional quality. In theory, there would always be a group of teachers at the school with knowledge and experience related to the school's goals and mission and a sense of history regarding what programs are most successful. Regardless of how a district resolves this issue, if school sites are held to total budget amounts, regardless of staff composition, then some kind of safety net will be needed to help schools deal with temporary highs and lows in teachers' salaries. The same issues need consideration in the employment of other certified and classified staff in schools. Differences in the unit cost of personnel, despite similar responsibilities, need to be taken into account if central districts are to continue to distribute funds to school sites.

Allocation of Nonstaff Resources

This section describes some of the difficulties school sites may encounter if they are given substantial responsibility for many of the functions now handled at the district level. Its purpose is to describe some of the complexities of shifting the fiscal management to schools. For more information on individual topics and how they are managed in today's school business office, see Wood and colleagues (1995).

Technology.   One of the most frequently discussed and most expensive items facing schools is the purchase, maintenance, repair, and updating of tools for instructional technology, particularly computers. The cost of placing computers and Internet connections in classrooms or in computer labs is substantial. Once the investment in equipment has been made, the expense of maintaining that equipment is considerable. It also is expensive to provide technical training and support for teachers so that they make maximum use of the technology, and a plan must be established to keep both the hardware and the software up to date. Providing equity for schools in making these purchases and then maintaining their investment is complicated. Moreover, unless schools are able to carry over funds from one year to the next, it may never be possible to establish a fund large enough to purchase enough computers to fund an entire computer lab at one time. This could lead to nonstandardization of hardware, further complicating the management of a school's technology program.

Transportation. The costs of transporting students to and from school vary with the distances children have to travel and the density of the population in the school's attendance boundaries. If school sites are held responsible for funding student transportation out of site funds, schools with fewer children to bus or shorter travel distances will have more money for alternative programs than schools with more expensive transportation needs. For this reason, districts typically keep transportation as a district-level function.

Maintenance and Operations. Although few have suggested that authority for transportation be given to school sites, Hentschke (1986) does suggest shifting authority for utilities to school sites, assuming they can keep all or part of any savings they generate. Again, this will not work well if each school were to receive a flat amount per pupil (or per classroom or per square foot) for utilities. Older and less energy-efficient buildings might require substantially higher expenditures per student for utilities than newer and more energy-efficient schools. Thus, formulas to distribute funds to school sites need to take site characteristics into account. Similar problems exist for the maintenance and repair of school facilities. Newer buildings require less expensive maintenance and repairs and are less likely to require expensive rehabilitation, such as roof repairs or the replacement of a boiler. It is important that either allocation rules take these differences into account or school-site decision makers have the foresight to establish reserves to pay for these items when they come due.

Risk Management. Another area critical to this discussion is risk management. For expenses on insurance and medical benefits, large risk pools are helpful in keeping costs down. There are some advantages to cooperative purchasing programs, across schools or districts. The advantage to letting school sites purchase their own benefit and insurance packages is that they can tailor their programs to meet the needs of their staff and students. The downside is that in smaller risk pools, the potential of one lengthy illness or catastrophic loss making future insurance very expensive is much greater. Thus, programs that provide more autonomy at school sites need to be structured very carefully so that these functions do not take away from funds available for direct instruction.

Food Services. Virtually every school in the United States provides food services for its students. In many schools, federal assistance pays for meals of low-income children. Although it is possible to shift authority for operation of food services programs to school sites, there may be little reason to do so. This is one area that frequently benefits from substantial economies of scale, particularly in the purchase of food. Moreover, it is unlikely that a school principal, or his or her staff, will have the skill and expertise to operate a food services program efficiently. Although school sites could consider contracting out for food services, again, there may be benefits of scale in allowing the district to handle this.

Purchasing. For years, districts have operated large purchasing operations, buying supplies in bulk and then distributing them to school sites. Although there are substantial savings in the purchase price of materials, the costs of maintaining inventory and distribution are significant. Today, many districts have eliminated the cost of inventories and warehouses through the decentralized purchasing of many office supplies. Widely available office supply stores make it possible for local school sites to manage their supplies needs more economically through arrangements with local providers who often are willing to distribute purchased materials to the school for free. Thus, districts not only save inventory expenses, but can reduce the costs of intradistrict shipping from the central warehouse to school sites.

This discussion shows that there are a number of alternative ways budget resources can be directed to school sites. Here we provide brief descriptions of the approaches used in two large urban school districts.

Seattle[5]

The Seattle Public School District is widely recognized as having developed a successful approach for allocating budget resources to school sites. The "weighted-student formula" developed by the district was first implemented for the 1997–98 school year. As described in district materials (see the district's website) there are three basic principles that guide the weighted-student methodology:

- resources follow the student,
- resources are denominated in dollars, not FTE staff; and
- the allocation of resources varies by the personal characteristics of each individual child.

For 2002–03, the district's budget totaled $423,083,787.[6] Of this, 58.4 percent or $246,941,284 was distributed directly to the schools through the formula, while the remaining funds were controlled centrally for these functions:

- centrally held instructional support;
- logistics and other support,
- central administration, and
- general reserves.

The funds distributed to the schools consist of two components. The first is a foundation allocation or allocation to each school based on the type of school. To be funded, a school must have a minimum enrollment. This figure ranged from $200,000 for elementary and nontraditional schools with a minimum enrollment of 250 students to $425,000 for middle schools with a minimum enrollment of 600 students, and $544,000 for high schools with a minimum of 1,000 students. These funds are to ensure the minimum operational viability of each school.

Seattle School
District

[5]Further details about Seattle's budget system can be found at the district's website.
[6]District "blue book," *www.seattleschools.org/area/finance/budget/bluebookwsfoverview/wsfoverview.pdf*, accessed February 2, 2003.

The balance of a school's funds is distributed through the weighted-pupil formula.[7] Each student receives a weight based on his or her characteristics. The formula provides different weights for regular-education students, plus additional weights for students based on special-education needs, bilingual education eligibility, and eligibility for free and reduced-price lunch. The sum of the weighted pupils is multiplied by the base funding factor, which in 2002–03 was budgeted at $2,680.73 for each weighted student.

A school's total allocation is the sum of the foundation allocation plus the funds generated through the weighted-student formula. Principals and the school community are responsible for managing the resources to provide the educational program. Because the district has an extensive system of school choice, supported in part through an excellent public transportation program that allows students to commute throughout the district, schools actually compete for students. Schools with enrollments falling below the minimum are eventually scheduled for closure. The system places substantial control for the educational program at a school in the hands of local school officials.

San Francisco[8]

The San Francisco Unified School District has also made efforts to devolve more budget authority to the school sites. The district has established these components as part of a school program:

- adequate administrative support;
- adequate secretarial/clerical support;
- library resources, including a skilled librarian;
- counseling resources, including a head counselor or dean in secondary schools;
- arts education and physical education programs;
- other services to meet the social, emotional, and psychological needs of students;
- supports for general education enrichment; and
- class sizes in various subject areas that are proportional to the goals set out in the district's negotiated contract with its teachers.

Under district guidelines, each school must fund a principal, assistant principals if enrollment exceeds minimum levels, and teachers at various ratios depending on the grade level and subject matter being taught. Unlike Seattle, funds are based on the average cost of staff, not actual dollars. Schools are allowed to allocate personnel funds in patterns different from those in the funding formulas as long as certain minimums are met. At least one middle school in the district with 300 students has elected to employ two assistant principals to focus attention on the needs of its students.

In addition, each school receives revenues based on the characteristics of individual children. Special education remains a central office function, while other needs such

---

[7]Chapter 6 contains a detailed discussion of weighted-pupil systems.
[8]The principle source of this information is Leigh, Myong, Memorandum to Principals regarding Budget Information Packet for Planning School Year 2002–03, April 3, 2002.

as bilingual instruction (within the requirements of California's Proposition 227, which places limits on such programs), free and reduced-price lunches, and any other of the many categorical programs available to students, schools, and districts in California. Table 8.6 shows the division of responsibility between schools sites and the central office in the district. Decisions about the allocation and use of resources that are the responsibility of the school site are under the control of the site administrators and their site councils.

TABLE 8.6   Central versus Site-Based Responsibilities in San Francisco Unified School District

Site Budget Responsibility	Central Office Budget Responsibility
General education teachers	Itinerant staff
Paraprofessionals	Boiler plant engineers' salary
Librarians	Transportation
Counselors	Business services
Building administration—leadership	Human resources
Building administration—office support	Legal services
Parent liaisons	Athletic coaches
Noontime supervisors (elementary)	Food and nutrition services
Elementary advisors	Telecommunications/telephones
Substitutes for staff development absences	Substitutes—nonstaff development
	Professional development
Extra-duty pay for student activities	Special-education teachers, aides, and related service providers
Special-education supplies	
Special-education professional development	Furniture
	Equipment
ELL school-based teachers and aides	Utilities
School supplies	Assistive technology for special education
Library books	Maintenance and grounds-keeping staff and supplies
Instructional materials and technology	
Extended learning opportunities	Districtwide assessment
Optional test preparation	Custodial staff supplies, salaries, and overtime
Replacement texts	
Benefits for all positions funded by site	Basic texts (new adoptions)
Security aides, other than those out of general funds	Language interpreters and translations
	Capital outlay
"Adjustment" teachers	Information technology and hardware
Specialty programs	General-fund security personnel
AP teachers	STAR schools staff
	Vocational-education staff
	Administrative interns (elementary schools)

Source: Ackerman, 2002.

5. SUMMARY

A school district's budget is a planning document that links programmatic decisions to financial information about the district's revenues and expenditures. As such, a budget document provides a description of the district's priorities and strategies along with a description of the resources to be used to meet those priorities. Budgets can also be used by school districts as a basis for long-range planning and as a management tool to ensure that resources are allocated and used on the basis of established policies and goals.

At the most basic level, a budget document should include an introduction describing the district's educational plans, the expected revenues and expenditures of the district, the number and type of personnel to be employed in carrying out those plans, and a description of the way funds are allocated to schools sites and programs within the district. In addition to providing revenue and expenditure estimates for the budget year, a budget document typically provides information for the previous year and the current operating year.

While there are many approaches to budgeting, most school districts rely on line-item budgets that provide information by object and often by program and function as well. All 50 states have established legal requirements for the format, timing, and publication of budgets. Many districts provide more information than the minimum required by their state seeking ways to make the information more useful to administrators and the public. Two large urban districts, Seattle and San Francisco, provide examples of districts that have devolved a large amount of budgeting control to school sites.

Allocation and Use of Funds at the District, School, and Classroom Levels

Distributing dollars to districts and schools in equitable ways, the subject of previous chapters, is a first step in providing educational resources for the purpose of educating children. Interdistrict resource allocation has dominated school finance for years. But we now need to know more about how to turn dollars into productive uses in districts, schools, and classrooms. The first step in this process is to understand how dollars currently are spent.

This chapter identifies what is now known about what happens to dollars once they reach districts. Since schools and classrooms are the "production units" in education, gathering data on resource allocation and use at these levels began to be the focus of research in the 1990s. For each level of schooling—elementary, middle, and high school—these types of data are needed:

- staffing and expenditures by program—the regular instruction program; programs for special-need students such as compensatory, bilingual, and special education; administration; staff development; and instructional materials,
- staffing and expenditures by educational strategy—class size, professional development, tutoring, pull-out resource room, core versus elective subjects, etc.,
- staffing and expenditures by content area—mathematics, language arts (reading in elementary schools), science, history/social science, foreign language, art, music, and physical education,
- interrelationships among these staffing and expenditure patterns, and
- relationships of these staffing and expenditure patterns to student performance.

The field of school finance is far from having this knowledge. Although more states are reporting expenditures by program area with their current accounting systems, data are not systematically collected at the school level (Busch and Odden, 1997a). A few states do collect these data, including Florida, Kentucky, Ohio, Oregon, and Texas. But in general, the total expenditure by level for elementary, middle, and high schools across the United States and within most of the 50 states is not known.

Collecting and analyzing these data is a first step toward addressing the productivity questions that policymakers now ask. They want to know where money goes, what resources—especially instructional and curriculum resources—it buys, and what impact those resources have on student performance. As discussed in this chapter and in Chapter 10, altering resource-use patterns at the school site might be the most promising way to improve education system productivity in the near future.

This chapter provides a brief overview of how education dollars are used. The first section describes expenditures by function and staffing patterns using national, state, and district data. One conclusion from this section is that there has been a remarkable stability in the overall use of educational resources across functional categories—and that for decades, about 60 percent of the education dollar has been spent for instruction. Section 2 discusses some of the dynamics of resource use, describing significant changes in the use of educational resources, particularly within the instructional category over the past several decades. Section 3 briefly discusses the results of several studies of expenditures at the school-site level. Finally, Section 4 begins to translate these overall findings on expenditure patterns to identify typical staffing patterns in elementary, middle, and high schools nationally, and within four different regions of the country, as a prelude to Chapter 10, which discusses how school-level resources could be used more effectively.

1. RESOURCE-USE PATTERNS IN EDUCATION

All 50 states collect some kind of fiscal data from their school districts. These data include information on district revenues and expenditures, as well as numbers and characteristics of district employees. The revenue data generally identify the sources (federal, state, or local) and amounts of revenue received by each school district. Expenditure data are most frequently collected by object of expenditure, such as professional salaries, classified salaries, employee benefits, materials and supplies, and capital expenditures. States now also collect and report expenditure data by broad functional areas—instruction, instructional support, student support, administration, transportation, plant operation and maintenance, and debt service—and several also report by program area—such as regular education, compensatory education, special education, bilingual education.

Staffing data usually include information on the number of licensed staff employed by each district, and their title such as teacher, administrator, principal, librarian, and counselor. Some states maintain databases with information on instructional aides as well. In a few states, data on teacher credentials and/or teaching assignments are also available. Staffing data usually include numbers of professional staff, and within that, numbers of administrators, teachers, librarians and counselors, instructional aides, and support staff. These data provide a starting point for identifying how districts use money.

Expenditures by Function Using National Data Sets

Annually, the National Center for Education Statistics (NCES) provides nationwide and individual state data on expenditures by function. But because definitions for functional categories differed across states, NCES reported expenditures across only a few very broad functional categories prior to 1990.

Table 9.1 provides data on expenditures by function at the national level from 1920 to 1980. Two points should be noted about these data. First, the distribution of expenditures by function changed over these 60 years. The data show that the percent spent on instruction declined, and that the percent spent on administration and fixed

TABLE 9.1   Percent Distribution of Expenditures by Function, 1920–80

	1920	*1930*	*1940*	*1950*	*1960*	*1970*	*1980*
	Percentage Distribution						
Total expenditures, all schools	100.0	100.0	100.0	100.0	100.0	100.0	100.0
Current expenditures, all schools	83.4	80.0	83.4	80.9	79.8	85.7	91.2
Public elementary							
and secondary schools	83.1	79.6	82.8	80.3	79.0	84.1	90.6
Administration	3.5	3.4	3.9	3.8	3.4	3.9	4.4
Instruction	61.0	56.9	59.9	53.3	53.5	57.2	55.5
Plant operation	11.2	9.3	8.3	7.3	6.9	6.2	(5)
Plant maintenance	2.9	3.4	3.1	3.7	2.7	2.4	10.2
Fixed charges	0.9	2.2	2.1	4.5	5.8	8.0	12.3
Other school services[1]	3.5	4.4	5.5	7.7	6.6	6.3	8.3
Summer schools	(2)	(2)	(2)	(2)	0.1	0.3	(4)
Adult education[2]	0.3	0.4	0.6	0.6	0.2	0.3	–
Community colleges	(2)	(2)	(2)	(2)	0.2	0.3	–
Community services	(1)	(1)	(1)	(1)	0.4	0.6	0.6
Capital outlay[3]	14.8	16.0	11.0	17.4	17.0	11.5	6.8
Interest on school debt	1.8	4.0	5.6	1.7	3.1	2.9	2.0

Source: National Center for Education Statistics, 2002, p. 188, Table 164.

Note: Beginning in 1959–60, includes Alaska and Hawaii. Because of rounding, details may not add to totals.

[1]Prior to 1959–60, items included under "Other school services" were listed under "Auxiliary services," a more comprehensive classification that also included community services.
[2]Prior to 1959–60, data shown for adult education represent combined expenditures for adult education, summer schools, and community colleges.
[3]Prior to 1969–70, excludes capital outlay by state and local school-housing authorities.
[4]Less than 0.05 percent.
[5]Plant operations includes plant maintenance.

TABLE 9.2   Current Expenditures by Function for the United States, 1991–95

	1990–91 *(%)*	*1995–96* *(%)*	*1998–99* *(%)*
Current expenditures			
Instruction	60.5	61.7	61.7
Instruction support	4.2	4.0	4.4
Student support	4.4	4.8	5.0
District administration	5.7	5.1	5.2
School administration	5.8	5.8	5.7
Operation and maintenance	10.5	10.1	9.7
Student transportation	4.3	4.1	4.0
Food	4.2	4.2	4.0
Other	0.5	0.3	0.3

Source: National Center for Education Statistics, 2002, p. 188, Table 164.

Note: Totals may not equal 100 percent due to rounding.

charges (benefits) increased over this period. Second, however, the percent spent on instruction remained about the same from about 1950 onward. Since the percentages in this figure are related to total expenditures, which include capital as well as operating expenditures, the percent spent on instruction as a percentage of current expenses needs to be calculated. The figure would be 60.8 percent for 1980, a figure quite close, as we shall show, to the percent of the operating budget that is spent on instruction today.

During the late 1980s and early 1990s, NCES began a project to collect more detailed expenditure data that were comparable across states. During this process, they also slightly modified the categories of data collected. Table 9.2 displays national data on expenditures by function for the 1990–91, 1995–96, and 1998–99 school years. The data show that instructional expenditures rose by about 1 percentage point from 60.5 percent in 1991 to about 61.7 percent of the operating budget by the end of the decade. The data also show what have become typical expenditure distributional patterns: about 10 percent for student and instructional support, 6 percent for district administration, 6 percent for site administration, 10 percent for operations and maintenance, and just under 10 percent for transportation, food, and other services.

Expenditures by Function Using Individual State Data Sets

Although states often define expenditure categories somewhat differently, research on expenditure patterns using state databases generally reach the conclusion that the major portion of the education budget is spent on instruction. As we will show, however, a large portion of instructional expenditures is spent outside the regular classroom on services for special-needs students. This strategy reflects a system characterized by good values but unimpressive results, because the typical "pullout" strategy of providing extra services has not had much positive impact on those students' learning (Odden, 1991; Borman, Stringfield, and Slavin, 2001; Reynolds and Wolfe, 1999). Districts also provide a host of noneducation services. Districts run buses, heat and clean buildings, serve meals, and administer a complex system. The result is that only a small portion of the education dollar is spent on regular education instruction.

Table 9.3 draws from studies of district-level expenditure patterns in three major states—Florida (Nakib, 1995), California (Picus, Tetreault, and Murphy, 1996), and New York (Monk, Roellke, and Brent, 1996)—and compares the results with national patterns provided by NCES. Not surprisingly, the data show that the districts in all three states spent about 61 percent on instruction, which includes both regular-education instruction in mathematics, language arts, writing, history, and science, as well as instruction for students with special needs such as the disabled. The proportion of 61 percent spent on instruction is quite consistent across the states, and squares with the figure from national studies. These researchers also examined the spending patterns across a number of different district characteristics, including spending level, rural and urban location, high and low percentages of minority students, and students from low-income families, and the patterns were remarkably consistent. The coefficient of variation for percent spent on instruction was just 10 percent, meaning the proportion varied from about 55 to 67 percent for two-thirds of all districts.

These figures are similar to the findings from other studies of school district expenditure patterns from the study by Odden, Palaich, and Augenblick (1979), to the New York state study discussed in Chapter 1 of this book, to two studies of districts in Pennsylvania (Hartman 1988a, 1988b, 1994), and to studies by Cooper (1993) and Speakman and colleagues (1997) in New York.

TABLE 9.3 Current Expenditures by Function (Percent) Across the Nation and in California, Florida, and New York

Expenditure Function	Nation NCES	California[1]	Florida	New York
Instruction	61.2	60.8	58.4	61.8
Instructional support and student services	8.7	7.9	9.9	8.6
Total administration	8.4	11.4	8.1	10.2
District administration	2.6	3.2	4.4	5.7
School administration	5.8	8.2	6.9	4.5
Operation and maintenance	10.3	13.4	10.7	9.3
Transportation	4.2	1.5	4.2	6.3
Short-term capital	–	0.4	0.3	1.1
Food services	4.2	4.6	5.2	2.7

Source: Monk, Roellke, and Brent, 1996; Nakib, 1995; Picus, Tetreault, and Murphy, 1996; National Center for Education Statistics, 1996, Table 160.

[1]Large unified districts

Expenditure Patterns by Expenditure Levels

An additional question often asked about school district expenditure patterns is whether they differ across high- and low-spending districts. Two studies of New York (Odden, Palaich, and Augenblick, 1979; Monk, Roellke, and Brent, 1996) and several more recent studies provide some evidence for answering this question. Table 9.4 displays expenditure data by high, medium, and low levels of operating expenditure levels in New York for the 1977–78 school year; the numbers include only state and local revenues. These data reveal two major patterns. First, instructional expenditures comprised about 60 percent of state/local operating expenditures per pupil, quite close to the national average. Second, instructional expenditures per pupil as a percent of total operating expenditures *increased* with spending levels, rising from 58 percent in the bottom decile, to 59 percent in the middle, and to 63 percent in the top spending decile. This pattern was different, however, from studies in Pennsylvania, and different from later New York studies in the 1990s, both discussed here.

It is important to note, though, that while the percent spent on instruction increased from just 58 to 63 percent from the bottom to the top decile, the dollar amount of the increase was larger, rising from $800 per pupil in the low-spending decile, to $1,107 in the middle, and to $1,822 at the high-spending decile. These differences produced different patterns in expenditures for teachers. Low-spending districts spent 77 percent on teacher salaries, compared with only 72 percent in the high-spending districts. But this allowed the high-spending districts to spend more than twice the amount per pupil on teachers—$1,303 to $619. These higher expenditures were mainly related to differences in salaries; the median salaries were almost twice as high in the high-spending districts as in the low-spending districts. Pupil-teacher ratios differed only marginally, ranging from 20.4 in the lowest-spending districts to 17.2 in the higher-spending districts. In general, pupil-teacher ratios were uniformly low. Thus, differences in spending on teachers were reflected primarily in differences in teacher salary levels.

TABLE 9.4   Expenditures by Function by Level of Spending in New York, 1977–78

Component of per-Pupil Expenditures	Level of Spending[1]		
	High	*Medium*	*Low*
Operating expenditures	$2,863	$1,850	$1,325
Instruction	1,822 (63%)	1,107 (59%)	800 (58%)
Central district administration	80 (3%)	42 (2%)	48 (3%)
Central district services	329 (11%)	240 (13%)	156 (11%)
Employee benefits	559 (19%)	373 (20%)	271 (20%)
Transportation	114 (4%)	105 (6%)	104 (8%)

Source: Odden, Palaich, and Augenblick, 1979.

[1]High is top-spending decile; middle is decile 6; low is lowest-spending decile.

TABLE 9.5   New York Expenditures by Function and by Spending Level, 1991–92

Function	Quintile 1	Quintile 2	Quintile 3	Quintile 4	Quintile 5	Total
Instruction	62.5	62.2	62.0	61.9	60.0	61.8
Instructional support	5.2	5.3	5.1	4.7	5.4	5.1
Administrative	9.9	10.2	9.9	10.1	11.0	10.2
District						
State						
Pupil services	2.9	3.2	3.3	3.4	4.2	3.5
Maintenance						
and operation	9.0	9.2	8.8	9.4	10.2	9.3
Transportation	6.4	6.1	6.4	6.5	6.3	6.3
Food	3.5	3.3	3.1	2.5	1.8	2.7
Debt service	0.6	0.7	1.4	1.3	1.1	1.1
Total expenditures	$6,067	$6,627	$7,309			

Source: Monk, Roellke, and Brent, 1996, Table 3A.

Note: Each quintile includes districts that enroll about one-fifth of all students.

Some of these New York expenditure patterns had changed by 1992. As shown by the data in Table 9.5, the major difference was that the percent spent on instruction decreased as overall expenditures increased in 1992, a pattern that was much more typical across the country in the 1970s and 1980s, and a pattern more typical today as well. The data also show that the percentage spent on some other categories then increased with overall expenditures. As expenditures per pupil rose, the percent spent on administration, pupil services, maintenance and operations, and debt service also rose. Since the absolute amount spent is the product of the percentage times the overall expenditure level, higher-spending districts not only spent more dollars on instruction (largely teacher salaries and benefits) but also on all of these other elements of the budget as well.

The expenditure patterns across spending levels for Pennsylvania in both 1984–85 (Hartman, 1988a, 1988b) and 1991–92 (Hartman, 1994) were similar to these latter patterns in New York. Instructional expenditures as a percent of current expenditures *decreased* as current spending increased. Further, a larger portion of teacher expenditures was spent on reducing pupil-teacher ratios than on increasing teacher salaries. But higher-spending districts also paid their teachers more, so higher-spending districts provided teachers both higher salary levels and smaller class sizes. In terms of other patterns, higher-spending districts had teachers with slightly more education and experience (though the differences were not as dramatic as in New York) and had more support and administrative personnel.

These studies show that higher-spending districts are able to purchase a different mix of educational services than low-spending districts. They hire more teachers, administrators, and support personnel, hire teachers with more advanced education and years of experience, pay them more (sometimes dramatically more), have smaller class sizes, provide more pupil-support services, and provide a greater variety of instruction-ally related support services.

In analyzing data from a larger and nationally representative sample of districts, Picus (1993a, 1993b) and Picus and Fazal (1996) came to similar conclusions. They found that higher-spending districts tended generally to spend the bulk of their extra funds on more staff, and a lesser portion on higher salaries. Their research found that higher-spending districts spent about 50 percent of each additional dollar on more teachers and the other 50 percent on noninstructional services. Of the 50 percent spent on teachers, 40 percentage points were used to hire more teachers, and only 10 percentage points were used to provide higher salaries. Barro (1992) found similar results with state-level data; the bulk of extra revenues was used to hire more staff rather than for higher salaries.

But the schools tend not to use much of the additional staff for the regular instructional program, as partially hinted by the New York and Pennsylvania information just discussed. In a fascinating analysis of 1991–92 teacher resources by core subject areas in New York secondary schools (English, mathematics, science, social studies, and foreign language), Monk, Roellke, and Brent (1996) showed that staffing in core subjects changed very little across district spending levels. Table 9.6 shows the remarkable stability of the number of teachers per 1,000 students by five subject areas. Yes, teacher resources spiked a bit in the highest-spending quintile, but only modestly. The average spending between the highest and lowest deciles differed by almost 100 percent, but teacher resources *for the core academic subjects* differed by only 20 percent. Teacher resources varied by negligible amounts across the four lowest-spending quintiles, though spending varied by thousands of dollars.

Although higher-spending districts did not systematically provide more resources for core academics, they did spend more on some subjects than lower-spending districts in New York. Monk, Roellke, and Brent (1996) found that higher-spending districts spent significantly more on mathematics, and somewhat more on language arts, science, and social studies. Across all spending levels, districts tended to spend the most per pupil on science and foreign language, the second most on music, and the least on health and physical education.

TABLE 9.6   Instructional Staff per 1,000 Pupils by Subject Area in New York Secondary Schools (Grades 7–12), 1991–92

Subject	Quintile 1	Quintile 2	Quintile 3	Quintile 4	Quintile 5
English	5.20	5.25	5.43	5.31	6.10
Mathematics	4.46	4.51	4.67	4.54	5.00
Science	3.86	3.98	4.01	4.18	4.95
Social studies	4.04	4.05	4.06	4.09	4.65
Foreign language	2.18	2.36	2.35	2.46	3.23

Source: Monk, Roellke, and Brent, 1996, Table 7a.

Note: Quintiles refer to spending levels, with quintile 1 being the lowest and quintile 5 being the highest.

Summary

In short, districts spend about 61 percent of their budget on instruction, although that percentage is a bit higher for lower-spending districts and a bit lower for higher-spending districts. But across all spending levels, instructional resources focused on the regular-education program (mathematics, science, language arts/reading/writing, history, and foreign language) might not change that much across spending levels. As spending rises, more of the dollar is spent on nonregular instructional services (i.e., "supports" for the regular instructional program)—specialist teachers in resource rooms, more pupil support, and so on. The end result is that less than 50 percent of the education budget is spent on regular instruction, at both secondary and elementary levels. This pattern also characterizes how the education system uses "new" money, an issue addressed in Section 2.

Finally, some studies show that variations in expenditures by function can also occur over time because of other factors. Picus (1988) found that expenditures for instruction increased slightly in California in the years after that state's large education reform program was enacted in 1983. Similarly, Hannaway, McKay, and Nakib (2002) found that expenditures for instruction nationally increased by about 1 percentage point (from 60 to 61 percent) over the 1990s, which was also a period of intense education reform. These findings mirrored those reported by the National Center for Education Statistics (2002). In a follow-up study, Hannaway, Fu, and Nakib (2002) showed that spending allocations by function also vary by whether districts are experiencing fiscal growth or decline, or rising or falling enrollments. But neither of these studies show dramatic variation from the overall general pattern of about 61 percent for instruction, 8 to 10 percent for instructional and student support, 9 to 12 percent for administration (both district and school), 10 percent for operation and maintenance, 10 percent for transportation, food services, and other. At times, the allocation of the education dollar varies by 1 to 2 percent from the norm, but often reverts back to the standard pattern over time. Still, the 1 percentage point increase in expenditures for instruction that occurred during the 1990s seems to be holding.

The relatively stable use of education dollars across districts, however, masks differences in resource use within the instructional budget. The fact is that even though the proportion of expenditures spent on instruction has been quite stable for over a century, the pattern of exactly how those instructional dollars are spent has changed dramatically, phenomena not revealed by most fiscal reporting systems that show expenditures by function.

2. CHANGES IN EDUCATIONAL RESOURCE USE OVER TIME

As Section 1 noted, real dollars per pupil for public schools rose consistently during the twentieth century. Despite the feeling of many educators as well as much of the public and even policy community, real dollars per pupil—that is, resources after inflation—increased by about 3.5 percent annually from 1890 to 1990, according to a 100-year analysis by Hanushek and Rivkin (1997).

This study not only tracked the change in educational resources over a 100-year period, but also investigated how those new dollars were used—for higher salaries, for more educational services, for lower pupil-teacher ratios, and so on. Their analysis reached several conclusions, all of which are worth noting:

- First, dollars per pupil after adjusting for inflation increased continuously during the last century, rising on an *inflated, per-pupil basis* through even large-scale service expansion times—such as the expansion to high school education in the 1920s and 1930s, the rising high school graduation rates after World War II, and the postwar enrollment growth of the 1950s and 1960s.
- Large portions of the real dollar increase, consistent with findings in Section 1, were consumed by adding more teaching staff, which could be used to provide instruction in additional classes of noncore subjects such as art and music, to lower class sizes, or to expand other education services. Except for special education, their analysis was not able to distinguish which of these uses of more staff were employed.
- More teaching staff were used both to expand services, such as special education, and to lower actual class sizes, but during the 1980s, expansion of special-education services constituted a particularly large portion of increased education revenues, even though class size reduction and teacher salary increases continued (though at a slower pace).
- Substantial portions of increased revenues were also used to increase teacher salaries, but this portion of the increase was less than that used to hire more teachers. Further, even substantial teacher salary increases did not keep teacher salaries on par with wages in other occupations. This failure to maintain wage parity was particularly problematic for women in the latter quarter of the twentieth century.
- Resource increases halted during the first half of the 1990s, even though special-education costs continued to rise, thus encroaching on the general education fund.

This aggregate analysis of the use of ever-rising educational resources shows that, contrary to popular understanding, education has been a fiscal growth industry overall for nearly a century, but that while educational services have expanded and teacher salaries have risen, there are still questions about the proportion of the increase that has been used for specialist teachers and special-needs programs. And it appears that even larger salary increases are needed in order to make education competitive in the labor market for quality teaching talent.

These conclusions are similar to three sets of studies of the uses of new or greater education resources, one set conducted in the 1970s, a second conducted in the 1990s on the use of school finance reform dollars, and a third conducted in the 1990s but on the use of new dollars over a decade and a half.

Two 1970s studies investigated what higher-spending districts bought in comparison with lower-spending districts (Alexander, 1974; Barro and Carroll, 1975). Generally, these studies found that higher-spending districts tended to use more money to increase nonteaching aspects of the budget, and that those dollars used to increase teacher expenditures were primarily used to reduce pupil-teacher ratios, with only a small portion used to raise average teacher salary levels. But it was not clear if the lower pupil-teacher ratios produced lower class sizes or just additional periods of non-core academic classes.

These findings paralleled those of Kirst (1977), who studied the use of school finance reform dollars in California in the 1970s. He analyzed how spending changed in K–12 districts in a Los Angeles county that received a 15 percent increase in state aid from a 1972 California school finance reform in response to the *Serrano* v. *Priest* court suit. He found that salary increases were marginal, in the 5 to 7 percent range. His study showed that the bulk of new funds were used to hire additional instructional personnel, with some funds used to reduce class size, some to add periods to the school day, and some to hire specialists. While the specific roles of the new staff varied across districts, all exhibited a pattern of hiring more professional personnel rather than hiking salaries.

Related research in the 1990s on the local use of new money from school finance reforms found similar patterns of resource use. Poor districts received more money and used it for clear needs (facilities, social services, compensatory education), but allocated little of the new money to the regular-education program (Adams, 1994; Firestone et al., 1994; Picus, 1994b).

A third set of studies investigated the micro-specifics of the uses of new dollars over time. Rothstein and Miles (1995) analyzed in detail the use of education dollars by nine school districts over a 24-year period, 1967–91. At the time, this was the most detailed analysis of the use of educational resources over time that had ever been conducted. The period covered by their analysis covered the years during which there was an expansion of many services for special-needs populations—including federal and state programs for students from low-income backgrounds, the disabled with the enactment in 1976 of the federal Education for All Handicapped Children law that provided a legal entitlement to education services for all handicapped students, students with limited English proficiency, and so on. Rothstein and Miles found that for all nine districts the vast bulk of new education resources were used to provide new education services for these special-needs students. Indeed, they found that expenditures for special-education students in these nine districts rose from 3.7 percent of the operating budget at the beginning of their analysis to 17 percent by the end, and that services for disabled students constituted the single largest use of the rising education dollars over the period analyzed.

In a similar longitudinal analysis of the changing uses of educational resources conducted by Lankford and Wyckoff (1995) for school districts in New York from 1980 to 1992, special-education spending also consumed the bulk of new education dollars. Outside of the Big Five districts in New York—New York City, Buffalo, Rochester, Syracuse, and Yonkers—about 20 percent of increased spending was attributed to special education. But the portion in the Big Five was much larger—60.5 percent in New York City and an average of almost 25 percent in the other districts. Since New York City enrolls about one-third of all students in the state, statewide figures including the Big Five would show that about one-third of all new money from 1982 to 1990 was allocated to special education.

What all these studies show is that there were substantial changes in the use of instructional dollars over the last quarter of the twentieth century, even though, as Section 1 showed, the instructional portion of the budget remained around 60 to 61 percent. Note that expenditures for special education, compensatory education, bilingual education, and all special-needs students are reported in the instructional function, as are expenditures for more teachers to decrease in class size and expenditures to increase teacher salaries.

By the close of the last century, and thus the beginning of the current century, the allocation of the educational dollar across functional categories was about what it was at mid-century, but the actual use of those dollars within the instructional category was quite different. In the first half of the twentieth century, most of instructional expenditures were for regular classroom teachers. That changed in the latter part of the century.

Although researchers disagree on the exact proportion of rising educational resources that were consumed by expenditures for special needs over the last 25 years, the fact is that today, a significant portion of instructional expenditures are used for providing extra services for students with extra needs, such as mental or physical disabilities, educational disadvantage from growing up in a lower-income environment, limited proficiency in English, and so on.

In addition, starting in the mid-1960s, school systems began to provide teachers with "planning and preparation" time during the regular school day by hiring art, music, physical education, library, and other teachers for non-core subjects. So even the proportion of the instructional budget that was not used for "special-needs" students was not completely used for "regular" teachers; about 15 to 20 percent was used to hire additional teachers, not to reduce class size, but to simultaneously teach other subjects (e.g., art, music, physical education) and provide time for "regular" teachers to plan and prepare lesson plans during the regular school day.

These are the "micro" realities of the use of instructional dollars. The exact proportions obviously vary by school district. But for districts on average, regular education will comprise about 45 to 60 percent of the instructional budget; art, music, physical education, and so on, about 10 to 20 percent; and programs for special-needs populations including special education about 20 to 30 percent, realities not shown by fiscal accounting systems that just report expenditures by function. [Note that if disabled students comprise about 12 percent of students, and cost about 1.9 times that of other students, total expenditures for the disabled would be about 22.8 percent of the budget (12 × 1.9)].

More Staff But Not Lower Class Sizes

The previous findings help explain why rising real dollars per pupil, which have been accompanied by declines in the pupil-staff ratio—from a high of 25 in 1960 to about 14 in 1990—stand beside actual class sizes of 30 or more students in many districts. Historically, schools have been organized bureaucratically, and tend to be organized similarly today. Jobs are defined narrowly—principals manage schools and teachers teach students often with a fairly set curriculum and assumed teaching strategies. As schools face new issues—for example, desegregation, children with disabilities, low achieving students, and English language learners—programs are created that provide money to enable schools to hire specialist staff to deal with the problems. Teachers remain in the regular classroom, and specialists are hired to teach or counsel children with these identified special needs in settings outside of the regular classrooms. Past examples of this same behavior are the specialists that were added to school staffs for vocational education, physical education, and even art and music. Growth by addition and specialization has characterized the education system for several decades (Odden and Massy, 1992).

Indeed, as these studies show, the majority of new dollars provided to schools over the past 30 years were not spent on staff for the core instructional program but on specialist teachers and other resource people to provide services to special-needs students usually outside of the regular classroom. Unfortunately, many other studies have shown that these programs and services have produced modest, if any, long-lasting impacts on student achievement (Allington and Johnston, 1989; Odden, 1991; Reynolds and Wolfe, 1999). The children who are targeted to receive these services are deserving and need extra services, but while the values that lead us to provide the extra dollars for these additional services should be retained, the productivity of the expenditure of these dollars needs to rise.

As a result of the increase of specialist staff and programs, regular classroom teachers—the primary service providers—comprise a declining portion of professional staff in schools. The National Commission on Teaching and America's Future (1996) found that regular classroom teachers as a proportion of all professional staff fell from 70 percent in 1950 to 52 percent in 1995, with 10 percent of the latter not engaged in classroom teaching. The fiscal implication is that a declining portion of the education dollar is being spent on the core activity in schools—teaching the regular instructional program. These findings reinforce the data discussed at the beginning of this chapter.

The end result is a system in which when money rises, services expand outside the regular classroom, but results in terms of student achievement stay flat or improve by only small amounts. We will return to this theme in Chapter 10 when we discuss how new school designs use site resources quite differently, with many fewer outside-of-the-regular-classroom specialists.

3. SCHOOL-LEVEL EXPENDITURES

The conclusions from the last section on district-level expenditures by function and the uses of education dollars are reflected in the few studies that exist on expenditures at the school-site level. Until recently, two major studies on expenditures by school and classroom formed the information base on how funds are used below the district level. Guthrie, Kirst, and Odden (1990) conducted a study of school-level expenditures in California for 1985–86. The numbers represented a statewide average for all schools, thus merging data for elementary, middle, and high schools, for which expenditure patterns undoubtedly differ. Nevertheless, it was one of the first studies that provided information on expenditures at the school level.

The figures showed that 63 percent of all expenditures were spent directly on classroom services, which is close to the percent spent on instruction in Sections 1 and 2. Only

50 percent was spent on classroom and specialized teachers. How was the other 13 percent spent in the classroom? Instructional aides constituted one large portion, at 5 percent; pupil personnel support such as guidance counselors constituted another 4 percent; and books, supplies, and equipment comprised the remaining 4 percent. Thus, the data indicated that about two-thirds of expenditures were on direct, classroom services.

What were the one-third noninstructional elements? First, about 31 percent was spent on other site-related items—site administration; site instructional support including curriculum support and staff development; and operations, maintenance, and transportation. Only 6 percent was spent on district, county, and state administration. Thus, 37 percent of California 1986–87 school-site expenditures were spent on nonclassroom activities. Hayward (1988) showed that for many of these expenditure items, the amount spent per item (such as per meal served, per student transported, per square foot of physical plant, etc.) was below norms in the private sector, suggesting that school system expenditures were not profligate.

These figures begin to take the mystery out of how educational dollars are spent at the site level. Although only 50 percent of each dollar was spent on teachers, the other 50 percent was not simply wasted. While the efficiency of expenditures in all categories can be examined, the fact is that all categories of expenditures are needed. Students must be transported to school. Schools must be operated, heated or cooled, and maintained. Some central administration is necessary, and 6 percent is not a large figure. Books, materials, supplies, and instructional support services are needed.

In short, nonteacher expenditures are not lost in an alleged "administrative blob," though these other expenditures are noninstructional. Though a dramatically restructured school could have different spending patterns and produce more student learning, actual spending patterns were not irrational. The route to improving school productivity is not in attacking administrative costs, although such costs are probably too high in many districts. The route is determining what works to boost student learning and making sure dollars support those strategies, issues addressed in Chapter 10.

National data on classroom expenditures generally confirmed these California patterns. Fox (1987) analyzed nationwide classroom expenditures for 1984–85, numbers that also reflected a merged elementary, middle, and high school classroom. Instruction and site administration comprised 58.6 percent of total expenditures, with classroom teachers and other specialist teachers comprising 40.4 percent of total expenditures. Actually, these national data showed that the percent of expenditures spent on teachers nationwide were lower than in California, and that the percent spent on instruction and site administration expenditures were somewhat below that spent in California. The figures showed that "other expenditures" including transportation, operation and maintenance, food services, and fixed charges constituted about one-third (33.2 percent) of total expenditures. Nonsite administration constituted another 7.2 percent.

One of the most recent attempts to investigate school-level data is the work of Picus (1993a, 1993b). By merging data from the Schools and Staffing Survey (SASS) with Census Bureau data on governmental expenditures, Picus was able to estimate spending patterns at the school level. Because fiscal data were not available at the school level, the analysis focused on the use of staff. What was particularly interesting in these analyses was the difference between the estimated pupil-teacher ratio and the teacher self-reported class size. He found that while the average pupil-teacher ratio reported in schools was in the vicinity of 16.5 or 17 to 1, similar to the Hanushek, Rivkin, and NCES results previously reported, self-reported class sizes ranged from 24 to 32 (Picus, 1994a; Picus and Bhimani, 1993) or from 50 to 100 percent higher than even school-level statistics indicated.

Two important findings emerged from this work. First, it was clear that many individuals classified as "teachers" in our public school systems have assignments other than spending the full day in a regular, core classroom. Second, it appears that as the size of the district increases, and as its wealth declines, the disparity between the calculated pupil-teacher ratio and the actual class size grows. Further school-level analyses were not possible with the SASS and Census data.

A number of studies have been conducted using databases with school-level data constructed from individual district records. Miles' (1995) study of Boston showed that if all individuals in the district classified as teachers were placed in regular classrooms, class size could be reduced from an average of 22 to 13. While this change may not really be possible due to the need to provide special services to children with severe disabilities, Miles also provided a number of different policy options showing how the average class size could vary even as some of the district's current special-education practices were continued. Her analysis provided information that a school board could use to make policy decisions on class size and the delivery of special education.

An emerging effort to track expenditures to the student level may further enhance our understanding of how educational resources are used. This work, which seeks to identify the actual resources devoted to each child in a school, may help untangle both the question of how money matters in terms of student outcomes, and provide further data on how school resources are allocated among core instructional practices and other services for children (see Picus, 2000; Picus et. al, 2002; and Picus and Robillard, 2000).

4. STAFFING PATTERNS

Translating these broad expenditure patterns into specific staffing patterns at the school level is the next step in the process of analyzing what happens to the education dollar. Table 9.7 presents national data on the distribution of school district staff by staffing category from fall 1960 to fall 1999. Administrators do not appear to represent a large portion of the total. District, or central office, administrators totaled just 1.7 percent of total staff in 1999 and site administrators just 2.4 percent. Combined, administrators comprised a total of just 4.1 percent of all staff, fairly small percentages given the charges that the education system spends so much on administration.

Instructional staff dropped from 69.8 percent in 1960 to 67.8 percent in 1999. But this small decline masked larger changes in the composition of instructional staff. Though not shown in the table, teachers constituted 74.1 percent of total staff in 1950. The table shows that the percentage of teachers declined to 64.8 percent in 1960 and then to only 51.7 percent in 1999. At the same time, the percentage of instructional aides rose from almost zero in 1960 to 9.9 percent in 1995, and 11.1 percent in 1999. Though well intentioned, one possible downside of this rise in instructional aides is that

TABLE 9.7   Staff Employed in the Public Schools, 1960–99 (Percent Distribution)

	1960	*1970*	*1980*	*1990*	*1995*	*1999*
District administrators	2.0	1.9	1.9	1.7	1.7	1.7
Instructional staff	69.8	68.0	68.6	67.9	67.1	67.8
Site administrators	3.0	2.7	2.6	2.8	2.4	2.4
Teachers	64.8	60.0	52.4	53.4	52.0	51.7
Teacher aides	–	1.7	7.8	8.8	9.9	11.1
Counselors	0.8	1.7	1.8	1.8	1.8	1.7
Librarians	0.8	1.3	1.2	1.1	1.0	1.0
Support staff	28.1	30.1	29.5	30.4	31.2	30.5

Source: National Center for Education Statistics, 2002, p. 91, Table 82.

research shows that the use of instructional aides typically does not lead to student learning growth (Gerber et al., 2001).

Similarly, the percentage of support staff also rose over this time period, from 28.1 percent in 1960 to 30.5 percent in 1999. These numbers show that about one-third of staff in the education system perform nonadministrative roles, such as secretaries, operation, maintenance, and transportation personnel. When policymakers and local taxpayers wonder why only 60 percent of the education dollar is spent on instruction, one answer is that operations, maintenance, transportation, and a small amount of district administration account for nearly a third of public school expenditures.

The bottom line, though, is that the percentage of regular classroom teachers has dropped nearly 33 percent in the latter half of the twentieth century. They have been "replaced" by instructional aides, pupil support staff, and as shown here, by specialist teachers within schools but not teaching in regular classrooms. The policy and productivity issue is whether this use of resources is the most effective.

In the late 1980s, NCES began a comprehensive School and Staffing Survey (SASS) to produce more detailed information on how schools and classrooms are staffed across the country. The data became available in late 1990 and can be used in future analyses to identify staffing patterns by state, level of education, primary field assignment, and a variety of teacher characteristics, such as sex, race, ethnic origin, age, marital status, level of education, major assignment field, and area in which licensed. Table 9.8 indicates the distribution of teachers by some gross categories of primary assignment field for both elementary and secondary schools as reported by NCES (2002). The data in this table show the subjects teachers actually taught, so caution should be given because we know that teaching out of subject is a problem all over the country (Ingersoll, 2001).

The data in Table 9.8 show that the majority of teachers in elementary schools were elementary school generalists, with very few having content-specific assignments. Also, 9.6 percent of elementary teachers were in special education, and 19.5 percent in "other" areas.

TABLE 9.8   Elementary and Secondary Teachers by Primary Assignment Field, 1993–94

	Percent of Total	
Primary Assignment Field	*Elementary*	*Secondary*
English/language arts	0.2	14.0
Mathematics	0.3	11.5
Social studies	NA	10.6
Science	NA	10.7
General elementary, prekindergarten, and kindergarten	70.5	–
Special education	9.6	9.0
Vocational education	0.2	9.2
Other	19.5	34.9

Source: National Center for Education Statistics, 2002, p. 77, Table 68.

At the secondary level, only 46.8 percent of the teachers in the sample were assigned to the academic core areas of English/language arts, mathematics, social studies, and science. This reflects the actual staffing in most comprehensive high schools. These nationwide data provide the beginnings of detailed information on staffing patterns in schools, but analyses disaggregating the data to local and school levels provide even more useful information on how dollars are transformed into staffing patterns.

School-Level Staffing Patterns

To begin to answer this question, we used the Schools and Staffing Survey (SASS) school-level data to determine the median staffing in elementary, middle, and high schools nationally, and in each major region of the country. We calculated staffing patterns for elementary schools with between 400 to 600 students (roughly averaging 500 students), middle schools with 900 to 1,100 students (about 1,000 students, on average), and high schools with 1,400 to 1,600 students (typically averaging 1,500 students). Table 9.9 shows the national average staffing resources for the elementary, middle, and high schools of interest. In addition, Table 9.9 indicates the dollar value associated with staffing, using the figure of $50,000 for salaries and benefits for each professional staff slot and $15,000 for each instructional aide, which reflect very roughly a national average figure in the mid-1990s.

At the elementary level, the numbers show that the school would need 20 teachers to provide regular class sizes of 25 students. Since the school on average has 27 teachers, that means it has seven additional teachers probably used for such purposes as music, art, and physical education to provide regular teachers "planning and preparation" time, as well as specialist teachers for special-needs programs. Elementary schools also have a librarian and a half-time media aide, and 2.5 counselors and other pupil sup-

TABLE 9.9   School Resources in *National* Average Elementary, Middle, and High Schools

Ingredient	Elementary School Grades K–5[1]	Middle School Grades 6–8[2]	High School Grades 9–12[3]
Average enrollment	~500	~1000	~1500
1. Principal	1.0	1.0	1.0
2. Assistant principals	0.0	2.0	3.0
3. Teachers	27.0	57.5	85.5
4. Librarians and media	1.5	2.0	3.0
5. Media aides			
6. Counselors and psychologists	2.5	4.0	6.0
7. Teacher aides	6.0	5.0	6.0
8. Total staff resources[4]	$1,690,000	$3,400,000	$5,015,000
9. Total core resources	1 principal; 20 teachers $1,050,000	1 principal; 40 teachers $2,050,000	1 principal; 60 teachers $3,050,000
10. Total above core			
(line 8 – line 9)	$640,000	$1,350,000	$1,965,000
(per 500 students)	($640,000)	($675,000)	($655,000)

Source: Staffing data from analysis of Schools and Staffing Survey, 1993–94.

[1]Enrollments from 400 to 600 students.
[2]Enrollments from 900 to 1,100 students.
[3]Enrollments from 1,400 to 1,600 students.
[4]Average professional staff cost at $50,000; average teacher aide cost at $15,000.

port personnel. The average elementary school also has six instructional aides. In sum, the national average elementary school has several professional resources above the "core" of one teacher for every 25 students. Using national average figures for salaries and benefits, the average elementary school has $640,000 over "core" resources.

Though the data do not show nonprofessional staff expenditures, the data provide additional insights into how the education dollar is spent. As can be seen from Table 9.9, the professional staffing resources in schools of these sizes reach into the millions (line 8); if the classified staff (secretaries, maintenance), operations, utilities, discretionary resources, and other funding were included, the totals would be even higher. Line 8 indicates the total dollar value of the professional and teacher aide staff. Line 9 indicates the total dollar amount for "core" staffing; "core" staffing is defined as one principal for each 500 students and one teacher for every 25 students. Line 10 indicates the total dollar value of the staffing resources in these schools above those required for core staffing; the amount in parentheses indicates the amount for each grouping of 500 students.

The results show two important findings. First, the extra resources above the core are about the same across each level of schooling, somewhat contrary to the belief that the United States staffs secondary schools at higher levels than elementary schools.

Second, the data show that there are substantial resources above core staffing, averaging about $650,000 for each level of schooling.

These resources should not be viewed as free resources, however. In some districts, a portion of these resources are spent on regular-education specialists such as art, music, physical education, library, home economics, and vocational-education teachers, who have been employed over time to provide planning and preparation time for regular-classroom teachers. Assuming teachers are given one planning period a day, the number of regular-classroom teachers would need to be increased by about 20 percent to approximate the number of regular-education specialists needed to provide that time; note also that each specialist would receive a daily planning period. Thus, each group of 500 students, with 20 regular teachers in classes of 25 students, would require four additional teachers (0.2 × 20) for requisite planning and preparation time. At $50,000 each, this would reduce the additional $650,000 by $200,000 to $450,000.

A portion of the latter figure also would need to be devoted to special-needs students, such as students eligible for compensatory education programs, and additional services for students with disabilities, or who need to learn the English language. Indeed, the median number of Title I teachers is two, and the median for Title I aides is one at each school level. Finally, another portion of the remaining $450,000 would be spent on student support personnel, such as guidance counselors, social workers, psychologists, and family outreach individuals.

Studies discussed in Chapter 10 will show how these resources above the core were used differently in the restructured schools that were studied. The data in Table 9.9 show, at the national average, the magnitude of such additional school-level resources.

But the level and types of school-level resources vary quite substantially across the country, and the national average might only be accurate for a few districts. Previous chapters have discussed the magnitude of resource disparities in fiscal terms, making the important point that the major factor causing disparities across school districts are cross-state rather than within-state differences. Though the Schools and Staffing Survey sampling frame does not allow identification of school-level staffing on a state-by-state basis, it does allow it to be calculated on a regional basis. Tables 9.10 through 9.13 provide the same information as Table 9.9, but the data are broken out into four regions of the country: the Northeast (Connecticut, Maine, Massachusetts, New Hampshire, New Jersey, New York, Pennsylvania, Rhode Island, and Vermont), the Midwest (Illinois, Indiana, Iowa, Kansas, Michigan, Minnesota, Missouri, Nebraska, North Dakota, Ohio, South Dakota, and Wisconsin), the South (Alabama, Arkansas, Delaware, District of Columbia, Florida, Georgia, Kentucky, Louisiana, Maryland, Mississippi, North Carolina, Oklahoma, South Carolina, Tennessee, Texas, Virginia, and West Virginia), and the West (Alaska, Arizona, California, Colorado, Hawaii, Idaho, Montana, Nevada, New Mexico, Oregon, Utah, Washington, and Wyoming). Though prices of staff differ by region, we provide these tables primarily to indicate the difference in staffing because again, as we show here, resource reallocation at the school site largely entails using extant staff resources differently. Thus, we used national average salary figures to calculate dollar levels, a process similar to adjusting actual dollar figures by price indices (see Chapter 6).

TABLE 9.10   Median School Resources in Elementary, Middle, and High Schools in the *Northeast*

Ingredient	Elementary School Grades K–5[1]	Middle School Grades 6–8[2]	High School Grades 9–12[3]
Average enrollment	500	1,000	1,500
1. Principal	1.0	1.0	1.0
2. Assistant principals	0.0	1.0	3.0
3. Teachers	29.0	64.5	101.5
4. Librarians	1.0	1.0	1.0
5. Media aides	0.0	0.0	2.0
6. Counselors and psychologists	3.0	4.5	10.5
7. Teacher aides	6.0	3.0	6.0
8. Total staff resources[4]	$1,790,000	$3,645,000	$5,970,000
9. Total core resources	1 principal; 20 teachers $1,050,000	1 principal; 40 teachers $2,050,000	1 principal; 60 teachers $3,050,000
10. Total above core (line 8 – line 9) (per 500 students)	$740,000 ($640,000)	$1,595,000 ($797,500)	$2,920,000 ($973,000)

Source: Staffing data from analysis of Schools and Staffing Survey, 1993–94.

[1]Enrollments from 400 to 600 students.
[2]Enrollments from 900 to 1,100 students.
[3]Enrollments from 1,400 to 1,600 students.
[4]Average professional staff cost at $50,000; average teacher aide cost at $15,000.

We should note, though, that actual average salaries are quite low in the South and that one of the reasons the staffing in the South is higher than some regions is because of the very low salary levels, making their expenditures per pupil the lowest of any region.

The data in these tables show that school-level resources vary substantially across the four different regions, and that each of the four regions represent staffing patterns different from the national average. For example, line 10 of Table 9.9 gives total resources above the core for each group of 500 students, which is about the same for elementary, middle, and high schools at the national average, but it is different in all of the four regional tables. The Northeast (Table 9.10) provides substantially more resources for its high schools than it does for either its middle or elementary schools. Indeed, the Northeast pattern is the stereotypical pattern: middle schools are resourced somewhat above elementary schools, and high schools are resourced to an even higher level above middle schools, and thus substantially above elementary schools.

In the Midwest (Table 9.11), middle schools, surprisingly, receive the highest level of staffing resources, with elementary schools having less than the national average and high schools about the national average of resources above the core. The resourcing patterns in the South (Table 9.12) are just the opposite of those in the Northeast; elementary

TABLE 9.11   Median School Resources in Elementary, Middle, and High Schools in the *Midwest*

Ingredient	Elementary School Grades K–5[1]	Middle School Grades 6–8[2]	High School Grades 9–12[3]
Average enrollment	500	1,000	1,500
1. Principal	1.0	1.0	1.0
2. Assistant principals	0.0	1.8	2.5
3. Teachers	24.5	62.0	87.0
4. Librarians	1.0	1.0	2.0
5. Media aides	0.5	1.0	1.0
6. Counselors and psychologists	2.5	4.0	7.0
7. Teacher aides	4.0	4.0	6.0
8. Total staff resources[4]	$1,517,500	$3,565,000	$5,080,000
9. Total core resources	1 principal; 20 teachers $1,050,000	1 principal; 40 teachers $2,050,000	1 principal; 60 teachers $3,050,000
10. Total above core (line 8 – line 9) (per 500 students)	$467,500 ($467,500)	$1,515,000 ($757,500)	$2,030,000 ($676,667)

Source: Staffing data from analysis of Schools and Staffing Survey, 1993–94.

[1]Enrollments from 400 to 600 students.
[2]Enrollments from 900 to 1,00 students.
[3]Enrollments from 1,400 to 1,600 students.
[4]Average professional staff cost at $50,000; average teacher aide cost at $15,000.

schools receive the greatest level of resources, followed by middle schools, with the high schools receiving the lowest level. This pattern could reflect the predominant Southern practice of providing students in grades K–3 with a weight above one. Finally, although there are differences in resources among different school levels in the West (Table 9.13), the predominant feature of these data is simply the lower level of resources above the core, generally less than half that of the national averages, and substantially below that in either the Midwest or the Northeast. These figures document that school-level resources are quite different in the various regions of the country, and that just using national averages to assess resource reallocation possibilities for different schools across the country could lead to inaccurate conclusions.

5. SUMMARY

The discussion in this chapter provides an overview of how the education dollar is allocated and used. As Chapter 1 showed, the good news about education dollars is that the country provides a large number of them. But then it makes a serious error. It distributes the money in highly unequal ways, and remedying these inequities has been the

TABLE 9.12   Median School Resources in Elementary, Middle, and High Schools in the *South*

Ingredient	Elementary School Grades K–5[1]	Middle School Grades 6–8[2]	High School Grades 9–12[3]
Average Enrollment	500	1,000	1,500
1. Principal	1.0	1.0	1.0
2. Assistant principals	0.0	2.0	3.0
3. Teachers	29.0	58.0	87.0
4. Librarians	1.0	1.0	2.0
5. Media aides	0.5	1.0	1.0
6. Counselors and psychologists	2.5	4.5	6.0
7. Teacher aides	7.0	6.0	4.0
8. Total staff resources[4]	$1,787,500	$3,430,000	$4,755,000
9. Total core resources	1 principal; 20 teachers $1,050,000	1 principal; 40 teachers $2,050,000	1 principal; 60 teachers $3,050,000
10. Total above core (line 8 – line 9) (per 500 students)	$737,500 ($737,500)	$1,380,000 ($690,000)	$1,705,000 ($568,333)

Source: Staffing data from analysis of Schools and Staffing Survey, 1993–94.

[1]Enrollments from 400 to 600 students.
[2]Enrollments from 900 to 1,100 students.
[3]Enrollments from 1,400 to 1,600 students.
[4]Average professional staff cost at $50,000; average teacher aide cost at $15,000.

focus of school finance for years. Then as this chapter shows, one could raise questions about how the dollars are used once they get to the district and school level; further, this question can be asked both about how higher-spending districts spend their fiscal advantage as well as about how any district spends new dollars that are provided over time. The combination of the stagnant nature of student performance in America, together with the rise of real resources over time, raises the question of whether dollars could be used more effectively. We expect that the answer is, Yes, at least to some degree, and Chapter 10 investigates this issue in more depth.

But the first step in determining how to better use educational resources is to understand how current educational resources are used and why they are used that way. This chapter has identified seven key aspects about current resources and their use:

- Real dollars per pupil rose by an average of 3.5 percent from 1890 to 1990, which represents substantial hikes in real education resources over time.
- The bulk of new dollars provided to public schools has been used to expand educational services, usually outside the core or regular-education program, rather than hiking teacher salaries. One result of this practice has been that teacher

TABLE 9.13   Median School Resources in Elementary, Middle, and High Schools in the *West*

Ingredient	*Elementary School* Grades K–5[1]	*Middle School* Grades 6–8[2]	*High School* Grades 9–12[3]
Average enrollment	500	1,000	1,500
1. Principal	1.0	1.0	1.0
2. Assistant principals	0.0	1.0	2.5
3. Teachers	23.0	41.5	67.0
4. Librarians	0.5	1.0	1.0
5. Media aides	0.5	0.5	1.0
6. Counselors and psychologists	2.0	3.5	5.5
7. Teacher aides	5.5	4.0	6.5
8. Total staff resources[4]	$1,415,000	$2,467,500	$3,962,500
9. Total core resources	1 principal; 20 teachers $1,050,000	1 principal; 40 teachers $2,050,000	1 principal; 60 teachers $3,050,000
10. Total above core (line 8 – line 9) (per 500 students)	$365,000 ($365,000)	$417,500 ($208,750)	$912,500 ($304,167)

Source: Staffing data from analysis of Schools and Staffing Survey, 1993–94.

[1]Enrollments from 400 to 600 students.
[2]Enrollments from 900 to 1,100 students.
[3]Enrollments from 1,400 to 1,600 students.
[4]Average professional staff cost at $50,000; average teacher aide cost at $15,000.

salary levels have not kept pace with salaries for jobs that compete with education for worker talent. The clear implication is that teacher salaries need to rise.

- The large portion of the education dollars used to expand education services, particularly during the past 40 years, can be divided into three uses: (1) providing extra services for special-needs populations; (2) providing planning and preparation periods for regular teachers by hiring specialist teachers who provide instruction in noncore subjects (art, music, physical education, library, etc.); and (3) lowering class size.

- It is difficult to determine just which of these expanded services has been given the most attention, but class sizes of 25 to 30 along with pupil-staff ratios of 15 suggest that the first two have dominated over class-size reduction. We should note, however, the data analyzed do not capture class-size reductions that occurred through new policies enacted by several states during the late 1990s.

- Despite the expansion of services for special-needs students, which represent good and admirable U.S. values, research shows that the students served in pull-out programs have not increased their learning all that much because of the extra services.

- This fact combined with the stagnant nature of student achievement generally (National Center for Education Statistics, 2000), suggest that it is reasonable to raise questions about the productivity of the use of education dollars.
- Finally, and related to the last point, research shows that the average elementary, middle, and high school in America has substantial staffing resources above those needed to provide for regular classes of 25 students. The productivity question is whether these additional staff resources (and even the staff resources of the core teacher) could be used more effectively to boost student learning to the levels required by standards-based education reform.

Chapter 10 tackles this productivity and resource reallocation issue.

We should note here that unlike the second edition, this edition does not include a chapter on teacher salaries. Readers are encouraged to read a book on this topic by Odden and Kelley (2002), which shows how teacher salary structures and salary levels can be changed.

Chapter 10

Using Education Dollars More Wisely to Improve Results

As Chapter 9 showed, schools across the country have substantial resources above the core of one principal and one teacher for every 25 students. Although the magnitude and kind of these additional resources varies by region, district, and school, the fact is that most schools have substantial staffing resources. Since the goal of standards-based education reform is to teach all students to high performance levels (which generally requires a doubling or tripling of educational results), attaining that goal will probably require additional resources, as well as using current school staffing resources differently. The latter is the focus of this chapter.

Astute readers will note that the previous paragraph refers to using *staffing* resources differently in schools. Many in education claim that because most of the education dollar is spent on salaries and benefits, schools are less able to engage in using resources differently. But as this chapter shows, resource reallocation in education today is fundamentally about using *staffing* resources differently. To be sure, the examples discussed here are not exhaustive. In a very real sense, the nation's education system and its schools are just beginning to understand how to programmatically restructure and reallocate resources to higher performance. We expect that many other more powerful strategies will be identified in the future. We also acknowledge the fact that some schools will need more resources to teach all students to higher standards, but we maintain that using current resources differently can be a starting point to boosting student achievement.

With that in mind, this chapter identifies and analyzes some of the strategies that currently exist for using education dollars better. Section 1 summarizes staffing in America's schools as background for the rest of the chapter. Section 2 discusses the key features of three approaches to using staffing resources differently: examples of school restructuring from the first part of the 1990s, the different staffing strategies involved in the comprehensive school designs that emerged during the middle of the 1990s, and a mixture of these two strategies studied during the latter part of the 1990s. Section 3 makes the point that resource reallocation is an example of large-scale educational change, and identifies the key change steps involved in implementing a resource reallocation initiative. Finally, Section 4 shows how resource reallocation strategies can be incorporated into an approach to defining school finance adequacy.

1. STAFFING IN AMERICA'S SCHOOLS

As Chapter 9 explained, the composition of instructional expenditures, and thus school staffing, changed dramatically between 1960 and 1995. In the midpart of the century, most instructional expenditures were for classroom teachers—that is, licensed teachers who taught a classroom of students the regular curriculum for most of the day—the typical elementary school teacher at the primary level and subject-matter teachers in mathematics, science, social studies, and English at the secondary level. As a result, the staffing in most elementary schools included a principal and one teacher for every 25 to 30 students—a fairly simple staffing structure.

By the close of the century, the portion of classroom teachers as a percentage of the instructional budget declined significantly. At the same time, the portion of specialist teachers providing instruction in subjects such as art, music, and physical education and/or instructing students with special needs, largely in resource rooms separate from the regular classroom, increased. As a result, school staffing included not only the principal and approximately one teacher for every 25 students, but also these:

- Specialist teachers (art, music, physical education, library, etc.) who taught these noncore academic subjects and simultaneously provided the regular or core academic teachers with a planning or preparation period (i.e., a period during which they did not instruct students).
- Specialist teachers trained to provide instruction for students with special needs, such as those with learning disabilities, those from low-income backgrounds, and those with limited English proficiency. Until recently, most of this instruction was provided in pull-out resource rooms, not in the regular classroom.
- Instructional aides who provided a variety of assistance to teachers, sometimes actually teaching small groups of students.
- Specialist professionals such as guidance counselors, social workers, and psychologists who provided supports for students' nonacademic needs.

Thus, although expenditures for instruction remained the same approximate percentage of overall expenditures, the pattern of spending within instruction changed. By the late 1980s, instructional expenditures were comprised of a smaller percentage of frontline education workers—regular-classroom teachers—and a larger percentage of specialist staff (both teachers and instructional aides) working outside of the regular classroom and providing extra help for students with special needs. Though some of the increase in education funding from 1960 to 1990 was used to raise teacher salaries and modestly reduce actual class sizes (Hanushek and Rivkin, 1997; Miles, 1997), the bulk was used for services outside of the classroom provided by individuals addressing a range of special student needs. In some cases, the vast majority of extra teachers provided services just for students with disabilities (Lankford and Wyckoff, 1995), a pattern that was especially prominent for large city school districts.

Two issues emerged with these practices. The first was that schools began to look like bureaucracies, with rising numbers of "specialized staff" working outside of the regular classroom to help accomplish overall organizational goals—and the more student achievement goals were not met, the greater the demand for more teacher and other staff resources outside of the regular classroom. The second was that while the appropriate students received the extra services, they tended not to learn much more from the extra help (i.e., the additional educational strategies were not very effective). By the end of 1980s, research showed that students receiving extra help from the federal Title I program achieved a tiny bit more than similar students who did not receive those services, but that the achievement bump eroded shortly after the students left the program (Odden, 1991); longitudinal research at the end of the 1990s documented the same findings (Borman, Stringfield, and Slavin, 2001). Research on students receiving special-education services reached the same conclusions; the appropriate students were served but achievement gains were hard to document (Odden, 1991; Reynolds and Wolfe, 1999). Without program restructuring, moreover, these two realities retained an education dynamic that demanded ever-more resources with little improvement in performance, a dynamic that could not last forever.

In fact, these realities lead in part to the education excellence reforms of the 1980s (Murphy, 1990), which evolved into the standards-based education reform movement of the 1990s (Fuhrman, 1993; Odden, 1995a). This movement had a two-part goal: (1) to make the regular curriculum program more rigorous for all students, and (2) to ensure that special-needs students were taught a more rigorous core curriculum initially in the regular classroom and then, if needed, with a more effective extra-help strategy to enable them to master the standards of that basic instructional program. Put differently, the excellence movement retained the values that led to the proliferation of resources for special-need students, but called for program restructuring for both special-needs and regular-education students, with the goal that all students achieve to much higher levels.

Many argued, however, that because schools were labor intensive, it was impossible for them to improve their productivity. It is true that schools are labor intensive. But as this chapter shows, determining how educational dollars can be used more effectively requires an analysis of how school *staff* members are used and entails using those resources for staff quite differently. Using dollars more effectively in schools largely requires changing the labor mix within schools. In other words, improving the use of education dollars requires changing the labor structure of schools, which means changing how schools are staffed and thus changing the "cost structure" of schools.

As just explained, in terms of resources, schools today are in a fairly good position to at least begin responding to these cost structure and performance challenges. But in order to use those resources differently, schools needed a set of new ideas. Fortunately, these ideas began to emerge in the 1990s, initially led by general calls for school restructuring (Elmore, 1990), then by the initiative of the New American Schools that created specific new school designs with different staffing structures (see Stringfield, Ross, and Smith, 1996), and finally by the popularity of class-size reduction at the end of the 1990s.

2. APPROACHES TO RESOURCE REALLOCATION

This section discusses three different approaches to resource reallocation practices actually being pursued around the country: general school restructuring, the different staffing structures that are part of most comprehensive school designs, and mixed strategies that often include major class-size reduction in kindergarten through grade 3.

Examples from School Restructuring

Research by Karen Hawley Miles and Linda Darling-Hammond (1997, 1998) provide good examples of the way schools' staffing resources can be used more effectively through school restructuring. In the early 1990s, they studied three elementary and two high schools across the country that adopted or created a new school vision and reallocated their extant resources to the needs of their new vision. All schools were in urban districts serving large numbers of low-income and, in some cases, disabled students. Three of the schools were "new starts," or schools created anew. Two schools restructured themselves from their previous to their new design. All schools produced large increases in student achievement and other desired results such as greater attendance, higher graduation rates, and more student engagement.

To varying degrees, the schools implemented five different resource reallocation strategies. They (1) increased the number of regular-classroom teachers, thereby devoting more of their budget to the core education service: teaching a classroom of students; (2) provided varied class sizes for different subjects; (3) grouped students differently from the age-grade strategy of most schools; (4) expanded common planning time for teacher teams; and (5) increased teacher professional development. Each of these strategies involved using resources differently. All of these different resource-use strategies were designed to help strengthen the schools' core instructional program. And each school produced higher levels of student performance as a result.

None of the schools studied were given extra resources above those provided through normal district budgeting; the schools were staffed with the same total number of professional positions and resourced the same as all other schools in the district, with similar numbers and characteristics of students. But these schools used their professional teaching resources differently.

First, they all expanded the number of regular-classroom teachers. Two of the schools traded administrative positions for more teachers, and then involved more teachers in the management of the school. Most of the schools converted the bulk of their categorical specialist teacher positions, largely funded with categorical program dollars (federal Title I, state and local special education, bilingual education, etc.), into regular-classroom teacher positions, which allowed them to lower actual class sizes.

Second, all schools had different class sizes for different subject areas. They provided the lowest class sizes—sometimes as low as eight—for reading and language arts. One strategy was to have almost all teachers, including reading tutors and sometimes even music, art, physical education, and library teachers, teach a reading class during the reading period; this practice allowed schools to lower class size to 15 or less for reading. Other schools had some large lecture-style classes that were supplemented by smaller discussion groups, as well as individual student advising. Rather than have the same class size for all subjects, the schools varied class sizes. They required everyone in the school to teach reading, thus providing quite small class sizes, and then required less than half the staff to teach larger classes such as music and physical education, thus freeing those not teaching for other activities, including both common planning time and professional development.

Third, most of the schools also grouped students differently from the traditional age-grade approach in most schools. Several schools created multiage and multiyear student groupings, putting students of two or three different ages in the same classroom, and having the same teachers work with those students over a two- to three-year period. This grouping strategy permitted teachers to build strong relationships and develop rapport with students, allowed them to provide a more personalized classroom atmosphere, and eliminated the need for the extended adjustment period at the beginning of each year when teachers get to know a new class of students.

The high schools created block schedules with longer class periods, which let them reduce the daily teacher-student load from over 150 to less than 100, even to less than 60 in one case. This arrangement provided teachers time to get to know a smaller number of students at a deeper level and thus to provide a more individualized instructional program. The high schools also assigned small groups of students to each teacher for ongoing advising and counseling, yet another strategy that enhanced the personal, caring nature of the school environment, which research shows helps to improve achievement (Bryk, Lee, and Holland, 1993; Newmann and Associates, 1996).

Fourth, all five schools created more planning time for teachers, or simply rescheduled the planning time that existed to allow teams of teachers to work together during some portion of the regular school day. Many schools across the country already provide teachers with planning and preparation time. Too often, however, schools do not schedule this time for all members of a teacher team at the same time during the day. Although rearranging the school schedule to provide common planning time for teacher teams is not an easy task, it is a way to reallocate current resources to provide more paid time for professional development. The schools studied underwent this process and were able to make such changes to their schedules. But these schools also used the flexibility provided by their different class sizes for joint planning. During those times when students were in larger classes, and in the case of one high school, during those times when students were out of the school working on community service projects, the schools scheduled common teacher planning time. In this way, each school was able to provide more common planning time for their faculty by using both money and time differently.

Fifth, all schools increased investments in professional development. The additional professional development for the teachers in these schools was an important new way of using their resources.

How did they finance these new staffing and resource deployment strategies? First, they traded specialist positions for regular-classroom teachers, including many specialist teachers for students with mild disabilities such as the learning disabled. As a result, each school had specific strategies for instructing low-achieving or learning-disabled students within the regular classroom or as part of the core features of the school design. For example, two schools not only taught reading in small classes of 15, but also provided one-on-one tutoring to any student, including learning-disabled students, not reading at grade level. One school that mainstreamed all special-education students trained the entire faculty to instruct students in this more inclusive environment. In order to make this approach to service provision for the disabled legal, each disabled student's individual education program was modified, with parental consent, to reflect the instructional strategies of the school. The achievement data showed that these special-needs students also improved their performance, a result often not produced by pull-out, resource-room programs (Allington and Johnston, 1989; Reynolds and Wolfe, 1999), the typical service identified by individualized education programs. It should be noted that changing the way special-education students are served is a difficult task and one that probably benefits many, but not all, special-education students.

Schools implemented these restructuring and resource reallocation strategies over a number of years. In no case were teacher positions eliminated precipitously; in fact, many teachers assumed new roles, with training to give them the required new expertise. Miles and Darling-Hammond (1997, 1998) noted that restructuring and reallocation processes would have been facilitated if the schools had had more authority over recruiting and selecting staff committed to the vision they were deploying.

In short, without any additional resources, these schools:

- reduced core class sizes,
- created even lower class sizes for reading,
- reduced the daily student-teacher contact numbers,
- personalized the teaching-learning environment,
- provided common planning time, and
- expanded professional development.

Although all schools faced obstacles and challenges in implementing these different resource-use strategies, they nevertheless made substantial progress and engaged in substantive resource reallocation. They also improved educational results for students, including students with special needs. In short, all five schools improved the productivity of their existing staffing resources through programmatic and organizational restructuring, accompanied with substantial resource reallocation.

Examples from New School Designs

While some questioned whether school restructuring could be scaled up and argued that the only way to improve the productivity of *the entire educational system* was to break up the educational bureaucracy by injecting choice into the public school system (see, for example, Chubb and Moe, 1990), others supported another initiative. This initiative, first called the New American Schools Development Corporation and now just New American Schools (NAS), commissioned several teams of experts around the country to create higher-performance, "break the mold" school designs. These schools would be planned around a "high-standards" curriculum program, with changes in both school and classroom structure, all targeted on teaching students to rigorous performance levels for the evolving standards-based education reforms adopted by nearly all states in the country (Stringfield, Ross, and Smith, 1996). The goal was to create a number of different "whole-school" designs that would cost about the national average expenditure per pupil.

Several new school designs emerged that actually met this fiscal constraint (Odden and Busch, 1998; Odden and Picus, 2000). Today, moreover, several organizations provide comprehensive or whole-school designs and the technical assistance to implement them, including, for example, the New American Schools (Stringfield, Ross, and Smith, 1996), Core Knowledge Schools (Hirsch, 1996), Accelerated Schools (Finnan et al., 1996), the Coalition of Essential Schools (Sizer, 1996), the School Developmental Program (Comer et al., 1996), and the Edison Project (1994). Research shows that these designs have various impacts on student performance (Borman et al., 2002; Herman et al., 1999).

Most of these schools use a different mix of staff from typical schools (Odden, 1997a; Odden and Busch, 1998) that reflect a reallocation of their instructional staff. Table 10.1 provides an example of these differences for a "typical" school and a New

TABLE 10.1   Staffing in a Typical versus a Restructured School: 500 Students, 50 Percent Poverty

Typical School before Restructuring	*Restructured School*
1 principal	1 principal
No assistant principal	2 instructional facilitators, focused on professional development
20 teachers in class sizes of 25 students	25 teachers with class sizes of 20 students
3 extra teachers	0 extra teachers
6 art, music, and PE teachers plus 1 librarian, who teach a content and provide planning and preparation time for teachers	5 art, music, PE teachers for planning and preparation time for teachers, plus 1 librarian
7 teachers in categorical programs for low-income students, gifted and talented, and mild disabilities (mainly learning disabilities)	4 teacher tutors offering one-on-one help to struggling students, whatever the specific reason for the struggle
4 instructional aides	0 instructional aides
4 pupil support (guidance counselor, social worker, nurse, etc.) working independently	4 person pupil-support/family outreach team
Almost no money for professional development	$100,000 for ongoing professional development provided by external experts

American Schools design. First, class sizes in the typical school on the left were 25. Second, the typical school had one category of specialist teachers (art, music, etc.) who taught nonacademic subjects; during that time core classroom teachers had a planning and preparation period. Third, this typical school had another and larger number of specialized staff "supporting" teachers outside of the regular classroom who were focused on various extra educational student needs. These included five teachers in categorical programs, mainly working in resource rooms, four instructional aides providing some version of the same service, and three professionals working independently providing various types of nonacademic student support. The school had no funds for schoolwide instructional improvement, school-based mentoring, or ongoing professional development. The school also had staff for severely disabled students but these staff and their services were not changed.

The New American Schools design used school and staffing resources quite differently, however both regular classrooms of one teacher for every 25 students remained, and the staff for music, art, physical education, and library remained, thus providing instruction for these subjects as well as a planning and preparation period for regular teachers. But, there was a large investment in ongoing training and professional development, including two full-time instructional facilitators who worked as within-school coaches, and an additional $100,000 for purchasing ongoing professional development from outside experts. In addition, students struggling to learn to high standards—whatever the particular reason for the struggle—received one-on-one tutoring from licensed teachers trained to be tutors, rather than remedial help in resource rooms with a less rigorous curriculum. Further, the pupil support and family outreach professionals were organized into a team that provided coordinated supports for these functions. Not shown is that when reading was provided for 90 minutes each day, nearly all licensed professionals taught such a class so reading class sizes could be reduced to just 15 students. And all these changes were implemented without any additional funding (i.e., via resource reallocation).

Though the specific staffing configurations varied across many of the restructured school designs (see Odden, 1997a; Stringfield, Ross, and Smith, 1996), and school designs that were not part of New American Schools emerged over time, the new school designs all had more of the features on the right-hand side of Table 10.1 than on the left-hand side. Instructional expenditures were the same for both sides, but the details of those expenditures were quite different, as were the use of staff during the day to implement the program. Not only did some programs provide smaller classes for targeted subjects such as reading but also some school strategies grouped students with the same teacher over the course of two years and scheduled common planning time for teams of teachers inside the school. This joint scheduling allowed teachers to collaboratively work on curriculum and instructional issues and to know students more deeply on both cognitive and personal levels.

The new school designs provided a high-standards curriculum to all students (except the severely disabled). The restructured schools shifted resources via professional development for regular teachers so they had more instructional expertise. The restructured school created more cohesive, effective, and integrated support programs—tutoring for academic needs and student/family health teams for nonacademic needs. And the restructured schools took ongoing professional development seriously with a large investment in both within-school coaches and outside expert trainers. All such differences are characteristic of higher-performing organizations in general (see Lawler, Mohrman, and Benson, 2001).

Both Odden and Busch (1998) and the second edition of this text (Odden and Picus, 2000, Chapter 8) showed that the average elementary, middle, and high school in America has sufficient resources to finance all of the New American Schools designs, including providing planning and preparation time. Note that after subtracting the resources needed for core staffing (one principal per school and one teacher for each 25 students) and for planning time (20 percent additional teachers), national average schools still had about $450,000 remaining, which is more than sufficient to finance even the most expensive school design described and costed-out at between $350,000 and $375,000 above these core resources (Odden, 1997a). But this conclusion varied by region of the country. The average school in the Northeast (Table 9.10) as well as, somewhat surprisingly, in the South (Table 9.12) would have more than sufficient resources to fund even the most expensive New American Schools designs. We should note again, however, that a major reason for the substantial staffing resources in the South is the lower teacher salaries, making expenditures per pupil much lower in the South, even after adjusting for the varying purchasing power of the education dollar.

The data in Table 9.11, however, show that middle and high schools in the Midwest on average would be able to afford both a high-performance school design and planning/preparation time, but that their average elementary schools would have a more difficult time financing both of these items. Table 10.2 shows an example of this situation for a Midwestern school with 540 students, 83 percent eligible for free or reduced-price lunch. The left side of the figure shows that class sizes are 32, above the typical 25 preferred by most designs, and also that the school has $560,000 above the core, where the core in this case provides for larger class sizes. This total also leaves the two teachers for the severely disabled and the school nurse in the school. The right side of the figure shows the costs of the Roots and Wings program and that the school could afford this design with $210,000 remaining. But these remaining funds would have two primary uses: one would be to lower class sizes to 25 and the other would be to provide planning and preparation time. Each of these strategies would require the full remaining amount, so the school would be able to fund only one or the other. In short, this school has the resources that would allow it to finance a New American Schools design, but then it would either have to have larger class sizes and planning and preparation time, or class sizes of 25 but no planning and preparation time. We should note that this example is for a school in an average spending district in an average spending state for this region, and that the school wanted the Roots and Wings design.

The situation in the Western region shows similar fiscal difficulties (see Table 9.13). Few schools in this region would be able to afford both a high-performance school design and planning and preparation time. Most would need to choose between these two strategies. Indeed, if they chose to finance any one of the school designs, they then would have very few remaining resources to deploy for extraordinary student needs. In short, financing a higher-performance design in the average elementary, middle, and high school in the West could be very difficult, and for most, it would require providing no planning and preparation time for teachers within the normal school day.

TABLE 10.2   Reallocating Resources to Fund a Comprehensive School Design: An Example of a Midwest Elementary School

540 Students, 83 Percent Low-Income	Roots and Wings/Success for All
• Core: 1 principal, 17 teachers • No AP (540 kids—32 per class) • Regular education: 1 each music, technology (2), PE, reading, math, librarian ($350,000) • Categorical education: 2 learning disability ($100,000) • 4 aides ($80,000) • Pupil support: 1 guidance counselor ($50,000), plus 1 nurse • $60,000 in desegregation funds • Total above core: $560,000 plus 1 nurse, 2 teachers for the severely disabled	• 1 principal, 23 teachers • 1 instructional facilitator ($50,000) • 4 tutors (two more than suggested) ($200,000) • 1 family liaison ($50,000) • $25,000 for professional development • $25,000 for materials Total design costs: $350,000 Remaining: $210,000

Teacher ($50,000); aide ($20,000)

Source: Analysis of data gathered by author.

As this discussion shows, the ability to reallocate school staffing resources to higher-performance school strategies, at least those represented by several of the designs developed by New American Schools, varies across the country. It appears to be the most feasible in the Northeast and the South. It also is feasible for middle and high schools in the Midwest. It is a fiscal tight squeeze for Midwest elementary schools, and difficult if not impossible on average in the West. In order to make it work, many schools in the West would need both to select the less-expensive, comprehensive school designs and not provide planning and preparation time.

To be sure, in the short run the restructuring and resource reallocation will be constrained by federal, state, and local rules, regulations, and contract provisions, which would need to be changed over the medium to long term. The changes will be easier for some districts than they will for others even within the same state because of such fiscal drivers as rising or falling enrollments. However, many districts and states already are providing waivers for schools and districts to implement these designs. And the federal government is encouraging schools to use categorical resources in these different ways. In 1998, for example, as many schools began implementing these designs under the new federal "Comprehensive School Reform" program, the federal government actually stated that these new resource use practices were within the federal guidelines and could be implemented without waivers.

Late 1990s Mixed Strategies for Resource Reallocation

During the late 1990s, Odden and Archibald (2000) and Tychsen (1999) studied several schools and districts that were involved in the type of resource reallocation processes

discussed in the preceding sections, but that often included a substantial class-size reduction strategy as well. The results discussed below pertain to two major new school
strategies that required resource reallocation:

- Adoption of a school design that included tutors, instructional facilitators, parent outreach, and substantially increased professional development, and
- Class-size reduction to as close to 15 as possible, usually for kindergarten
  through grade three.

For just the school design portion, the extra-cost items were instructional facilitators, tutors, a family outreach strategy, extensive professional development, and sometimes instructional technology, which generally equated to about 7.5 additional professional positions in the school.

The second strategy was the result of schools, and in one case a district, deciding
for instructional reasons that their program would be stronger if they reallocated some
specialist staff to regular teaching positions to allow them to reduce class size to 15 or
less. In all cases studied, the schools identified the Tennessee STAR study as the research basis for this strategy (Achilles, 1999), citing that the study showed that class-size
reduction to 15 for grades K–3 was associated with higher student achievement, and that
the impact was even larger for low-income and minority students. The cost of this strategy varied by district and school, depending on the regular class size and number of
classes in kindergarten through third grade.

A K–6 school of about 500 students with class sizes of 25 would have about three
classes of about 25 students in each of kindergarten through grade 3. They would need
two additional teachers in each grade to reduce class size to 15, or a total of eight extra
positions.

Thus, the costs of these two strategies were quite high and about the same. Assuming the average cost of a teacher is $50,000 for salaries and benefits, the cost of these
strategies over the standard core of a principal and one teacher for every 25 students is
between $350,000 and $400,000, a significant amount of money.

We provide here a short summary of what Odden and Archibald (2000) found
about the specifics of the resources reallocated by these schools. Since the schools retained a principal and all of the regular teachers, the research findings focus on the three
categories of specialist staff. First, they found that the schools did not reallocate their
regular-education specialists, such as their art, music, physical education, or librarian
teachers. In all cases studied, schools eliminated none of these teacher positions; in two
cases, the number of these staff was increased. These staff persons were retained both
because the schools valued the content these teachers taught and because collective
bargaining required the schools to provide a daily planning and preparation period for
all teachers.

Second, schools made significant change in the use of their categorical program
specialist staff. These staff primarily were teachers and instructional aides supported
with federal and state compensatory education money, with bilingual education funds,
and with the learning disabilities portion of funds for providing services to students with

disabilities. The vast majority of Title I remedial reading and math teacher positions were eliminated; many of the actual individuals were retrained and either became instructional facilitators or reading tutors. For the class-size reduction strategy, they became regular-classroom teachers. In some cases, the number of instructional aides was dramatically reduced; it took about two to three aide positions to fund a fully certified teacher tutor. But in some cases, the aides took on new roles, such as becoming reading tutors, even though some research suggests they have less of a positive impact on student achievement than professional teachers (Slavin, Karweit, and Wasik, 1994).

Most schools traded a portion of their specialist teachers for the disabled (in most cases learning disability [LD] teachers) either for regular-classroom teachers or for teacher tutors. But the general practice was to retain 60 percent or more of these positions. In several instances, the LD teachers were dually certified in special education as well as regular education; when given a regular classroom, they often were given the lowest-level reading class (which tended to have the most students with a required Individual Education Program [IEP]) or the classes with the most number of IEP students. Though this was not required, school staff nevertheless thought that it provided the best educational strategy for these students. Teachers at these schools reported that mainstreaming even the LD special-education students was quite challenging and thought that the changes were beneficial for some, but not all, such students.

One school that had 35 percent of students with limited English proficiency (LEP) and reduced class size to 15 traded all pull-out ESL specialists for regular-classroom teachers. In the first year, these and other teachers with dual certification in ESL had the classes with the highest percentage of LEP students, but the school also implemented a professional development strategy to dually certify all teachers as regular and ESL teachers. Again, there were those in the school who questioned whether mainstreaming these students was the best option, but the majority of teachers believed it was in these students' best interests. One sign that these students were learning more came in the same year that the changes were made: many more LEP students took standardized tests than had in the past, showing that they were more a part of the regular curriculum.

Third, only a small number of pupil-support specialist staff at any of the schools were reallocated. Some of these staff were moved into new roles (e.g., to become a parent-outreach coordinator), but most were simply retained. They tended to represent staff positions that schools believed were necessary to serve their population of students.

All schools studied also had access to from $25,000 to $100,000 of additional funds from a variety of sources—state reading and school-improvement grants, state compensatory education funds, federal Goals 2000 and Eisenhower training grants, and federal Obey-Porter comprehensive school reform funds, which they cobbled together to support their new school strategies.

All schools also rewrote every IEP for each disabled student so it conformed to the new service strategy of their restructured school. This task required extra effort in the first and second year of the school's restructuring process but was absolutely necessary in the cases where schools used a portion of their disability funds to finance their new school strategy. IEPs had to be changed, or the schools would have been out of compliance with state and federal requirements. Indeed, in the state where the schools had reduced their class size, and received both state and federal waivers to do so, another school that was not part of this study implemented the same strategies but did not seek the required waivers. Its strategies were found to be out of compliance, and the school was required to reverse its resource reallocation actions.

In sum, the schools studied were able to finance quite expensive new school strategies via substantial resource reallocation. Federal Title I and state compensatory education funds were the largest sources that schools reallocated. But schools also reallocated a portion of learning disabilities staff, a small portion of pupil-support staff, and a large portion of other small grants they controlled. Nearly all regular-education specialist staff remained, as did the bulk of special-education staff and most pupil-support staff. Finally, some schools propelled instructional aides into reading tutor roles rather than make the more difficult decision to redeploy these funds for more effective teacher tutors; this is often the more difficult decision because of personal and contractual issues, but some schools did eliminate instructional aide positions.

Finally, we note that districts played significant roles in helping schools implement these creative, ambitious resource reallocation strategies. Odden and Archibald (2000) describe in more detail the roles played by school districts. But in the most effective instances, districts viewed resource reallocation as part of a large-scale change process and structured consciously and directly the key elements of such a fundamental change process (see Mohrman 1994; Odden and Archibald, 2001). As part of this process, most districts also changed leadership in many of the schools, created school-based funding formulas to provide schools with authority over lump-sum budgets and began to create school-based information systems, particularly systems that included school revenues and expenditures.

Simulating the Feasibility of Resource Reallocation

CPRE School
Redesign
Simulation

The website of the Consortium for Policy Research in Education provides a simulation for a school to assess its ability to implement new educational strategies via resource reallocation. The simulation requires the reader to input a school's staffing and other resource information and then provides an instantaneous report that indicates whether it can afford one of several comprehensive school designs. One design is a variation of the school staffing identified by the evidence-based approach to school finance adequacy, discussed in Chapter 3 (see also, Odden 2000). The simulation also allows a selection of class size in elementary schools of either 15 or 25. Readers are encouraged to enter the resources for the school in which they work, or for a school that needs to dramatically improve performance, in order to determine what new designs the school could afford if it engaged in the program restructuring and resource reallocation process.

As an example, we entered this staffing and fiscal information for a local school:

a K–5 school, with 600 students, 500 eligible for free and reduced lunch
one principal
one assistant principal
two instructional/curriculum support specialists
twenty-three classroom teachers

six regular education specialists (art, music, library, etc.)
six categorical program teachers (learning disabilities, Title I, etc.)
four pupil-support specialists (guidance counselors, social workers, etc.)
eight instructional aides
average principal salary and benefits: $80,000
average teacher salary and benefits: $60,000
average instructional aide salary and benefits: $20,000
discretionary funds: professional development: $50,000 (comprehensive school
　　reform grant), instructional materials: $10,000, equipment and technology:
　　$15,000, and other: $13,000
targeted class size: 25

The simulation results, available immediately, showed that these resources represented a total of $2,848,000 in revenues. It then showed that the school could afford, via resource reallocation, the Odden (2000) comprehensive school design, with $128,000 left over, as well as every other school design included in the simulation, with a minimum of $645,000 left over from each design. We should note, however, that unlike the Odden design, very few of the other designs required planning and preparation time for teachers provided by art, music, and other specialist teachers, and some had insufficient strategies for struggling students. These strategies would clearly have the first draw on the "left over" $645,000.

As shown in this example, this simulation can help school leaders think about the kinds of school reform that they might adopt and determine the fiscal feasibility of different options.

3. THE PROCESS OF RESOURCE REALLOCATION

In a book on resource reallocation, Odden and Archibald (2001) discuss several other examples of resource reallocation, and describe the processes in more detail. As important, they show that resource reallocation is part of a large-scale educational change process that has five key steps (see also Fullan, 2001; Mohrman, 1994).

First, the stimulus for change was faculty dissatisfaction with their old educational strategies. Faculties concluded that the old strategies were both ineffective for their old goals and not strong enough to accomplish their new goals—generally the ambitious goals associated with standards-based education reform. Most important, school faculties were particularly unsatisfied with their instructional strategies for educating their students with special needs; many concluded those strategies simply did not work.

Second, the faculties then engaged in various versions of self-study by analyzing both student achievement and other socioeconomic school data; the purpose was to determine the performance position of the school and to identify other problems that were related to performance deficiencies. This step usually included surveys and one to two weekend retreats with parents, which resulted in joint faculty and parent understanding of the condition of the school. This "needs assessment" process also produced teacher "ownership" of the problems that emerged from the joint analysis.

Step three entailed identifying, adapting, or creating a new, cohesive educational strategy, usually one quite different from their previous strategy. Oftentimes, this search and adoption process resulted in the school's adopting a "comprehensive school design" and/or substantial class-size reduction. Because this adoption process was faculty led, it represented strong faculty commitment to the new educational strategy; faculty believed that the new strategy would allow them to boost student performance, including the performance of its special-needs students.

Step four involved a parallel implementation and resource reallocation process that sometimes took two to three years to complete. Each school had to implement some type of shift of resources from the left-hand side of Table 10.1 to the right-hand side as it put its new educational strategy into place. Since these shifts entailed eliminating certain staff positions in the school and creating others, and sometimes "cashing out" staff positions for professional development contracts, schools had to phase in the new program and reallocate resources as personnel changes could be made. In some cases, staff were shifted to new roles, but in many cases staff were released and new staff for new roles had to be hired. The new educational strategy "drove" the resource reallocation process, both by identifying new types of staff that were needed and, by implication, the old types of staff that were not.

Because nearly all schools restructured how they served special-needs students, all student individual education programs (IEPs) that were provided for disabled students had to be written so the new service strategy was legally prescribed. Longitudinal analysis of the achievement of these special-education students would be useful to identify how these changes affected their academic performance.

Finally, during the process of resource reallocation, each school encountered various problems—such as regulatory constraints, personal connections to individuals whose jobs were eliminated, appeals to local teacher unions to block the changes. And in each instance, faculties were able to overcome the problems because of the ownership of the schools' performance problems that emerged from the needs assessments and because of faculty commitment to the new educational strategies. Rather than glitches halting progress, glitches became something that joint faculty action overcame in order for the faculty as a whole to realize the new educational vision for the school.

In this program restructuring and resource reallocation process, there usually was a shift from specialist staff to more regular teachers and to more professional development and training. This shift was the strongest for schools that reduced class sizes to 15 for the entire day (see, for example, Odden and Archibald, 2001). Assistant principals, usually found only in larger schools, were often eliminated as schools first divided themselves into smaller, relatively independent units of no larger than 500 students, each headed by one to two instructional facilitators who provided ongoing training and coaching for these schools within schools. Finally, the professional development pot was enlarged to engage outside expert trainers, often individuals associated with the comprehensive school design adopted by the school. Only small changes were made with classified staff (secretaries, custodians, etc.); and the numbers of student-support staff usually remained though sometimes they were reorganized into more cohesive teams.

4. RESOURCE REALLOCATION AND SCHOOL FINANCE ADEQUACY

The type of resource reallocation discussed in this chapter has now become a central feature of one state's school finance reform agenda, and could become part of others in the future. In early 1998, New Jersey became the first state in the country to join the issues of school finance equity and adequacy with comprehensive school designs and resource reallocation to higher-performing education strategies. As discussed in Chapter 2, New Jersey's school finance program was litigated over the 25 years from 1973 to 1998. In 1997, the New Jersey State Supreme Court required the state to provide its poorest districts (called the Abbott districts and comprising largely the urban districts that enrolled 25 percent of the state's students) with the same level of dollars per pupil as spent by its wealthiest districts; it also asked a remand court to determine whether any supplemental programs were needed for the special needs of the low-income and minority students in the poorest districts. Supplemental programs were those over and above what could be funded with the existing New Jersey compensatory education programs (called Demonstrably Effective Programs) and full-day kindergarten and pre-school programs (called Early Childhood Education Programs).

Of course, the resultant proposals would depend on what could be funded in the "core" program and which supplemental programs were needed. And the state testified that an approach to this analysis was to identify a school design specifically created for a low-performing school in an urban environment, which was the case for almost all Abbot schools. After a lengthy trial, the remand court, supported by a subsequent state supreme court decision, ruled that with the aforementioned finance provisions, there appeared to be sufficient money for schools in the Abbott districts to implement the most expensive school design at that time: the Roots and Wings/Success for All design. Subsequently, the state allowed schools to select from a number of designs, but the "default" design was Roots and Wings, both because it was specifically designed for the types of schools in the Abbott districts, had a track record of success (Borman, et al., 2002), and because it was the most expensive.

It turned out that because of the high level of resources in New Jersey, the state showed during the remand trial that the funds in a typical Abbott district could provide these for an elementary school with 500 students:

- half-day preschool for 4-year-olds;
- full-day kindergarten for 5-year-olds;
- one instructional facilitator and one technology coordinator;
- thirty teachers, which was sufficient to provide class sizes of 21 students, and additional teachers to provide at least one period a day for planning and development for each teacher;
- five tutors;
- one each: social worker, counselor, nurse, and parent liaison for not just a parental-outreach program but a full family health team;
- one library/media teacher;

- one security officer;
- three preschool teacher aides and four additional teacher aides;
- technology at about $83,000 per year; and
- professional development at over $100,000 per year, including funds for substitute teachers.

This level of resources was substantially above those found in a typical Roots and Wings school. In fact, the New Jersey proposal in a sense expanded the Roots and Wings model in these ways:

- smaller classes (21 versus 25),
- five versus four tutors in a school of 500 low-income students,
- a technology coordinator in addition to an instructional facilitator,
- family health team rather than just one parent-outreach person,
- more professional development,
- a full complement of technology (the Roots and Wings programs does not have a substantial technology program), and
- an unallocated sum of $400,000 to be used for other identified needs.

In sum, the state claimed that the level of resources already in the system would allow the typical elementary school in an Abbott district to select one of the most expensive and effective school designs in the country, and to implement it via resource reallocation.

Only time will tell whether this approach to settling a school finance adequacy case will work. The expectation is high. As the New Jersey Supreme Court stated in its final decision, the state can now begin to transform the school finance debate from the historical focus on equity of resources to how the money is used to fund a program that is effective in teaching students to the New Jersey content and performance standards.

But the process is complex. Many Abbott schools in New Jersey are struggling with both how to choose an appropriate school design and how to engage in the program restructuring and resource reallocation process. Two studies of implementation of this process is showing how complicated it actually is (Erlichson, Goertz, and Turnbull, 1999; Erlichson and Goertz, 2001). Many schools do not understand or do not have the cohesive staff necessary to create a new educational vision nor how to put it into place via educational program restructuring and resource reallocation. There has also been confusion about how to provide schools with the budget discretion to engage in resource reallocation. And the allocation of leadership for this process among the state department of education, local school districts, and school leaders is unclear. Nevertheless, New Jersey is an example of one state that has decided that school finance adequacy includes the intertwined issues of an adequate level of dollars and the most effective ways to use them via resource reallocation.

Other states are also likely to try this approach. In a 2002 study of school finance adequacy in Kentucky, commissioned by the department of education with the concurrence of both the legislature and the governor, Odden, Fermanich, and Picus (2002) used a merged model of staffing for high-performance school designs (Odden, 2000) to assess whether schools in that state had sufficient resources to adopt a wide variety of school designs, including class sizes of 15 in kindergarten through grade 3. The authors concluded that to do so the state would need to provide approximately $600 million more, and that implementation in any school would require both program restructuring and resource reallocation. Although this is one approach to defining school finance adequacy, if implemented it also would require the twin struggles that are emerging in New Jersey—resource reallocation as a part of educational program restructuring.

5. SUMMARY

Most but not all schools in America altered their internal staffing structure from the mid-twentieth century to about 1990. Schools became characterized by much reduced pupil-staff ratios, from something like 25 to 1 at mid-century, to closer to 15 to 1 at the end of the century. Class sizes became somewhat but not all that much smaller, as the bulk of the staff were used for educational strategies outside of the regular classroom—teaching specialist subjects like art, music, and physical education, or providing extra services for students struggling to learn the regular curriculum, such as those from lower-income backgrounds, those with learning disabilities, or those who spoke a language other than English. Though these resource levels and extra service strategies reflected good American values, achievement data showed that the special-needs students did not learn that much more from the extra service and that the achievement of students in the regular program was also not adequate.

These realizations led to a series of reforms, beginning with the education excellence reforms of the 1980s, standards-based education reforms of the 1990s, and then "whole-school" reforms of the late 1990s and early twenty-first century, that now are working their ways into definitions of school finance adequacy. Undergirding these reforms are two notions: first, that there are better ways to use extant fiscal and staffing resources in schools and second, that many of them could be financed via resource reallocation. This chapter profiled several such resource reallocation strategies, and showed that such resource reallocation usually entails significant changes in the use of instructional aides and three categories of "specialist" staff: (1) regular-education specialists such as art, music, physical education, and library teachers; (2) categorical program staff providing services for students from low-income backgrounds, with limited English proficiency or with various physical and cognitive learning disabilities; and (3) pupil-support staff such as guidance counselors and social workers.

This chapter also showed that resource reallocation constitutes a large-scale educational change effort, as it entails both considerable educational program restructuring (eliminating educational strategies that did not work and adding new strategies that will work better) and resource reallocation (i.e., the shifting of staffing resources from the old to the new strategies). The change process entailed these five steps: (1) concluding that the old educational strategies were not working or were not powerful enough for new, ambitious achievement goals; (2) analyzing the specific achievement problems/challenges for the school; (3) finding or adapting strategies to produce the desired performance objectives; (4) beginning the restructuring and resource reallocation process; and (5) persevering in the implementation process when problems or obstacles were encountered.

The chapter also identifies a school redesign simulation available online that can be used by any school to determine whether it can afford several new school designs, including the evidence-based design discussed in more detail in Chapter 3 (see suggested assignment at the end of the chapter for more information).

Finally, this chapter explained how resource reallocation and whole school designs are now, in at least one state, a part of court-ordered education reforms that are designed to increase the performance of all students, but especially those low-income students in urban areas that have not been adequately served in the past.

6. SUGGESTED PAPER TOPIC

CPRE School
Redesign
Simulation

Using the CPRE School Redesign Simulation, conduct your own resource reallocation exercise. Enter data for your school, or any school, to see whether that school can afford—via resource reallocation—several different school-wide designs. Then, write a paper summarizing your findings. The paper should identify problems or issues at the school, discuss why a particular design would help remedy the problems, determine whether the school could afford the design, and list the key implementation challenges.

Financing Educational Facilities

Up to this point, the text has focused on current revenues and expenditures—money raised and spent in a single year. In fact, the focus on current resources has been typical in most school finance activity and research over the last 30 or more years. However, there is another important finance issue that all states and school districts must deal with—the financing of school facilities.

This chapter looks at the issue of capital funding for schools, discussing the differences between financing current and capital expenditures. It also describes how school districts raise funds to build new schools, renovate existing schools, and finance long-term capital improvements to their facilities and grounds. We will discuss the complexities of bond financing, the equity issues surrounding the use of property taxes to pay off the principal and interest on bonds levied by school systems, current court rulings on capital funding for schools, and the alternative finance options available to states and school districts as they strive to build and maintain adequate school facilities. This chapter is divided into four sections. Section 1 discusses the condition of school facilities in the United States. Section 2 delves into the topics of how those facilities are financed. Section 3 examines the literature on whether school facilities affect student performance. The chapter concludes with a summary of the current literature on the impact of school facilities on student learning. The chapter begins with a discussion of the current state of school facilities across the United States. For more detailed information related to school facilities, see Crampton and Thompson, 2003.

1. THE CONDITION OF SCHOOL FACILITIES IN THE UNITED STATES

There has been a great deal of discussion about the condition of school facilities in the United States since 1990. The work of the Education Writers Association (Lewis et. al, 1989) emphasized the need to consider the condition of school facilities. The existence of tremendous disparities in the conditions of school building was highlighted by Jonathan Kozol in his book *Savage Inequalities* (1992). Since that time a number of organizations have attempted to get a better understanding of how many school buildings are substandard and what it might cost to upgrade them to a more acceptable condition.

A number of difficulties are associated with determining the facility needs of our nation's schools, including:

1. Lack of good data on facilities and their conditions in many states.
2. Few clear standards on what constitutes an "adequate" school facility.
3. How to account for routine—but deferred—maintenance and repairs.
4. Understanding the costs of upgrading existing school facilities to meet the demands of schooling today. This is particularly an issue in relation to the growing demands of technology on the infrastructure of school buildings.

While each of these represents an important issue in ascertaining what it will cost to bring all school facilities up to standard, the biggest problem is a lack of clear data on exactly what is needed.

The National Education Association (2000) identifies six specific components of school infrastructure needs:

1. new construction,
2. deferred maintenance,
3. renovation,
4. retrofitting,
5. additions, and
6. major improvements to grounds.

The costs of each of these can be substantial, and individual school and district needs vary depending on the age of existing school buildings and the current population needs of each school district and state.

The National Center for Education Statistics (Lewis et. al. 2000) estimated that in 1999 one-quarter of school campuses in the United States had at least one building in less than adequate condition. These campuses enrolled some 11 million children of which 3.5 million attended school on a campus where at least one building was in poor condition or needed to be replaced because it was nonoperational. Many other schools have adequate facilities, but need upgrades to provide enough electricity for the number of computers used in schools today or infrastructure improvements for networks within the school and connections to the Internet. One of the problems with assessing school facility needs is the somewhat subjective nature of what constitutes an adequate facility.

The National Center for Education Statistics (NCES) survey of school facilities did not find substantial differences in the condition of school buildings related to school characteristics such as instructional level, or school size (enrollment), location in a city, suburb, or rural area. However, schools with more than 70 percent of students eligible for free and reduced-price lunch had more buildings that were reported to be in less than adequate condition. These schools were typically located in urban areas where the buildings tended to be older (Lewis et. al. 2000).

This description of facility needs leads to the question of how much it might cost to upgrade or modernize school facilities today. Unfortunately, data about school facilities and construction needs are not kept uniformly by the states—and even many districts do not have accurate assessments of the conditions of their facilities. Thus, estimates have been hard to find. The U.S. General Accounting Office (GAO) conducted a number of studies on the condition of school facilities in the early 1990s (General Accounting Office, 1995a, 1995b, 1995c, 1996, 2000). They estimated that the construction and deferred maintenance needs of the public schools was $112 billion (General Accounting Office, 1995a).

In 2000, the GAO issued a report indicating that between 1990 and 1997, there had been a considerable increase in school construction expenditures in most of the states. Table 11.1 shows the percentage increase in school construction between 1990 and 1997 by state as well as the average annual per-pupil expenditures for school facilities during that same period. New Jersey's increase of over 433 percent was by far the largest change during these years. Two other states, Idaho and Alaska, had increases in excess of 200 percent, while 12 more states had spending increases of 100 percent or more. On the other end of the spectrum, six states—Maine, Kansas, Oklahoma, Montana, Louisiana, and New Hampshire—spent less on school construction in 1997 than they did in 1990. Arizona, despite a court ruling related to school facilities (discussed more later in this chapter), had an increase of just 2.6 percent.

The third column of Table 11.1 shows the average annual expenditure for school construction for each of the 50 states. Nevada, Florida, Washington, and Minnesota had the highest average per-pupil expenditures for school construction between 1990 and 1997. In each of those four states average annual per-pupil expenditures for school construction exceeded $800. On the other hand, per-pupil expenditures for school construction averaged less than $100 in three states—Massachusetts, Rhode Island, and Connecticut.

The National Education Association also conducted an analysis of school modernization needs. In 2000, the NEA estimated that a total of $321.9 billion would be needed nationwide to fully modernize school facilities. It broke this figure into two major components, $268.2 billion for school infrastructure and $53.7 billion for educational technology (National Education Association, 2000). Moreover, it found considerable differences in the facility needs by state. New York had the largest funding need among the 50 states, with modernization requiring over $50 billion ($47.6 billion for infrastructure and $3 billion for technology). California had the second largest total need, amounting to nearly $33 billion ($22 billion for infrastructure and $10.9 billion for technology). Seven states were estimated to need more than $10 billion to meet their school modernization needs, and more than 40 percent of the total need was accounted for by five states—New York, California, Ohio, New Jersey, and Texas (National Education Association, 2000).

In contrast, Vermont's total school facility needs were estimated to be $333 million (roughly two-thirds for infrastructure and one-third for technology), and North Dakota's

TABLE 11.1   Percentage Change in Expenditures for School Construction and Average Annual Expenditures for School Construction by State, 1990–97

State	Percent Change in Expenditures for School Construction 1990–97 (Constant Dollar Comparison) (%)	Average Annual Expenditure per Pupil for School Construction 1990–97 ($)
Alabama	25.9	265
Alaska	208.1	759
Arizona	2.6	773
Arkansas	36.3	258
California	15.1	417
Colorado	140.4	667
Connecticut	90.2	37
Delaware	135.9	399
District of Columbia	11.4	352
Florida	11.3	877
Georgia	41.3	523
Hawaii	100.0	491
Idaho	241.4	410
Illinois	49.6	357
Indiana	38.8	490
Iowa	51.9	308
Kansas	−52.0	203
Kentucky	12.0	155
Louisiana	−14.0	180
Maine	−61.8	330
Maryland	31.3	491
Massachusetts	92.6	49
Michigan	116.3	450
Minnesota	73.2	825
Mississippi	92.6	218
Missouri	16.5	420
Montana	−40.7	275
Nebraska	33.4	493
Nevada	51.7	934
New Hampshire	−5.8	399
New Jersey	433.3	379
New Mexico	74.1	575
New York	25.4	614
North Carolina	37.8	491
North Dakota	9.9	223
Ohio	82.5	274
Oklahoma	−43.7	308

TABLE 11.1   Percentage Change in Expenditures for School Construction and Average Annual Expenditures for School Construction by State, 1990–97 (continued)

State	Percent Change in Expenditures for School Construction 1990–97 (Constant Dollar Comparison) (%)	Average Annual Expenditure per Pupil for School Construction 1990–97 ($)
Oregon	193.4	378
Pennsylvania	10.5	623
Rhode Island	172.7	41
South Carolina	40.9	414
South Dakota	14.3	321
Tennessee	104.5	286
Texas	30.8	631
Utah	171.8	452
Vermont	166.9	449
Virginia	21.7	494
Washington	20.0	854
West Virginia	165.5	303
Wisconsin	151.4	496
Wyoming	141.2	395
U.S. Total	38.7	473

Source: General Accounting Office, 2000, Appendix II, and Appendix IV.

needs were estimated at $545 million ($420 million for infrastructure and the balance for technology).

What's clear from this discussion is that there is a tremendous need for more money to build and modernize school buildings. The need varies considerably from state to state, and within states there are vast differences in the condition of local school facilities. These disparities in the quality of school facilities stem from the Federalist approach we use in this county to govern education with a strong sense of local authority and control.

2. FINANCING SCHOOL FACILITY CONSTRUCTION AND REPAIR

This section describes various approaches to financing school facilities. The most commonly used tool is general obligation bonds issues by the local school district. Because there are a number of important equity issues associated with the use of local bond measures, many states have developed programs to reduce these inequities, either on their own or under pressure from the courts. Following a brief summary of the court rulings that directly impact school facility construction, there is a discussion of these models and how they are used today.

General Obligation Bonds

Financing school facilities has traditionally been a local responsibility. The most common approach has been to use general obligation bonds to pay for the costs of construction. In general, with voter approval, a school district is authorized to "borrow" a given sum of money through the sale of general obligation bonds. This "loan" is then repaid through a property tax assessment in excess of the district's property taxes for general operations. Districts receive favorable interest rates both because as a government, investors' income from the bonds (i.e., the interest paid to investors), is generally not subject to income taxation, and because repayment of the bonds is guaranteed by the district's property tax base and a legal commitment to raise the property taxes to pay for the principal and interest on the bonds.

This approach makes sense for a number of reasons. Just like the purchase of a family home, district budgets rarely have enough cash to pay for the construction of a facility while it is being built. Moreover, since the life span of a new school facility is usually 30 or more years, it makes sense to pay for its construction over some portion of its life—the duration of most bond issues is 20 years. Interest paid on school district–issued bonds is tax free to the purchaser of those bonds, enabling districts to take advantage of low interest rates.

An equity problem arises because of variations in the ability of school districts to raise funds through the property tax to make the payments on bonds they issue. It is exactly the same issue we have discussed throughout this text—variations in the local tax base lead to considerable differences in how much a district can raise with a given tax rate. Just as in our discussion of current expenditures, high-wealth districts (those with a high property value per pupil) are able raise considerably more money for a given tax effort than are low-wealth districts. Therefore, low-wealth school districts often have lower-quality facilities, overcrowded schools, and/or considerably higher tax rates than their more wealthy neighbors. We will discuss models for correcting these inequities below.

The mechanics of school bond issues vary from state to state. In most states, voter approval is required, and in many there is a limit to the amount of debt a district can incur. Alaska requires state approval of local district bond issues, while in other states the bonds are issued by another taxing jurisdiction such as a municipality or county.

Voter Approval.   Table 11.2 shows that 41 of the 50 states require local districts to gain voter approval of local bond issues. Nine of these states (California, Idaho, Iowa, Mississippi, New Hampshire, Nebraska, North Dakota, Oklahoma, and Oregon) require a super majority for passage of bonds. This super majority is most commonly 60 percent, although in California there are two passage thresholds. Traditionally in California, the requirement was a two-thirds majority for passage of a bond measure. A recent voter-approved change, however, allows school districts to obtain passage of a bond measure with 55 percent of the vote provided: (1) the election takes place during a regularly

TABLE 11.2 Bond Programs and State Aid for Debt Service

State	Bonds	Conditions	Debt Limits	State Aid for Debt
Alabama	X	Municipality may issue bonds	None reported	None
		Districts may issue revenue warrants		
Alaska	X	State approval	None reported	Reimburses up to 70%
Arizona	X	Voter approved for projects that exceed state standards	10%—unified districts	None
Arkansas	X	Voter approved 2nd lien bonds	30% AV	None
California	X	Voter approved; super majority	None reported	None
Colorado	X	Voter approved	None	Part of basic program
Connecticut	X	Issued by municipality not school district	None reported	Limited
Delaware	X	Voter approved	10% AV	None
Florida	X	Voter approved	Not reported	None
Georgia	X	Voter approved	10% AV	Yes—Equalized funding to pay for bond issues, funds for new classrooms, and additional help for low wealth districts
Hawaii		Full state funding		
Idaho	X	Voter approved; super majority	10–20 years	Partial subsidy—interest
Illinois	X	Voter approved	None reported	10% principal × grant index
Indiana	X	No approval but subject to remonstration	2%	Flat grant—$40/ADA in 1–12
Iowa	X	Voter approved; 60% majority	5% AV; 20 years	None
Kansas	X	Voter approved	None reported	Equalized grants—AV/p
Kentucky	X	Districts sell bonds with state oversight	20 years	Yes—flat grant, equalized assessments and grants based on un-met needs
Louisiana	X	Voter approved	10–20% AV; 40 years	None
Maine	X	Voter approved	State approval	Yes—equalized based on local need

(continued)

TABLE 11.2   Bond Programs and State Aid for Debt Service (*continued*)

State	Bonds	Conditions	Debt Limits	State Aid for Debt
Maryland		Only state issued bonds		Not reported
Massachusetts	X	Voter approved	2.5% AV	None
Michigan	X	Voter approved	15% AV; 30 years	Equalized
Minnesota	X	Voter approved	15% market value	Included in flat grant—$24/ADA
Mississippi	X	Voter approved; 60% majority	15% AV	None
Missouri	X	Voter approved	15% tax base; 20 years	Yes—equalized funding for debt service
Montana	X	Voter approved	45% AV	
Nebraska	X	Voter approved; 55% majority	None	None
Nevada	X	Voter approved	15% AV	None
New Hampshire	X	Voter approved; 60% majority	None reported	None
New Jersey	X	Voter approved	None reported	Formula that considers debt service, district basic aid percentage, eligible costs, and LEA fulfillment of maintenance requirements
New Mexico	X	Voter approved	6% AV	None
New York	X	Voter approved	Not reported	Equalized funding available
North Carolina	X	Voter approved	Not reported	Yes—funding based on wealth, and enrollment growth; also a flat grant based on corporate income tax receipts
North Dakota	X	Voter approved; 60% majority	10% AV	None
Ohio	X	Not reported	Not reported	None
Oklahoma	X	Voter approved; 60% majority	10% AV	None
Oregon	X	Voter approved; 50% voters w/50% majority	Based on AV and school grade level	None

330

TABLE 11.2 Bond Programs and State Aid for Debt Service (*continued*)

State	Bonds	Conditions	Debt Limits	State Aid for Debt
Pennsylvania	X	Voter approved	No limit	Reimbursement based on approved payment schedule
Rhode Island	X	Not reported	Not reported	State share calculated; minimum state funding is 30%
South Carolina	X	Voter approved	8% AV	Not reported
South Dakota	X	Voter approved	10% AV	None
Tennessee	X	Voter approved; issued by local municipalities, counties, etc.	None reported	Part of basic state aid
Texas	X	Voter approved	None reported	Part of Instructional Facility Allotment Distributed as a guaranteed yield program
Utah	X	Voter approved	40% market value	Equalized based on local effort
Vermont	X	Voter approved	None reported	Based on guaranteed yield provisions of basic aid formula
Virginia	X	Voter approved for county schools	None	Lottery allocation and maintenance supplement program
Washington	X	Voter approved	None reported	None; bonds are local required share
West Virginia	X	Voter approved	5% AV	Lottery proceeds dedicated to debt service
Wisconsin	X	Voter approved	10% AV; 20 years	Part of basic state aid formula
Wyoming	X	Voter approved	10% AV	Supplements mill levy if AV/ADM is <150% state average

Source: Sielke (2002).

scheduled statewide primary or general election, (2) the district establishes an oversight committee to monitor the expenditure of the bond funds, and (3) the district meets certain other accountability standards. In Oregon, in addition to obtaining a majority vote, at least 50 percent of the registered voters must vote in the bond election.

Debt Limits.   Many states impose a limit on the amount of bonded indebtedness a school district may incur. This is typically imposed as a percentage of a district's assessed valuation. While designed to protect school districts from incurring more debt than they can reasonably pay back, these limits again present equity problems. A district with a low assessed value per pupil cannot raise as much money through the bond process as a wealthier district. So, even if the voters of that poor district are willing to tax themselves at a high rate to build school facilities, they may be constrained by the state. Table 11.2 shows that half the states impose limits of this type.

Other Jurisdictions.   Table 11.2 shows that in a number of states, jurisdictions other than local school districts actually issue the bonds. This process can make the approval and issuance of bonds more complex. However, to the extent that the greater resources of a county or municipality can equalize tax rates across school districts, or that the higher total assessed value of the government can provide a higher debt limit, it may be possible to reduce the inequities inherent in a property tax based system. By the same token, dependent school districts may also have to compete with other service needs for bond financing.

This discussion shows that when districts can only rely on school bonds to finance school facilities, substantial inequities exist. As shown here, the courts have also noted this problem in some states.

Court Rulings on School Facilities

Many state school finance cases have included some discussion of school facilities.[1] However, the pressure to resolve the general school funding issues in these cases (whether successful or not) overshadowed facility issues, so, in most instances, little attention was paid to financing school facilities.[2]

In other states, facilities have played a greater role in court rulings. *Roosevelt Elementary School* v. *Bishop,* 179 Ariz. 233, 877 P.2d 806 (1994) in Arizona focused pri-

---

[1]These include New Jersey (*Robinson* v. *Cahill* 303 A.2d. 273 [1973]), California (*Serrano* v. *Priest* Cal. 3d 584, 487 P.2d 1241, 96 Cal. Rptr. 601 [1971 or 1976]), Colorado (*Lujan* v. *Colorado State Board of Education,* 649 P.2d 1005 [1982]), Texas (*Edgewood Independent School District* v. *Kirby,* 777 S.W.2d 391 [1989]), and Montana (*Helena Elementary School District No. One* v. *Montana,* 236 Mont. 44, 769 P.2d 684 [1989]).

[2]One exception to this was California. It was not the court ruling in *Serrano,* however, but rather passage of Proposition 13 in 1978 that forced the state to help with facility construction costs. Because Proposition 13 prohibited the levying of ad valorem property taxes in excess of one percent of assessed value for any purpose, property tax guaranteed bond issues could not be issued in that state for eight years, until another constitutional amendment was passed allowing bond measures for capital construction purposes.

marily on school facilities, with the court requiring the state to implement a program to help school districts finance their school facilities. Recent adequacy cases in Ohio[3] have stated that facilities are an essential component of an adequate education. While Wyoming has undertaken an exhaustive analysis of its facilities and developed a sophisticated system for maintaining and constructing school facilities, the issue has received considerably less attention in Ohio to date. The Arkansas ruling led to the establishment of a major study in 2003, but the long-term implications for facility financing in Arkansas were unknown at the time this book was published.

In California, plaintiffs in a school finance adequacy suit have taken a somewhat different approach. In the complaint filed in *Williams* v. *California,*[4] the plaintiffs allege that deteriorating and unsanitary facilities prove that school funding in California is inadequate. In an interesting development, the state of California in a cross complaint alleged that the districts have adequate funding, and the problem is poor management on the part of some school districts. Whether this case will lead to changes in the way California funds its school facilities is probably years from being determined.

What is clear from this discussion is that the courts have, in a number of states, recognized that school facilities are both important to the educational process, and that there are substantial inequities in how new facilities, repairs, and modernization are funded. In some states, programs to mitigate the disequalizing effects of differing property wealth have been implemented. The next section discusses those models.

State Assistance for School Facilities

On the surface, it would seem that funding for school facility construction could be equalized using the same formulas that are described in Chapter 5. There are a number of difficulties with this approach, however. These include variations in the timing of facility needs among school districts, and the long-term costs of such programs.

District Facility Needs

School district facility needs among school districts vary over time. While all school districts need at least a certain amount of funding each year to provide for ongoing expenditures, some districts have vastly greater facility needs than others. Factors that impact a district's facility needs include the school district's current enrollment and projected changes in that enrollment, the age of current school buildings, the physical condition of those buildings, and the need for major repairs and renovations to existing facilities, either to improve their condition or enable them to better accommodate today's instructional practices—in particular the increasing power supply demands of technology.

School districts experiencing rapidly growing student enrollments need to build new schools to accommodate this growth. The need to avoid overcrowding in schools

---

[3](*DeRolph* v. *State* 78 Ohio St. 3d 193, 677 N.E.2d 733 [1997]), Wyoming (*Campbell County School District* v. *State,* 907 P.2d 1238 [1995]), and Arkansas (*Lakeview* v. *Huckabee* 01-836 [Ark. Sup. Ct. November 21, 2002]).

[4]*Williams* v. *California* 312 236, dept. 16, Cal. Sup. Ct. City and County of San Francisco.

may require building new schools immediately. Many state formulas provide aid for district facilities on the basis of some figure, such as unhoused student need (i.e., the number of students exceeding the intended capacity of the schools in the district). Assuming a state has limited funds available to equalize school facility construction, how should it prioritize between districts that need to replace existing schools, and districts that need to build new facilities to keep up with enrollment? Moreover, what impact does timing have on the state's decision?

In California, many suburban districts have been able to identify a site for a new school and begin the application process for obtaining state funding relatively quickly. On the other hand, large urban districts such as Los Angeles have had difficulty finding suitable sites for new schools because of their population density. Finding a site requires either moving people from their homes or apartments, or finding an industrial site that is not being used or is underutilized and available for sale. The problem with the first option is it displaces families and is very unpopular, and as the district has found, the second option often leads to acquisition of sites with substantial environmental hazards that must be mitigated before construction can begin—often at considerable additional cost.

The delays caused by these urban problems led the Los Angeles School District to sue the state of California over the timing of school facilities funding decisions. The court forced the state to set aside some of the money it had available for school construction for large districts such as Los Angeles. While helpful to those districts, the decision was very unpopular in fast-growing suburban districts that suddenly did not qualify for funding they hoped would be available to meet their needs.

Finding a fair way to distribute limited resources to schools on the basis of changes in enrollment is challenging, but even more difficult is making decisions about when funds should be made available for replacement of school buildings, and for major repairs and renovations. Determination of what constitutes an "adequate" school facility is a subjective matter, leading to the potential for heated debates and arguments about which districts qualify for funding. Some states have established standards for school facilities that provide an objective set of measurements which can be used to assess the quality of a school facility. North Carolina has established a number of standards for school construction, maintenance, and renovation that are frequently used as a model for other states. The information provided by the North Carolina Department of Public Instruction can be found on their website.

North Carolina
Facilities
Standards

Long-Term Costs of State Facility Programs

As previously mentioned, there are also substantial costs involved in equalizing the property tax levies used to pay for school facility bond issues. For example, if a state decides that it would like to devote $200 million a year to equalization of property taxes levied for school construction it faces some difficult choices. First, assuming an acceptable formula can be developed (which should be relatively easy to do using the models and principles discussed in Chapter 5) and all of the $200 million is allocated to school districts in the state, the state will need to commit that amount of money to those recipient districts for the life of the bonds they issue. If the typical bond measure is paid

TABLE 11.3   Hypothetical Costs of a State Facility Equalization Program

Year	State Annual Commitment to the Equalization Program (in Millions)	Total State Cost per Year (in Millions)
1	$200	$ 200
2	200	400
3	200	600
4	200	800
5	200	1,000
6	200	1,200
7	200	1,400
8	200	1,600
9	200	1,800
10	200	2,000
11	200	2,200
12	200	2,400
13	200	2,600
14	200	2,800
15	200	3,000
16	200	3,200
17	200	3,400
18	200	3,600
19	200	3,800
20	200	4,000

Assumptions:
1. State commits $200 million in new funding annually.
2. All bond measures have a 20-year payback period.

for over 20 years, this means the state has committed something on the order of $200 million a year to the qualifying districts for 20 years.[5]

If the state wanted to provide similar opportunities in the following years, it would need to find an additional $200 million in the second and each subsequent year until the first group of bonds were paid off in 20 years. If the state committed $200 million a year, after 20 years the program would cost $4 billion a year. This hypothetical example is displayed in Table 11.3. The fundamental difference between equalizing current expenditures and facility expenditures is this "multiplicative" effect resulting form the 20-year life of a bond issue.

Other options for state assistance for school facilities are in use in some states. These include: flat grants, categorical grants, equalization aid, support within the basic

---

[5]The estimate is approximate as the actual assistance to a school district would vary with variations in the district's assessed value each year.

state support program for current expenditures, and full-state funding. The use of each of these models in 2000–01 in each of the states is summarized in Table 11.4.

Flat Grants.   Identical to the flat grants described in Chapter 5, nine states use some form of flat grants to support school facilities. For example, Indiana provides $40 per pupil in funding for debt service to all school districts. Flat grants for facility construction suffer from the same problems as flat grants used for current operations: they are disequalizing in that they provide the same amount of money to all districts regardless of need and/or wealth. If districts receive this money regardless of wealth or existing debt, it is clear some benefit more than others from the state program. Districts without facility construction needs would be advantaged as they could use the funds for maintenance and renovation. This method works best once it is agreed that all districts have adequate facilities.

Equalization Aid.   This program, used by most states, provides funds generally in inverse relationship to a district's property wealth. The disadvantage of an equalization program was previously described above and is shown in Table 11.3 where to fully fund the state's intent, the expenses over 20 years can grow considerably. This typically results in relatively low equalization efforts on the part of the state.

Basic Support.   Only two states, Colorado and Wisconsin, fund facilities within the basic school support funding program. In both cases, funding per pupil for facilities is provided to districts as part of the distribution of state money to schools.

Full-State Support.   In Hawaii, which is a state-operated school system, the state provides full funding for facilities.

Other Approaches to Facility Funding.   Table 11.5 displays for each of the states other approaches that have been used to finance school facilities. These include lease-purchase agreements, leases, and rentals of school space, local option sales taxes, developer fees and sinking funds. Sielke (2002) provides a summary of the methods used in each of the states.

While it is clear that funding for facilities will continue to be an important issue in schools finance, likely becoming more important as school finance adequacy issues move to the forefront on more states, the question that remains is what impact school facilities have on student performance. We address this issue briefly in Section 3.

3. THE IMPACT OF SCHOOL FACILITIES ON STUDENT PERFORMANCE[6]

Conventional wisdom suggests that a school's physical environment has an effect on student learning, but researchers have had difficulty demonstrating a statistically significant relationship. Despite the fact that several hundred studies have been conducted on how

[6]This section draws heavily on Picus et al., 2003.

TABLE 11.4 State School Infrastructure Funding Programs, 2001–02

State	State-Funding Program	Flat Grant	Equalized	Basic Support	Full Funding	Categorical Grant	None
Alabama	Guaranteed tax yield for capital improvements.		X				
Alaska	Grants with required local contribution ranging from 5–35%.		X				
Arizona	Reimburses debt up to 70%. Debt must be preauthorized.		X				
	Full-state funding within required state standards.				X		
Arkansas	Per-pupil amount for "soft," short-term capital needs.	X					
	Provided within basic state aid—ADM × wealth index × $39.		X				
California	State provides approximately 55–66% of costs.					X	
Colorado	Included in basic support program—$223–$800 per pupil.			X			
Connecticut	Equalized funding for 20–80% of eligible costs. Magnet schools receive 100%.		X				
	Additional funding for initiatives such as early childhood, reduced class size, full-day kindergarten.					X	
Delaware	State pays 60–80% of costs. Equalized based on taxing ability.		X				
Florida	PECO funds projects based on need.					X	
Georgia	Equalized funding based on AV/p ranging from 75–90%. SPLOST funds are also included in the formula.		X				
	Grants for new classrooms, reduced class-size initiatives.					X	
	Additional incentives available for low-wealth districts.					X	
Hawaii	Full-state funding.				X		
Idaho	Subsidies for debt retirement based on mill rate, health and safety issues.					X	
Illinois	Equalized grants based on EAV/p at the 90th percentile.		X				
	Grants for debt service equaling 10% of principal × grant index.		X				
Indiana	Flat grant of $40 per pupil ADA in grades 1–12. Purpose —debt service.	X					

(continued)

337

TABLE 11.4 State School Infrastructure Funding Programs, 2001–02 (continued)

State	State-Funding Program	Flat Grant	Equalized Grant	Basic Support	Full Funding	Categorical Grant	None
Iowa	Grants based on enrollment size and inverse relationship with sales tax proceeds. Required local equalized match based on district fiscal capacity. Minimum match is 20%.		X				
Kansas	Weighting per pupil in basic aid of 0.25 for costs of new facility.	X					
Kentucky	Grants for debt service equalized inversely to AV per pupil.		X				
	Flat grant of $100 per pupil.	X					
	District levy of 5¢/$100 AV equalized if property wealth is <150% of state average.		X				
	Grants for debt service based on percent of district unmet needs compared with state unmet needs.		X				
Louisiana	No state funding.						X
Maine	Funding for debt service based on local share for approved projects.		X				
Maryland	Funding based on state share of minimum foundation/pupil. Minimum is 50% of costs.		X				
Massachusetts	Reimbursement of 50–90% for approved projects. Funding based on calculation of property value, average income, district poverty level, and incentive points (type of construction, project manager, efficiency, maintenance history).		X				
Michigan	No state funding.						X

TABLE 11.4 State School Infrastructure Funding Programs, 2001–02 (continued)

State	State-Funding Program	Flat Grant	Equalized Grant	Basic Support Funding	Full Funding	Categorical Grant	None
Minnesota	Funding by weighted ADM × ($173 + district average building age).					X	
	Equalized debt service aid.		X				
	Incentive grants such as $30 per year round pupil served, health and safety issues.					X	
Mississippi	Flat grant of $24 per ADA.	X					
	Other grants based on specific needs.					X	
Missouri	No state aid.						X
Montana	Funding for debt service only. Based on ratio of district mill value per pupil enrollment and the state mill value per pupil.		X				
Nebraska	Funding for accessibility and environmental issues: $0.052 per $100 AV.					X	
Nevada	No state funding with the exception of special appropriations for two districts due to extreme need.						X
New Hampshire	State funds 30–55% of building costs depending on number of towns. Funding is not equalized.	X					
New Jersey	Abbott districts receive 100% funding.				X		
	Non-Abbott districts receive equalized funding (minimum of 40%) based on district wealth (personal income and property tax base).		X				
	Some districts may be eligible debt service aid.						
New Mexico	Equalized funding for voter approved 2 mill levy.		X			X	
	Grants for critical needs if district is bonded to 65% of capacity.					X	

(continued)

TABLE 11.4 State School Infrastructure Funding Programs, 2001–02 *(continued)*

State	State-Funding Program	Flat Grant	Equalized	Basic Support	Full Funding	Categorical Grant	None
New York	Equalized funding based on building aid ratio and approved building expense.		X				
North Carolina	Funding provided based on ADM, growth, and low wealth. Additional flat grant from proceeds of corporate income tax.	X	X				
North Dakota	No state funding.						X
Ohio	Funds Ohio School Facilities Commission. Equity list developed based on 3-year average property wealth—local district must pass levies. State design manual requirements.		X				
Oklahoma	No state funding.						X
Oregon	No state funding.						X
Pennsylvania	Funding (reimbursement) based on the greater of district's market value aid ratio, capital account reimbursement fraction, or density.		X				
Rhode Island	Funding for debt service. State share ratio = 1– ((district wealth per pupil/state wealth per pupil) × 62%). Minimum funding 30% of cost.		X				
South Carolina	Funding allocated per pupil based on available funding divided by K–12 ADM.	X					
South Dakota	No state funding.						X
Tennessee	Funding through the basic education program. Based on cost per square foot/ADM + 10% for equipment + 5% for architect fees + debt service at state bond rate.					X	
Texas	Guaranteed yield funding through the instructional facility allotment, which is based on size of district, property value, ADA, and amount of annual debt service.		X				

340

TABLE 11.4 State School Infrastructure Funding Programs, 2001–02 (continued)

State	State-Funding Program	Flat Grant	Equalized	Basic Support	Full Funding	Categorical Grant	None
Utah	Equalized funding based on local effort (.0024), Av/p and need.		X				
Vermont	Funds about 30% of cost of project based on prioritized needs.					X	
	Debt service reimbursed based on the guaranteed yield provisions of the general aid formula.		X				
Virginia	Flat grant of $200,000 per district.	X					
	Remaining amount prorated based on enrollment and ability to pay.		X				
	Per-pupil supplement for maintenance and debt service.	X					
Washington	Funding is based on eligible area, area cost allowance, and matching ratio. Required local effort (matching ratio) is determined by comparing district AV/p to state AV/p.		X				
West Virginia	State funding is based on need: efficiency, adequate space, educational improvement, educational innovations, health and safety, changing demographics.					X	
	Lottery money is dedicated to debt service.						
Wisconsin	Funding is included in the basic support program.			X		X	
Wyoming	State supplements mill levy if AV/ADM is below 150% of state average.		X				

Source: Sielke, 2002.

TABLE 11.5   Other School Infrastructure Programs

State	Additional Funding Availability
Alabama	Revenue warrants that do not exceed 80% of pledged revenue
Alaska	None
Arizona	None
Arkansas	State loan program
California	Developer fees
Colorado	Voter approved mill levies up to 10 mills for 3 years
Connecticut	State loan program
Delaware	May assess a tax rate without referenda for state match requirements
Florida	Up to 2 mill levy without voter approval; voter approved 1/2 ¢ sales tax
Georgia	Grants; voter approved 1¢ local option sales tax up to 5 years
Hawaii	None
Idaho	2/3 majority–approved tax levies
Illinois	None
Indiana	Leases, rentals
Iowa	County local option sales tax, 1¢ up to 10 years
Kansas	Additional mill levies with approval of state board of tax appeals
Kentucky	None
Louisiana	None
Maine	State revolving loan fund
Maryland	None
Massachusetts	None
Michigan	State loan fund, sinking funds of 5 mills up to 20 years
Minnesota	State loans
Mississippi	3 mill levy up to 20 years without voter approval; state loan fund
Missouri	Lease purchase up to 20 years
Montana	Building reserves
Nebraska	Voter approved mill levies
Nevada	Voter approved mill levies, developer's fees
New Hampshire	None
New Jersey	Lease purchase
New Mexico	None
New York	None
North Carolina	Local option sales tax
North Dakota	Voter approved building funds up to 20 mills annually
Ohio	None
Oklahoma	Mill levy up to 5 mills annually
Oregon	None
Pennsylvania	Some nonelected debt allowed
Rhode Island	Leases, reserve funds

TABLE 11.5 **Other School Infrastructure Programs** *(continued)*

State	Additional Funding Availability
South Carolina	Children's Education Endowment Fund; funding based on total revenue available, basic aid support formula, weighted pupils, and need
South Dakota	None
Tennessee	Lease purchase, capital outlay notes
Texas	Lease purchase
Utah	Revolving loan fund
Vermont	Sinking funds
Virginia	Revolving loan fund; pooled bond issues
Washington	Fund reserves; special levies
West Virginia	None
Wisconsin	State loan fund, sinking funds
Wyoming	None

Source: Sielke, 2002.

school buildings affect student achievement, there are no conclusive findings. Many of the studies were based on the open schools movement of the 1970s and are no longer relevant to today's schools. Most of the rest are plagued with severe methodological problems and, not surprisingly, produce conflicting, ambiguous results.

It is difficult to study the relationship between school building quality and student achievement. To begin with, there are measurement problems. School building quality is composed of numerous factors, many of which are hard to separate and most of which are hard to measure objectively. Some studies have attempted to look at each factor separately, independently assessing how paint color, carpeted or noncarpeted floors, lighting, thermal control, acoustics, and other factors affect student learning. Other studies take one composite measure such as building age and use it as a proxy for general building condition. Both approaches are problematic. When researchers attempt to independently assess each factor, they may run into difficulties controlling for the other factors and understanding how they relate to one another. On the other hand, using a composite variable like building age may create difficulties as well, since schools are built with different life spans. A 40-year-old building that was initially constructed to last 35 years will likely be in significantly worse condition than a similarly aged building designed to last 100 years. Also, the deferred maintenance decisions made by school officials have a profound affect on building upkeep, further obscuring the relationship between building age and condition.

In addition to measurement difficulties, school building quality studies suffer from data availability problems. When examining how the building environment affects student learning, ideally researchers would like to control for a host of other factors such as parents' education level, parents' occupation, percent of the student body on free lunch, median family income, percent of single-parent families, number of student transfers, school size, length of school day, amount of instructional time, principals' experience, how districts allocate operating funds, entry-level student achievement, school climate, motivation, class size, homework and attendance policies, teacher experience and credentials, and others. Unfortunately these data, along with an objective measure of building quality and student achievement, are rarely all available for large-scale studies. The studies that have been completed so far control for only a tiny fraction of all these factors—they might take into account only the percent of students on free lunch, for instance—making it impossible to draw definitive conclusions about the effects of building quality alone on student learning. Given these problems, it is not surprising that researchers have not conclusively demonstrated a relationship between school building condition and student achievement.

Several attempts have been made to summarize the research in this field, most recently by Earthman and LeMasters (1996). They encapsulate the findings from two previous literature reviews, Weinstein (1979) and McGuffey and Brown (1978), who together covered 232 separate studies on how buildings influence students. Their main conclusion is that "even with this large number of studies, it is difficult to determine any definite line of consistent findings" (p. 3). After cautioning that there are serious methodological problems and difficulties in interpreting the studies, McGuffey examines the "preponderance of the evidence" and draws two major conclusions: (1) old, obsolete buildings have a detrimental effect on student achievement, while modern buildings facilitate learning; and (2) building conditions have a differing impact across grades and subjects. Specifically, McGuffey found that the research supported school building age, thermal factors, lighting quality, color, acoustic factors, school size as factors affecting student achievement, while no relationship was found for open space, amount of space, windowless facilities, and underground facilities.

McGuffey's finding that building conditions have a differing impact across grade levels and subjects is a difficult finding to explain, given that the underlying theory suggests that facilities affect behavior, which in turn affects learning. The theoretical base is best summarized by a 1989 Carnegie Foundation for the Advancement of Teachers report. "The report acknowledged that a good building does not necessarily make a good school, but points out that students' attitudes toward education and the prospect of educational success, are a reflection of their environment. The report notes that the tacit message of the physical indignities in many urban schools is not lost on students. It bespeaks neglect, and students' conduct seems simply an extension of the physical environment that surrounds them' " (as quoted in Berner, 1993, p. 9).

There is nothing in this theory to explain why some grade levels would be more affected by building condition than others. The more puzzling issue is why some subjects, such as math and social studies, would be affected differently. The theory runs into further difficulty because the link between facilities and student behavior is even more tenuous than the link between facilities and achievement. For example, some of the studies which claim to find a positive relationship between building condition and student learning also report finding a negative relationship between facility quality and student behavior.

McGuffey acknowledges that facilities have a very small potential impact on student learning, but they are still one of the variables over which school officials have complete control, unlike many of the other factors thought to influence student learning.

Given this, shouldn't schools make every effort to ensure high-quality facilities? The answer may be no. It is extremely costly to build, maintain, and renovate facilities, and it is possible that it would be more cost-effective to use that money elsewhere. The amount of funding for education is limited, and school officials must chose how to best allocate their resources. Improved carpeting in a school may come at the expense of hiring more, or better teachers. If future studies concentrate on specific elements of building structure and maintenance, and do so in a way that takes cost into consideration, schools may be able to assess whether installing air-conditioning, painting the walls certain colors, or adding better lighting will raise student scores, or whether they are better off buying new textbooks. Future studies would do well to take costs into consideration, and some type of cost-benefit analyses might be a productive line of research.

Researchers have obtained contradictory results on whether building age is related to student achievement. Because it is an objective measure with readily available data, researchers would like to be able to use building age as a proxy for building condition. While several early studies found a relationship between the two, some more recent studies have not. Building age is not necessarily a sound reflection of condition because buildings are built with different projected life spans and receive differing amounts of maintenance.

One solution that researchers should consider is using the percent of the life span attained rather than age itself as the independent variable, perhaps controlling for the level of maintenance funding. Another issue is that building age is not a particularly useful variable even if it does turn out to have a direct relationship to student achievement, because it would be impractical to replace schools every 10 years or so to ensure they were constantly "modern." As already noted, it is more important to discover what aspects of building condition in particular are important to student achievement, and thus know what areas of maintenance (or levels of funding) are most key.

Finally, several studies have suggested that cosmetic building condition has a greater effect on student achievement than structural condition, for which the reported effect seems to range from weak to none at all. The authors of these studies fail to discuss the implications of these findings, which appear to support routine maintenance efforts rather than the construction of state-of-the-art new schools. This approach is actually in line with the underlying theory, because while students would be expected to notice cosmetic features, they would be less likely to be affected by structural problems on a day-to-day level. This is not to say that structural factors are unimportant. Whether or not structural factors have a direct influence on student achievement, it is important to maintain buildings for safety reasons and for financial reasons—a little bit of maintenance funding goes a long way in forestalling major repairs down the road.

4. SUMMARY

Most of this book, as well as most studies of school finance focus on current expenditures—the ongoing expenditures of school systems to provide educational services to children. Despite this focus, considerable educational resources are devoted to the construction and renovation of school facilities each year. These expenditures occur on an irregular basis depending on a number of factors including school enrollments, the age of existing facilities, and the capability of those buildings to meet today's educational standards and expectations. As a result, school districts typically resort to the use of long-term payment plans for their facility needs.

The most common approach to facility (and other capital) financing is the issuance of general obligation bonds, guaranteed by the property wealth and tax-raising capacity of the school district. While this approach makes sense, reliance on local property taxes, and the willingness of local voters to approve the use of local property taxes to finance facilities, leads to disparities in the quality of local facilities.

The problem with property tax–based financing of school facilities are identical to those identified earlier in this book for financing the current operations of schools. It is made more complex by the long-term obligation created by the sale of bonds for school facilities, and the fact that individual school district capital construction needs vary considerably. The result is that it is harder to develop programs that equalize these differences, and many of the solutions come with considerable costs.

This is further made more complex because there is relatively little data on the impact of school facilities on student learning. While clean, modern facilities would seem to be important to a quality education, evidence suggests that if such a relationship exists at all, it has a very small impact on student learning.

Appendix

This appendix provides initial documentation for the use of the simulation that accompanies this book. Students are encouraged to download the simulation from this text's website (www.mhhe.com/odden3e) and use it in conjunction with the material in Chapters 5, 6, and 7. The simulation requires that you have Microsoft Excel available and running on your computer. Any version of Excel from Excel 97 through Excel XP will operate the simulation; earlier versions of Excel will not work with the simulation. Students do not need to be familiar with Excel to run the simulation, but the program itself must be installed for the simulation to operate correctly.

Additionally, the state-level simulations can be used to estimate the impact of school finance proposals on your own state in the future. *Because we view the simulation as a dynamic product that will continue to change as school finance in the 50 states changes, it is important that you carefully read the documentation pages provided at the website before using the simulation.* These pages will contain information documenting the status of each state simulation. This will include information as to the date and source of the finance data available, as well as information on any updates that have been made to state simulations and to the 20-district simulation. The balance of this appendix describes the system requirements for using the simulation and provides an introduction to its use.

SYSTEM REQUIREMENTS

The program relies on the Visual Basic Application language that is part of Excel. Consequently the simulation will not operate without the Excel software. Microsoft made a number of changes to that language with the introduction of Excel 97. As a result, the macros written for this simulation in Visual Basic will not run on older versions of Excel. The simulation will run on any Windows-based computer that has Microsoft Excel 97 or higher installed. The simulation will operate in Excel for the Macintosh, but the computations for correlation and elasticity will not function properly because Excel for the Macintosh does not currently support computation of the regression equations required for computing those statistics.

RUNNING THE SIMULATION THE FIRST TIME

Before you run the simulation the first time, you will need to install two of Excel's built-in add-ins. These two add-ins provide Excel with substantial data analysis capabilities that the simulation uses to calculate the equity statistics displayed in the printouts.

To install the add-ins, start Excel on your computer. When you have an empty file, do this:

1. Click on the **Tools** menu.
2. From the menu that appears below the word **Tools,** select the **Add-Ins** option.
3. You will see a dialogue box with the title "Add-Ins" in the bar across the top. The dialogue box contains a list of Add-Ins available to Excel. Place a check mark in two of them—**Analysis ToolPak** and **Analysis ToolPak—VBA.** You can place these check marks simply by clicking in the box to the left of each title.
4. Click on the box marked **OK.**

This will install the **Analysis ToolPak** on your version of Excel. Note that on Macintosh versions of Excel, you will only see the Analysis ToolPak option, the Analysis ToolPak—VBA is not available. On the Macintosh, just install that one option.

You only need to do this the first time you run the simulation. After that, Excel will automatically include these functions when it starts. *Remember that if you are using the simulation from a computer on a network installation at your institution, you will have to make sure the **Analysis ToolPak** is installed on each computer you use.* You should be able to do this following the previous instructions. If that does not work, contact your network administrator for instructions on how to use these two Excel add-ins.

Once the Analysis ToolPak is installed, you can start the simulation. Follow the instructions on the website to download the simulation you want to run. Once the file has been downloaded, double click on the file's icon and it will start. Because the files are relatively large, if you are given the option, be sure to save the simulation to your local computer's hard drive rather than trying to run the simulation directly from the text's website.

An Important Note on Security

Because macros (which are used extensively in the simulation) are a common source of computer viruses, Excel offers a number of security protections. Unfortunately, the highest level of security will not allow you to run the simulation. At the highest level of security, Excel will not allow macros in the simulation to load and run, so you need to change the security settings in Excel. To do this, click on the **tools** menu and highlight **macro.** From the menu that appears to the side, select **security.** In the security dialogue box select the medium level of security.[1] This allows you to choose whether or not

---

[1]At the high level of security, Excel will not allow macros to load or run, and in that case you won't be able to run the simulation.

to enable macros in Excel spreadsheets when they are started. When you double click on the icon for the simulation, and the simulation loads, you will be prompted as to whether or not you want to enable the macros. Choose the option that says "enable macros" and the simulation will continue to load. Note that if you don't choose to enable the macros at this point, the simulation will not operate correctly.

The authors and McGraw-Hill have gone to great lengths to ensure that the simulations are virus-free. Moreover, your own virus check program should test the files that you download from the web for viruses as they download. With these protections, there should not be a virus problem. If you don't have a virus protection program, we recommend that you install one on your computer.

RUNNING THE SIMULATION

Once the simulation has loaded you will see the greeting screen which tells you which version of the simulation is running. Simulation options are chosen by using control commands. You access these by typing the <ctrl> key plus one of the letter keys. Thus if told to press <ctrl> B, you would hold down the <ctrl> key and press B. The commands you will need are very simple.

> View base data <ctrl> B: This displays the base data for the simulation.
> Flat Grant <ctrl> L: This gives you a dialogue box for simulating a flat grant.
> Foundation Program <ctrl> F: This gives you a dialogue box for simulating a foundation program.
> GTB <ctrl> G: This gives you a dialogue box for simulating a GTB.
> Combination <ctrl> K: This gives you a dialogue box for simulating a combination program.
> To calculate the results <ctrl> Q: This runs the simulation and computes the results.

> *Note:* It is essential to run <ctrl> Q after every change in the simulation parameters.

After making a simulation selection using one of the control key combinations just outlined, you will see a box with the simulation parameters displayed. Simply replace the numbers in that box with the values you want to use in your simulation and press

<ctrl> Q

This will run the simulation. You will be returned to the Base Data view. To see the results of you simulation, type the control key (<ctrl>) and a letter for the relevant simulation option again, and the results will be displayed. You may need to scroll around the screen to see all of the results depending on the size of your display and the resolution the display is using.

> *Note:* When running the simulation on a Macintosh, you will get a macro run-time error because the Analysis ToolPak—VBA is not available. When you get this error

box, simply choose the "continue" option. The simulation will complete its calculations, but the data presented for the correlation and elasticity will be wrong. Unfortunately, we cannot fix this bug until regression computations are available on the Macintosh version of Excel. If you have a very current version of Excel for the Macintosh, and the Analysis ToolPak—VBA option is available, select it when you set up Excel the first time as just described, and your calculations should be correct.

Printing Your Results

Pull down the **view** menu.
Highlight **Page Break Preview.**
Your screen will change.
Highlight the portion of the spreadsheet you want to print and click on the print
   button.

State Simulations

The individual state simulations operate the same way. For each simulation, however, there are two identical summary boxes. Only one should be changed. When you type the <ctrl> commands just listed, you are placed at the location of the correct summary box. If you accidentally try to change something in the wrong box, you will not be allowed to make the change. If this happens, simply type the <ctrl> command for the simulation you wish to run and make the changes in that summary box.

Viewing the Graphs

Across the bottom of the screen there are a series of tabs with labels identifying the various graphs (charts) that are available through the simulation. To view one of the graphs, click on one of the tabs. To return to the simulation, click on the tab labeled sim20 (or the tab related to the state simulation you are using).

Before typing <ctrl> Q to make calculations, it is important that you click on the sim20 (or state simulation) tab. If you fail to do so, errors will occur and the simulation will be corrupted. If this happens, delete the simulation from your computer and download a new copy. Be sure to check for update notices as well.

PUPIL WEIGHTS

If you want to use the pupil-weight feature of the simulation, click on the pupil-weights tab. You will see a new worksheet. At the top is a question, which asks, "Do you want to use pupil weights?" Replace the word "no" with the word "yes."

In the screen that appears, you will see two boxes. In the first you can determine the weight for each student category. In the second box you can assign the percentage of students in each weighting category for each district. If you want to make changes to the values presented, simply type them in the respective cells on the worksheet.

When you have finished making your weighting selections, click on the sim20 tab, and the press <ctrl> Q.

Before typing <ctrl> Q to make calculations, it is important that you click on the sim20 (or state simulation) tab. If you fail to do so, errors will occur and the simulation will be corrupted. If this happens, delete the simulation from your computer and download a new copy. Be sure to check for updated notices as well.

EXITING FROM THE SIMULATION

To exit from the simulation, either click the X box in the upper-right-hand corner of the screen, or go to the **file** menu and choose **exit.** You will be asked if you want to save your changes. If you select yes, the most recent simulation options you selected will be saved. If you select no, you will have the data that was downloaded from the website. Since more than one simulation option cannot be saved, either choice is fine. To recreate a simulation, all you have to do is use the command key for the simulation you want to run (i.e., <ctrl> F for a foundation program simulation), enter the parameters you want to simulate and press the <ctrl> Q button.

SUMMARY OF STEPS FOR OPERATING THE SIMULATION

1. Make sure Microsoft Excel for Office 97 or higher is installed on your computer.
2. Be sure that the Analysis ToolPak add-ins have been installed on Excel.
3. Log in to the text's website (www.mcgraw-hill.com/odden3e).
4. **Read the documentation update available on the website.**
5. Download the simulation you want to run. We suggest you start with the 20-district simulation to become familiar with the operation of this program.
6. Run the simulations you want to analyze.
7. Exit from Excel.

Enjoy the simulation. If you have comments or suggestions, please send an e-mail to Lawrence O. Picus at the address listed on the text's website.

Glossary

This glossary contains a number of tax, education, and statistical terms that are used in school finance research and policy analysis. In order to make comparisons of tax and expenditure data among school districts, adjustments must be made in many measures. The purpose of these adjustments is to create a set of comparable numbers and a set of common terms. Standard procedures are used to make these adjustments, and the glossary indicates how some of the adjustments are made.

ADA, ADM   ADA is an abbreviation for student average daily attendance and ADM is an abbreviation for student average daily membership. ADA and ADM are the official measures that most states use to represent the number of students in a school district for the purpose of calculating state aid. ADA is always less than ADM.

adequacy   Adequacy entered the educational arena primarily in the 1990s. For school finance, it means providing sufficient funds for the average district/school to teach the average child to state standards, plus sufficient additional revenues for students with special needs to allow them to meet performance standards as well. Many school finance court cases have shifted from challenging fiscal disparities to challenging the adequacy of the funding system.

assessment ratios   The assessed valuation of property in most states is usually less than the market value of the property. In other words, owners are able to sell property for a price higher than the assessed valuation of that property. Although most states have a legal standard at which all property should be assessed, assessed valuations are usually below even the legal level and may vary widely among jurisdictions in a state. The actual assessment level or assessment ratio is determined by comparing actual assessed valuations to market values.

assessed valuation   The assessed valuation is the total value of property subject to the property tax in a school district. Usually, it is established by a local government officer and is only a percentage of the market value of the property.

assessed valuation, adjusted or equalized   Because local assessing jurisdictions in a state usually have different actual assessment ratios, the reported assessed valuations need to be adjusted or equalized in order to compare them among school districts. The best way to make such adjustments is to convert the assessed valuations to what they would be if all counties assessed at 100 percent of market value and then adjust them to the legal standard (for example, 33⅓ percent). The mathematical way to make the adjustment is to divide the assessed valuation by the assessment ratio and multiply the result by 0.333. The result is called the adjusted or equalized assessed valuation. The following is an example:

Consider two school districts, A and B.

District A has an assessed valuation of $200,000.
District B has an assessed valuation of $250,000.

G

Focusing just on assessed valuations, district A would appear to be poorer in property wealth than district B. However, assume that the actual assessment ratio in district A is 20 percent while it is 25 percent in district B.

Assuming that the legal ratio is $33^{1}/_{3}$ percent, the computation of the adjusted assessed valuation for district A is as follows:

$$\text{adjusted assessed valuation} = \frac{\$200,000 \times 0.333}{0.20} = \$333,333$$

The computation of the adjusted assessed valuation for District B is:

$$\text{adjusted assessed valuation} = \frac{\$250,000 \times 0.333}{0.25} = \$333,333$$

Both school districts have the same adjusted assessed valuation. That is, both school districts effectively have the same total tax base, despite the differences in the reported assessed valuation.

Adjusted assessed valuations must be used to compare property wealth among school districts and should be the basis on which state equalization aid is calculated.

assessed valuation per pupil, adjusted The adjusted or equalized assessed valuation per pupil is the adjusted assessed valuation for a school district divided by the district's total ADA or ADM.

categorical programs Categorical programs refer to state aid that is designated for specific programs. Examples would be transportation aid, special-education aid, and aid for vocational education. Equalization formula aid is not an example of categorical aid. Formula funds provide general aid that can be used for any purpose.

correlation Correlation is a statistical term indicating the relationship between two variables. When two variables are said to be positively correlated, as one variable increases the other variable also tends to increase. When two variables are said to be negatively correlated, as one variable increases, the other variable tends to decrease.

correlation coefficient The correlation coefficient is a number indicating the degree of relationship between two variables. Because of the way a correlation coefficient is calculated, it always will have a value between -1.0 and $+1.0$. When the correlation coefficient is around $+0.5$ to $+1.0$, the two variables have a positive relationship or are positively correlated—when one variable gets larger, the other tends to get larger. When the correlation coefficient is around zero, the two variables do not appear to have any relationship. When the correlation coefficient is around -0.5 to -1.0, the variables have a negative relationship or are negatively correlated—as one gets larger, the other tends to get smaller.

current operating expenditures Current operating expenditures include education expenditures for the daily operation of the school program, such as expenditures for administration, instruction, attendance and health services, transportation, operation and maintenance of plant, and fixed charges.

district power equalization (DPE) See *guaranteed tax base.*

elasticity of tax revenues The elasticity of tax revenues refers to the responsiveness of the revenues from a tax to changes in various economic factors in the state or nation. In particular, policymakers may want to know whether tax revenues will increase more rapidly, as rapidly, or less rapidly than changes in personal income. The revenues from an elastic tax will increase by more than 1 percent for each percent change in personal income. Income taxes are usually elastic tax sources. In general, elastic tax sources have progressive patterns of incidence, and inelastic tax sources have regressive patterns of incidence. Expenditure elasticity may be defined similarly.

equalization formula aid   Equalization formula aid is financial assistance given by a higher-level government—the state—to a lower-level government—school districts—to equalize the fiscal situation of the lower-level government. Because school districts vary in their abilities to raise property tax dollars, equalization formula aid is allocated to make the ability to raise such local funds more nearly equal. In general, equalization formula aid increases as the property wealth per pupil of a school district decreases.

expenditure uniformity   Expenditure uniformity is part of the horizontal equity standard in school finance requiring equal expenditures per pupil or per weighted pupil for all students in the state. (See *fiscal neutrality.*)

fiscal capacity   Fiscal capacity is the ability of a local governmental entity, such as a school district, to raise tax revenues. It is usually measured by the size of the local tax base, usually property wealth per pupil in education.

fiscal neutrality   Fiscal neutrality is a court-defined equity standard in school finance. It is a negative standard stating that current operating expenditures per pupil, or some object, cannot be related to a school district's adjusted assessed valuation per pupil, or some fiscal capacity measure. It simply means that differences in expenditures per pupil cannot be related to local school district wealth. (See *expenditure uniformity.*)

Flat Grant Program   A flat grant program simply allocates an equal sum of dollars to each public school pupil in the state. A flat grant is not an equalization aid program because it allocates the same dollars per pupil regardless of the property or income wealth of the local school districts. However, if *no local* dollars are raised for education and all school dollars come from the state, a flat grant program becomes equivalent to full-state assumption.

foundation program   A foundation program is a state equalization aid program that typically guarantees a certain foundation level of expenditure for each student, together with a minimum tax rate that each school district must levy for education purposes. The difference between what a local school district raises at the minimum tax rate and the foundation expenditure is made up in state aid. In the past, foundation programs were referred to as minimum foundation programs, and the foundation level of expenditure was quite low. Today, most newly enacted foundation programs usually require an expenditure per pupil at or above the previous year's state average. Foundation programs focus on the per-pupil expenditure level and thus enhance the state government's fiscal role in education.

Full-state assumption   Full-state assumption (FSA) is a school finance program in which the state pays for all education costs and sets equal per pupil expenditures in all school districts. FSA would satisfy the expenditure per-pupil "uniformity" standard of equity. Only in Hawaii has the state government fully assumed the costs of education, except for federal aid.

guaranteed tax base program (GTB)   Guaranteed tax base (GTB) refers to a state equalization aid program that "equalizes" the ability of each school district to raise dollars for education. In a pure GTB program, the state guarantees to both property-poor and property-rich school districts the same dollar yield for the same property tax rate. In short, equal tax rates produce equal per-pupil expenditures. In the property-poor school districts, the state makes up the difference between what is raised locally and what the state guarantees. In property-rich school districts, excess funds may or may not be "recaptured" by the state and distributed to the property-poor districts. Most GTB state laws do not include recapture provisions. However, Montana and Utah included recapture mechanisms in their school finance laws. GTB programs are given different names in many states, including district power equalizing programs (DPE), guaranteed yield programs, and percentage equalizing programs. GTB programs focus on the ability to support education and, thus, enhance the local fiscal role in education decision making. GTB would satisfy the "fiscal neutrality" standard without achieving "uniformity" of expenditures among school districts.

guaranteed yield program   See *guaranteed tax base.*

median family income   Median family income usually is reported in the decennial U.S. census. It reflects income for the year before the census was taken (i.e., 1989 income for the 1990 census, or 1999 income for the 2000 census). If the income of all families in a school district were rank ordered, the median income would be the income of the family midway between the lowest- and the highest-income families.

municipal overburden   Municipal overburden refers to the fiscal position of large cities. Municipal overburden includes the large burden of noneducation services that central cities must provide and that most other jurisdictions do not have to provide (or at least do not have to provide in the same quantity). These noneducation services may include above-average welfare, health and hospitalization, public housing, police, fire, and sanitation services. These high noneducation fiscal burdens mean that education must compete with many other functional areas for each local tax dollar raised, thus reducing the ability of large-city school districts to raise education dollars. The fiscal squeeze caused by the service overburden, together with the concentration of the educationally disadvantaged and children in need of special education services in city schools, puts central-city school districts at a fiscal disadvantage in supporting school services.

percentage equalizing programs   See *guaranteed tax base.*

progressive tax   A progressive tax is a tax that increases proportionately more than income as the income level of the taxpayer increases. Under a progressive tax, high-income taxpayers will pay a larger percent of their income toward this tax than low-income taxpayers.

property tax circuit breaker program   A property tax circuit breaker program is a tax relief program, usually financed by the state, that focuses property tax relief on particular households presumed to be overburdened by property taxes. That is, it is intended to reduce presumed regressivity of the property tax. A typical circuit breaker attempts to limit the property tax burden to a percent of household income and applies only to residential property taxes. The percent usually rises as income rises in an attempt to make the overall burden progressive. Initially, most states enacted circuit breaker programs just for senior citizens, but a few states have extended circuit breaker benefits to all low-income households, regardless of the age of the head of the household. The circuit breaker is based on actual or estimated taxes paid on residential property and generally takes the form of a credit on state income taxes.

property tax incidence or burden-traditional and new views   The traditional view of property tax incidence divided the tax into two components: that which fell on land and that which fell on improvements (i.e., structures). Property taxes on land were assumed to fall on landowners. The part on improvements was assumed to fall on homeowners in the case of owned homes, to be shifted forward to tenants in the case of rented residences and to be shifted forward to consumers in the case of taxes on business property. Nearly all empirical studies based on the traditional view found the incidence pattern to result in a regressive burden distribution, markedly regressive in lower income ranges. The new view of property tax incidence considers the tax to be, basically, a uniform tax on all property in the country. Such a tax is borne by owners of capital and, thus, the burden distribution pattern is progressive. Although the new view allows for modifications caused by admitted tax-rate differentials across the country, adherents of the new view hold that even with the modifications, the tax would exhibit a progressive pattern of incidence over much of the range of family incomes.

proportional tax   A proportional tax is a tax that consumes the same percent of family income at all income levels.

pupil-weighted system or weighted-pupil programs   A pupil-weighted system is a state-aid system in which pupils are given different weights based on the estimated or assumed costs of their education program; aid is allocated on the basis of the total number of weighted students.

Usually, the cost of the education program for grades 4–6 is considered the standard program and weighted 1.0. For states, such as Florida, that choose to invest more dollars in the early school years, pupils in grades K–3 are given a weight greater than 1.0, typically around 1.3. In other states, high school students are weighted about 1.25, although these secondary weightings are slowly being eliminated. The two major programmatic areas where numerous weightings have been used are special and vocational education. Weighted-pupil programs, therefore, recognize that it costs more to provide an education program for some students than for others and includes the extra costs via a higher weighting. State aid is then calculated and distributed on the basis of the total number of weighted students in each school district. Determining the appropriate weight is a difficult matter.

regressive tax   A regressive tax is a tax that increases proportionately less than income as the income level of the taxpayer increases. Under a regressive tax, low-income taxpayers will pay a larger percent of their income toward this tax than high-income taxpayers.

revenue gap   A revenue gap exists when projected expenditures exceed projected tax revenues. Although revenue gaps usually are not allowed to exist in fact for current fiscal years, of importance are the projected values. If revenue gaps are projected, tax rate increases or expenditure cuts, both politically difficult, will be required. Revenue gaps usually occur when the elasticity of expenditures exceeds the elasticity of revenues. This often happens at the state and local level because state and local taxes are, in most instances, less elastic than expenditures. If states want to eliminate the occurrence of revenue gaps and the constant need to increase tax rates or decrease projected expenditure levels, attention must be given to ways to increase the elasticity of state tax systems, usually by increasing reliance on income taxes. (See *elasticity of tax revenues*).

school district tax rate   School district tax rate is the term states use to indicate the local school property tax rate. The tax rate often is slated as the amount of property tax dollars to be paid for each $100 of assessed valuation or, if given in mills, the rate indicates how much is raised for each $1,000 of assessed valuation. For example, a tax rate of $1.60 per hundred dollars of assessed valuation means that taxpayers pay $1.60 for each $100 of their total assessed valuation: a tax rate of 16 mills indicates that $16 must be paid for each $1,000 of assessed valuation. The tax rate can also be expressed as a percent, so a tax rate of 1.6 percent would be the same as a tax rate of 16 mills or $1.60 per hundred dollars of assessed valuation.

state aid for current operating expense   State aid for current operating expenses is the sum of the equalization formula aid and categorical aid for vocational education, special education, bilingual education, transportation, and other categorical aid programs. (See *categorical programs.*)

tax burden (or sometimes tax incidence)   Tax burden typically refers to the percent of an individual's or family's income that is consumed by a tax or by a tax system. Usually, one wants to know whether a tax or tax system's burden is distributed in a progressive, proportional, or regressive manner. In the United States, a tax system that is progressive overall seems to be the most acceptable to a majority of people. Tax burden analysis takes into account the extent of tax shifting.

tax incidence   See *tax shifting* and *tax burden.*

tax price   The tax price generally is the tax rate a district must levy to purchase a given level and quality of school services. Poor districts generally have to levy a higher tax rate, and thus pay a higher tax price, to purchase such a given bundle of school services than a wealthy district, because, at a given tax rate, the poor district would raise less dollars per pupil than the wealthy district.

tax shifting or tax incidence   Tax shifting refers to the phenomenon wherein the party that must legally pay a tax (for example, a store owner) does not in fact bear the burden of the tax but shifts the tax to another party (for example, the consumer of an item that is sold in the store). Taxes can be shifted either forward or backward. For example, landlords might be able to shift their property taxes forward to tenants in the form of higher rents, and a business might be able to shift property or corporate income taxes backward to employees in the form of lower salaries. The ability to shift taxes depends on a variety of economic factors and there is great debate among economists over the extent to which some taxes are shifted. It is usually agreed, however, that individual income taxes are not shifted and rest on the individual taxpayer. It also generally is agreed that sales taxes are shifted to the consumer. There is argument over the extent to which corporate income taxes are shifted to consumers in the form of higher prices or to employees in the form of lower wages versus falling on the stockholders in the form of lower dividends. There is also debate about who effectively pays the property tax. Tax incidence analysis examines how various taxes may or may not be shifted.

References

Please note: Visit the text's website at www.mhhe.com/odden3e for updates to any URLs included in the References section.

Aaron, Henry J. (1975). *Who Pays the Property Tax? A New View*. Washington, D.C.: The Brookings Institution.

Achilles, Charles. (1999). *Let's Put Kids First, Finally; Getting Class Size Right*. Thousand Oaks, CA: Corwin Press.

Ackerman, A. (2002). *San Francisco Unified School District: Academic Plan Development and Site-Based Budgeting Guide, School Year 2002–2003*. San Francisco: San Francisco Unified School District.

Adams, E. Kathleen, and Allan Odden. (1981). "Alternative Wealth Measures." In K. Forbis Jordan and Nelda H. Cambron-McCabe (Eds.), *Perspectives in State School Support Programs*. Cambridge, MA: Ballinger, pp. 143–165.

Adams, E. Kathleen. (December 1980). *Fiscal Response and School Finance Simulations: A Policy Perspective* (Report No. F80-3). Denver: Education Commission of the States.

Adams, Jacob E. (1994). "Spending School Reform Dollars in Kentucky: Familiar Patterns and New Programs, But Is This Reform?" *Educational Evaluation and Policy Analysis* 16(4), 375–390.

Adams, Jacob. (1997). "School Finance Policy and Students' Opportunities to Learn: Kentucky's Experience." *The Future of Children: Financing Schools* 7(3), 79–95.

Advisory Commission on Intergovernmental Relations (ACIR). (1995). *Tax and Expenditure Limits on Local Governments*. Washington, D.C.: Author.

Advisory Commission on Intergovernmental Relations. (1989a). *Significant Features of Fiscal Federalism, 1989 Edition* (Vol. 1). (Report M-163). Washington, D.C.: Author.

Advisory Commission on Intergovernmental Relations. (1989b). *Local Property Taxes Called Worst Tax. News Release of 18th Annual ACIR Poll*. Washington, D.C.: Author.

Alexander, Arthur J. (1974). *Teachers, Salaries and School District Expenditures*. Santa Monica, CA: The RAND Corporation.

Alexander, Kern. (1982). "Concepts of Equity." In Walter McMahon and Terry Geske (Eds.), *Financing Education*. Urbana: University of Illinois Press.

Alexander, Kern, John Augenblick, William Driscoll, James Guthrie, and R. Levin. (1995). *Proposals for the Elimination of Wealth-Based Disparities in Public Education*. Columbus, OH: Department of Education.

Alexander, Kern, and Richard Salmon. (1995). *Public School Finance*. Boston: Allyn and Bacon.

Allington, Richard. L., and Peter Johnston. (1989). "Coordination, Collaboration, and Consistency: The Redesign of Compensatory and Special Education Interventions." In Robert E. Slavin, Nancy L. Karweit, and Nancy A. Madden (Eds.), *Effective Programs for Students at Risk*. Needham Heights, MA: Allyn and Bacon, pp. 320–354.

R

Altman, Daniel. (2003, January 21). "Doubling Up of Taxation Isn't Limited to Dividends." *New York Times,* C1, C8.

Andrews, Matthew, William Duncombe, and John Yinger. (2002). "Revisiting Economies of Size in American Education: Are We Any Closer to a Consensus." *Economics of Education Review* 21(3), 245–262.

Augenblick, John. (1991). *Report Concerning the SEEK Program.* Mimeo.

Augenblick, John. (1997). *Recommendations for a Base Figure and Pupil-Weighted Adjustments to the Base Figure for Use in a New School Finance System in Ohio.* Columbus: Ohio Department of Education.

Augenblick, John, and E. Kathleen Adams. (1979). *An Analysis of the Impact of Changes in the Funding of Elementary/Secondary Education in Texas: 1974/75 to 1977/78.* Denver: Education Commission of the States.

Augenblick and Myers, Inc. (2001a). *Calculation of the Cost of an Adequate Education in Maryland in 1999–2000 Using Two Different Analytic Approaches.* Report prepared for the Maryland Commission on Education Finance, Equity and Excellence.

Augenblick and Myers, Inc. (2001b). *A Procedure for Calculating a Base Cost Figure and an Adjustment for At-Risk Pupils that could be Used in the Illinois School Finance System.* Report prepared for the Education Funding Advisory Board.

Barro, Stephen. (1989). "Fund Distribution Issues in School Finance: Priorities for the Next Round of Research." *Journal of Education Finance* 11(1), 17–30.

Barro, Stephen M. (1992). *What Does the Education Dollar Buy? Relationships of Staffing, Staff Characteristics, and Staff Salaries to State Per-Pupil Spending.* Los Angeles: The Finance Center of CPRE, Working Paper.

Barro, Stephen M., and Stephen J. Carroll. (1975). *Budget Allocation by School Districts: An Analysis of Spending for Teachers and Other Resources.* Santa Monica, CA: The RAND Corporation.

Barnett, W. Steven. (1995). "Long-Term Effects of Early Childhood Programs on Cognitive and School Outcomes." *The Future of Children: Long-Term Outcomes of Early Childhood Programs* 5(3), 25–50.

Barnett, W. Steven. (2000). "Economics of Early Childhood Intervention." In Jack Shonkoff and Samuel Meisels (Eds.), *Handbook of Early Childhood Intervention* (2d ed.). Cambridge: Cambridge University Press.

Bell, Michael E., and John H. Bowman. (1986). "Direct Property Tax Relief." In *Final Report of the Minnesota Tax Study Commission* (Volume 1). St. Paul and Boston: Butterworth's, pp. 291–326.

Berke, Joel. (1974). *Answers to Inequity: An Analysis of the New School Finance.* New York: Russell Sage Foundation.

Berne, Robert, and Leanna Stiefel. (1979). "Taxpayer Equity in School Finance Reform: The School Finance and Public Finance Perspective." *Journal of Education Finance* 5(1), 36–54.

Berne, Robert, and Leanna Stiefel. (1984). *The Measurement of Equity in School Finance.* Baltimore: Johns Hopkins University Press.

Berne, Robert, and Leanna Stiefel. (1999). "Concepts of School Finance Equity: 1970 to Present." In Helen Ladd, Rosemary Chalk, and Janet Hansen (Eds.), *Equity and Adequacy in Education Finance: Issues and Perspectives.* Washington, D.C.: National Academy Press.

Berne, Robert, Leanna Stiefel, and Michelle Moser. (1997). "The Coming of Age of School-Level Finance Data." *Journal of Education Finance* 22(3), 246–254.

Berner, Maureen M. (1993). "Building Conditions, Parental Involvement, and Student Achievement in the District of Columbia Public School System." *Urban Education* 28(1), 6–29.

Black, D. E., K. A. Lewis, and C. K. Link. (1979). "Wealth Neutrality and the Demand for Education." *National Tax Journal* 32(2), 157–164.

Bolton, Denny G., and W. Gary Harmer. (2000). *Standards of Excellence in Budget Presentation.* Reston, VA: Association of School Business Officers International.

Borg, Mary O., Paul M. Mason, and Stephen L. Schapiro. (1991). *The Economic Consequences of State Lotteries.* New York: Praeger.

Borman, Geoffrey, and Jerome D'Agostino. (2001). "Title I and Student Achievement: A Quantitative Analysis." In Geoffrey Borman, Samuel Stringfield, and Robert Slavin (Eds.)., *Title I: Compensatory Education at the Crossroads.* Mahwah, NJ: Lawrence Erlbaum Associates, pp. 25–27.

Borman, Geoffrey D., G. Hewes, L. T. Overman, and S. Brown. (2002). *Comprehensive School Reform and Student Achievement: A Meta-Analysis* (CRESPAR Report No. 59). Baltimore: Johns Hopkins University, Center for Research on the Education of Students Placed at Risk.

Borman, Geoffrey, Samuel Stringfield, and Robert Slavin. (Eds). (2001). *Title I: Compensatory Education at the Crossroads.* Mahwah, NJ: Lawrence Erlbaum Associates.

Bowman, John H. (1974). "Tax Exportability, Intergovernmental Aid, and School Finance Reform." *National Tax Journal* 27(2), 163–173.

Brackett, J., J. Chambers, and T. Parrish. (1983). *The Legacy of Rational Budgeting Models in Education and a Proposal for the Future* (Report No. 83-A21 [August]). Stanford, CA: Institute for Research on Educational Finance and Governance.

Bransford, John, Ann Brown, and Rodney Cocking. (1999). *How People Learn.* Washington, D.C.: National Academy Press.

Brazer, Harvey E. (1974). "Adjusting for Differences Among School Districts in the Costs of Educational Inputs: A Feasibility Report." In Ester Tron (Ed.), *Selected Papers in School Finance: 1974.* Washington, D.C.: U.S. Office of Education.

Break, George F. (1980). *Financing Government in a Federal System.* Washington, D.C.: The Brookings Institution.

Brown, Lawrence L., et al. (1977). *School Finance Reform in the Seventies: Achievements and Failures.* Washington, D.C.: U.S. Department of Health, Education and Welfare, Office of the Assistant Secretary for Planning and Evaluation and Killalea Associates, Inc.

Bruer, John. (1993). *Schools for Thought.* Cambridge, MA: MIT Press.

Bryk, Anthony, Valerie E. Lee, and P. Holland. (1993). *Catholic Schools and the Common Good.* Cambridge, MA: Harvard University Press.

Buday, Mary, and James Kelly. (November 1996). National Board Certification and the Teaching Profession's Commitment to Quality Assurance. *Phi Delta Kappan* 78(3), 215–219.

Burtless, Gary (Ed.). (1996). *Does Money Matter?* Washington, D.C.: The Brookings Institution.

Busch, Carolyn, and Allan Odden. (1997). "Collection of School-Level Finance Data." *Journal of Education Finance* 22(3).

Busch, Carolyn, Karen Kucharz, and Allan Odden. (1996). "Recognizing Additional Student Need in Wisconsin: A Re-Examination of Equity and Equity Analysis." In Barbara LaCost (Ed.), *School Finance Policy Issues in the States and Provinces.* Lincoln, NE: University of Nebraska and American Education Finance Association, pp. 109–126.

Cardenas, Jose, J. J. Bernal, and N. Kean. (1976). *Bilingual Education Cost Analysis: Texas.* San Antonio: Intercultural Development Research Association.

Carey, Kevin. (2002). *State Poverty-Based Education Funding: A Survey of Current Programs and Options for Improvement.* Washington, D.C.: Center on Budget and Policy Priorities.

Carpenter-Huffman, P., and S. M. Samulon. (1981). *Case Studies of Delivery and Cost of Bilingual Education Programs.* Santa Monica, CA: The RAND Corporation.

Chaikind, Steve, Louis C. Danielson, and Marsha L. Braven. (1993). "What Do We Know about the Costs of Special Education? A Selected Review." *Journal of Special Education* 26(4), 344–370.

Chambers, Jay G. (1978). *Educational Cost Differentials Across School Districts in California.* Denver: Education Commission of the States.

Chambers, Jay G. (1980). *The Development of a Cost of Education Index for the State of California.* Final reports, Parts 1 and 2, prepared for the California State Department of Education.

Chambers, Jay G. (1981). "Cost and Price Level Adjustments to State Aid for Education: A Theoretical and Empirical View." In K. Forbis Jordan and Nelda Cambron-McCabe (Eds.), *Perspectives in State School Support Programs.* Cambridge, MA: Ballinger.

Chambers, Jay G. (1995). "Public School Teacher Cost Differences Across the United States: Introduction to a Teacher Cost Index (TCI)." In *Developments in School Finance.* Available online: www.ed.gov/NCES/pubs/96344cha.html.

Chambers, Jay G., Allan Odden, and Phillip E. Vincent. (1976). *Cost of Education Indices Among School Districts.* Denver: Education Commission of the States.

Chambers, Jay, and Thomas Parrish. (1983). *The Development of a Resource Cost Model Funding Base for Education Finance in Illinois.* Stanford, CA: Associates for Education Finance and Planning.

Chambers, Jay, and Thomas Parrish. (1994). "State-Level Education Finance." In *Advances in Educational Productivity.* Greenwich, CT: JAI Press, pp. 45–74.

Chambers, Jay, Thomas Parrish, and Cassandra Guarino (Eds.). (1999). *Funding Special Education.* Thousand Oaks, CA: Corwin Press.

Chambers, Jay G., Thomas B. Parrish, and Jennifer J. Harr. (2002). *What Are We Spending on Special Education Services in the United States, 1999–2000?* (Report 02-01.) Palo Alto: American Institutes for Research, Center for Special Education Finance.

Chubb, John, and Terry Moe. (1990). *Politics, Markets and America's Schools.* Washington, D.C.: The Brookings Institution.

Clune, William. (1994a). "The Shift from Equity to Adequacy in School Finance." *Educational Policy* 8(4), 376–394.

Clune, William. (1994b). "The Cost and Management of Program Adequacy: An Emerging Issue in Education Policy and Finance." *Educational Policy* 8(4).

Clune, William. (1995). "Adequacy Litigation in School Finance Symposium." *University of Michigan Journal of Law Reform* 28(3).

Coeyman, Marjorie. (November 24, 1998). "Small-Town Schools: Changing Times and Budgets Put the Squeeze On." *Christian Science Monitor* 90(252), 15.

Cohen, Matthew C. (1997). "Issues in School-Level Analysis of Education Expenditure Data." *Journal of Education Finance* 22(3), 255–279.

Cohn, Elchanan. (1974). *Economics of State Aid to Education.* Lexington, MA: Heath Lexington Books.

Cohn, Elchanan, and Terry G. Geske. (1990). *The Economics of Education* (3d ed.). Oxford, England: Pergamon Press.

Comer, James P., Norris M. Haynes, Edward T. Joyner, and Michael Ben-Avie. (1996). *Rallying the Whole Village: The Comer Process for Reforming Education.* New York: Teachers College Press.

Coons, John, William Clune, and Stephen Sugarman. (1970). *Private Wealth and Public Education.* Cambridge, MA: Belknap Press of Harvard University Press.

Cooper, Bruce. (March 1993). *School Site Cost Allocations: Testing a Microfinancial Model in 23 Districts in Ten States.* Paper presented at the annual meeting of the American Education Finance Association, Albuquerque, NM.

Crampton, Faith E., and David C. Thompson (Ed.). (2003). "Saving America's School Infrastructure." In *Research in Education Fiscal Policy and Practice,* Christopher Roellke and Jennifer King Rice (Series Editors). Greenwich, CT: Information Age Publishing.

Cubberly, Elwood Patterson. (1905). *School Funds and Their Apportionment.* New York: Teachers College Press.

Cubberly, Elwood Patterson. (1906). *School Funds and Their Apportionment.* New York: Teachers College Press.

Cummins, James. (1980). "The Exit and Entry Fallacy in Bilingual Education." *NABE Journal 4* 25–60.

Danielson, Charlotte. (1996). *Enhancing Professional Practice: A Framework for Teaching.* Arlington, VA: Association for Supervision and Curriculum Development.

Darling-Hammond, Linda. (1997). *The Right to Learn.* San Francisco: Jossey-Bass.

Dayton, John, C. Thomas Holms, Catherine C. Sielke, and Anne L. Jefferson. (2001). *Public School Finance Programs of the United States and Canada, 1998–99* (NCES-2001-309). Washington, D.C.: National Center for Education Statistics.

Downes, Thomas, and Thomas Pogue. (1994). "Adjusting School Aid Formulas for the Higher Cost of Educating Disadvantaged Students." *National Tax Journal* 47(1), 89–110.

Doyle, Denis, and Terry Hartle. (1985). *Excellence in Education: The States Take Charge.* Washington, D.C.: American Enterprise Institute.

Due, John F., and John L. Mikesell. (1994). *Sales Taxation: State and Local Structure and Administration* (2d ed.). Washington, D.C.: The Urban Institute.

Duncombe, William, John Ruggiero, and John Yinger. (1996). "Alternative Approaches to Measuring the Cost of Education." In Helen F. Ladd (Ed.), *Holding Schools Accountable: Performance-based Reform in Education.* Washington, D.C.: The Brookings Institution, pp. 327–356.

Dye, Robert F., and Teresa I. McGuire. (1991). "Growth and Variability of State Individual Income and Sales Taxes." *National Tax Journal* 44, 55–66.

Earthman, G., and Linda LeMasters. (1996). *Review of Research on the Relationship Between School Buildings, Student Achievement, and Student Behavior.* Paper present at the annual meeting of the Council of Educational Facility Planners, International, Santa Fe, NM.

Ebel, Robert D., and James Ortbal. (1989). "Direct Residential Property Tax Relief." *Intergovernmental Perspective* 16, 9–14.

Edison Project. (1994). *An Invitation to Public School Partnership.* New York: The Edison Project.

Elmore, Richard. (1990). *School Restructuring: The Next Generation of Educational Reform.* San Francisco: Jossey-Bass.

Enrich, Paul. (1995). "Leaving Equality Behind: New Directions in School Finance Reform." *Vanderbilt Law Review* 48, 100–194.

Erlichson, Bari Anhalt, and Margaret Goertz. (2001). *Implementing Whole School Reform in New Jersey, Year Two.* New Brunswick: Rutgers, the State University of New Jersey, Bloustein School of Planning and Public Policy.

Erlichson, Bari Anhalt, Margaret Goertz, and Barbara Turnbull. (1999). *Implementing Whole School Reform in New Jersey, Year One in the First Cohort Schools.* New Brunswick: Rutgers, the State University of New Jersey, Bloustein School of Planning and Public Policy.

Evans, William, Sheila Murray, and Robert Schwab. (1997). *State Education Finance Policy After Court Mandated Reform: The Legacy of Serrano. 1996 Proceedings of the Eighty-Ninth Annual Conference on Taxation.* Washington, D.C.: National Tax Association-Tax Institute of America.

Farland, Gary. (1997). "Collection of Fiscal and Staffing Data at the School Site Level." *Journal of Education Finance* 22(3), 280–290.

Feldstein, Martin. (1975). "Wealth Neutrality and Local Choice in Public Education." *American Economic Review* 64, 75–89.

Ferguson, Ronald F. (Summer 1991). "Paying for Public Education: New Evidence on How and Why Money Matters." *Harvard Journal on Legislation* 28, 465–497.

Finkelstein, Neil, William Furry, and Luis Huerta. (2000). "School Finance in California: Does History Provide a Sufficient Policy Standard?" In Elizabeth Burr, Gerald C. Hayward, Bruce Fuller, and Michael W. Kirst (Eds.), *Crucial Issues in California Education 2000: Are the Reform Pieces Fitting Together?* Berkeley: Policy Analysis for California Education, pp. 45–78.

Finn, Jeremy. (1996). *Class Size and Students At Risk: What Is Known? What Next?* Paper prepared for the National Institute on the Education of At-Risk Students, Office of Educational Research and Improvement, U.S. Department of Education.

Finn, Jeremy. (2002). "Small Classes in America: Research, Practice, and Politics." *Phi Delta Kappan* 83(7), 551–560.

Finnan, Christine, Edward St. John, Jane McCarthy, and Simeon Slovacek. (1996). *Accelerated Schools in Action.* Thousand Oaks, CA: Corwin Press.

Firestone, William A., Margaret E. Goertz, Brianna Nagle, and Marcy F. Smelkinson. (1994). "Where Did the $800 Million Go? The First Years of New Jersey's Quality Education Act." *Educational Evaluation and Policy Analysis* 16(4), 359–374.

Fortune. (2002). The 2002 Fortune 500: America's Largest Companies. New York: *Fortune Magazine.* Available online: www.fortune.com/lists/F500/ (November 10, 2002).

Fowler, William Jr., and David Monk. (2001). *A Primer for Making Cost Adjustments in Education.* Washington, D.C.: U.S. Department of Education, National Center for Education Statistics.

Fox, James. (1987). "An Analysis of Classroom Spending." *Planning and Changing* 18(3), 154–162.

Fox, William F. (1981). "Reviewing Economies of Size in Education." *Journal of Education Finance* 6(3), 273–296.

Fuhrman, Susan H. (Ed.). (1993). *Designing Coherent Education Policy: Improving the System.* San Francisco: Jossey-Bass.

Fullan, Michael. (2001). *The New Meaning of Educational Change.* New York: Teachers College Press.

Gallagher, H. Alix. (June 2002). "Vaughn Elementary's Innovative Teacher Evaluation System: Are Teacher Evaluation Scores Related to Growth in Student Achievement?" Submitted to *Educational Evaluation and Policy Analysis.*

Garcia, O. (1977). "Analyzing Bilingual Education Costs." In G. Banco, et al. (Eds.), *Bilingual Education: Current Perspectives.* Arlington, VA: Education Center for Applied Linguistics.

Garms, Walter I. (1979). "Measuring the Equity of School Finance Systems." *Journal of Education Finance* 4(4), 415–435.

General Accounting Office. (1995a). *School Facilities: Conditions of America's Schools.* Washington, D.C.: Author. GAO/HEHS-95-61.

General Accounting Office. (1995b). *School Facilities: American's School Not Designed or Equipped for 21st Century.* Washington, D.C.: Author. GAO/HEHS-95-95.

General Accounting Office. (1995c). *School Facilities: State's Financial and Technical Support Varies.* Washington, D.C.: Author. GAO/HEHS-96-27.

General Accounting Office. (1996). *School Facilities: America's Schools Report Differing Conditions.* Washington, D.C.: Author. GAO/HEHS-96-103.

General Accounting Office. (1997). *School Finance: State Efforts to Reduce Funding Gaps between Poor and Wealthy Districts.* Washington, D.C.: Author.

General Accounting Office. (2000). *School Facilities: Construction Expenditures Have Grown Significantly in Recent Years.* Washington, D.C.: Author. GAO/HEHS-00-41.

Gerber, Susan, Jeremy Finn, Charles Achilles, and Jane Boyd-Zaharias. (2001). "Teacher Aides and Students' Academic Achievement." *Educational Evaluation and Policy Analysis* 23(2), 123–143.

Goertz, Margaret E. (1979). *Money and Education: How far have we come? Financing New Jersey Education in 1979.* Princeton, NJ: Education Policy Research Institute, Educational Testing Service.

Goertz, Margaret. (1983). "School Finance in New Jersey: A Decade after Robinson v. Cahill." *Journal of Education Finance* 8(4), 475–489.

Goertz, Margaret. (1988) *School District's Allocation of Chapter 1 Resources.* Princeton, NJ: Educational Testing Service.

Goertz, Margaret. (1997). "The Challenges of Collecting School-Based Data." *Journal of Education Finance* 22(3), 291–302.

Goertz, Margaret, Margaret McLauglin, Virginia Roach, and Suzanne Raber. (1999). "What Will It Take: Including Students with Disabilities in Standards-Based Education Reform." In Jay Chambers, Thomas Parrish, and Cassandra Guarino (Eds.), *Funding Special Education.* Thousand Oaks, CA: Corwin Press, pp. 41–62.

Goertz, Margaret, and Allan Odden (Eds.). (1999). *School-Based Financing.* Thousand Oaks, CA: Corwin Press.

Gold, Steven. (1994). *Tax Options for States Needing More School Revenue.* Washington, D.C.: National Education Association.

Gold, Steven D., David M. Smith, and Stephen B. Lawton. (1995). *Public School Finance Programs of the United States and Canada: 1993–94.* New York: American Education Finance Association of Center for the Study of the States, The Nelson A. Rockefeller Institute of Government.

Gold, Stephen D., David M. Smith, Stephen B. Lawton, and Andrea C. Hyary. (Eds.). (1992). *Public School Finance Programs in the United States and Canada, 1990–1991.* Albany: State University of New York Center for the Study of the States.

Goldhaber, Dan, and Karen Callahan. (2001). "Impact of the Basic Education Program on Educational Spending and Equity in Tennessee." *Journal of Education Finance* 26(4), 415–436.

Gonzalez, Rosa Maria. (1996). *Bilingual/ESL Programs Evaluation, 1995–96* (Publication No. 95-01). Austin: Austin Independent School District. (ERIC Document Reproduction Service No. ED 404877).

Greenwald, Rob, Larry V. Hedges, and Richard D. Laine. (1996a). "The Effect of School Resources on Student Achievement." *Review of Educational Research* 66(3), 361–396.

Greenwald, Rob, Larry V. Hedges, and Richard D. Laine. (1996b). "Interpreting Research on School Resources and Student Achievement: A Rejoinder to Hanushek." *Review of Educational Research* 66(3), 411–416.

Grissmer, David. (1999). "Class Size: Issues and New Findings." *Educational Evaluation and Policy Analysis* 21(2). (Entire issue.)

Grubb, W. Norton, and Stephan Michelson. (1974). *States and Schools: The Political Economy of Public School Finance.* Lexington, MA: Lexington Books.

Grubb, W. Norton, and J. Osman. (1977). "The Causes of School Finance Inequalities: Serrano and the Case of California." *Public Finance Quarterly* 5(3), 373–392.

Guss-Zamora, M., R. Zarate, M. Robledo, and Jose Cardenas. (1979). *Bilingual Education Cost Analysis: Utah.* San Antonio: Intercultural Development Research Association.

Guthrie, James W. (1979). "Organizational Scale and School Success." *Educational Evaluation and Policy Analysis* 1(1), 17–27.

Guthrie, James, Walter Garms, and Lawrence Pierce. (1988). *School Finance and Education Policy.* Englewood Cliffs, NJ: Prentice Hall.

Guthrie, James W., Michael W. Kirst, and Allan R. Odden. (1990). *Conditions of Education in California, 1989.* Berkeley: University of California, School of Education, and Policy Analysis for California Education.

Guthrie, James W., and Richard Rothstein. (1999). "Enabling 'Adequacy' to Achieve Reality: Translating Adequacy into State School Finance Distribution Arrangements." In Helen Ladd, Rosemary Chalk, and Janet Hansen (Eds.), *Equity and Adequacy in Education Finance: Issues and Perspectives*. Washington, D.C.: National Academy Press, pp. 209–259.

Guthrie, James, et al. (1997). *A Proposed Cost-Based Block Grant Model for Wyoming School Finance*. Davis, CA: Management Analysis and Planning Associates, LLC. Available online: *http://legisweb.state.wy.us/school/cost/apr7/apr7.htm*.

Haller, Emil, David H. Monk, Alyce Spotted Bear, Julie Griffith, and Pamela Moss. (1990). "School Size and Program Comprehensiveness: Evidence from *High School and Beyond*." *Educational Evaluation and Policy Analysis* 12(2), 109–120.

Hamilton, Stephen F. (1983). "The Social Side of Schooling: Ecological Studies of Classrooms and Schools." *The Elementary School Journal* 83(4), 313–334.

Hannaway, Jane, Helen Fu, and Yasser Nakib. (2002). *Signs of the Times: Effects of Good Times and Bad Times, Growth and Decline on School District Staffing Patterns*. Washington, D.C.: The Urban Institute.

Hannaway, Jane, Shannon McKay, and Yasser Nakib. (2002). "Reform and Resource Allocation: National Trends and State Policies." *Developments in School Finance, 1999–2000*, 57–75. Washington, D.C.: U.S. Department of Education, National Center for Education Statistics.

Hanushek, Eric A. (1981). "Throwing Money at Schools." *Journal of Policy Analysis and Management* 1(1), 19–41.

Hanushek, Eric. (1986). "The Economics of Schooling: Production and Efficiency in Public Schools." *Journal of Economic Literature* 24(3), 1141–1177.

Hanushek, Eric. (1989). "The Impact of Differential Expenditures on Student Performance." *Educational Researcher* 18(4), 45–52.

Hanushek, Eric A. (1994). "Money Might Matter Somewhere: A Response to Hedges, Laine, and Greenwald." *Educational Researcher* 23(3), 5–8.

Hanushek, Eric A. (1997). "Assessing the Effects of School Resources on Student Performance: An Update." *Educational Evaluation and Policy Analysis* 19(2), 141–164.

Hanushek, Eric. (2002). "Evidence, Politics and the Class Size Debate." In Lawrence Mishel and Richard Rothstein (Eds.), *The Class Size Debate*. Washington, D.C.: Economic Policy Institute, pp. 37–65.

Hanushek, Eric, and Associates. (1994). *Making Schools Work: Improving Performance and Controlling Costs*. Washington, D.C.: The Brookings Institution.

Hanushek, Eric, and Steven Rivkin. (1997). "Understanding the Twentieth-Century Growth in U.S. School Spending." *Journal of Human Resources* 32(1), 35–68.

Hartman, William. (1980). "Policy Effects of Special Education Funding Formulas." *Journal of Education Finance* 6(2), 135–139.

Hartman, William. (1988a). "District Spending: What Do the Dollars Buy?" *Journal of Education Finance* 13(4), 436–459.

Hartman, William T. (1988b). *School District Budgeting*. Englewood Cliffs, NJ: Prentice Hall.

Hartman, William T. (1994). "District Spending Disparities Revisited." *Journal of Education Finance* 20(1), 88–106.

Hartman, William. (2002). *School District Budgeting* (2d ed.). Reston, VA: Association of School Business Officers International.

Hayward, Gerald C. (1988). *The Two Million Dollar School*. Berkeley: University of California, School of Education, Policy Analysis for California Education.

Hedges, Larry. V., Richard D. Laine, and Rob Greenwald. (1994a). "Does Money Matter? A Meta-Analysis of Studies of the Effects of Differential School Inputs on Student Outcomes." *Educational Researcher* 23(3), 5–14.

Hedges, Larry V., Richard D. Laine, and Rob Greenwald. (1994b). "Money Does Matter Somewhere: A Reply to Hanushek." *Educational Researcher* 23(3), 9–10.

Heise, Michael. (1995). "State Constitutions, School Finance Litigation and the "Third Wave": From Equity to Adequacy." *Temple Law Review* 68(3), 1151–1176.

Hentschke, Guilbert C. (1986). *School Business Administration: A Comparative Perspective.* Berkeley: McCutchan.

Herman, R., D. Aladjem, P. McMahon, E. Masem, I. Mulligan, and A. O'Malley, et al. (1999). *An Educator's Guide to School Reform.* Arlington, VA: Educational Research Service.

Hertert, Linda. (1996). "Does Equal Funding for Districts Mean Equal Funding for Classroom Students? Evidence from California." In Lawrence O. Picus and James L. Wattenbarger (Eds.), *Where Does the Money Go? Resource Allocation in Elementary and Secondary Schools.* 1995 Yearbook of the American Education Finance Association, Newbury Park, CA: Corwin Press, pp. 71–84.

Hertert, Linda, Carolyn A. Busch, and Allan R. Odden. (1994). "School Financing Inequities Among the States: The Problem from a National Perspective." *Journal of Education Finance* 19(3), 231–255.

Hickrod, G. Alan, Ramesh B. Chaudhari, and Ben C. Hubbard. (1981). *Reformation and Counter-Reformation in Illinois School Finance: 1973–1981.* Normal, IL: Center for the Study of Education Finance.

Hinrichs, William L., and Richard D. Laine. (1996). *Adequacy: Building Quality and Efficiency into the Cost of Education.* Springfield: Illinois Board of Education.

Hirsch, E. Donald. (1996). *The Schools We Need and Why We Don't Have Them.* New York: Doubleday.

Hirth, Marilyn. (1994). "A Multistate Analysis of School Finance Issues and Equity Trends in Indiana, Illinois, and Michigan, 1982–1992." *Journal of Education Finance* 20(2), 163–190.

Hodge, Michael. (1981). "Improving Finance and Governance of Education for Special Populations." In K. Forbis Jordan and Nelda Cambron-McCabe (Eds.), *Perspectives in State School Support Programs.* Cambridge, MA: Ballinger.

Ingersoll, R. (2001). "Teacher Turnover and Teacher Shortages: An Organizational Analysis." *American Educational Research Journal* 38(3), 499–534.

Johns, Roe, Kern Alexander, and K. Forbis Jordan (Eds.). (1971). *Planning to Finance Education, Vol. 3.* Gainesville, FL: National Education Finance Project.

Johnson, Gary, and George Pillianayagam. (1991). "A Longitudinal Equity Study of Ohio's School Finance System: 1980–89." *Journal of Education Finance* 17(1), 60–82.

Johnson, Nicholas. (2000). "State Low-Income Tax Relief: Recent Trends." *National Tax Journal LIII* (3, Part I), 403–416.

Johnston, Jocelyn, and William Duncombe. (1998). "Balancing Conflicting Policy Objectives: The Case of School Finance Reform." *Public Administration Review* 58(2), 145–157.

Kakalik, James. (1979). "Issues in the Cost and Finance of Special Education." *Review of Educational Research, Vol. 7.* Washington, D.C.: American Educational Research Association.

Kakalik, James, W.S. Furry, M.A. Thomas, and M.F. Carney. (1981). *The Cost of Special Education.* Santa Monica, CA: The RAND Corporation.

Kearney, Phillip, Li-Ju Chen, and Marjorie Checkoway. (1988). *Measuring Equity in Michigan School Finance: A Further Look.* Ann Arbor: University of Michigan, School of Education.

Kelley, Carolyn. (1998a). "The Kentucky School-Based Performance Award Program: School-Level Effects." *Educational Policy* 12(3), 305–324.

Kelley, Carolyn, and Jean Protsik. (1997). "Risk and Reward: Perspectives on the Implementation of Kentucky's School-Based Performance Award Program." *Educational Administration Quarterly* 33(4), 474–505.

Kenny, L., D. Denslow, and Irving Goffman. (1975). "Determination of Teacher Cost Differentials among School Districts in the State of Florida." In Ester Tron (Ed.), *Selected Papers in School Finance.* Washington, D.C.: U.S. Office of Education.

Kirst, Michael. (1977). "What Happens at the Local Level after School Finance Reform?" *Policy Analysis* 3(1), 302–324.

Kozol, Jonathan. (1992). *Savage Inequalities: Children in America's Schools.* New York: Harper Perennial.

Krashen, Steve, and Douglas Biber. (1988). *On Course: Bilingual Education's Success in California.* Sacramento: California Association for Bilingual Education.

Kreuger, Alan. (2002). "Understanding the Magnitude and Effect of Class Size on Student Achievement." In Lawrence Mishel and Richard Rothstein (Eds.), *The Class Size Debate.* Washington, D.C.: Economic Policy Institute, pp. 7–35.

Ladd, Helen. (1975). "Local Education Expenditures, Fiscal Capacity and the Composition of the Property Tax Base." *National Tax Journal* 28(2), 145–158.

Ladd, Helen, and John Yinger. (1994). The Case for Equalizing Aid. *National Tax Journal* 47(1), 211–224.

Laine, Richard D., Rob Greenwald, and Larry V. Hedges. (1996). "Money Does Matter: A Research Synthesis of a New Universe of Education Production Function Studies." In Lawrence O. Picus and James L. Wattenbarger (Eds.), *Where Does the Money Go? Resource Allocation in Elementary and Secondary Schools.* Thousand Oaks, CA: Corwin Press, pp. 44–70.

Lankford, Hamilton, and James H. Wyckoff. (1995). "Where Has the Money Gone? An Analysis of School Spending in New York." *Educational Evaluation and Policy Analysis* 17(2), 195–218.

Lawler, E. E, S. A. Mohrman, and G. Benson. (2001). *Organizing for High Performance.* San Francisco: Jossey-Bass.

Lee, Valerie, and Julia Smith. (1997). "High School Size: Which Works Best, and for Whom?" *Educational Evaluation and Policy Analysis* 19(3), 205–228.

Levacic, Rosalind. (1999). "Case Study 2: United Kingdom." In Kenneth Ross and Rosalind Levacic (Eds.), *Needs-Based Resource Allocation in Schools via Formula-Based Funding.* Paris: UNESCO, International Institute for Educational Planning.

Levin, Betsy. (1977). "New Legal Challenges in Educational Finance." *Journal of Education Finance* 3(1), 53–69.

Lewis, A., D. Bednarek, L. Chion-Kenney, C. Harrison, J. Kolodzy, K. McCormick, J. Smith, D. Speich, and L. Walker. (1989). *Wolves at the Schoolhouse Door: An Investigation of the Condition of Public School Buildings.* Washington, D.C.: Education Writers Association.

Lewis, L., K. Snow, E. Farris, B. Smerdon, S. Cronen, and J. Kaplan. (2000). *Condition of America's Public School Facilities: 1999* (NCES 2000-032). Washington, D.C.: U.S. Department of Education, National Center for Education Statistics.

Linn, Robert L., Eva L. Baker, and Damian W. Betebenner. (2002). "Accountability Systems: Implications of Requirements of the No Child Left Behind Act of 2001." *Educational Researcher* 31(6), 3–16.

Madigan, Timothy. (1997). *Science Proficiency and Course Taking in High School: The Relationship of Science Course-Taking Patterns to Increases in Science Proficiency between 8th and 12th Grades.* Washington, D.C.: National Center for Education Statistics.

Management Analysis and Planning, Inc. (2001). *A Professional Judgment Approach to Determining Adequate Education Funding in Maryland.* Report prepared for the New Maryland Education Coalition. Davis, CA: Author.

Management Analysis and Planning, Inc. (2002). *A Professional Judgment Approach to Determining Adequate Education Funding in Wyoming.* Davis, CA: Author.

Massell, Diane, Margaret Hoppe, and Michael Kirst. (1997). *Persistence and Change: Standards-Based Reform in Nine States.* Philadelphia: University of Pennsylvania, Graduate School of Education, Consortium for Policy Research in Education.

McDonnell, Lorraine M., Margaret J. McLaughlin, and P. Morison. (Eds.). (1997). *Educating One and All: Students with Disabilities and Standards-Based Reform* (A report by the National Research Council Committee on Goals 2000 and the Inclusion of Students with Disabilities). Washington, D.C.: National Academy Press.

McGuffey, C., and C. Brown. (1978). "The Impact of School Building Age on School Achievement in Georgia." *The Educational Facility Planner,* 2/78.

McGuire, C. Kent. (1982). *State and Federal Programs for Special Student Populations.* Denver: Education Commission of the States.

McLauglin, Margaret. (1999). "Consolidating Categorical Educational Programs at the Local Level." In Jay Chambers, Thomas Parrish, and Cassandra Guarino (Eds.), *Funding Special Education.* Thousand Oaks, CA: Corwin Press, pp. 22–40.

McLaughlin, W. Milbrey, and Sylvia Yee. (1988). "School as a Place to Have A Career." In Ann Lieberman (Ed.), *Building a Professional Culture in Schools.* New York: Teachers College Press.

McMahon, Walter W. (1994). "Intrastate Cost Adjustment." In *Selected Papers in School Finance.* Available online: www.ed.gov/NCES/pubs/96068ica.

McUsic, M. (1991). "The Use of Education Clauses in School Finance Reform Litigation." *Harvard Journal on Legislation* 28(2), 307–340.

Mieszkowski, Peter. (1972). "The Property Tax: An Excise Tax or Profits Tax?" *Journal of Public Economics* 1, 73–96.

Mikesell, John L. (1986). *Fiscal Administration: Analysis and Application for the Public Sector.* Homewood, IL: Dorsey.

Miles, Karen Hawley. (1995). "Freeing Resources for Improving Schools: A Case Study of Teacher Allocation in Boston Public Schools." *Educational Evaluation and Policy Analysis* 17(4), 476–493.

Miles, Karen Hawley. (1997). *Spending More at the Edges: Understanding the Growth in Public School Spending from 1967 to 1991.* Unpublished Doctoral dissertation, University of Michigan, Ann Arbor.

Miles, Karen Hawley, and Linda Darling-Hammond. (1997). *Rethinking the Allocation of Teaching Resources: Some Lessons from High Performing Schools* (CPRE Research Report Series RR-38). Philadelphia: University of Pennsylvania, Graduate School of Education, Consortium for Policy Research in Education.

Miles, Karen Hawley, and Linda Darling-Hammond. (1998). "Rethinking the Allocation of Teaching Resources: Some Lessons from High-Performing Schools." *Educational Evaluation and Policy Analysis* 20(1), 9–29.

Miner, Jerry. (1963). *Social and Economic Factors in Spending for Public Education.* Syracuse, NY: Syracuse University Press.

Minorini, Paul, and Stephen Sugarman. (1999a). "School Finance Litigation in the Name of Educational Equity: Its Evolution, Impact and Future." In Helen Ladd, Rosemary Chalk, and Janet Hansen (Eds.), *Equity and Adequacy in Education Finance: Issues and Perspectives.* Washington, D.C.: National Academy Press.

Minorini, Paul, and Stephen Sugarman. (1999b). "Educational Adequacy and the Courts: The Promise and Problems of Moving to a New Paradigm." In Helen Ladd, Rosemary Chalk, and Janet Hansen (Eds.), *Equity and Adequacy in Education Finance: Issues and Perspectives.* Washington, D.C.: National Academy Press.

Mohrman, Susan. (1994). "Large Scale Change." In Susan Mohrman and Priscilla Wohlstetter (Eds.), *School-Based Management: Organizing for High Performance.* San Francisco: Jossey-Bass.

Monk, David. (1987). "Secondary School Size and Curriculum Comprehensiveness." *Economics of Education Review* 6(2), 137–150.

Monk, David. (1990). *Educational Finance: An Economic Approach.* New York: McGraw-Hill.

Monk, David H. (1992). "Educational Productivity Research: An Update and Assessment of Its Role in Education Finance Reform." *Educational Evaluation and Policy Analysis* 14(4), 307–332.

Monk, David H. (1997). "Challenges Surrounding the Collection and Use of Data for the Study of Finance and Productivity." *Journal of Education Finance* 22(3), 303–316.

Monk, David H., and Brian O. Brent. (1997). *Raising Money for Schools: A Guide to the Property Tax.* Thousand Oaks, CA: Corwin Press.

Monk, D.H., Christopher F. Roellke, and Brian O. Brent. (1996). *What Education Dollars Buy: An Examination of Resource Allocation Patterns in New York State Public School Systems.* Madison: University of Wisconsin, Wisconsin Center for Education Research, Consortium for Policy Research in Education.

Monk, David, and Billy Walker. (1991). "The Texas Cost of Education Index." *Journal of Education Finance* 17(2), 172–192.

Moody, Scott (Ed.). (2002). *Facts and Figures on Government Finance* (36th ed.). Washington, D.C.: Tax Foundation.

Moore, Mary, T. E. William Strang, Myron Schwartz, and Mark Braddock. (1988). *Patterns in Special Education Service Delivery and Cost.* Washington, D.C.: Decision Resources Corporation.

Murnane, Richard, and Frank Levy. (1996). *Teaching the New Basic Skills.* New York: The Free Press.

Murphy, J. (1990). *The Educational Reform Movement of the 1980s.* Berkeley: McCutchan.

Murphy, John, and Lawrence O Picus. (1996). "Special Program Encroachment on School District General Funds in California: Implications for Serrano Equalization." *Journal of Education Finance* 21(3), 366–386.

Murray, Shelia E. (2001). "Kentucky." In John Dayton, C. Thomas Holms, Catherine C. Sielke, and Anne L. Jefferson. (Eds.), *Public School Finance Programs of the United States and Canada, 1998–99* (NCES-2001-309). Washington, D.C.: National Center for Education Statistics.

Murray, Sheila, William Evans, and Robert Schwab. (1998). "Education Finance Reform and the Distribution of Education Resources." *American Economic Review* 88(4), 789–812.

Musgrave, Richard, and Peggy Musgrave. (1989). *Public Finance in Theory and Practice.* New York: McGraw-Hill.

Nakib, Yasser. (1995). "Beyond District-Level Expenditures: Schooling Resource Allocation and Use in Florida." In Lawrence Picus and James Wattenbarger (Eds.), *Where Does the Money Go?* Thousand Oaks, CA: Corwin Press, pp. 106–131.

National Center for Education Statistics. (1990). *Financial Accounting for Local and State School Systems* (NCES 97096R). Washington, D.C.: U.S. Department of Education.

National Center for Education Statistics. (1996). *Digest of Education Statistics, 1996.* Washington, D.C.: U.S. Department of Education.

National Center for Education Statistics. (1997). *Time Spent Teaching Core Academic Subjects in Elementary Schools.* Washington, D.C.: U.S. Department of Education.

National Center for Education Statistics. (1998a). *Digest of Education Statistics, 1997.* Washington, D.C.: U.S. Department of Education.

National Center for Education Statistics. (1998b). *Federal Support for Education: Fiscal Years 1980–1998.* (NCES 98-155). Washington, D.C.: U.S. Department of Education.

National Center for Education Statistics. (2002). *Digest of Education Statistics, 2001.* Washington, D.C.: U.S. Department of Education.

National Commission on Excellence and Equity in Education. (1983). *A Nation At-Risk: The Imperative of Educational Reform.* Washington, D.C.: U.S. Department of Education.

National Commission on Teaching and America's Future. (1996). *What Matters Most: Teaching in America.* New York: Teachers College Press.

National Education Association. (2000). *Modernizing Our Schools: What Will It Cost?* Washington, D.C.: Author.

National Education Association. (2001). *Rankings and Estimates: Ranking of the States 2000 and Estimates of School Statistics 2001.* Washington, D.C.: Author.

National Research Council. (1999). *Report of the Panel on Special Education.* Washington, D.C.: Author.

Nelson, F. Howard. (1984). "Factors Contributing to the Cost of Programs for Limited English Proficient Students." *Journal of Education Finance* 10(1), 1–21.

Netzer, Dick. (1966). *Economics of the Property Tax.* Washington, D.C.: The Brookings Institution.

Newmann, Fred, and Associates. (1996). *Authentic Achievement: Restructuring Schools for Intellectual Quality.* San Francisco: Jossey-Bass.

Norman, Jack. (2002). *Funding Our Future: An Adequacy Model for Wisconsin School Finance.* Milwaukee: Institute for Wisconsin's Future.

O'Neill, G. Patrick. (1996). "Restructuring Education: Lessons from Chicago, Edmonton and Wellington." *House* 70(1), 30–31.

Odden, Allan. (1978). "Missouri's New School Finance Structure." *Journal of Education Finance* 3(3), 465–475.

Odden, Allan. (1988). "How Fiscal Accountability and Program Quality Can Be Insured for Chapter I." In Denis Doyle and Bruce Cooper (Eds.), *Federal Aid to the Disadvantaged: What Future for Chapter I?* New York: Falmer Press.

Odden, Allan (Ed.). (1991). *Education Policy Implementation.* Albany: State University of New York Press.

Odden, Allan. (1995a). *Educational Leadership for America's Schools.* New York: McGraw-Hill.

Odden, Allan. (1995b). *Missouri School Finance System: Fiscal Equity after S.B. 380.* Paper prepared for the Missouri Performance Commission.

Odden, Allan. (1997a). *The Finance Side of Implementing New American Schools.* Paper prepared for the New American Schools, Alexandria, VA.

Odden, Allan. (1997b). "Having to Do More With Less: Stretching the School Budget Dollar." *School Business Affairs* 63(6), 2–10.

Odden, Allan. (1998). *Improving State School Finance Systems: New Realities Create Need to Re-Engineer School Finance Structures* (CPRE Occasional Paper Series OP-04). Philadelphia: University of Pennsylvania, Graduate School of Education, Consortium for Policy Research in Education.

Odden, Allan. (1999). "Case Study 3: School Based Formula Funding in North America." In Kenneth Ross and Rosalind Levacic (Eds.), *Needs-Based Resource Allocation in Schools via Formula-Based Funding.* Paris: UNESCO, International Institute for Educational Planning.

Odden, Allan. (2000). "Costs of Sustaining Educational Change Via Comprehensive School Reform." *Phi Delta Kappan* 81(6), 433–438.

Odden, Allan, and Sarah Archibald. (2000). "Reallocating Resources to Support Higher Student Achievement: An Empirical Look at Five Sites." *Journal of Education Finance* 25(4), 545–564.

Odden, Allan, and Sarah Archibald. (2001). *Reallocating Resources: How to Boost Student Achievement Without Asking for More.* Thousand Oaks, CA: Corwin Press.

Odden, Allan, Sarah Archibald, and Anita Tychsen. (1998). *Can Wisconsin Schools Afford Comprehensive School Reform?* Madison: University of Wisconsin, Wisconsin Center for Education Research, Consortium for Policy Research in Education.

Odden, Allan, and John Augenblick. (1981). *School Finance Reform in the States: 1981.* Denver: Education Commission of the States.

Odden, Allan, Robert Berne, and Leanna Stiefel. (1979). *Equity in School Finance.* Denver: Education Commission of the States.

Odden, Allan, and Carolyn Busch. (1995). "Costs and Impacts of Alternative Plans for Reforming Wisconsin School Finance and Providing Property Tax Relief." In Carla Edlefson (Ed.), *School Finance Policy Issues in the States and Provinces.* Columbus: The Ohio State University, Policy Research for Ohio Based Education and American Educational Research Association, pp. 192–203.

Odden, Allan, and Carolyn Busch (Eds.). (1997). "Special Issue: Collection of School-Level Finance Data." *Journal of Education Finance* 22(3).

Odden, Allan, and Carolyn Busch. (1998). *Financing Schools for High Performance: Strategies for Improving the Use of Educational Resources.* San Francisco: Jossey-Bass.

Odden, Allan, and William Clune. (1998). "School Finance Systems: Aging Structures in Need of Renovation." *Educational Evaluation and Policy Analysis* 20(3), 157–177.

Odden, Allan, and Van Dougherty. (1984). *Education Finance in the States, 1984.* Denver: Education Commission of the States.

Odden, Allan, Mark Fermanich, and Lawrence O. Picus. (2003). *A State-of-the Art Approach to School Finance Adequacy in Kentucky.* Report prepared for the Kentucky State Department of Education.

Odden, Allan, and Carolyn Kelley. (2002). *Paying Teachers for What They Know and Do: New and Smarter Compensation Strategies to Improve Schools* (2d ed.). Thousand Oaks, CA: Corwin Press.

Odden, Allan, and William Massy. (1992). *Education Funding for Schools and Universities: Improving Productivity and Equity.* Los Angeles: University of Southern California, Center for Research in Education Finance, Consortium for Policy Research in Education.

Odden, Allan, Robert Palaich, and John Augenblick. (1979). *Analysis of the New York State School Finance System, 1977–78.* Denver: Education Commission of the States.

Odden, Allan, and Lawrence O. Picus. (1992). *School Finance: A Policy Perspective.* New York: McGraw-Hill.

Odden, Allan, and Lawrence O. Picus. (2000). *School Finance: A Policy Perspective* (2d ed.). New York: McGraw-Hill.

Office of Bilingual Education, California State Department of Education. (1984). *Schooling and Language for Minority Students: A Theoretical Framework.* Los Angeles: California State University, Evaluation, Dissemination and Assessment Center.

Ornstein, Allen C. (1990). "How Big Should Schools and Districts Be?" *Education Digest* 56(2), 44–48.

Park, Rolla Edward, and Stephen J. Carroll. (1979). *The Search for Equity in School Finance: Michigan School District Response to a Guaranteed Tax Base.* Santa Monica, CA: The RAND Corporation, R-2393-NIE/HEW.

Parrish, Thomas B. (1994). "A Cost Analysis of Alternative Instructional Models for Limited English Proficient Students in California." *Journal of Education Finance* 19(3), 256–278.

Parrish, Thomas. (1996). "Special Education Finance: Past, Present and Future." *Journal of Education Finance* 21(4), 451–476.

Parrish, Thomas B. (1997). *Special Education in an Era of School Reform.* (Product of the Federal Resource Center.) Palo Alto, CA: Center for Special Education Finance.

Parrish, Thomas, and Jean Wolman. (1999). "Trends and New Developments in Special Education Funding: What the States Report." In Jay Chambers, Thomas Parrish, and Cassandra Guarino (Eds.), *Funding Special Education.* Thousand Oaks, CA: Corwin Press, pp. 203–229.

Pechman, Joseph A. (1985). *Who Paid the Taxes, 1966–85.* Washington, D.C.: The Brookings Institution.

Pechman, Joseph A. (1986). *Who Paid the Taxes, 1966–85, Revised Tables.* Washington, D.C.: The Brookings Institution.

Phares, Donald. (1980). *Who Pays State and Local Taxes?* Cambridge, MA: Oelgeschlager, Gunn and Hain.

Phillips, Robyn. (1988). "Restoring Property Tax Equity." *California Policy Choices* 4, pp. 143–169. Los Angeles: University of Southern California, School of Public Administration.

Picus, Lawrence O. (1988). *The Effect of State Grant-In-Aid Policies on Local Government Decision Making: The Case of California School Finance.* Santa Monica, CA: The RAND Corporation.

Picus, Lawrence O. (1993a). *The Allocation and Use of Educational Resources: School Level Evidence from the Schools and Staffing Survey.* Los Angeles: USC Center for Research in Education Finance, Working Paper No. 37.

Picus, Lawrence O. (1993b). *The Allocation and Use of Educational Resources: District Level Evidence from the Schools and Staffing Survey.* Paper prepared for the Consortium for Policy Research in Education Finance Center, University of Wisconsin–Madison.

Picus, Lawrence O. (1994a). "Estimating the Determinants of Pupil/Teacher Ratios: Evidence from the Schools and Staffing Survey." *Educational Considerations* 21(2), 44–52.

Picus, Lawrence O. (1994b). "The Local Impact of School Finance Reform in Texas." *Educational Evaluation and Policy Analysis* 16(4), 391–404.

Picus, Lawrence. (1997). "Using School-Level Finance Data: Endless Opportunity or Bottomless Pit?" *Journal of Education Finance* 22(3), 317–330.

Picus, Lawrence O. (2000). "Student Level Finance Data: Wave of the Future." *The Clearing House,* 74(2), 75–80.

Picus, Lawrence O., and Minaz Bhimani. (August 1993). "Estimating the Impact of District Characteristics on Pupil/Teacher Ratios." *Journal of the American Statistical Association.* Proceedings of the annual conference of the American Statistical Association, San Francisco.

Picus, Lawrence O., and M. Fazal. (1996). "Why Do We Need to Know What Money Buys? Research on Resource Allocation Patterns in Elementary and Secondary Schools." In Lawrence O. Picus and James L. Wattenbarger (Eds.), *Where Does the Money Go? Resource Allocation in Elementary and Secondary Schools* (1995 Yearbook of the American Education Finance Association). Newbury Park, CA: Corwin Press, pp. 1–19.

Picus, Lawrence O., and Linda Hertert. (1993a). "A School Finance Dilemma for Texas: Achieving Equity in a Time of Fiscal Constraint." *Texas Researcher* 4, 1–28.

Picus, Lawrence O., and Linda Hertert. (1993b). "Three Strikes and You're Out, Texas School Finance After Edgewood III." *Journal of Education Finance* 18(3), 366–389.

Picus, L. O., S. Marion, N. Calvo, and S. Oshman. (2003). *Understanding the Relationship between Student Achievement and the Quality of Educational Facilities.* Paper presented at the annual meeting of the American Education Finance Association, Orlando.

Picus, L. O., J. McCroskey, E. Robillard, J. Yoo, and L. Marsenich. (2002). "Using Student Level Data to Measure School Finance Adequacy: An Exploratory Analysis." In Christopher Roellke and Jennifer King Rice (Eds.), *Fiscal Issues in Urban Schools. Volume 1 of Research in Education Fiscal Policy and Practice.* Greenwich, CT: Information Age Publishing, pp. 181–201.

Picus, Lawrence O., Allan Odden, and Mark Fermanich. (2001). *Assessing the Equity of Kentucky's SEEK Formula: A Ten-Year Analysis.* Los Angeles: Lawrence O. Picus and Associates. Paper prepared for the Kentucky Department of Education.

Picus, L. O., and E. Robillard. (2000). "The Collection and Use of Student Level Data: Implications for School Finance Research." *Educational Considerations* XXVIII(1), 26–31.

Picus, L. O., and L. Toenjes. (1994). "Texas School Finance: Assessing the Impact of Multiple Reforms." *Journal of Texas Public Education* 2(3), 39–62.

Picus, Lawrence O., Donald R. Tetreault, and John Murphy. (1996). *What Money Buys: Understanding the Allocation and Use of Educational Resources in California.* Madison: University of Wisconsin, Wisconsin Center for Education Research, Consortium for Policy Research in Education.

Pompa, Delia. (March 26, 1998). *Testimony on the Fiscal Year 1999 Budget Requests for Bilingual and Immigrant Education.* Available online: www.ed.gov/speeches.

Porter, Andrew. (1991). "Creating a System of School Process Indicators." *Educational Evaluation and Policy Analysis* 13(1), 13–30.

Prince, Henry. (1997). "Michigan's School Finance Reform: Initial Pupil-Equity Results." *Journal of Education Finance* 22(4), 394–409.

Puelo, V. T. (1988). "A Review and Critique of Research on Full-Day Kindergarten." *Elementary School Journal* 88(4), 425–439.

Pulliam, John D. (1987). *History of Education in America* (4th ed.). Columbus: Merrill.

Pyhrr, P. (1971). "Zero-Based Budgeting." *Harvard Business Review* 48(4), 111–121.

Reschovsky, Andrew. (1994). "Fiscal Equalization and School Finance." *National Tax Journal* 47(1), 185–197.

Reschovsky, Andrew, and Jennifer Imazeki. (1998). "The Development of School Finance Formulas to Guarantee the Provision of Adequate Education to Low-Income Students." In William J. Fowler (Ed.), *Developments in School Finance 1997.* Washington, D.C.: National Center for Education Statistics. NCES 98-212.

Reschovsky, Andrew, and Jennifer Imazeki. (2001). "Achieving Educational Adequacy through School Finance Reform." *Journal of Education Finance* 26(4), 373–396.

Reynolds, Arthur. J., and Barbara Wolfe. (1999). "Special Education and School Achievement: An Exploratory Analysis with a Central-City Sample." *Educational Evaluation and Policy Analysis* 21(3), 249–269.

Riew, John. (1986). "Scale Economies, Capacity Utilization and School Costs: A Comparative Analysis of Secondary and Elementary Schools." *Journal of Education Finance* 11(4), 433–446.

Robledo, M., M. Zarate, M. Guss-Zamora, and Jose Cardenas. (1978). *Bilingual Education Cost Analysis: Colorado.* San Antonio: Intercultural Development Research Association.

Rosen, Harvey S. (1992). *Public Finance* (3d ed.). Homewood, IL: Irwin.

Rosen, Harvey S. (2001). *Public Finance* (6th ed.). Boston: Irwin/McGraw-Hill.

Rossmiller, Richard, and Lloyd E. Frohreich. (1979). *Expenditures and Funding Patterns in Idaho's Programs for Exception Children.* Madison: University of Wisconsin.

Rossmiller, Richard, et al. (1970). *Educational Programs for Exceptional Children: Resource Configurations and Costs.* Madison: Department of Educational Administration, University of Wisconsin.

Rotberg, Iris, Mary Futrell, and Joyce Lieberman. (1998). "National Board Certification: Increasing Participation and Assessing Impacts." *Phi Delta Kappan* 79(6), 462–466.

Rothstein, Richard, and Karen Hawley Miles. (1995). *Where's the Money Gone?* Washington, D.C.: Economic Policy Institute.

Rubenstein, Ross. (1998). "Resource Equity in the Chicago Public Schools: A School-Level Approach." *Journal of Education Finance* 23(4), 468–489.

Rubenstein, Ross. (2002). "Providing Adequate Educational Funding: A State-by-State Analysis of Expenditure Needs." *Public Budgeting and Finance,* 22(4), 73–98.

Rubenstein, R. (2002). "Who Pays and Who Benefits? Examining the Distributional Consequences of the Georgia Lottery for Education." *National Tax Journal* 55, 223–238.

Rubenstein, Ross, Dwight Doering, and Larry Gess. (2000). "The Equity of Public Education Funding in Georgia, 1988–1996." *Journal of Education Finance* 26(2), 187–208.

Ruggiero, John. (1996). "Efficiency of Educational Production: An Analysis of New York School Districts." *Review of Economics and Statistics* 78(3), 499–509.

Salmon, Richard, Christina Dawson, Steven Lawton, and Thomas Johns. (1988). *Public School Finance Programs of the United States and Canada: 1986–87.* Sarasota, FL: American Education Finance Association.

Sample, Patricia Ritchey, and William Hartman. (1990). "An Equity Simulation of Pennsylvania's School Finance Simulation." *Journal of Education Finance* 16(1), 49–69.

Schick, A. (1971). *Budget Innovation in the States.* Washington, D.C.: The Brookings Institution.

Schwartz, Myron, and Jay Moskowitz. (1988). *Fiscal Equity in the United States: 1984–85.* Washington, D.C.: Decision Resources Corporation.

Seal, Kenna R., and Hobart L. Harmon. (1995). "Realities of Rural School Reform." *Phi Delta Kappan* 77(2), 119–124.

Shanahan, Timothy. (1998). "On the Effectiveness and Limitations of Tutoring in Reading." *Review of Research in Education* 23, 217–234. Washington, D.C.: American Educational Research Association.

Sher, Jonathan, and Rachel B. Tompkins. (1977). "Economy, Efficiency and Equality: The Myths of Rural School and District Consolidation." In Jonathan P. Sher (Ed.), *Education in Rural America.* Boulder: Westview Press.

Sherman, Joel. (1992). Review of School Finance Equalization Under Section 5(d) of P.L. 81-874, The Impact Aid Program. *Journal of Education Finance* 18(1).

Siegler, Robert. (1998). *Children's Thinking.* Upper Saddle River, NJ: Prentice Hall.

Sielke, Catherine C. (2002). "Financing School Infrastructure Needs: An Overview Across the 50 States." In Faith E. Crampton and David C. Thompson (Eds.), *Saving America's School Infrastructure* (Vol. II in the Series, Research in Education Fiscal Policy and Practice: Local, National, and Global Perspectives). Greenwich, CT: Information Age Publishing.

Sielke, Catherine, John Dayton, C. Thomas Holmes, and Ann Jefferson (Eds.). (2001). *Public School Finance Programs in the U.S. and Canada: 1998–99.* Washington, D.C.: U.S. Department of Education, National Center for Education Statistics.

Sizer, Theodore. (1996). *Horace's Hope.* Boston: Houghton Mifflin.

Slavin, Robert, and Margarita Calderon. (Eds.). (2001). *Effective Programs for Latino Students.* Mahwah, NJ: Lawrence Erlbaum Associates.

Slavin, Robert, and Olatokunbo Fashola. (1998). *Show Me the Evidence! Proven and Promising Programs for America's Schools.* Thousand Oaks, CA: Corwin Press.

Slavin, Robert, Nancy Karweit, and Barbara Wasik. (1994). *Preventing Early School Failure: Research Policy and Practice.* Boston: Allyn and Bacon.

Slavin, Robert, Nancy Madden, Lawrence Dolan, and Barbara Wasik. (1996). *Every Child, Every School.* Thousand Oaks, CA: Corwin Press.

Smith, Marshall S., and Jennifer O'Day. (1991). "Systemic School Reform." In Susan Fuhrman and Betty Malen (Eds.), *The Politics of Curriculum and Testing.* Bristol, PA: Falmer Press, pp. 233–267.

Sparkman, William. (1994). "The Legal Foundations of Public School Finance." *Boston College Law Review* 35(3), 569–595.

Sparkman, William. (1990). "School Finance Challenges in State Courts." In J. Underwood and D. Verstegen (Eds.), *The Impacts of Litigation and Legislation on Public School Finance.* Cambridge, MA: Ballinger, pp. 193–224.

Speakman, Sheree, Bruce Cooper, Hunt Holsomback, Jay May, Robert Sampieri, and Larry Maloney. (1997). "The Three Rs of Education Finance Reform: Re-Thinking, Re-Tooling and Re-Evaluating School-Site Information." *Journal of Education Finance* 22(4), 337–367.

Stern, David. (1973). "Effects of Alternative State Aid Formulas on the Distribution of Public School Expenditures in Massachusetts." *Review of Economics and Statistics* 55, 91–97.

Stringfield, Samuel, Steven Ross, and Lana Smith. (1996). *Bold Plans for School Restructuring: The New American School Designs.* Mahwah, NJ: Lawrence Erlbaum.

Swanson, Austin, and Richard King. (1997). *School Finance: Its Economics and Politics.* New York: Longman.

Texas State Board of Education. (1986). *1985–96 Accountable Cost Study.* Austin: Texas Education Agency.

Tiebout, Charles M. (1956). "A Pure Theory of Local Expenditures." *Journal of Political Economy* 54, 416–424.

Tsang, Mun C., and Henry R. Levin. (1983). "The Impacts of Intergovernmental Grants on Education Spending." *Review of Educational Research* 53(3), 329–367.

Tyack, David, and Elizabeth Hansot. (1982). *Managers of Virtue.* New York: Basic Books.

Tychsen, Anita. (1999). *The Power of the Purse: An Examination of How Schools Reallocated Resources to Implement Reform Strategies.* Unpublished Ph.D. dissertation.

Underwood, Julie, and W. Sparkman. (1991). "School Finance Litigation: A New Wave of Reform." *Harvard Journal of Law and Public Policy* 14(2), 517–544.

Underwood, Julie. (1995a). "School Finance Litigation: Legal Theories, Judicial Activism, and Social Neglect." *Journal of Education Finance* 20(2), 143–162.

Underwood, Julie. (1995b). "School Finance as Vertical Equity." *University of Michigan Journal of Law Reform* 28(3), 493–520.

U.S. Department of Education, Office of Special Education Programs, Data Analysis System (DANS). Data based on December 1, 2001 count, updated as of August 30, 2002. Available online: www.ideadata.org/tables25th/ar_aa13.htm.

Verstegen, Deborah. (1996). "Concepts and Measures of Fiscal Inequality: A New Approach and Effects for Five States." *Journal of Education Finance* 22(2), 145–160.

Verstegen, Deborah. (1999). "Civil Rights and Disability Policy: An Historical Perspective." In Jay Chambers, Thomas Parrish, and Cassandra Guarino (Eds.), *Funding Special Education.* Thousand Oaks, CA: Corwin Press, pp. 3–21.

Verstegen, Deborah. (2002). "Financing the New Adequacy: Towards New Models of State Education Finance Systems that Support Standards Based Reform." *Journal of Education Finance* 27(3), 749–782.

Verstegen, Deborah, Thomas Parrish, and Jean Wolman. (1998). A Look at Changes in the Finance Provisions for Grants to States under the IDEA Amendments of 1997." *The CSEF Resource.* Palo Alto, CA: Center for Special Education Finance.

Verstegen, Deborah, and Richard Salmon. (1991). "Assessing Fiscal Equity in Virginia: Cross-Time Comparisons." *Journal of Education Finance* 16(4), 417–430.

Vincent, Phillip E. and Kathleen Adams. (1978). *Fiscal Response of School Districts: A Study of Two States—Colorado and Minnesota* (Report No. F78-3). Denver: Education Finance Center, Education Commission of the States.

Weinstein, C. S. (1979). "The Physical Environment of the School: A Review of the Research." *Review of Educational Research* 49, 577–610.

Wendling, W. (1981a). "Capitalization: Considerations for School Finance." *Educational Evaluation and Policy Analysis* 3(2), 57–66.

Wendling, Wayne. (1981b). "The Cost of Education Index: Measurement of Price Differences of Education Personnel among New York State School Districts." *Journal of Education Finance* 6(4), 485–504.

Wenglinsky, Harold. (1997). *When Money Matters.* Princeton, NJ: Education Testing Service.

Wildavsky, Aaron. (1988). *The New Politics of the Budgetary Process.* Glenview, IL: Scott Foresman.

Wise, Arthur. (1968). *Rich Schools–Poor Schools: A Study of Equal Educational Opportunity.* Chicago: University of Chicago Press.

Wise, Arthur. (1983). "Educational Adequacy: A Concept in Search of Meaning." *Journal of Education Finance* 8(3), 300–315.

Wohlstetter, Priscilla, Amy Van Kirk, Peter Robertson, and Susan Mohrman. (1997). *Organizing for Successful School-Based Management.* Alexandria, VA: Association for Supervision and Curriculum Development.

Wood, R. Craig, David Honeyman, and Verne Bryers. (1990). "Equity in Indiana School Finance: A Decade of Local Levy Property Tax Restrictions." *Journal of Education Finance* 16(1), 83–92.

Wood, R. Craig, David Thompson, Lawrence O. Picus, and Don I. Tharpe. (1995). *Principles of School Business Administration* (2d ed.). Reston, VA: Association of School Business Officials International.

Wyckoff, J. H. (1992). "The Interstate Equality of Public Primary and Secondary Education Resources in the U.S., 1980–1987." *Economics of Education Review* 11(1), 19–30.

Yinger, John. (2002). *Helping Children Left Behind: State Aid and the Pursuit of Educational Equity.* Unpublished manuscript.

Zodrow, George R. (2001). "The Property Tax as a Capital Tax: A Room with Three Views." *National Tax Journal* LIV(1), 139–156.

Author Index

Subject Index